How To Restore Your
Chevrolet Pickup

How To Restore Your
Chevrolet Pickup

Tom Brownell

Dedication

Dedication: This book is dedicated to the memory of Irv Neubert who loved vintage trucks and their owners enough to serve tirelessly and uncompensated for years as the secretary of the Light Commercial Vehicle Association. We miss you, Irv.

First published in 2004 by Motorbooks, an imprint of Quarto Publishing Group USA Inc., 400 First Avenue North, Suite 400, Minneapolis, MN 55401 USA

© Tom Brownell, 2004

Motorbooks titles are also available at discounts in bulk quantity for industrial or sales-promotional use. For details write to Special Sales Manager at Quarto Publishing Group USA Inc., 400 First Avenue North, Suite 400, Minneapolis, MN 55401 USA.

ISBN-13: 978-0-7603-1634-4

Editorial: Heather Oakley and Peter Bodensteiner
Design: LeAnn Kuhlmann

Printed in China

On the front cover:
Main: Chevrolet pickups from the Advance Design series are a perennial favorite with collectors. *Dennis Parks*
Small: Rust repair begins by cutting out the bad metal. Rotary cutoff tools make this job easy, but eye protection must be worn.

On the back cover: A 1972 Chevrolet pickup.

CONTENTS

ACKNOWLEDGMENTS

I wish to thank the following people who helped make this book possible:

Bruce Horkey who once again provided photos of bed wood replacement; John Milliman, editor of the Stovebolt Page website, who provided the focus and catchy wording for this edition's Big Iron chapter and sending an SOS for photo help to his website's readers; Bob Adler for reading and critiquing several chapters as well as photo help; Jim Carter for tips on distinguishing model characteristics; Jens Rick for spending afternoons in my shop buffing headlight rims and helping stuff a 133 in. wheelbase truck in a Carbag; Rich Jensen who upgraded the Longhorn to power disc brakes, give it a TPI transplant, and set up his shop for powder coating so we could do a photo shoot of the process; Anthony Brownell for letting his old truck urge lead him to a 1968 C-50 dump truck; Jeremy VanHoven whose passion for 1973-1987 working trucks showed me their collector status Vic Fowler and his auto body students for letting me pester them for photos; Tom Langdon for technical and photo help; Gene Beck, also for technical and photo help; Alvin Shier for lots of technical advice over the years; Many former LCVA members who sent me photos of their trucks during the years I served as editor for that organization; And most especially my wife, Joyce, who found it in her heart to overlook the time I spent putting out another book.

So you've bought an old truck and are thinking of fixing it up, maybe even planning to restore it. If this is your first older vehicle, you're probably looking for tips and guidance. If you've restored other old cars or trucks before, you're may be looking for advice on pitfalls when approaching a Chevrolet. Either way, this book is for you. It will show what needs to be done to bring the typical older Chevrolet truck back to first-class condition and how to go about it.

As a Chevrolet light truck owner or admirer, you're probably not far from where Mike Cavey was when he bought a clean-looking Chevrolet pickup that had spent most of its life in Florida and had only recently been brought to Michigan The truck had a fresh repaint and appeared to be a sound southern truck. It ran well and proved serviceable enough for Mike to run a couple years in his business. Then he started to think about fixing it up. "I didn't plan a restoration, certainly not what I ended up doing," Cavey observes. But one thing led to another so that over a two-year period, with a time investment of 2,000 hours, Cavey turned his respectable 1951 Chevrolet pickup into one of the best restored trucks in the world. That's a tall claim but he's got the trophy hardware to back it up: Antique Automobile Club of America's (AACA)

Junior, Senior and Grand National awards, plus several Preservation recognitions.

You might not be aiming for Mike Cavey's level of perfection, but looking at what he did and how he did it will guide your fix up or restoration to whatever stage you wish. Although Advance Design Chevrolet trucks like Mike's 1951 are popular, your truck may be of the later 1955-1959 Task Force series, or a 1960s design, or an earlier 1941-1946 Art Deco model—the year doesn't make any difference. This book doesn't focus just on early 1950s Chevrolets. You will see models of various years in the restoration steps, but we'll let Mike Cavey's approach be our guide.

One might ask why Cavey chose a 1951 Chevrolet pickup to restore, as he says, to the standards one would follow in building a show Corvette to compete for the Bloomington Gold. The magic, to Mike, was the fact that it was a pickup. What else represents a past era better than an old truck, and what truck is more universally recognizable than a Chevrolet? Look at the ads on TV that depict down-home scenes and you'll see what I mean. Invariably, the action centers around an old pickup and the truck, almost always, is a Chevrolet—usually from the Advance Design series of the late 1940s to mid-1950s.

Not all older Chevrolet trucks present as much of a challenge as this rare, but decrepit, Suburban. John Hart

Through the years Chevrolet has built consistently memorable trucks. The styling treatment has been varied, but the Chevrolet parentage has always been there. In the early 1940s, a toothy chrome grille made a Chevrolet pickup instantly recognizable at any distance. In the later forties, the sedate styling of the Advance Design series made a conservative, value-first statement. By the mid-fifties Chevrolet trucks set out to promote a modern image with the stylish wraparound windshield, similarly contoured front and rear fenders and, of course, the showy Cameo.

An appealing feature of any older truck, but particularly a Chevrolet, is its simplicity. Fenders unbolt, the Stovebolt six cylinder engines, used through 1962, are practically as easy to work on as a Briggs and Stratton lawn mower engine, and trucks continued the easy-to-rebuild straight axle front end up to 1960. To a restorer, simplicity is always easier to deal with than complexity. Another strong plus for Chevrolet is the enormous parts availability. Just as parts vendors have made practically every part needed to build an entire vehicle available for Model A and T Fords, so too are nearly all needed parts being remanufactured for Chevrolet light trucks, particularly those in the 1947-1955 Advance Design and 1967-1972 Custom Sport Truck series.

Another bonus of owning a Chevrolet is the continued value associated with the name. Chevrolet trucks lead the pack in rising collector values. This means that if you buy and fix up or restore a Chevrolet truck, you stand a good chance that you will be able to recoup your investment. For any number of reasons, styling, design, availability of parts, nostalgia, collectors like Chevrolet trucks. Certain models, like the low production and style-leading Cameo are rising in value as quickly as the more popular Chevrolet cars.

If you have a hankering to add an older truck to your vehicle stable, you can't go wrong with a Chevrolet. If you own a vintage Chevrolet truck, then you've picked a winner. In either case, questions you're likely to be asking are where and how to begin the fixing up process. First, though, some even more basic questions must be answered. These include your goal for your truck, what do you have available in the way of tools, equipment and shop space? What financial resources are you willing to invest in the project? And perhaps most important, what amount of the time you can commit to rebuilding an old truck? We will take you through the process of answering these questions and get you started on your truck's restoration or rebuild —whichever approach you decide to take.

A big part of a Chevrolet truck's appeal is that at one time or another, it's been in nearly every truck admirer's life. I first drove a Chevrolet truck while working at a dairy during summers while in college. The truck was a 1957 panel, painted white—the dairy's color—and I used it to haul ice from the ice plant, bottles from the warehouse and milk from our processing plant to stores. My memories of this truck have mostly to do with shifting without the clutch. Enough miles had tallied on the odometer that this truck was limber as a gymnast. Let off on the gas, plant both feet on the floor and the shift lever would go into most any gear you wanted. Obedient would be the best way to describe that truck. It didn't ooze hydraulic fluid out of its brakes, as did some of our other trucks. It started on the first twist of the switch, purred along the highway like a sewing machine and shifted like an automatic. What more could you want?

Chances are you've got memories of a vintage Chevy truck, too. This book's purpose is to help you turn those memories into a truck you can drive and enjoy.

Following the guidelines in this book, this can be the result. You'll see photos of this truck's transformation in the chapters that follow. John Hart

Chevrolet built its first trucks in 1918. These were one ton models on which buyers could mount a variety of delivery or express bodies. The first half-ton pickup wear to the bow tie emblem appeared in 1928. This light duty hauler was actually a roadster with a cargo box stuffed into the trunk. Chevy's first true roadster pickup, with a special open cab and standard pickup box, appeared in 1930, while the first closed cab pickup debuted in 1931. Chevrolet's first pickup

Most of Chevrolet's early light duty commercial models were set up as delivery trucks. George Childs, Jr.

By the 1930s, Chevrolet was building pickups that used forward sheet metal closely resembling the car models. Rene Chapotel

models, like their counterparts from arch-rival Ford, shared car body and mechanical parts extensively. Early Chevrolet trucks are very rare and present more than the usual challenges to those who find and decide to restore one. Replacement sheet metal for the one ton commercials is virtually non-existent. When Winross Restorations, a specialty truck restoration shop in Palmyra, NY, restored a 1926 Series X one ton, they had to fabricate the much of the sheet metal, including the fenders, hood sides and running boards, and remake the entire wooden cab and express body with little else but pictures for patterns.

1935-1938: Car Styling

By the mid-thirties, Chevrolet pickups had established a reputation for dependability and were sold in larger numbers, but since the nation was now in economic depression, these trucks were far from plentiful. During this period Chevy trucks still shared car front-end sheet metal, but the trucks always wore the previous year's car styling and in some cases truck body metal is just enough different that similar looking parts from a car won't fit. In 1936 Chevy sold two separate styles of trucks in the same year. Because of a change in cab design, the early 1936 models were called high cab and the later models are referred to as low cab. On the early models, carried over from 1935, the cab had a very high crown—hence the high cab name. The new models, introduced mid-year, had a substantially lower cab roof line, which explains the low cab nickname. Hydraulic brakes first appeared in the Chevrolet truck line on these low roof models. Chevrolet trucks continued to wear grilles that closely resembled the car line. The most substantial change during this period was the introduction, in 1937, of a completely reworked overhead valve (ohv) six-cylinder engine, now displacing 216.5 cubic inches and fitted with four main bearings instead of three. This basic engine would remain the light truck power plant until 1953.

1939-1940: Streamlined Design

A new tall, rugged-looking grille made the 1939 and 1940 light trucks look less like an extension of the car line. These trucks were also fitted with a new cab that now had a two-piece Veed windshield for improved visibility and a more streamlined look. Chevrolet trucks would use this cab with minor modifications until early 1947. At first glance, Chevy's 1939 and 1940 trucks appeared nearly identical, but there are ways to tell them apart. In 1939, the gauge cluster consists or three round individual gauges. In 1940, all gauges are grouped into one rectangular pod. Another difference is

The tall, rugged-looking grille and two-piece Veed windshield marked a styling departure for Chevrolet's 1939 and 1940 pickup models.

the top grille bar. On a 1940 model, this bar is wider than on '39. On half-ton 1939 pickups, the bed as also slightly longer on 1940 models.

Although not available in as great a quantity as the 1941 and later models, Chevy's 1939 and 1940 pickups are popular with collectors. Attractions are the distinctive grille, more modern cab, and for 1940, the larger box and sealed beam headlights. Parts availability is also an advantage. The basic mechanicals are the same as those on Chevy trucks through the next decade, and since the cab was also used on the next

styling series, a wide assortment of patch and replacement sheet metal is available—though the availability of these helpful metal repair pieces is growing for earlier Chevrolet pickup models as well.

1941-1947: Art Deco Styling

The flashy multi-toothed grille gives 1941-47 Chevrolet trucks a far less conservative look than the earlier models. On the 1941, 1946 and 1947 models, the grilles, bumpers, headlight rims and other decorative items are chrome plated. On trucks built during the short production run of 1942, a few assembled during wartime, and those built in 1945, the grille and other trim were painted. This so-called "blackout" look is unusual, and for that reason is considered desirable.

Besides their styling appeal, these trucks also offer collectors the benefit of a wide range of reproduction sheet metal as well as easily available mechanical parts. Collectors of this model enjoyed the crank-out windshield (which provides refreshing ventilation for summer driving) as well as these trucks' business-like, no nonsense simplicity.

1947-1955: Advance Design Era

Chevrolet introduced its all new post-war "Advance Design" trucks in the middle of the 1947 calendar year. In fact, both the earlier and newer style trucks were built simultaneously for a short two-month period as these trucks were being introduced. The overlapping production occurred because with the extreme demand for new trucks, GM didn't want any lag in production. The Advance Design series represented the first completely restyled postwar car or truck offering from any of the Big Three (GM, Ford and Chrysler). Also of significance, although Chevy's new trucks appeared nearly two years before

Chevrolet's pickups from the World War II era featured a pronounced Art Deco styling influence.

Post-war Advance Design models are very popular with collectors. No wonder, the styling is handsome and harmonious.

Among the rarest of the Advance Design models is the canopy express. The large canvas sheet toward the rear of the truck covers an opening through which the driver could sell his goods, which were often fresh produce.

GM's restyled postwar cars, the truck line clearly shows the major styling features of the corporation's coming car line.

To the public, Chevrolet's Advance Design models, particularly those built between 1947 and 1953, are coming to represent the classic old truck. Chevrolet's Advance Design series have become among the most sought after collector trucks. As witnessed with Model T and A Fords, a vehicle doesn't need to be rare to be desirable.

Several reasons account for the large and growing interest in this Advance Design series. The relatively plentiful supply plays a factor, as do the ease of repair and supply of parts. But nostalgia plays a big role as well; most of today's collectors grew up with these trucks—and to many, a 1947-1955 Chevy truck represents an instant flashback to the days of their youth.

Two significant mechanical changes occurred toward the end of this series. In 1954, Chevy installed its full-pressure lubrication, 235 ci. six in its light-duty trucks. This year also saw a styling facelift that replaced the former split windshield with a single-piece curved glass and added a more massive grille. Trucks with this styling revision were sold in parts of two years, 1955 production being cut short by the introduction of a completely restyled Chevrolet truck line. The carryover models are referred to as First Series, while the restyled 1955 line is called the Second Series. Besides the fact that the short production run makes them rather rare and unusual, First Series 1955 half ton models are also desirable because they used an open driveshaft in place of Chevy's familiar torque-tube driveshaft. Open drive appeared on 3/4 ton trucks in 1954 and on one-tons in 1946. The advantage of open drive is the ease of access to all driveline parts for service.

The earlier years (1947-1953) in the Advance Design series were more difficult to distinguish from one another—though there are some tell-tale differences: 1947 and 1948 Chevy pickups had gas tanks under the front of the bed; in 1949 the tank was moved into the cab. The 1947-1950 light trucks were fitted with chromed front *and* rear bumpers, standard. Advance Design models from 1947-1950 had left-hand cowl vents. Vent windows appeared in 1951. Most all chrome was discontinued in 1952, due to materials shortages caused by the Korean War. Push button door handles also first appeared in 1952.

1955-1959: Task Force Era

Chevrolet's cars and light trucks received a total restyling and major chassis changes for 1955. The changes were so sweeping that even a corporation with GM's resources couldn't launch both Chevy's new car and trucks lines simultaneously. Cars got the priority, delaying the new Task Force trucks until mid-year. This new truck line represented the height of contemporary styling—complete with panoramic windshield, Frenched headlights, two-tone paint schemes, and prominent chrome on deluxe models. A new special pickup called the Cameo Carrier sported even more styling gimmicks, including a hidden spare tire, split rear bumper, and a pacesetting flat sided pickup bed. Actually, the Cameo camouflaged Chevy's narrow box to look like a wide, smooth-sided box by applying full-length fiberglass fenders that matched the contours of the cab.

GM had a heyday with light truck styling in the mid-1950s. Probably its most exuberant model was the smooth-sided pickup that Chevrolet called the Cameo and GMC a Safari. The GMC variant is shown here.

Chevy broke tradition with its new Task Force trucks, just as it had done with its new 1955 cars, by introducing a totally new, 265 ci. V-8 that had all kinds of hop-up potential. The early 265 had some design weaknesses; for example, it lacked an oil filter and had oil passage limitations, although both problems were corrected by the 1956 production year. In 1957, Chevy boosted the V-8 displacement to 283 ci. As many owners and past owners of Chevrolet trucks or cars with this engine know, the 283 ci. V-8 is one of the toughest engines of all time.

There is almost no visible difference between the 1955 and 1956 light trucks. Both had 12 volt electrical systems, the egg crate grille, and shared the same styling and mechanical options. The trained eye noticed a slightly different hood emblem and on the 1956 trucks, and the side emblem was moved up above fender crease. The 1957 models were easy to recognize by the trapezoid-shaped outline in the center of the grille.

Chevrolet's 1955-1957 trucks are favorites among collectors, with the Cameo being one of the most sought after models. Restorers of standard trucks benefit from easy availability of mechanical, interior, and body parts. Cameo pickups can present some real parts hunting nightmares, however, since many of the trim parts are unique to this model.

During 1958, an all-steel, wide-box pickup called the Fleetside replaced the Cameo. In keeping with the styling trends, Chevrolet trucks now carried quad headlights. A new grille extended across the front of the truck. Changes in the standard 1959 pickup models were most easily seen in a redesigned hood emblem and model designation spears moved forward on the front fenders.

The 1959 El Camino with its gull-wing fins and star-ship front-end can easily draw a crowd and has attracted collector interest for two reasons. Cars, including this car-truck, representing the pinnacle of 1950s styling excesses are very much in vogue today. The other reason for the first series El Camino's popularity is the availability of high performance engines. Although Chevrolet installed its dependable six as the base engine, an El Camino could be special ordered with any of the V-8s including the Rochester fuel injected 283 and the tri-power (triple carbureted) 348. Transmission offerings also ran the gamut from standard three-speed, to Powerglide, to Turboglide, to the close-ratio four-speed of Corvette fame. *Hot Rod* magazine ran a new 1959 El with a tri-carburetor 348 up to 90 mph in a standing start quarter mile and turned a respectable 0-60 time of 8.7 seconds.

1960-1966: *Modern Trucks*

The 1960-1966 model run represents the first truly modern light trucks. Although Chevrolet trucks of these years consistently broke sales records, their styling—which mixes aircraft appearing pods and intakes with basically boxy and conservative

The 1960s marked Chevrolet's first truly modern trucks. A 1964 panel model is shown here. The side windows are an owner add-on.

designs—has yet to excite collectors. However, the use of modern engines, comfortable suspension and plentiful supply is bringing these trucks into the collector limelight.

Three facelifts occurred during this series' six-year styling run, the most popular of which seemed to be the slant windshield cab of 1964 and later. Some collectors have been puzzled by later-style hoods on earlier 1960 and 1961 trucks. There's an easy explanation for this: Chevrolet listed only the 1962 and later hoods as replacement parts.

From 1961 to 1963 the El Camino disappeared from production. The official reason was lack of a suitable two-door station wagon as the body platform. Actual reasons included sluggish sales of the 1960 El Camino and Ford's down sizing its Ranchero to the Falcon platform. A second El Caminos series, based on the mid-sized Chevelle, began in 1964. These trucks are popular among collectors, due in part to the variety of engine offerings, but also to the increasingly deluxe trim and interiors.

Not to be overlooked among Chevrolet's early 1960s pickups are the novel Corvair trucks. Two models, called Loadside and Rampside, were offered. Of the pair, the Rampside with its swing-down side-loading ramp is the more desirable. Both have a stepped box floor (necessitated by the rear engine) that proved awkward for carrying long, flat loads. Today Corvair pickups are quite rare, yet they sell at reasonable prices. Besides their unusual engineering and design, benefits of these trucks include good riding qualities and excellent maneuverability.

Of the Corvair-based pickups, the Rampside with its swing-down side-loading ramp is the more desirable. These Series 95 trucks are quite rare, yet they sell at reasonable prices. Besides their unusual engineering and design, benefits include good riding qualities and excellent maneuverability.

1967-1972: *Custom Sport Trucks*

Probably the second most popular Chevy trucks, after the Advance Design models of 1947-1955, are the 1967-1972 models. The styling of these trucks, with its blending of angular lines and rounded contours, seems to have a timeless look. To many collectors, this design series represents the Chevrolet's first success in bringing the front end styling, the cab, and the lines of the Fleetside box into an integrated whole. Earlier

Chevrolet trucks, including the snazzy Cameo Carrier, still belonged to the two-box school of pickup truck styling.

Although the eight cylinder models are a bit heavy on fuel consumption, there is plenty to recommend Chevrolet light trucks in this styling series to would-be collectors. Well-preserved examples are still available, reproduction, good used, and factory original parts are plentiful, these trucks are comfortable touring/travel vehicles, they're ruggedly built, and are appreciating in value—particularly the deluxe Cheyenne models.

If you enjoy the go-anywhere ability of four-wheel-drive, a Blazer from this series warrants consideration, though easily restorable examples are becoming few and far between.

1967-72 Chevy/GMC Build Sheet
On 1967-72 GM trucks, if the R.P.O. list on the inside of the glove box door is unreadable (or missing), look under or on the back side of the seat. Sometimes you'll find the factory build sheet slipped under the seat springs.

1973-1987: *Working Trucks*

Chevrolet trucks in the more recent styling period of 1973-1987 are beginning to be looked at by collectors. If you own one of these trucks, you'll find plenty of tips and techniques in the pages that follow that will help you preserve, recondition, or even restore your vehicle.

Most popular with collectors after the Advance Design models are trucks from GM's 1967-1972 styling series. Their integrated design seems to improve with age.

Low production and high performance are attracting collectors to the later model 454 SS.

1990-On: Super Sports

In 1990, Chevrolet entered the performance truck arena with a limited-production 454 SS sport pickup. Equipped with the Fleetside short box and 7.4-liter (454 ci) heavy duty engine, plus a performance handling package and locking rear axle, the 454 SS came in one color combination: Chevrolet's racing black with black trim. There was no mistaking a 454 SS for other than what it is—a high-image muscle trucks. Outside, 454 SS decals on the rear flanks denoted this special model while inside Silverado trim décor consisting of high-back, sport bucket seats and center console with a Garnet Red interior scheme dressed he 454 SS fittingly for its high-profile image. Just 10,000 of this special model were made in 1990, but Chevrolet lifted the cap in 1991 allowing production to meet buyer demand. Still, with an EPA fuel mileage rating of 10 mpg city and 11 mpg highway, not a lot were sold. The 454 SS was discontinued after the 1992 model year. Many of these high profile trucks have escaped hard work and warrant collector interest.

Driving Impressions

Two impressions struck me as I slid across the well Armor-All'd vinyl seat covering of an all-original 1972 Chevrolet Cheyenne shortbox pickup. Power steering and power front disc brakes made for feather-light steering and quick, sure stopping. Although my driving experience came on a pleasantly mild fall day, the cab remained comfortably cool with just the air circulation provided by the foot vents. Had it been a torrid July afternoon, I'd have summoned a chilling blast from the truck's built-in air conditioning .

The Cheyenne dress-up package has embossed and pleated vinyl seat coverings, fabric insert seats were also available and would probably be more comfortable on cold mornings. The Cheyenne's carpeted flooring and padded headliner

---

1972 Chevy Cheyenne

Seeking a dramatic styling statement to update its light truck line for 1971, Chevrolet once again applied the simple, Ferrari-inspired, egg crate grille it had used with great effectiveness in 1955. To keep the frontal area uncluttered, stylists moved the bow tie from the hood back to the center of the grille and placed the parking lights in the front bumpers.

A second feature that distinguishes 1971 and 1972 Chevrolet trucks is the optional two tone paint scheme on the Cheyenne and other deluxe models. Previous two-toning had painted the roof a contrasting white. Now the contrasting color could also be applied between the trim moldings on the sides of the cab and Fleetside bed, and across the tailgate.

The Cheyenne dress-up package addressed the growing up-scale pickup market. More and more truck buyers were showing interest in other than a basic cargo hauler. They were as interested in style as a new car buyer. Along with attractive outside trim, the Cheyenne presented a more comfortable looking interior fitted with embossed vinyl covered seats, door panels, and headliner. The growing interest in up-scale trucks can be traced to two trends: the continuing camper craze and buyers who didn't need a truck for business, but who wanted a pickup for its versatility, and travelers seeking greater luxury for the obvious reason that if they were going to spend several weeks or months on the road toting your "home" in the pickup box, they wanted their surroundings to be comfortable and pleasant looking.

Shortbox pickups with the upscale Cheyenne trim are the most sought after Chevrolet light truck model.

Spit and Polish GMC

"I was looking for an Advance Design Chevy pickup when I found my 1954 GMC. It was still owned by the original purchaser and had spent most of its life in Mississippi, so it wasn't rusted like most of the Michigan truck's I'd looked at." In a nutshell, that's the story Jim Toogood of Big Rapids, Michigan, tells of how he came to own and restore one of the rarer mid-50s trucks, an end-of-the-series Advance Design GMC.

Like Columbus sailing west to reach the east, probably many of us have started out looking for one thing and discovered another. In Jim's case his GMC pickup turned out to be a real find. Unlike Chevrolet, which built its curved-windshield trucks part of two years (all or 1954 and the first half of 1955), GMC built its version only one year, 1954. Add to the one-year production the fact that as a premium truck, GMC pickups sold in relatively small numbers and you're not likely to see a duplicate of this truck anytime soon.

Like Chevrolet, the two most prominent features of 1954 GMC trucks are a more massive grille and one-piece curved windshield. In keeping with its up-class image, GMC provided chrome plated grilles and front bumpers on deluxe trucks; standard models had painted trim. The grille now enclosed the parking lights and extended around the front contour of the front fenders. For 1954, the overhead valve six cylinder engine displaced 248.5 cubic inches and produced 125 hp.

Unlike Chevrolet, GMC did not build a transition 1955 model. All 1955 GMCs have the new styling.

For 1954 both GMC and Chevrolet pickups got a new box, which remained basically unchanged until 1988 and features a two-inch lower loading height, functional flat-top side panels, deeper sides with a grain-tight tailgate the same height, and a new tailgate latch to eliminate rattling. The tail lamp has a circular design and incorporates a single, double filament bulb covered with a plastic reflex-type lens. The license plate mounts in the center of the box below the tailgate on a special bracket, which also holds a license plate light when the optional rear bumper is fitted.

According to the original bill of sale, the dark green GMC cost $1,463. That price included $134.87 for extra-cost accessories: a side mounted tire, oil filter, oil bath air cleaner, turn signals, and deluxe equipment package. As early as 1954 Michigan had a sales tax, which then was charged at 3 percent, so the original buyer paid $42.10 in tax plus $27.20 for his license plates.

Although the GMC has received a full frame-off restoration, all the truck's bright work—except the parking lights—is original. Chrome plating on trucks must have been a lot higher quality than 1954 vintage cars, because the massive chrome grille, bumpers, door handles, and other plated metal looks factory-new.

improve the cab's insulation, while the wood appliqué door panel and dashboard trim make for a rich-looking interior.

Riding Impression

"Climb in," Jim said, so I swung open the passenger door and swung myself up into the cab. The six-volt starter ground that slow, deliberate growl, coaxing the 248 cubic inch six to life. Jim pulled the column-mounted gearshift lever into low and we motored down his driveway and onto the country road at a pace that would scarcely disturb a nearby napping dog. In terms of engine rpms and gearing, trucks of the mid-1950s and earlier vintage are happier in the field than on the highway. In fact, the field is where we headed, looking to show off the truck in a familiar setting

GMC's trademark through the 1950s was a massive grille, which for 1954 encloses the parking lights. The 1954 GMC harmonizes nicely with its rural Michigan setting.

15

There are two ways to approach the repairs and cosmetic upgrading needed by most older trucks. One is to leave the truck as intact as possible while making whatever repairs are needed to various mechanical components (the engine, brakes, front end, steering and so on), then doing body work and refinishing, replacing the flooring in the bed and redoing the interior. We'll call this approach *rebuilding*. The other is to disassemble the vehicle to the last nut or bolt and then overhaul all mechanical assemblies, strip off all paint, root out all traces of rust and, in effect, reduce the vehicle to a collection of parts that can then be reworked to better than factory condition. This approach we will call *restoration*. The goal of restoration is to bring your truck as close as possible to what it was like when it what rolled off the assembly line, but with the quality finish and workmanship that could be expected on a Rolls-Royce or other craftsman-built vehicle. The decision whether to rebuild or restore should be based on thoughtful consideration of the plusses and minuses to each approach. To help you make that decision, the merits of both approaches will be examined in five categories: your goal for the vehicle; its intended use; the amount of money you are able (and willing) to put into the vehicle; the amount of time you have to spend on the rebuilding or restoration process; and your patience or endurance. Weighing both approaches by these criteria should help you decide which direction to take.

Rebuilding Approach

Although your truck will be inoperable for short periods during the rebuilding process (while the engine is being over-hauled, for example), this piece-meal approach allows you to drive the truck during most of the rebuilding steps. Another benefit of rebuilding is being able to spread the cost of most repairs over as long a period of time as necessary, while still using the truck. Rebuilding also takes less shop space than restoration because the truck is never completely apart. If this is your first experience reworking a vintage vehicle, you're not as likely to lose interest in the project if you take it one component at a time rather than scattering the parts all over your garage and then having to muster the endurance to stick with the project for two, five, or even ten years (depending on your time commitment) while every part is cleaned, rebuilt, painted, and reassembled into the finished truck.

If you're fortunate enough to find (or own) a vehicle that has escaped the ravages of time and hard use, you'll impress far more people by doing just those necessary cosmetic and mechanical repairs than if you take it all apart and strip and paint every inch of metal so that it shines like a newborn. Any truck can be restored, but only an exceptionally well cared for truck can and should be preserved in its original condition. Both the Antique Automobile Club of America (AACA) and the Vintage Chevrolet Club of America (VCCA)

Trucks owned by fire departments are often in well-preserved original condition. Although it looks restored, the information with this 1954 GMC panel truck said, "No rust, new tires. Runs good. Unrestored original condition. Has been garaged when not in use." The mileage isn't listed, but it is certain to be low.

now have historic preservation classes for original unrestored vehicles. The purpose of the historic preservation classes to encourage people not to restore vehicles whose history should be preserved.

A goal of rebuilding, especially if you are starting with a truck that's in fairly good condition, is to bring your truck back to what it looked like when it was two or three years old. It won't be so perfectly manicured that you'll have to shoo the neighbor kids away from and you won't be afraid to leave it in a parking lot. However, people will still stop and tell you how good your truck looks, and many will probably tell you that

your truck reminds them of one they owned. That's what rebuilding accomplishes. It doesn't build a monument; it rekindles the past. For many collectors, that's the kind of old truck they want.

The steps to rebuilding a "typical" older truck include removing the fenders and pounding out the dents, repairing rust (typically found in the cab cowl and rear corners), most likely overhauling the engine, definitely reworking the brakes, replacing the wiring, upgrading the interior, and repainting the exterior. Of course, numerous other jobs may also be called for—from replanking the box to replacing the window glass.

The one major drawback to the rebuilding approach is the likelihood that there will always be something you wish you had done more thoroughly. For example, you're likely to repair only visible body damage and overlook deteriorated cab supports and rusted inner body panels. Repairing hidden damage is just as important in rebuilding as it is with restoration, but since the truck isn't taken apart, not all problems are likely to get noticed during the appropriate phase of the work. Later, when you're hooking up an exhaust system, you may glance at the cab supports and suddenly realize that the body is supported by Swiss cheese. Welding new metal into the support brackets at that stage can be a lot harder, especially if the nearby exterior surfaces have just been freshly painted.

Restoration Approach

Unless you ship your truck off to a professional restorer, you can plan on a ground-up restoration taking from 3-5 years. The "average" restoration requires 2,000 hours to complete. That's a man-year (40 hours a week times 50 weeks). A person

Some trucks shouldn't be restored. This Advance Design one ton model had been with its original owner until John Milliman, editor of the Stovebolt page website, bought it. Everything about the truck is original. The Antique Automobile Club of America (AACA) has established a Preservation class for such original condition vehicles.

Milliman's truck still has the assembly line inspector's markings on the firewall.

With trucks that have been worked hard and in cold weather climates where the metal is eaten by road salt, the amount of rebuilding required essentially amounts to restoration and is better planned as such.

working a full-time job may be able to devote 10 to 15 hours a week on an old truck restoration project, or 500 to 650 hours a year three years minimum, more likely longer since sustaining the work pace week after week is likely to produce emotional and marital strains. Mike Cavey, whose prize winning 1951 Chevy pickup is shown here, logged over 2,000 hours restoring what had been a quite well preserved, original truck. Cavey managed to complete his truck in just about two years, doing all work on his spare time. To make this goal possible, he had a friend's help on a regular basis, his son reworked the engine and he has a very understanding wife.

The benefit of restoring is that every part of the truck needing attention gets it. When the restoration is finished, the truck should be better than new. At that point you will face the restorer's dilemma. Can you drive and enjoy your truck, and endure the inevitable scratches, chipped paint, and oil film on the formerly immaculate engine compartment, and grime on the undercarriage, or must the truck now be an object to be looked at and not touched or driven?

Determining Standards

If your plans are to restore your truck so that it can compete in the show circuit, you will do everything possible to make sure every detail, up to and including the placement of the seam on the door weather stripping, matches exactly with original standards. If, however, you are restoring or rebuilding your truck so that it can be driven and enjoyed on the highway you will

Although looking a little dilapidated, the gray Advance Design truck in this photo's foreground could be a candidate for either rebuilding or restoration, especially as the body does not show much rust.

be more inclined to consider modifications that will increase your driving comfort and bring the truck up to modern highway standards. A complaint of most older truck owners is the low-speed rear axles installed in the days when a pickup may have seen the open highway only once or twice a week taking its owner to town. A pickup of 1930s or 1940s vintage is likely to feel uncomfortable at speeds much over 50 mph. During this same time period, Chevrolet didn't offer a higher (lower numerical ratio) rear end gearing for highway use.

What's the answer? For light duty Chevrolet trucks from 1940 through 1965, Patrick's Chevy Pickup Restorations in Casa Grande, Arizona, offers a higher speed gear set that can be installed in your truck's differential. Lower numerical (higher speed) rear end gearing can also be obtained by installing an overdrive transmission; however, the torque tube drivelines that Chevrolet used through 1954 don't allow bolt-in overdrive installation.

Converting the electrical system to 12 volts is another popular upgrade among collectors who plan to drive their trucks. If you change to a 12-volt electrical system, you'll have plenty of capacity for power-hungry accessories such as air conditioning and a modern radio and sound system. The higher voltage will also spin the starter faster, making the engine start more easily. You can modernize in these ways and still have a truck that looks stock.

Restoring an older truck to original standards requires extensive research. If your truck has been repainted, and chances are it has, you'll want to determine its original color. If there's another color you prefer, you'll need to find out whether it was offered for your year and model truck, and if not, what were the other color options. You will also need to research original engine-color schemes as well as whether the engine that's in your truck now is the one installed at the factory. If pinstripes were used on the wheels and cab, you'll need to find out the location, size, and color options for the stripes. Sometimes pinstripes will show up during the paint removing process. If not, you will need to determine the stripe's location from a truck with its original finish or a correctly striped show truck. When restoring a truck for show competition, there'll be a myriad of details including the proper style cap on the tire air valves, the correct spark plugs with painted or plated bases, original-style markings on the door and windshield glass, the right coating for the bed wood and all sorts of similar facts that will require research to establish authenticity

It's misleading to think that entering the show circuit is the only reason for restoring a truck as close to original condition as possible. Maintaining originality can also be personally satisfying—by giving you the sense when you're preserved a reminder of a bygone era, and is the best assurance for maximizing your truck's value. Anyone can rework an older truck with new parts and coat it with any color their heart desires; its takes stamina to track down original parts and to stick consistently to the original colors and overall appearance.

Gathering Information

Before you scatter your truck all over the garage, you should acquire a set of shop manuals, which should include Chevrolet Shop manual for your year and model truck. Chevrolet printed a shop manual for each year, also in some years the manual is a supplement so the previous year's full manual is also needed. The Master Parts catalog is also available in reprint form for many years. This book's exploded diagrams can be helpful with assembly sequences. If you buy a parts book a few years newer than your truck, you will get a good idea of what parts interchange. Another helpful information source is the Restoration Package available from General Motors (800) 222-1020. This package includes an invaluable specifications booklet.

Before approaching your truck with wrenches in hand, you need to assemble a collection of shop manuals.

Shop manuals are available from the literature dealers and can often be found at swap meets. You will use the shop manual to take the truck apart, as well as put it together. By following the disassembly steps in the manual, you'll find that things come apart easier—and you're less likely to break hard-to-replace items. Besides the Chevrolet service manual, it's also advisable to have a copy of the Motor's or Chilton's manual covering your year and model truck. To gain full understanding of how a component operates, and to learn the assembly or disassembly sequence, it is often helpful to be able to read the instructions from more than one vantage point.

While you're at it, order catalogs from several parts vendors specializing in vintage Chevrolet trucks. The catalogs often show exploded views of mechanical assemblies that can also help with disassembly, and when you've identified parts needing replacement the catalogs will suggest sources and prices for these parts.

To get a sense of what your truck looked like when new, you should scout and purchase sales literature for your year truck. These brochures will show original engineering and styling features, upholstery style, engines and interior and exterior colors. Sales brochures will help you spot changes that have been made to your truck over the years and will guide you toward its authentic preservation. Sales literature for Advance Design and later Chevy trucks is quite widely available and reasonably priced. Earlier literature is harder to find and correspondingly more expensive. In addition to the sales literature, you should also purchase one or more of the Chevrolet light truck reference books available from this publisher.

For Chevrolet trucks starting with the 1947 Advance Design series reprints of the original Factory Assembly Manuals are also available. These books, which consist largely of illustrations showing detailed views of chassis and body assemblies, are helpful guides to restorers who want to make sure that their trucks are as close to original as possible. Unfortunately, the Assembly Manuals are somewhat incomplete. However, they are good for the pages they contain, which are considerable.

Estimating Parts Costs

Whether you decide to restore or rebuild your truck you should prepare an estimate of expenses you expect to incur. Included in this cost estimate will be amounts for parts, labor, transportation and supplies. You can estimate parts costs by going through a catalog from a major Chevy parts vendor like Jim Carter's Classic Chevrolet Parts, based in Independence, Missouri. List all the items you think may be needed for your truck and price each item. Then add up the total amount. In actuality, you will probably shop around for parts, finding some at swap meets, others at auto supply stores and some at salvage yards, rather than place a shopping order from a single vendor's catalog. It's unlikely, however, that your parts bill will be less than the estimate because unanticipated replacement or repairs are inevitable. In fact, it will almost certainly exceed your estimate—the question is by how much. I suggest a fifty, even 100 percent fudge factor—perhaps even more if this is your first restoration.

Labor charges you will pay others, such as metal repair on the truck's body, mechanical or trim work and painting can grow very large, very fast. For this reason, most collectors try to do as much work on their trucks as they can. The problem many first-time rebuilders and restorers encounter in trying to redo their trucks themselves is the lack of proper tools and the skills to use them. Bodywork is an example. You can't do much in the way of metal repair without a welder and even if you invest a few hundred dollars in a suitable capacity welder, the tool isn't much use until you know how to use it.

Gathering catalogs from parts suppliers will help determine what parts are needed and their cost. You'll also enjoy and learn from publications addressing the old truck hobby.

Labor Costs

In estimating labor costs, make a list of the jobs you want to do yourself, then indicate whether your current tool assortment will be adequate for this work, or if additional tools and skills are needed. For example, most of the mechanical repair on a vintage Chevy truck can be done with a 3/8 or 1/2 in. drive socket set, assorted wrenches, pliers, screwdrivers, a file, hammer, chisel, and hacksaw, hydraulic jack, jack stands, and a few specialty tools like a gear puller. But for an engine overhaul and body work you will need a larger stock of specialized tools and equipment.

The question here is how large a tool investment are you willing to make to do as much of the work on your truck as possible? If you find working with your hands to be a therapeutic pastime (and many do), then you'll find the tool investment to be a great savings over the cost of having others do this work. Besides, once you've made the initial investment, the tools are yours—probably for a lifetime. If you plan to do as much of the work on your truck as possible, include the tool and training costs in the labor expenses category.

There will always be some work you will need to hire out and for this you should get estimates. In many cases, shops will be reluctant to quote a price for mechanical or repair work on an older vehicle, not wanting to be held to the quote when unforeseen problems develop. You can explain that for now, you're just looking for a ball-park figure which will probably be on the high side. In the labor cost category you will include specialty work such as chrome plating, and jobs better left to experts like instrument gauge repair and windshield replacement.

There are other ways, besides doing the work yourself, to shave labor costs. One is to share work with friends. The times I've been able to do this have been among my most enjoyable restoration experiences. As an example, a friend and I both needed to rebuild the steering and front end on our collector vehicles. So we took the front ends on both our vehicles apart, determined the parts we needed, pooled our orders and got a small discount for placing the larger order, then set up an assembly-line operation for cleaning, refinishing, and rebuilding both front-end and steering assemblies. This approach was much more efficient than if we had overhauled each vehicle separately, but more importantly, we learned from each other and had a great time in the process.

Another cost-saving alternative, sometimes available, is to have major mechanical or body work done by students in a vocational-technical program. Admittedly, there are some risks here. Parts can be lost and the quality of the instruction will determine the outcome of the finished product. I teach at a technical college which trains students in engine rebuilding, bodywork, machining and similar trades, and have consigned my truck to these programs for all of its body work and painting, plus some engine and other mechanical work. The process is not very speedy and problems do arise, but any lower quality work, such as a heavy "orange peel" texture that appeared in the paint near the bottom of the driver's door, has always been made right. The big plus to having a vo-tech

One option for saving costs is to consign mechanical or body repair to students in a vocational-technical program.

program assist in a vehicle's rebuild or restoration is the nominal labor charges. A hoped-for offshoot is giving the students an appreciation of older vehicles.

Supply Costs

Your expense estimate must also include a listing of supplies. This category covers everything from sandpaper and painting supplies, to masking tape, miscellaneous nuts, bolts and fasteners, weather stripping glue, plastic sheeting to protect parts from dust, sand for sandblasting, reference literature including sales brochures and service and parts manuals—in short all the odds and ends that you will need to complete your truck's restoration or rebuilding project. There's really no way you can accurately project supply expenses in advance, but all-told this figure will probably approach $1,000 by the time your truck is finished.

Transportation Costs

The last category in your cost estimate is for transportation expenses. These may include hauling the cab to a chemical stripping facility, traveling to scrap yards and swap meets to hunt for parts, UPS or freight charges for parts you may order from parts vendors, as well as travel to look at original, restored, or "in process" trucks. You may think of these travel expenses as part of the enjoyment of your hobby, but they are also part of the cost of restoring or rebuilding your truck, so you might as well project some figures and tally them in. Whether or not you will be using your truck in any business capacity, be sure to keep a log of travel and related expenses to use in calculating an accurate appreciation figure should you decide to sell your truck sometime in the future.

Exploring swap meets looking for parts can be a pleasant pastime but travel experiences for these forays are also part of the restoration expense.

When you add up all the expense estimates you may want to take a deep breath before you hit the total key on your calculator. Even rebuilding an older truck can be a more costly an undertaking than you would think—and restoring is likely to run considerably more. But don't let that sour you on sprucing up your old truck. You'll find that some of the costs can be trimmed and overall the expenses will be spread over the duration of the project. If restoration seems outside your budget, you might consider the rebuilding approach.

Shopping for Parts

Whether your approach is rebuilding or restoration, you'll spend a sizeable part of the your time hunting parts. The quicker you develop reliable parts sources, and tap into a good parts network, the smoother your parts hunting will be and the less likely you are to be taken on price and inferior quality. In a hobby where over 90% of the businesses are reputable and are as concerned about their reputations as you or I, there are, unfortunately, still a few shysters and often their catalogs are the ones that newcomers find first. One of your best supplier recommendations is the reference to preferred vendors you'll see in articles offering restoration tips in magazines like *Vintage Truck*. But even here it pays to shop around. A good policy is to order catalogs from several suppliers, then compare prices and place small orders at first to test the service. When you are satisfied that you've found a supplier whose service and quality you can trust, then you've got a green light to go ahead with your larger orders.

In shopping for parts, don't overlook the local auto parts stores. NAPA auto parts stores, a nationwide network of independently owned stores served by a massive warehousing system, have probably the most complete listings of parts for older vehicles. Not only are the items usually less expensive through a NAPA outlet than a restoration supplier, but there are no separate handling and shipping fees. Usually your local store can have the part within twenty-four hours after placing your order, if the part is not already on the store's shelves. If your area doesn't have a NAPA store, check parts availability at other large auto parts outlets.

Whether you're rebuilding or restoring, you'll also want to explore that most enjoyable parts source—the scrap yard. Unfortunately, old-fashioned salvage yards filled with vintage vehicles are fast disappearing. Serious collectors shroud these haunts with the secrecy of a gold prospector—but once they've picked their parts most will share their discovery with you. The question is who to ask. That's where joining a truck club for old-truck collectors comes in. Here truck enthusiasts will share their "finds" and help one another in that all-important parts search.

With the exception of some body and trim parts that have all but disappeared from circulation, Chevrolet truck parts are really quite easy to find. One reason, besides the fact that during nearly the entire collector period Chevrolet trucks were

Salvage yards can be a source of hard-to-find parts, especially for those restoring or refurbishing larger trucks.

Chevrolet trucks benefit from an extensive supply of reproduction parts. Making a grocery list of needed parts and totaling their cost will help you estimate one facet of your truck's overall restoration or rebuilding expense. You'll need to add a 50-100 percent fudge factor to approximate the actual cost.

the nation's best-seller, is the interchangeability of engine parts, as well as body parts in certain years, with the Chevrolet car line. Most body parts also interchange between Chevrolet and GMC. You'll find needed interchange information in Hollander manuals that are the mechanic's bible of parts substitution. Although copies can sometimes be found in general repair shops, the easiest access to this valuable interchange information is to buy a reprinted copy. You need the Hollander that is slightly newer than your truck. Popular reprints are 1949, 1956, 1966 and 1972.

Working at Your Own Pace

Working on your truck can be great therapy from the pressures of everyday life if you follow a few common sense guidelines. The first, of course, is don't let the truck become the driving compulsion of your life. If this happens, then daily life will become an escape from your truck, not the other way around. The simplest way to turn working on your truck from a relaxing pastime to a compulsion is to set deadlines on your work. Repair or restoration of an older vehicle never agrees with deadlines. Sometimes jobs will go smoother than expected, but not often. More commonly, the unexpected will throw your work off pace. The most common schedule saboteurs are missing or incorrect parts, but setbacks can also arise that seem providentially placed to test your patience. An acquaintance had a fly ball hit from a field across the street from his house land in the center of a freshly painted tailgate that he was preparing to remount on his truck. The ball left a dish shaped indent in the metal that had to be pounded out and the tailgate refinished. Heartbreaks like this often strike in the final stages, often the night you're putting on the last touches in preparation for tomorrow's show.

Scheduling the Work

The second guideline to making the time you spend working on your truck enjoyable is to take the jobs in manageable chunks. While it's smart to keep an eye out for parts and information you may need for later jobs, even a frame-up restoration should be handled one job at a time. If the current stage of work is sandblasting, then give your attention to that step and deal with concerns about metal repair later. If while working on larger projects, such as rebuilding the drivetrain, metal repair or refinishing, you sense frustration or impatience setting in, it's a good idea to break off and concentrate on a smaller, more manageable job that you can complete in one or two evenings or a weekend. That way, you'll have the satisfaction of seeing something through to completion and you'll return to the larger project with renewed confidence in achieving your goal.

As mentioned earlier it also helps to work with a partner or friend. Besides getting more than twice as much accomplished working with someone else has the benefit that most often when one gets discouraged the other will provide the encouragement to move ahead. Mike Cavey said that he would never have been able to restore his Grand National award winning 1951 Chevy pickup without the help of his friend, Brad Rose. Not only does Rose possess skills and equipment that Cavey does not, but Cavey says he stuck more faithfully to his project knowing that someone else would be at the shop waiting for him to show up. Cavey also says that he couldn't have driven himself to achieve his truck's level of perfection—"best in the world". Details like putting in those extra hours to assure a perfect fit on the front end metal and hood, took a buddy's saying, "Let's give that one more try."

Another way to avoid old truck burnout is to alternate between smaller jobs and larger projects. If you live in a

Interspersing small jobs like rebuilding the starter with larger projects helps reduce stress.

Disassembly should be slow and deliberate, one major assembly like the pickup box at time, not a weekend frenzy of wrenches that leaves the truck strewn apart in your garage

northern climate, winters may be a dead time as far as working in your shop is concerned. But you can keep your truck progressing by rebuilding smaller assemblies like the starter, generator or carburetor in your basement. You can also take time to send instruments out for rebuilding, or have the chrome plating done. That way, you'll feel like your truck is progressing, even if you aren't standing, toes numb, on bone chilling concrete, gripping an icy wrench.

Choosing the Rebuilding Approach

Whether your goal is rebuilding or restoration, you're going to be taking the truck apart, but not in a flurry of wrenches, chisels, and cutting torch. Instead the disassembly process needs to be slow and deliberate—one major assembly at a time, not a feverish weekend that leaves the truck scattered in pieces all over the garage. Disassembly is slow for three reasons: first to document each disassembly step, second to keep the disassembly from getting ahead of your enthusiasm and financial resources and third, so as not to break anything.

Disassembly for Repair

If you have decided to make your truck presentable and driveable by the repair approach, you will limit disassembly to just those parts or sheet metal that need reworking. A must-do job on any older vehicle is inspecting and overhauling the brakes. If you're working through a brake system for the first time, it's good advice to take only one side apart at a time. That way, if you get stuck putting a front or rear brake back together—and the instructions in the service manual don't make themselves clear—you can always pull off the drum on the opposite side of the truck and use its brakes for a reassembly guide

When rebuilding paired assemblies like brakes if you take apart one side at a time you can use the parts on the opposite side of the truck for a guide to reassembly.

(providing, of course, that someone hasn't cobbled up the brakes in a previous repair). When doing sheet metal repair, installing patch panels in the cab for example, it is sometimes advisable to do some further disassembly to make the job easier. With the patch panels, you might also want to remove the doors. Always remove the gas tank before doing any welding in its vicinity. You'll need to remove the pickup box to get to the back of the cab and to replace its cross braces and wooden floor. The engine will be removed from the truck for rebuilding, and the list goes on.

The basic guideline here is to take apart only one or two assemblies at the same time. While the engine is out of the truck for rebuilding, it makes sense to overhaul the brakes and replace the wiring. Overall, though, you will keep the truck as intact as possible so that you can continue to use and enjoy it while doing the upgrades. As the parts come off, tag them individually or if you're less meticulous sort and store each item in labeled boxes—"engine head bolts". Sure you'll need lots of boxes, large and small, coffee cans, jars and bottles. Collect the containers ahead of time. Also keep a log or journal. "Tuesday, removed engine. Disconnected throttle linkage (stored on middle shelf, garage south wall)...etc." In addition to the notes, photographs taken at each major disassembly step are also a great help when you're putting things back together. After the photos are processed, arrange them in an album to show the disassembly sequence. If you have a camcorder, ask a spouse, neighbor, or family or neighborhood teenager to videotape of the disassembly stages. You can watch the tapes for entertainment when you're bogged down with at a later stage, and the tapes can be a lifeline when you're trying to piece things back together. As much as possible, have replacement parts on hand before starting the repair. This way your truck won't be laid up while a supplier back orders out of stock parts.

One more disassembly caution—*don't throw anything away until the project is completely finished*, maybe not even then. You'll be amazed at the "value" some worn out parts may have. Not all of today's replacement parts exactly match originals. If a reproduction fender or hood won't fit, you can compare it to the damaged or rusted original. Perhaps the new part won't fit because the mounting holes are drilled incorrectly or a flange is missing or in the wrong location. When you are building a truck to enter in national competition this can mean pounding jig marks into reproduction sheet metal parts.

Sometimes you may even wind up re-using a part you thought sure you'd throw away. I did this once with a piece of headliner after I carelessly creased the item for that location that came with a kit. Not wanting to buy another headliner kit for just one piece, I sorted through the old headliner I'd removed from the truck was able to cut a new section from one of the better preserved originals and finish the project.

The other cardinal rule is *don't do anything you can't undo*. Observing this rule is going to take judgment on your skills, but essentially it says: don't get over-enthusiastic about what you take apart.

Choosing the Restoration Approach

Most first-time restorers begin by taking their vehicle apart. This is totally the wrong approach. It's true that the vehicle will have to be disassembled, but this is *not* the first step. You should begin by researching your truck as thoroughly as possible. This research begins with writing down as much information as you can find on the truck itself. This includes data codes, the original color scheme (usually visible underneath the hood, on the back of the cab behind the seat, and other places that aren't

When a truck is disassembled for restoration, space is needed to store the parts.

Frame-up restoration means eventually disassembling the truck to the bare frame and rebuilding from there. Richard Matott

likely to be repainted), engine and chassis numbers, and details such as mileage, accessories, tire sizes, and the like. Researching is also done by taking clear color photos of the truck from every conceivable angle, front and back, top and bottom. Note such details as the location of the weather strip around the doors and the location of the seam if the weather stripping is original, the location and width of striping on the wheels or body reveals, the presence or absence of welting between the fenders and body—everything you can think of. From your research you will also make a list of everything about the truck that you find to be unoriginal. Examples might include incorrect tail lights (from a hardware or auto supply store), signal lights on trucks not originally so fitted, an incorrect engine, missing hubcaps and the list goes on.

Disassembly for Restoration

Despite the cautions against impetuous disassembly, the process of restoration requires that we take things apart. The question is what's the right way? Do we just proceed by intuition: loosen a bolt here, pry a little there, try to make the parts come loose? If intuition is our approach, we're sure to do more damage as we take things apart.

A better approach is to know the right way to get the pieces to come apart. Window crank handles, for example, are typically held in place by little "C" clips that are easily popped off (and popped back on again) with a window crank handle removal tool. Without the right tool removing jobs like this can be very frustrating. Early handles to 1966 used a set screw, sometimes two set screws jammed in series down the same hole in the handle.

Body assembly manuals provided to dealerships by manufacturers and available today through automotive literature vendors, show the steps for removing window crank handles and the tool to use. Likewise, shop manuals detail mechanical disassembly steps—both in the right sequence and specifying the correct tools. The problem with disassembling components of an old truck using body or shop manuals as a guide is that age often causes things to come apart very differently (and more difficulty) than they did when new. Here tricks passed down by old timers can be of great help. Often these "tricks" are published in technical articles in club magazines and can be learned in restoration clinics and classes such as the technical seminars offered at some national club events.

Storing Parts After They've Been Removed

As parts are removed they need to be labeled and stored so that they won't be damaged and can be easily located. Small items like nuts and bolts should be placed in labeled containers. Large mouth jars with lids are ideal because the jars can be sealed to keep the parts from spilling out and being lost. Plastic containers are recommended over glass, which will break if dropped. Besides jars, cardboard boxes are needed to hold larger items. The extra-thick cardboard boxes from liquor stores are useful for holding smaller assemblies like carburetors, headlight and tail light assemblies, or trim items. The boxes should also be labeled with the items they contain. A roll of wide masking tape and a felt marker are ideal for labeling. Parts should be stored on shelves or a storage loft so that they're not underfoot.

Each assembly should be restored as it is removed from the truck. For example, lets say that we begin by removing the bumpers and chrome plated trim so that these items can be sent out for replating. The bumpers attach by brackets and are removed most easily by unbolting the brackets where they attach. The brackets can be removed more easily with the bumpers lying on the shop floor. So now you have the bumpers ready to pack and ship to the plater and the brackets and bolts. Before packing away the brackets, they should be stripped of paint and rust, metal prepped to prevent rerusting, primed, and finish painted. The bolts are similarly cleaned and painted if that's how they looked at the factory, or set aside for plating. When the brackets are finish painted they can be wrapped in pairs, placed in durable plastic bags, wrapped and securely sealed with duct tape, labeled, boxed with the other similarly wrapped and labeled bracket sets, and stored until needed. This piece-by-piece, restoration, sorting, and storage procedure may seem more time consuming, but is actually the most efficient way to go. It will prevent parts from being lost—with consequent lost time and frustration, possibly cost, to locate or purchase replacements.

When the windshield and rear window glass are removed these items should be stored standing up. Even though glass appears solid, it is actually liquid. (Tests have shown this by placing a wire with weights attached to the ends over one end of a vertically positioned sheet of glass. Over time, the wire will cut through the glass.) Lying curved glass flat risks distortion.

Fabric items, like headliner or seat coverings that will be re-used, also require proper storage. These items should lay flat and not be folded. Folds may show as creases when the fabric is re-installed. Likewise, new fabric seat coverings should be unpacked as soon as they are received and stored flat. Otherwise the folds from shipping may be difficult to remove. Avoid storing fabric in direct sunlight which can cause fading or where rodents may decide to use your new seat covering for a nest. Rodents can be difficult to keep out of shop areas, but a fully enclosed area is the first step. Some people also report success using moth balls to repel rodents.

When disassembling an early Advance Design (1947-53) grille, look for notches on the back side that were made in the factory so that you can get the bars back in the right locations.

If at all possible, avoid outside storage for any part of the truck, including body and chassis. Decay will set in a lot more quickly than you think. Parking your restoration project outside on damp ground for just one season—maybe while the engine is out and being rebuilt—can cause a coating of mildew to develop on the interior, rust scale to form on the underbody surface, and, brake cylinders or calipers seize—not a pretty picture. If you lack inside storage, look into renting space or some other solution.

As you remove the truck's sheet metal, be sure to save all bolts and as much as possible avoid breaking bolts during disassembly. Ways to keep rusty bolts from seizing on the nut and breaking are to soak the bolt and nut well with penetrating oil for several days before attempting to turn them loose. Then, if the nut still refuses to turn, apply heat with a welding torch.

Although shop manuals provide fairly detailed disassembly and rebuilding instructions for your truck's mechanical components, working on a 30-60 year old vehicle is different than overhauling the same vehicle when new. The rebuilding instructions in this book will take those differences into account and will guide you through difficulties you may experience and provide tips for making old parts work like new.

Disassembly and Restoration Sequence

The typical restoration sequence proceeds in the following steps:

1. Remove and send out chrome items for replating.

This step begins the restoration process because replating chrome items can take several months—a half-year or more. Restoring an old truck is like cooking a meal. It's important that everything be ready at the same time. Consequently it makes sense to begin with items that are going to take the longest time to progress through the restoration process. Note

that we're talking about chrome-plated items such as grille bars, diecast marker trim, door handles and latches. Stainless steel trim can be removed and restored separately.

In some cases you may decide to buy new, rather than have old chrome parts replated. This is especially true of bumpers where a new replacement may be available at a fraction of the cost of straightening and replating the original. If you make this decision, order the new chrome parts while you're having the others replated. This way all chrome plated items will be on hand when you're ready for reassembly. Shopping for chrome plated pieces by price is a mistake. Instead use length of warrantee and reputation of the supplier as your guides.

2. Gut the interior.

Remove the seats, door and other interior panels and headliner. This step is in preparation for body work, but as each component comes out, the same "restore before removing the next item" philosophy prevails. This means that the seat

When rebuilding, getting the truck running takes precedence over body repair. Hank Fresonke

When rebuilding, it helps to remove the forward sheet metal for easier access to the engine.

A benefit or restoration is that every part will be rebuilt as new.

assembly should be disassembled, repaired, built back up, and recovered before removing any sheet metal. Once the seat cushions that have been rebuilt and recovered, they should be sealed in plastic bags and stored for installation back in the car at a later date. This is a good time to order new interior coverings and headliner, if your truck is so-equipped.

3. Remove sheet metal and perform all necessary metal repair.

At this stage you will unbolt the box from the frame, remove the fenders, grille, hood and other parts of the front clip and, finally, remove the cab from the frame. Note: Unbolting and removing the steering column makes removing the cab much easier. Metal repair may require cutting out and redoing earlier repairs, straightening dents, and filling holes drilled in the fender, cab or doors to mount lights or mirrors. If these accessories will be replaced on the car later, the holes can be re-drilled. It's easier to re-drill a hole than to have to fill a hole after the car has been finish painted.

As fenders are removed, they are straightened, any rust damage repaired, the old finish stripped off or prepared for

priming. Then the metal is coated with a rust proof primer and the part is carefully stored (hanging fenders by wires run through bolt holes can distort the part's shape).

4. Remove and overhaul the engine, gearbox, suspension, and wiring.

This step typically interrupts work on the interior and body work/refinishing. On a frame-up restoration, all mechanical components will typically be removed, disassembled, and rebuilt. Again, keeping with our one component at a time philosophy, we'll focus our attention on one mechanical assembly at a time (though the engine and transmission are often removed as a unit).

If you decide to send the engine out to be rebuilt (as opposed to rebuilding it yourself), or while waiting for machine work to be done, you can rebuild the carburetor, generator, and other engine accessories—sealing and storing each as they're finished. Likewise other driveline and suspension parts, including the rear end, springs, and other assemblies.

With a frame-up restoration, mechanical work may proceed apace with body work. In a rebuilding scenario where the truck is not going to be completely overhauled, mechanical work should precede body work. It's important to get the truck running before investing in expensive body repair.

On trucks of 1950s vintage and earlier with cloth-insulated wiring, the insulation has probably deteriorated, necessitating that the wiring harness be replaced. On later model trucks with plastic insulated wiring, if the insulation is intact and harness is in good condition with all circuits operating, the connectors may be cleaned or replaced if corroded and the wiring left otherwise undisturbed.

5. Clean and refinish the frame for reassembly

This marks the turn-around step. From this point onward, the truck will be going back together.

Restored trucks appear as new, inside as well as out. Rob Pederson

27

6. Prepare the body for finish painting.

Depending on the condition of the finish and the number of times the truck has been repainted, all layers of paint and primer may be stripped off to bare metal. This process can be accomplished chemically or mechanically—either way being relatively tedious and time consuming, and therefore something you'll probably do yourself rather than hiring it out. If you've invested in an air compressor and spray painting gun, you're also likely to prep and prime the cab, fenders and other sheet metal—though you may leave finish painting for a professional. There are two reasons for having the finish paint professionally applied: a top quality finish takes skill and special equipment; the painting products may be highly toxic.

All mechanical work is completed prior to finish painting so as not to damage the paint. However, mechanical assembly and painting may proceed in stages, with underbody, underhood and interior surfaces being primed and finish painted, then the cab and box re-mounted on the chassis, after all mechanical assemblies are back in place, then the wiring installed. Now the cab, box, fenders, hood, grille and other sheet metal can be painted and window glass refitted.

Whether rebuilding or restoring, it's important to have a system for organizing parts. Trent Stephan

7. Remount trim and exterior accessories.

The truck is gathering a completed look. Remounting the bumpers and other exterior items like headlights and mirrors goes fast and hastens the finished appearance. Now you see the reason for restoring each item as it's removed from the car. If you reach this stage only to remember that the bumpers are still lying dented and rusted in a corner of the shop, you're in for a big disappointment. How much better to pull these restored items from inventory and put them back on the truck. Indeed, the end is in sight.

8. Replace the interior.

We've reached the final step. However, we're going to have to be very careful. While installing the door and interior panels, replacing the seats, and fitting the headliner, it's very easy to mar the finish. Use plenty of protective cloths (old sheets and blankets) and work very carefully. The consensus is that it's easier to install the interior without damaging the finish than it is to apply the finish without damaging the interior. If you haven't already done so, you'll also glue new weather seal in place around the door openings.

Note: On Chevrolet trucks 1947 and up, the door weather seal must be replaced before the door is hung. Bob Adler, owner of Adler's Antique Autos in Stephentown, NY, notes, "I glue on the door weatherstrip right after painting the interior

Tip: Loosening Rust-frozen Bolts
To remove rusted bolts, heat each bolt red hot with an acetylene torch and apply a sponge soaked in cold water. The heat removes hydration from the rust, shrinking it and opening space at the threads.

While pickup boxes interchange over various series, other parts also fit multiple years. For instance, the 1964 grille shown here was also used in 1966.

panel with the door on my paint table before flipping the door over to paint the exterior. To gain some clearance, I put bolts in the hinge and trim holes to hold the door off the table."

Looking Ahead

The chapters that follow describe the major restoration/ rebuilding steps that are typically followed in refurbishing an older truck. Each is presented as a do-it-yourself process that is easily within the capability of anyone with an inclination to learn and the do-it-yourself spirit. Where special tools are required, these are mentioned with the jobs. If a substantial tool investment is required (as is the case with sandblasting), alternative sources to getting the job done are suggested.

One bit of advice. Don't wait until your truck is finished to show it off to your family and friends. A repainted chassis deserves display as much as the finished truck. When the body and box are back in place, who will see that undercarriage on which you lavished so much time and attention? Some restorers have even been known to haul their truck's chassis to shows. Spectators will be amused, and some will later remember the time when your truck rolled in as just a black framework. If you find yourself getting too serious, remember, you're working on that old truck because it's *fun*.

Rebuild or Restore, Which Approach To Take?

REBUILDING

Goal:
To make a reliable running truck that looks
    as it might

Approach:
Start with a well preserved truck.

Advantages:
Spread costs over as long a period of time as
    necessary
Takes less shop space than total disassembly
Less likely to lost interest.

Disadvantages:
Can't drive the truck most of the time while
    repairs are in progress
Requires space equivalent to two-car garage.

Results:
Likelihood there will be some things you wish
    you had done more thoroughly or overlooked

RESTORATION

To bring the truck to showroom or better than
    new originally in use.condition.

Start with any condition truck.

Lack of funds at any critical stage will delay
    completion of project

Truck will be inoperative through most of
    restoration period.
For average hobbyist, a frame-up restoration
    will take 2 to 5 years

Every part needing attention will get it.
When finished the truck will be better than new

In many cases restoration is necessity. Much of this 1926 Chevrolet Series X delivery had disintegrated and had to be hand fabricated.
Winross Restorations

Preparation Steps Checklist

To decide whether rebuilding or restoration is the correct approach for you:

- **Establish standards:**
  Will the truck be modified or stock?
  If modified, what non-stock components will it have?
- **Document the truck with notes and photos on:**
  Weather stripping location
  Original colors
  Pinstripe locations (if any)
  Original and non-original accessories
  Repair work needed (if any)

- **Purchase parts and service manuals, locate sales brochures and resource books.**

- **Begin research:**
  Decode truck's data plate
  Determine original color

  Learn correct coating for bolts and fasteners
  Find out if engine is correct/original
  Determine if drivetrain is original

- **Estimate costs:**
  Estimate parts costs
  Determine tool investment
  Estimate cost of professional services
  Factor-in travel expenses

- **Set up supply network:**
  Order reproduction parts supplier catalogs
  Gather scrap yard references

- **Decide where to begin:**
  Restoration requires complete disassembly
  Rebuilding puts priority on mechanical/safety concerns
    over cosmetics

Restoring 1960-1966 Chevrolet Pickups

Chevrolet's new 1960 truck line introduced a completely redesigned and restyled light pickup truck. These trucks featured improved handling and styling. The new cab was 11 inches lower than the 1950's models and offered more interior room for the driver and passengers. Engineering design changes included the introduction of independent front suspension and torsion springs. The rear axle had deep coil springs with a control arm attached between each end of the axle housing. These control arms helped distribute the force of steering and braking. The new suspension provided a smoother, passenger car type ride.

Chevy's early to mid-sixties trucks are starting to catch on with collectors. Due to the improved riding and handling qualities of independent front suspension, these trucks can be driven comfortably for long distances. Parts are plentiful and reproduction items for these trucks are beginning to appear. Collectors are attracted primarily to the half-ton pickup, either with the narrow Stepside short (6 ft.) box, or wide Fleetside long (8 ft.) box and deluxe trim. Because of their utilitarian nature, Panels and Suburbans also have appeal. The low roofline makes the styling of the Panel and Suburban a vast improvement over the former Task Force models.

The C-10 model half ton truck came standard with the 230 six cylinder. Two optional engines were available, the 292 six and 283 V-8. Transmission selections included 3-speed standard, heavy duty 3 or 4-speed and Powerglide "B" (aluminum case) transmissions. Overdrive was also available with the three-speed standard on some years of this series. The buyer could further improve performance through the purchase of an optional Positraction. The Custom Cab package included armrests, sun visors, chrome accents and body trim, deluxe heater, and a full-size rear window.

Chevrolet's 1960-66 light trucks proved popular with the public and over 3 1/2 million were produced during this period.

In 1964 Chevrolet made a substantial mid-series styling change by replacing the wrap around windshield with a flat windshield. The windshield change resulted in a redesigned cab and new doors. The 1964 model also featured a new interior with restyled gauges, knobs, and dash layout. The exterior cab molding, grille and hubcaps were also changed. For the first time, factory installed in-dash air conditioning was available.

Manuals

Your first purchase (after the truck) should be a 1963 shop manual and a 1964 update. These manuals will provide you with specifications, serial and unit number locations, lubrication and service information, and illustrated repair procedures. A parts book is also very useful. Parts numbers define the differences between the various 1960-66 models. Some things (such as the engine, transmissions, and box) changed very little on this series of trucks, while other items (electrical and body parts) vary a great deal . You will need to know exactly what parts you are looking for (this is why you need access to parts numbers) and how to remove or install them correctly. These manuals can save hours of agony.

GVW Plate

The vehicle rating plate is attached to the left inner cowl panel of the cab, between the door and the air vent on the driver's side. The Gross Vehicle Weight is listed along with certified net engine horsepower, body trim, paint code, wheelbase and cab-axle dimensions of the truck. Coding references are found in the Chevrolet service manual for your year truck.

Color Options

The following GM colors were available to new truck buyers during this series:

1960
Garrison Gray, Golden Yellow, Grenadier Red, Hemlock Green, Klondike Gold (metallic), Marlin Blue, Neptune Green, Brigade Blue, Cardinal Red, Tartan Turquoise.

1961
Neptune Green, Brigade Blue, Flaxen Yellow, Romany Maroon, Tahiti Coral (metallic), Tampico Turquoise, Woodsmoke Blue, Balboa Blue, Cameo White, Woodlawn Green.

1962
Brigade Blue, Balboa Blue, Cameo White, Woodland Green, Tangier Gold (metallic), Crystal Turquoise (metallic), Desert Beige, Georgian Gray, Glenwood Green, Seamist Jade (metallic), Yuma Yellow.

1963
Brigade Blue, Balboa Blue, Cameo White, Woodland

(continued)

Green, Crystal Turquoise (metallic), Desert Beige, Georgian Grey, Glenwood Green, Seamist Jade (metallic), Yuma Yellow.

1964

Coppertone (metallic), Fawn, Gray Green (metallic), Light Green, Dark Blue, Dark Green, Dark Yellow, Grey, Ivory, Light Blue, Turquoise (metallic).

1965

Light Green, Dark Blue, Dark Green, Dark Yellow, Grey, Ivory, Light Blue, Turquoise (metallic), Fawn, Maroon (metallic), Yellow.

1966

Dark Aqua (metallic), Light Green, Saddle (metallic), Silver (metallic), Dark Blue, Dark Green, Dark Yellow, Grey, Ivory, Light Blue, Turquoise (metallic).

Two-tone paint schemes with the cab top and sides painted white were available as options with the Custom Cab series trucks. Black does not appear on the GM paint list.

Whether chromed or plated, front grille had the block letters spelling Chevrolet done in black paint.

Rust Areas

The 1960-1966 Chevrolet pickups have their favorite rust areas. These are the cab corners, lower edges of the cab doors, floor pans, rocker panels, the areas behind the headlight grille, the upper edge of the windshield and inside corners of fenders and box. Rust repair panels are available from many vendors. These are weld in panels or patches and include fenders, cab corners, rocker panels and bed parts.

Some rust areas are difficult to spot. Rust can develop under the door sill plate and spread into the floor and side of the cab as well. The insides of doors are also potential rust targets, especially if deteriorated window or door weather stripping has allowed water to seep into the bottom of the doors. If the door bottoms are rusted through, or spongy, repair panels will have to be purchased and welded in.

You are not likely to spot rusting cab supports unless you crawl underneath the truck and poke at the support brackets. Rusted supports can endanger the stability of the cab. Depending upon the extent of the damage, the supports may be repaired by using patch metal. Severe rust will call for their total replacement—a job that will require loosening the cab from the frame.

The rear floor corners of the cab have drain holes (you will need to pull back the cardboard gas tank liner to see into this area), which often become clogged with debris, allowing water to build up. This area is a common rust-out spot, which is repaired by welding in cab corner patches.

Accessories

Many accessory items were available to buyers who wanted them. These included a windshield washer, air conditioning, seat belts, outside rear view mirrors (right and left in several sizes), power brakes, locking gas cap, fire extinguisher, grille guard, chrome grilles and bumpers, front bumper guards (painted or chrome), deluxe heater, emergency tool kit, backup lights, cigarette lighter, inside (non-glare) rear view mirror, deluxe rear view mirror with day/night feature, manual radio and antenna, passenger side arm rest, radiator screen, hand operated spotlamp, auxiliary springs, rear step bumper, hazard flasher switch and light package, ventshades, and passenger side sun visor. Many of these were grouped together and sold by the dealer as part of the "Custom Cab" package.

Desirable accessories can be found at swap meets or in scrap yard or parts trucks.

Interchangeable parts:

Bed parts and rear fenders are virtually the same throughout this series of trucks. The hoods can also be interchanged. Bumpers are the same for 1960-1962 and 1963-1966 and grilles are the same between 1964 and 1966. On GMC trucks, the grille is the same from 1960-1966. On Stepside models, the rear bumper is the same from 1955-1966.

Chevrolet discontinued the 1960-1961 style truck hood in 1963 and used the 1962-1963 hood as a replacement. The part number was 3820650 and this included all necessary parts for a complete installation (parking lamps, etc.). This way, GM made only one hood fit more years, plus most felt the later hood was more attractive. If your 1960-61 Chevy truck has the later hood, front end damage that required a replacement hood is probably the reason.

Vehicle Identification Number

Each truck has a unique Vehicle Identification Number (VIN). Decoding this number can provide some interesting information. Sample VIN: 4C144F101586 decodes as follows

4	C	14	4	F
Model Year	Vehicle Type	Series designation	Model Type	Assembly Plant
1964	C-Conventional	First numeral	3-Cab-Chassis	A-Atlanta
	K-Four Wheel drive	denotes rating	4-Cab and pickup box	B-Baltimore
		1-1/2 ton		F-Flint
		2-3/4 ton	5-Panel body	G-Framingham
			6-Suburban	J-Jonesville
			9-Cab,platform	K-Kansas City
				L-Los Angeles
				N-Norwood
				O-Oakland
				S-St. Louis
				T-Tarrytown

Translation: This truck is a 1964 conventional drive, 1/2 ton cab with pickup box. It was assembled at the Flint, MI plant. The last digits refer to the truck's production number at that plant. All plant production numbers started at 100001. This is the 1,586th truck to be assembled at the Flint plant in 1964.

CHAPTER 3
SHOP AND TOOLS

Three differences separate the average hobbyist restorer and the restoration professional. Typically these differences lie in the nature of the shop facility where the work is to be done, the completeness of the tool set used to do the work, and the level of the skills in performing various mechanical and body repair techniques as well as familiarity with special tools such as welding outfits and spray painting equipment. Although hobbyists are very resourceful in solving their shop space needs (its not uncommon to hear of vehicles having been restored out of doors, though this approach isn't recommended), before starting a restoration or the repair jobs needed to bring an older truck back to prime, you should take a close look at your work space and compare what's available to the recommendations given here.

Needless to say, you don't expect to purchase every tool that might be useful in restoring an older truck—after all, resourcefulness is part of the game here too. But some jobs such as abrasive blasting do require the necessary tools. In this chapter you will learn what tools should be considered the basic tool set for extensive repair or restoration of an older vehicle, as well as recommendations for specialized tools that you should either consider purchasing, plan to rent, or work out an arrangement where they can be borrowed.

In the process of restoring or extensively repairing (rebuilding) an older truck you will develop and discover skills through trial and error, practice, reading, and getting help and guidance from more experienced friends. Finding those who can guide you through this new territory will be one of the most important steps you can take to help assure that your old truck will end up the beauty of your dreams rather than a half-completed project that has consumed your energies and finances with nothing in return. Experts who will help you in your restoration can be found at the parts counters of auto parts stores, general repair shops, adult auto instruction courses and through involvement in a local old-car or truck club.

As you're sure to discover along the way, many difficult or seemingly impossible jobs are made easy by knowing the right approach. You'll discover some of these tips in this book; you will learn others from the experts you have found to help you when the going gets tough. If enthusiasm overshadows your mechanical and body repair experience, you may find it beneficial to enroll in adult auto mechanics, welding, or body work classes at a nearby skill center, vocational high school, or vo-tech college. Often the instructor will let you work on whatever part of your truck relates to the skills being taught (in a welding class you might install patch panels, for example). Where this is the case, for the small outlay of a tuition fee, you receive not only valuable instruction, but also the use of expensive tools and warm, dry, well-lighted shop space as well.

One of the basic skills for working on any older vehicle is knowing how to light and handle a gas welding outfit. As you take your truck apart there will be many times when a gas wrench, as mechanics often call a gas welding outfit, seems to be an indispensable tool. Welding as a metal repair process is discussed in detail in Chapter 5.

Shop Needs

The space needed to store and work on an old truck grows as the truck is taken apart. For a while you can economize on space by storing dismantled parts in the bed, but sooner or

Critical to restoring or rebuilding an old truck is working space. Here the rebuilder has working room as long as the daily driving vehicles that normally occupy these stalls sit outdoors.

In contrast, this restorer has a clean, spacious area in which to work and storage cabinets in which to organize and store parts.

When you're working on older trucks, chances are you're going to acquire one or more parts vehicles. In many areas zoning would prohibit this restorer's parts collection.

later that comes off too. Then there are the spares and replacements, which sometimes include a parts truck or two, that need to be housed—or at least parked . In some localities zoning regulations require that parts vehicles be stored indoors or may not be allowed at all. Before bringing a parts vehicle home, be sure your local zoning code allows its storage on your premises. And you'll really kick yourself if you toss out rusted or damaged original parts from your truck, only to find that you need them to check a fit or paint scheme after they're gone. The best policy is to save *everything* until the restoration

is finished and all this, plus room to work on the truck amounts to more shop space than many hobbyists have available. What's to be done? The first step is to realize that shop space is likely to be a problem. If you have a two-car garage, you can get by but the daily driver(s) may be parked outside for a long while. But even if you have the space, you may be restricted in your activities by local zoning, covenants or other regulations.

For my restoration and storage needs I lease a nearby barn which was once the carriage building to the town's former mansion, now a fraternity house. The barn provides space to store my collector vehicles and is adequate, if not an altogether suitable facility, in which to do mechanical work. The building is not heated, so I have to schedule projects for warm weather.

Another alternative that works for several collectors I know, is to work with others who have the facilities you don't. Members of a local antique car club take turns bringing their collector vehicles into the "club house"—a member's three-car plus garage—for specific restoration projects. Another collector I know does restoration projects in a friend's shop, with the understanding that he will assist on the friend's projects. There are undoubtedly hundreds of stories of how resourceful restorers have solved their garaging problems. The challenge is for you to solve yours.

Besides the physical space in which to park the truck, store the parts you remove and others you acquire along the way, and work on the parts you have dismantled, a restoration shop also needs some special facilities. In order to remove the engine, you will either need a strong overhead support beam from which to suspend a come-along or chain fall, or you will

If zoning codes allow, one of the least expensive storage solutions is an old semi-trailer. Since it's not a permanent structure, it won't raise your property taxes.

This car enthusiast built a workshop out of a distressed mobile home. The structure had been gutted due to a kitchen fire. The only needed modifications were heavier duty wiring and a garage door on one end. At a later date when this collector moved, he sold the mobile home garage, which was simply trucked off his property.

need to rent a "cherry picker" engine hoist. For spray painting, you should rig a spray booth (this can be done by putting up "walls" of sheet plastic and installing a ventilation system). For welding, some portion of the floor should be concrete or other non-combustible. Parts storage will take less space and be more organized if you set up shelving. Paint and chemicals should be stored in locked cabinets to prevent their access by children. You will need a sturdy workbench, storage places for tools, 220-volt service for an arc welder and air compressor, good lighting, and a heat source if you live in a seasonal climate and plan to work in cool weather.

If you are in the position to construct a shop for restoration purposes, then you have the opportunity of considering helpful extras like running water with a sink for cleaning up after work, a floor drain for washing your vehicles, and a set of permanent ramps or a hoist for servicing your truck and doing repairs. You'll also find it very helpful to run galvanized pipe for air compressor lines with outlets in various locations in the shop. Running pipe for the main compressor lines has at least three advantages over uncoiling a length of air compressor hose each time you use air tools. First, you avoid the nuisance of having to uncoil and coil the hose; second, you won't lose air supply through restrictive hose connections; and third, the pipe will assist with moisture condensation, helping prevent water from passing into air tools or sandblasting and spray painting equipment.

Those who plan to do their own sandblasting are advised to construct a three-sided pen outside the building to catch the dust and conserve the sand. This is assuming you don't live in a residential neighborhood where the dust and noise of a sand-blasting operation would not be allowed. If you set up a degreasing bath of the type described in the stripping and derusting chapter, then you should also construct an enclosure for the alkaline bath. It is crucial that you take every measure to prevent children (your own or those in the neighborhood) from gaining access to harmful chemicals that you may be using in the restoration process. You will also need to plan and work out an environmentally sound means for disposing of an alkaline degreasing solution and other chemicals that if simply dumped out would leach into the soil and contaminate ground water. Look for a waste disposal facility in the Yellow Pages of the phone book.

Basic Tools

Having a vehicle professionally restored can be a very expensive experience. The only way I know that you can avoid a professional shop's fee is to restore or repair the vehicle yourself. Very likely, the repair or restoration will take you substantially longer than if you hired out the work. But when the job is done the feeling of accomplishment will be rewarding and the money saved will be substantial.

The drawback to doing your own restoration and repair work is the investment required to purchase needed tools.

Your workshop is going to need plenty of storage shelving. Notice the engine stand, an essential tool when doing an engine overhaul.

Approaching restoration with an inadequate tool set is bound to produce frustration, damaged, or incorrectly repaired parts. It isn't necessary to own every tool in the professional's shop, but the home handyman's tool set won't be adequate either. The tool set described below will get you through most restoration and repair jobs. Remember, that money spent on tools can be considered a lifetime investment and you can short cut some of the tool costs either by renting from a rent-all store, or by teaming with friends or club members to buy more expensive tools on a cooperative basis.

Socket Wrenches

The single most used tool for mechanical repair is the 3/8 in. drive ratchet and sockets. The 3/8 in. drive ratchet is big enough to tackle most jobs on a light truck, yet is still small enough to get into tight spots. The socket set should contain 10 sockets ranging from 3/8 to 15/16 in. in increments of 1/16 inch. Sockets generally come with either twelve-point or six-point grip openings. Unless you have a specific need for twelve-point sockets, I recommend six-point. Six-point sockets have more surface area to grab the nut or bolt making it easier to remove the fastener without slipping or damaging it. For this reason, they are far more effective with rusted bolt heads and nuts than twelve-point sockets. It is also a good idea to have a swivel coupling and a range of extension bars.

Adding to this basic set, a 1/4 in. drive ratchet and socket set is handy for really small jobs while a 1/2 in. drive socket set is needed for larger jobs. On a light truck you can get by without the 1/4 in drive set, but you'll need the 1/2 inch drive bar and sockets to loosen larger, rust frozen nuts and bolts.

Combination Wrenches

On these wrenches one end is open and the other end is boxed—hence the name. This style of wrench is very handy in a hard-to-reach location where if you can't turn the bolt or nut with the box end, you can usually get a bite with the open end. A set of combination wrenches should range from 3/8 in. to 1 in. in increments of 1/16 in.

Chisels and Punches

Chisels will be used to remove rivets and corroded nuts and bolt heads that are too rusted or have rounded over and so as not to hold a wrench. A set of four chisels ranging in width from 3/8 in. to 3/4 in. should cover all jobs. The punch set should include starting and drift punches that are used to drive out rivets and roll pins, an aligning punch for lining up holes and a center punch used to mark a spot for identification or centering a drill. A brass drift is also very a valuable tool and is used for tapping into place bearings or other parts that are easily damaged.

Pliers

A variety of pliers are needed for various jobs requiring holding, pinching, removing, cutting and squeezing. Pliers that should be found in the basic tool set include standard slip-joint pliers, 9 in. channel locks, needle-nose pliers and diagonal cutters.

Hammers

Two ball peen hammers are needed: a 12 oz. for light jobs, and a 24 oz. or a 32 oz., for big jobs. A plastic-tipped or a brass hammer is absolutely critical for any job where it is possible to scratch or damage the part with a steel ball-peen hammer.

Screwdrivers and Miscellaneous Hand Tools

The basic tool set should also contain a variety of screwdrivers, ranging in shank length and blade size and with Phillips as well as slot heads. Cluchhead screwdrivers are also useful for working on Chevrolet trucks. Hobby suppliers and SnapOn have them. Other miscellaneous hand tools include a hacksaw and selection of flat and round files. If you're building your tool inventory from scratch, you can buy tool sets containing most of these items at relatively low cost from Sears.

Jack Stands and Jack

To support the truck chassis during restoration and repair, professional-grade jack stands are a necessity. Avoid light duty jack stands sold in discount marts. The heavier duty stands have a ratchet release for the load-head and thicker gauge steel legs and braces. *Never* support the truck on a stack of blocks. Jack stands are relatively inexpensive items and should be selected as though your life depended on the quality of their design and construction—since that is literally the case.

Although a regular platform-style hydraulic jack will be adequate for raising the truck off the floor, you will find that a repair-shop style floor jack on rollers is a much more convenient tool to use. It also has the advantage of letting you wheel the truck around on the shop floor, sometimes enabling you to park the truck in an otherwise inaccessible space.

Specialty Tools

In the process of your truck's restoration or repair, you will probably invest in several specialty tools needed to perform specific jobs or to make those jobs easier. Specific tools for specialized jobs are identified in the various chapters. The

Here's a very helpful device. This cab rests on a low crib that has rollers to make moving around in the shop easy.

Tools should be well organized and within easy reach.
Richard Matott

It's important to keep the shop floor clean and to leave uncluttered work space around the truck.

specialty tools listed below should be considered musts if you are considering a ground-up restoration.

Brake Tools

Nearly all older vehicles need a thorough brake overhaul. Brake tools needed for this job include a tubing bender and flaring tool for creating replacement brake lines with the right length and shape to match the originals, as well as a tubing cutter and brake spring spreaders.

Puller and Engine Overhaul Tools

Pullers will be needed to remove the steering wheel, the crankshaft pulley (if you decide to rebuild the engine), and taking apart other mechanical assemblies.

Engine overhaul will also necessitate its own tool list including valve spring and piston ring compressors. A gasket scraper and wire brush are handy items for parts cleanup. Important to most work and critical to engine work are measuring tools. Digital calipers are becoming low-cost and are precise and easy to use.

Torque Wrench

One of the most important specialty tools is a torque wrench. This tool, which attaches to 1/2 in. drive sockets, is used to tighten nuts and bolts to proper torque specifications. A torque wrench should be used on everything from head bolts to lug nuts and will prevent stripped threads from over tightening, or damage that results from parts coming loose due to under tightening.

Gas Welder and Air Compressor

Although they require a larger investment than any of the tools mentioned previously, a welding torch and air compressor are

virtually indispensable for any serious restoration or repair work on an older vehicle. If you have to stagger the purchase of these two items, buy the torch first. You will use it during disassembly. The air compressor can be used for sandblasting and painting, and is an excellent power source for a variety of air tools.

When you buy a gas welding outfit you typically purchase the gauges, hoses and torch, and rent the tanks. The oxygen and fuel gas tanks come in a variety of sizes and are best transported around the shop on a cart (also purchased). As an alternative to a full-sized welding outfit, you can purchase portable gas welding outfits like the Toteweld by Arco. This small-scale gas welding outfit has the same capability as the bigger setups, but a more limited capacity. When selecting a gas welding outfit, it is essential to pick one using oxygen cylinders (the cheap

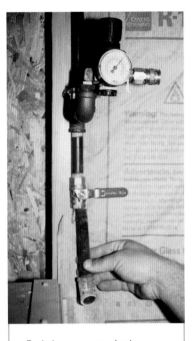

Each drop or connection has a pressure gauge showing the pressure reading at that juncture and a drain to bleed off moisture.

Air line pipe diameters (minimum)

Compressor	Horsepower	Air line piping	
"hobby" compressor	1 ½-2 hp	¾ in.	over 50 ft.
small portable compressor	3-5 hp	¾ in.	up to 200 ft.
		1 in.	over 200 ft.
stationary compressor	5-10 hp	¾ in.	up to 100 ft.
		1 in.	over 100 ft.
		1 ¼ in.	over 200 ft.
professional compressor	10-15 hp	1 in.	up to 100 ft.
		1 ¼ in.	over 100 ft.
		1 ½ in.	over 200 ft.

Airline pipe diameter chart

pelletized-oxygen units have neither the capacity nor the durability for the heat applications you will encounter while disassembling your truck). For the fuel gas, acetylene is preferred to MAPP (short for stabilized methylacetylene-propadiene and a trademark of Dow Chemical Corp.) because of the greater heat. Avoid propane, which does not produce enough heat.

In selecting an air compressor you need to consider the air supply rate (cubic feet per minute or CFM) size of the air storage tank. Hobby-size portable air compressors producing 10 CFM will power a spray gun or sander. A small air grinder requires 15 CFM. For sandblasting the amount of air required depends on the nozzle size, which increases with use and wear. To sandblast the frame and other large parts on your truck, you'll need a two stage, two cylinder air compressor with about a 15 CFM rating. A larger air tank, a longer run of hose, and moisture traps will help cool and dry the air. With sandblasting, moisture in the air is an enemy as it wets and clogs the sand. The longer hose is also important so that the compressor can be placed away and upwind of the blasting area. A tip from Bob Adler, coiling the hose in a washtub of water cools the air and condenses moisture.

Air Tools and Spray Painting Equipment

Air tools save time with both mechanical and body work. Among the more popular air tools are impact and socket wrenches, die-grinder, drill, cut off tool and sanders. These tools need a large volume of air to operate efficiently; hence the concern for large air storage and recovery capability.

Even if you have a professional paint your truck (good decision), you will save a great deal of money (and transportation hassle) if you do the preparation steps, which can include applying the primer coat. For automotive painting, you need to make a decision between a high pressure paint spraying gun and an HVLP (high volume low pressure) gun. The HVLP gun is going to require a 15 cfm air compressor recommended for air tools and sandblasting, but the pressure requirements are lower with painting. If you plan to spray paint, you will need a professional-grade charcoal respirator. The air line will need a moisture filter at the compressor outlet and quick-connect couplings on the spray gun and air hose.

Sandblaster

As you will learn in the next chapter on cleaning and derusting, there are two types of sandblasters: siphon and pressurized. If you purchase an air compressor, you will most likely want to add a sandblaster to your tool inventory. Siphon sandblasters are quite inexpensive and work well for smaller jobs. You will find that owning a sandblaster boosts your popularity with fellow old truck restorers.

Since the restoration of a vintage vehicle calls for a body and mechanical repair work that is quite different than that done on newer trucks, you will find a number of other specialty tools to be helpful for work such as buffing bright trim, cutting and shaping body repair panels, and many other jobs. A wide assortment of specialty tools for restoration work are available from The Eastwood Company in Malvern, Pennsylvania . Ordering Eastwood's catalog will familiarize you with tools that apply for specific applications. When specialty tools are needed, or advised, for various repair or restoration procedures, they will be listed in the chapter.

Tool Storage

If you are going to build up a good set of tools you will want to take care of them. The three basic choices for tool storage are a tool box, a roller cabinet, or a combination of both. The tool box must have easily working drawers, a functional lock and enough room so that the tools don't lie on top of each other. After that, it is really personal preference. The basic tool set should fit into a tool box. As you add to your tool collection, however, you will find a roller cabinet is better suited to your tool storage needs. Beware of low-quality roller cabinets often seen in discount marts that are undersized, flimsily built, and have such small rollers that they do not move around easily. Quality roller cabinets and accompanying tool boxes that are designed to sit on the top of the cabinet are available from Sears as well as professional tool suppliers like Snap-on.

Tool Quality Versus Price

Tools can be found in three ways: bad, good and excellent. Bad tools are the cheapest, both in cost and quality. Examples are the non-brand tools often found in discount marts. Many of

Sandblasting cabinets, shown in this photo's foreground, are very useful tools. This restorer has piped compressed air to several locations in his shop. He has used black pipe, which is the correct material. Never pipe compressed air through plastic or copper.

these tools aren't worth bringing home. I bought one of the cheap screwdriver sets once and chipped the blade the first screw I attempted to turn.

Good tools are the Sears Craftsman line. These tools come with a lifetime guarantee, have a high standard of quality, and sell at a reasonable price. An added attraction of Craftsman tools is that they are offered at low sale prices periodically during the year. Another benefit is that most Sears stores will replace broken tools on-the-spot with no questions asked.

In the excellent tool category are Snap On, Mac or other professional brands. These are the highest quality tools made—and the most expensive. They not only have a look of quality, but feel different in your hand: like a well broken-in baseball glove. These tools also come with a lifetime guarantee and in most cases will out perform any other make of tool, including Craftsman. One measure of tool performance is the tool's fit on a rusted bolt. A Snap-on dealer once had me try one of his wrenches on a rusted bolt that my Craftsman wrench would simply slip off. The Snap-on wrench not only took a firm grip, but turned the bolt loose.

The quality-to-price ratio of Craftsman tools is hard to beat. If you are working from a budget, Craftsman tools are the best way to go. But if you truly enjoy mechanical work and expect to work on vehicles for years to come, and can afford them, then Snap On, Mac or other professional tools are what you want. Their quality look will increase your pride in your work and you will find that once you have developed the "feel" of working with high quality tools, picking up a lesser quality tool will give you the feeling that you're just holding a chunk or steel in your hand.

Safety: Bringing Up the Hobbyist's Shop to Professional Standards

Safety begins by adopting a professional's outlook, which means doing everything by the book.

Rule 1. Keep a clean shop. Mess and clutter invites accidents, whether a snarled air hose, tangled electrical cords, or other clutter lying about the shop floor. Paint the shop walls and ceiling a light color, preferably white, and install lots of lighting. It's easier to keep things clean and avoid accidents working in a well lighted shop.

Rule 2. Store chemicals, especially hazardous painting products, in locked, fireproof cabinets. Keeping the cabinets locked prevents the chemicals from being reached by children.

Rule 3. Don't smoke inside your shop and don't allow others to smoke. Gasoline and painting solvents are highly flammable. Don't bring matches or a lighter into the work area either. Post no-smoking signs to alert others of shop policy.

Rule 4. Mount fire extinguishers within easy reach. The fire extinguishers need to be foam or dry powder. Do not attempt to extinguish chemical fires with water.

Keep a first aid kit in the shop to treat cuts or burns. For medical emergencies resulting from harmful exposure to toxic chemicals, draw up and post a list of first aid procedures. This list includes:

- Irregular or halted breathing‹
- Immediately remove the person to fresh air, Call 911, keep him/her warm and at rest; administer artificial respiration.
- Eye contact
- Flush eyes with clean water for at least 10 minutes.
- Skin contact
- Wash skin around contact area with soap and water. Remove contaminated clothing.

It is very helpful if the shop has a sink or other washing facility (a hose). If not, post directions for the quickest route to a washing facility.

Rule 6. Do not bring food or beverage into the work area. Always wash hands after using or handling chemicals.

Rule 7. Wear protective clothing and equipment when ever working with toxic chemicals, including most modern painting products.

Clothing should include:
- Lint free coveralls with elastic wrist and ankles
- A painter's cap with elastic or adjustable band
- Rubber gloves offering chemical resistance to solvents and hardeners. Nitrile is best.
- These clothing items are available from the painting supplier.
- Equipment should include
- An approved respirator—to be used when spraying acrylic enamel painting products.
- A full face piece respirator is preferred to a respirator alone
- An air supplied hood or full facepiece, air supplied respirator and oilless compressor—to be used when spraying two-part paints with urethane/isocyanate hardener.

Rule 8. Confine paint spraying to booths or enclosures with a filtered ventilation system. Make sure air is exhausted away from buildings and/or people. Remove painting vapors not just from the person doing the spraying, but from others who may be in or near the building where the spraying is occurring.

Rule 9. Properly decontaminate and dispose of all left-over painting and filler product that has been mixed with hardener, also "empty" paint cans and hardening agents that have reached the end of their relatively short shelf-life. Don't store expired and non-usable product. Never pour coating products or solvents into drains or dump them into the soil. Once catalyzed products have hardened, they are no longer haxardous.

Rule 10. Remember, Safety is a personal and daily decision. Post safety reminders.

As you take the truck apart you will encounter years of caked grease and grime on mechanical parts and most likely rust on the body metal. Removing grease coatings from mechanical parts not only make rebuilding assemblies like the engine and chassis components easier, but thorough cleaning is also important if your truck is to have that fresh from the showroom look. Welding doesn't work well on rusted panels and paint won't adhere over rust, so stripping off old paint coatings and thorough derusting body metal are the preparation steps to body work and refinishing.

Cleaning and derusting are one of the biggest challenges facing any old-truck rebuilder or restorer. Your thoroughness with this step will determine the outcome of all subsequent rust repair and refinishing steps as well as the truck's overall appearance when you're done. Actually, cleaning and derusting consist of three different processes that can either be done separately, or in some cases in combination. These processes are degreasing, paint removal and derusting.

There are various methods for cleaning and derusting that you can use to prepare your truck for the next stages of mechanical and metal repair. If you are taking the restoration approach, cleaning and derusting is the first major step after complete disassembly. If you are taking the repair approach, you will clean various mechanical components as you overhaul them. Derusting may occur at isolated stages as you repair and refinish your truck's sheet metal. As you will discover, cleaning and derusting can be time-consuming processes that are done more efficiently all at once rather than piecemeal. This means that if you are taking the repair approach, you may find it expedient to clean or derust as much of your truck as possible without taking the truck apart.

Degreasing

The typical chassis on an older truck is coated with grease and road debris an inch or more thick in places. It may also be covered with a scale of rust. There are several methods for cleaning heavy grease from engine and chassis components. The easiest is to take the chassis (or the whole truck if you are

On large panels like doors, paint can be removed with paint remover and a D/A sander.

Sanding is also effective where rust or paint only needs to be removed from selected areas

As an alternative to a pressure washer, you can use the high pressure spray at a car wash to remove grime and grease.

using the rebuilding approach) to a shop that does steam cleaning—if such a place exists in your community.

If a steam jenny isn't available from a local tool rent-all, you may find a power washer to be nearly as effective. This tool can be connected to a hot-water faucet and also mixes detergent with high-pressure water spray for fast, effective cleaning. A power washer is a tool you may wish to own. A power washer can also be rented from most any tool rent-all.

Another alternative is to haul your truck's mechanical parts to a nearby car wash and use the engine cleaner cycle to degrease the parts. You will find this approach to be more effective if you scrape off heavy grease buildup first with putty knife. The car wash method works essentially like a power washer. The difference is that you bring the parts to the wash location, as opposed to the other way around.

If you are working with a small budget and time is of less concern than expense, you can clean the chassis the old fashioned way with a putty knife, scrub brush, and solvent. This approach can be time consuming, but the only cost may be a few scrub brushes and several gallons of solvent. When degreasing engine and chassis parts by hand, you'll save yourself a lot of time by first scraping off the build up, using a good grease-cutting solvent like Gunk, and working in warm temperatures. If the grease coating is fairly thin and you work the solvent into the grease residue with a scrub brush, when you hose off the solvent the metal will wash clean enough for sandblasting. If the metal doesn't need derusting, you should inspect the degreased area very closely for any traces of grease buildup, then remove whatever grease remains, and wash off

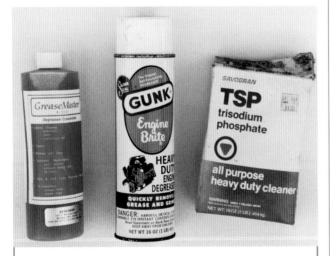

Here are three common degreasing agents you can use safely. Gunk is sprayed on, allowed to soften caked on grease and washed or scrubbed off. TSP and GreaseMaster are used in solutions. GreaseMaster has the advantage of being biodegradeable.

the degreaser with a painting preparation solvent. At this point the metal should be ready for refinishing.

Because gasoline is very flammable it shouldn't be used as a degreasing solvent. Instead, use a less flammable fuel like kerosene or a commercial parts cleaning solvent. To protect your skin, rubber gloves and full clothing should be worn when working with any solvent. It is also important to protect your eyes by wearing safety glasses or preferably a face shield.

Alkaline Degreaser Bath

An effective degreasing bath for cleaning smaller parts can be made by mixing an alkaline solution in a large metal pail, old oil drum, or even as large a container as a livestock watering tank. The alkaline degreasing solution consists simply of household lye (sold in grocery stores either as lye or Drano) and water in a mixture of approximately 24 oz. of lye per gallon of water. A metal container is advised because then heat can be applied to raise the temperature of the degreasing bath.

To set up an alkaline bath for my parts degreasing needs, I have used a 55-gallon oil drum in which I have poured about 40 gallons of water and 96-120 oz. of lye, or about 10 twelve oz. containers. The lye is always added to water, not water to lye as this will cause the mixture to boil, likely exposing skin and face to the caustic chemical. To heat the alkaline solution, I placed the oil drum on concrete blocks and built a small wood fire underneath. Alternatively, a propane heater can be used. When heated to near boiling, the lye solution will remove even heavily caked-on grease coats in just a few minutes. The alkaline solution works equally well removing paint. I found that the 55-gallon oil drum would hold wheels, front end assemblies, transmission housings, and engine blocks, as well as other smaller parts. Caution: Do not immerse mechanical assemblies in the alkaline solution unless they are taken apart or will be disassembled and rebuilt later.

After parts are removed from the caustic solution they must be washed thoroughly. A garden hose works well to rinse off the slimy alkaline film. Thorough cleaning is important for two reasons: even a slight alkaline film left on the part's surface gives the metal poor wetting or paint-bonding properties; and any chemical remaining in seams may eventually leach out, lifting the paint. However, washing presents another problem Cleaned metal is prone to rapid rusting. To protect against rusting and provide the wetting necessary for painting, cleaned parts can be wiped with an acid-etch solution (typically containing dilute phosphoric acid) available from auto parts stores selling refinishing products.

As the caustic chemical solution is used it will gradually lose its strength. This decline does not occur rapidly. I have cleaned parts in a lye tub over a period of several days before noticing an appreciable loss in degreasing potency. When the decline does occur, the solution can be restored to full strength by adding more chemical. However, the caustic chemical degreasing bath will eventually become contaminated with sludge and have to be disposed of by transferring the solution to a sealed container that can be taken to an appropriate toxic chemical dump.

Numerous other concerns apply to the alkaline bath degreasing method. Always wear rubber gloves and a full covering of clothing. Tie lengths of wire to the parts before dipping them into the bath so that you won't have to fish the parts out of the solution. Small parts can be immersed in a wire mesh container. Always wear face protection to prevent the alkaline solution from splashing into your eyes. It is extremely important to make sure that children and animals cannot reach the alkaline bath. Options are to set up the alkaline solution inside your shop and make sure the container is covered and access doors are locked when the alkaline bath is not in use, or to build a secure enclosure around the bath if it is outside. You will also need to dispose of the spent solution in a legally and environmentally safe fashion when the degreasing work is finished. Although the alkaline degreasing method is very effective, if you question your ability to follow these safety demands you should use another approach.

Dissolving Grease Safely with Environmentally Friendly GreaseMaster®

While all the previously described degreasing methods will remove the heavy buildups typically found on older car parts, none is completely harmless to the environment and all pose a health hazard to some degree if prolonged contact occurs with exposed skin, or if the chemicals splash into the eyes or are ingested. In contrast, a commercial product called GreaseMaster is safe, non-toxic, has an almost neutral pH, is

biodegradeable and can legally be disposed of in waste water or used as a plant fertilizer.

Unlike detergents that emulsify or solvents that dissolve grease, GreaseMaster lifts the buildup—leaving no oily film on the surface of the part. The cleaned surface can simply be rinsed and painted. The product works extremely well with a power washer or can be used as a bath. A pint size container will yield 50 gallons of cleaning solution, which can be re-used by allowing the sediment to settle and the periodically skimming oil off the top. If used with a power washer, a bed of hay or straw under the wash area will collect oil and grease leaving the runoff clear with no oil film rainbow effect on the water's surface.

For thick coatings, GreaseMaster gel can be applied to loosen the coating. After soaking for several hours, the thick grease can be power washed off.

Sandblasting

Following degreasing, most parts will need to be cleaned of what remains of the old finish and whatever rust lies on the surface or has penetrated more deeply into the metal. As with degreasing, paint and rust can be removed by several methods. The most common and inexpensive paint- and rust-removal method is sandblasting. Other methods use chemicals. Attempting to remove paint and rust by a sanding, grinding or wire brushing is not very effective since these mechanical methods can abrade the metal and leave seeds of rust in visible or microscopic pits that will fester and bleed through after the metal is repainted.

Sandblasting is an effective way to remove paint and other coatings. Here the sheet metal as well as the chassis has been cleaned by sandblasting; however, mechanical assemblies like the driveline should not be sandblasted unless these components will be disassembled and rebuilt.

When using chemical solutions for degreasing or paint stripping, lay down plastic sheeting to collect the chemical residue.

43

In many communities you will find commercial sandblasting outfits listed in the Yellow Pages. These businesses will strip paint and rust from chassis parts, wheels, bumpers and sheet metal for generally reasonable prices. The main disadvantage to commercial sandblasting is your lack of control over the sandblasting process. While a commercial sandblaster isn't likely to damage a bumper or frame, high-pressure sandblasting can easily warp sheet metal. If you will be resorting to sandblasting to strip and derust body parts, you either need to make sure the commercial sandblaster agrees to be very careful with these parts to avoid warpage (and then expect to have to do some straightening) or sandblast the sheet metal yourself, taking great care not to stress the metal.

If you live in a suburban development, sandblasting at home may be against zoning regulations and is sure to upset your neighbors (the process is both noisy and dirty), but if you live in a more rural setting the equipment investment to do your own sandblasting is reasonable enough that you may well decide to set up your own sandblasting operation. To do so, you will need an air compressor of the capacity described in the Shop and Tools chapter. An air compressor should be considered a basic shop item as it is also used to power air tools (impact wrenches, sanders, grinders, drills, buffers) and spray painting equipment, as well as a sandblasting outfit.

Sandblasting puts a great strain on the compressor, often causing the compressor to run continuously to keep up with the demand for air. A continuously running compressor produces hot, air which holds a greater quantity of moisture keeps the moisture as a vapor. Moisture is the enemy of sandblasting because wet sand won't flow through the sandblaster nozzle. To eliminate the moisture, you may want to use Bob Adler's wash tub tip (coil a section of hose from the air compressor in a metal washtub filled with cold water to cool the air in the hose and condense the moisture) described in the Shop and Tools chapter. At the sandblaster end of the air compressor hose you'll want to install a moisture separator, which does what the name says—it removes moisture from the air stream, allowing only dry air to travel down the air hose. These are inexpensive devices that can be purchased from the company selling the air compressor. Large bore air hose also helps slow down the air flow so that more cooling can occur. Bob Adler recommends 100 ft. of hose to make sure the compressor does not inhale sand from the blasting area. See accompanying chart on hose diameters for various compressor applications. . Sections of hose should not be spliced together due to the air restriction at the connection.

Siphon and Pressure-Feed Units

Sandblasting units are of two types: siphon and pressure feed. Both are available from restoration tool suppliers like Tip Sandblasting, The Eastwood Company, and others. The siphon-style sandblaster is cheaper, but also less effective than the pressure unit. Basically, a siphon sandblaster sucks sand into the air stream that is blown through the nozzle by the air compressor. A siphon sand blast is not as strong as a pressurized blast and uses more air—an important factor considering the limited capacity of smaller, home-shop-sized air compressors. This does not mean you should rule out a

Sandblasting provides a roughened surface for painting, but on body panels also risks stretching the metal.

Inside surfaces, such as this cab, interior should also be cleaned and stripped of paint.

siphon sandblaster. If you will primarily be sandblasting small parts (either your truck is largely rust free or you plan to have the larger parts commercially sandblasted or chemically derust is a more powerful blast and more efficient use of compressed air and sand.

Sandblasting Basics

There isn't much art to sandblasting. Basically, you point the nozzle at the part and blast off the paint and rust. Sandblasting isn't very effective against grease, which is the reason that heavy grease buildup has to be removed first. You will find that blasting at an angle seems to wash off the paint and rust and is not so likely to stress and warp the metal. However, on large relatively flat panels like the hood, it is best to sandblast only on reinforced areas and strip the paint from the rest of the panel with paint remover or a D/A (dual action) sander or more efficiently with a National Detroit Model 900 gear drive 8 in. sander or equivalent with 36 grit paper. Other than that, basic sandblasting precautions are to wear full-length clothing, protective gloves (welding gloves work well), a sandblasting hood and a dust mask. Some tie their shirt sleeves and pants cuffs when sandblasting in an attempt to prevent dust from blowing inside their clothing, but not much is gained as the dust sifts in anyway. Be sure to take everything out of your pockets. Sand is destructive of credit cards.

Coarse sandblasting sand is available from most auto parts stores, but regular sand from a building supplier, beach or sand pit works nearly as well and is less expensive—often free. The main advantage of sandblasting sand is the sand's extra course grit that enables it to be reused, sometimes several times. If you shovel your own sand from a beach or sand pit, be sure the sand has dried thoroughly before sandblasting. Nothing produces greater frustration than trying to sandblast with moist sand. The nozzle will clog as soon as you start, and each attempt to unclog the blockage will soon be followed by reclogging. If the sand is damp when you are ready to start blasting, spread a tarp a sunny area of your driveway and cover it with a thin layer of sand. When the sand turns white it is dry and ready to be used. If you decide to blast with sand you've gathered yourself (from a beach or sand pit) you will need to strain the sand through a window screen or similar fine mesh before using. If you don't stain the sand, larger pebbles and debris will clog the sandblaster's nozzle.

Problems

The biggest problem a restorer encounters when trying to sandblast at home is an insufficient air supply. You will probably need to allow the compressor to rest periodically for the tool to cool down. If you find the air compressor you own to be inadequate for the amount of sandblasting you are doing, one solution is to borrow a friend's portable compressor (or rent a portable unit from a tool rent-all) and power the sandblaster

from both compressors. (You can connect the air lines from the two compressors with a Y-fitting.) Borrowing a friend's compressor might be an occasion for you to work together sandblasting parts for both of your vehicles. Sandblasting with two people will be a faster operation since one can keep the blaster full while the other handles the parts. The other answer to a limited compressed air supply is to rent a commercial size air compressor and use this rig while you are doing larger sandblasting jobs like stripping the frame.

Another of the problems with sandblasting is the volume of dust it produces. One way to avoid this, and to economize on sand, is to build a two- or three-sided pen in which the sandblasting will be done. The pen walls need be no higher than 3-4 ft and 8-10 ft. long. You will place parts to be sandblasted in the center of the pen and blast toward the walls. This way most of the sand and much of the dust will settle inside the pen. The sand can be scooped up and reused at least once. If sandblasting has been used to remove rust, the fine dust can be swept up and disposed of on the garden, lawn or other spot where it can work into the soil. When sandblasting is used to remove paint, the paint pigment residue may contain heavy metals, in which case the sand should be swept up and hauled to a toxic waste disposal site. It's best to sand off

Sandblasters are of two types, siphon and pressure-fed. The siphon type shown here is less expensive, but also less effective and best suited for small parts.

Pressure-fed sandblasting requires a large capacity air supply. The process is noisy and dusty and should be done outside and not in a residential zone.

paint and use the blaster for rust and crevices that can't be reached by the sander.

Sandblasting is an effective way to rid metal parts of rust because the tiny sand grains penetrate into pits and scour out all traces of corrosion, however microscopic. Nonetheless, sandblasting is not very effective for cleaning hidden areas like the insides of doors, rocker panels and boxed frames. If rust is left unchecked in these hidden areas, you're likely to find corrosion blistering through the metal in a few years. Ways to remove or neutralize rust on hidden surfaces are described in the chemical cleaning methods that follow.

Treating Sandblasted Parts

The bare metal that is exposed by sandblasting needs to be treated to prevent rerusting, which will occur very rapidly if any moisture is present. For rust protection and to assure good paint adhesion, prime the parts right away with a self-etching primer. Clean metal parts can also be given short-term rust protection with metal prep—a dilute phosphoric acid solution available from auto parts stores as a painting preparation product under a variety of names including Metal Prep, Metal Etch and others. Tell the counter clerk that you are looking for a dilute acid product to etch bare metal in preparation for painting. Apply the acid solution with a pump spray bottle. Just spray it on liberally (while keeping it off your clothes) and let the solution run into seams and crevices. When the chemical dries, the treated metal has a dull gray color. The parts should then be primed using a base primer that is compatible with the topcoat system, meaning the type of painting product to be used for the truck's final finish. To select the right base

primer, you should talk to your painter and select the finish even at this early stage of the project.

Be very careful not to sandblast mechanical parts such front end or rear end assemblies unless these units will be completely disassembled and rebuilt. Never sandblast the engine or transmission. Sandblasting will leave the bearings of mechanical assemblies packed full of grit, which will quickly grind these delicate parts to scrap. Finally, don't touch sandblasted parts. Perspiration can corrode the metal and body oil can damage the paint. You should continue to wear your blasting gloves while handling the parts.

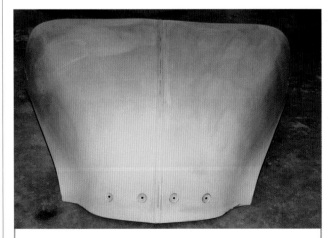

Metal that has been stripped should be coated promptly to avoid re-rusting.

Chemical Paint Stripping

Alternatives to sandblasting use chemicals to clean off paint and rust. We'll discuss paint stripping first, since older paint coatings should be removed before applying a new finish A number of commercial chemical paint stripping products are available from auto supply stores as well as specialty restoration supply companies. Most are brushed on or sprayed, allowed to work, and the paint is then scraped off using a plastic scraper. Don't use a metal putty knife as a scraper. You'll be filling gouge marks you cut into the metal.

The problem with these chemical paint removal products is that the layers of old paint usually don't scrape clean to bare metal. More often, the stripper will lift one layer at a time. This means tedious scraping to remove each layer. Often, you'll end up sanding off a paint coating that no amount of stripper seems to loosen.

Chemical strippers are of two types: liquid and paste. The paste type is generally favored and thought to be more effective. To remove the paint, you apply the stripper (by spreading or squirting), wait the time period recommended on the product label, and attack the bubbled up coating with a scraper. Older baked-enamel finishes, especially, can be very difficult to remove, usually requiring extensive sanding.

As you're peeling off the paint, it's a good idea to save a sample. If the paint supplier has difficulty matching the original color, the sample can be electronically scanned with a spectrophotometer to make an exact color match.

In preparation for the any paint removing process, first take off any decorative trim: hood ornaments, die cast series or model markings from the sides of the hood, which are usually held in place with clips. Be sure to find out how these trim pieces are fastened before trying to pry them off.

If the metal isn't rusted, paint remover can be used to strip the truck.

Chemicals in Paint Stripping Products and Their Dangers*

Methylene chloride—causes cancer in laboratory animals, considered a potential cancer causing agent in humans. Evaporates quickly so is easily inhaled. High concentrations can cause irritation to eyes, skin, nose, and lungs. Use only in well ventilated areas. High exposures over extended periods can cause liver and kidney damage. May be combined with other flammable materials, or nonflammable.

Acetone, toluene, methanol—all highly flammable. Do not use near sparks or flame. Inhaling high concentrations can be harmful to unborn children. Very high levels for prolonged periods can cause brain damage. Use in well-ventilated areas.

Nñmethylpyrrolidone (MNP)—can cause skin swelling, blisters, and burns. Absorbed through the skin, can cause health problems, including harm to unborn children. Very important to wear chemical-resistant gloves. Even when wearing gloves, wash hands immediately after use. Use only in well-ventilated areas.

Dibasic esters (DBE)—repeated inhalation causes damage to cells and respiratory damage in laboratory animals. Wear respirator; use only in well-ventilated area. Always wear protective clothing.

*Health warning information is from the U.S. Environmental Protection Agency, http://www.epa.gov/iaq/pubs/paintstr.html47

Commercial Metal Cleaning

Because paint stripping can be a time consuming task, many restorers prefer to sandblast metal parts (eliminating both paint and rust at the same time) or use a commercial chemical stripping method that not only removes paint and rust, but will also dissolve Bondo and any other non-metal coatings. This stripping and derusting process, which combines caustic chemicals with electroly-sis, is done by commercial establishments that often call themselves "metal laundries." Many belong to the RediStrip franchise chain. The locations of chemical metal stripping firms can be found in the Yellow Pages telephone directories of larger cities and in listings that appear in old car hobby magazines.

With commercial metal cleaning, the parts to be cleaned are placed in large tanks (many establishments have tanks large enough to submerse the entire truck cab or box) containing caustic chemicals. A combination of chemical action and electrolysis dissolves paint and eats away rust in anywhere from a few minutes to a few hours, depending on the condition of the parts. The advantages of commercial metal cleaning are that all the metal is cleaned, even hidden inside surfaces, that the

Commercial metal cleaning uses tanks large enough to immerse the entire truck.

When parts emerge from the cleaning tanks, the metal is as fresh as new.

process does not abrade or eat away good metal, and that the only work you have to do is transport the parts to the derusting establishment. As mentioned above, the chemical bath will dissolve any body filler, leaving the parts ready for metal repair and finishing. Many firms will apply a protective phosphoric coating to the parts after cleaning to retard rerusting and improve paint adhesion.

Despite the benefits of commercial metal cleaning, this method is not without disadvantages. The service can be quite expensive, and there have been reports of the caustic chemicals leaching out of body seams after painting. If chemicals are trapped in seams where the body panels are joined, they will eventually work to the surface of the metal where they can lift the paint. If this should happen the only way to repair the damage would be to remove the finish in the area where it is lifting and try to bake the chemical out of the seam—a process that has no assurance of success. In most cases, the likelihood of this paint-lifting scenario are slim. On a Chevrolet truck cab, the only visible seam is usually along the back portion of the roof, and this is a welded seam. The cab belt line through Advance Design years was a welded lap joint and very rust prone. On a pickup box where the sections are bolted together, the possibility of stripping chemicals being trapped if the box metal is painted shortly after stripping could pose a greater risk.

Derusting

Besides commercial metal cleaning, there are two chemical derusting processes you can do at home. One uses a mild acid to eat away the rust; the other converts the rust into a stable, protective coating. Acid derusting works best with smaller parts that can be dipped in a plastic container holding a mild solution of phosphoric acid. While other acids can also be used to derust ferrous metal parts, phosphoric acid is preferred because it is inexpensive, less dangerous than other more caustic acids like sulfuric or hydrochloric, works in a relatively short time frame, and leaves a protective coating that actually improves the paint bond with the metal. Dilute phosphoric acid is available from local automotive painting supply stores and restoration suppliers like The Eastwood Company under product names such as Twin Etch and OxiSolv. Instructions on the container give mixing proportions with water—typically 1:1. A lidded plastic pail makes the best container for the acid derusting solution since the chemical quickly develops a rotten egg smell.

Rusted metal should be completely immersed if possible and checked be checked at frequent intervals (every hour or

Mild acid solutions are effective at removing rust.

Although mild acids or acid jells can be effective derusting agents, there are two drawbacks to their use. One is the fact that acid removes rust by eating into the metal. This means that, along with the rust, some good metal is lost. If the metal is thin, due to severe rusting, it's possible that in the process of getting rid of the rust, the acid treatment may also destroy what good metal remains. The other problem with acid derusting is that the acid can cause a condition called "hydrogen embrittlement" which weakens the metal and can cause parts that are stressed to crack and break. For this reason, suspension parts, wheels, brake drums, or other components on which the car's mechanical safety depends, must not be derusted using the acid method. Acid is not a problem, however, for mild body steel.

Rust Stabilizing

Sometimes rust can't be conveniently removed by abrasive or chemical processes either because the vehicle isn't being disassembled for sandblasting or the corrosion is inaccessible. In these situations, the rust should be stabilized using a product that converts active rust into an inert coating. While not a total solution to the corrosion problem, these stabilizing products are effective at preventing the rust from spreading.

Popular rust stabilizer/converter products include POR-15 (the product name literally means Paint Over Rust), Corroless, Rust Ender and ChemSafe CSM 66. Since rust stabilizers are liquid, they can be brushed, rolled or sprayed onto the metal. POR-15 and Corroless react chemically with

so for a fresh acid bath; older acid works more slowly). Acid derusting will eat away the metal as well as the rust and if the parts are left too long, they can be destroyed. It's good to try a few scrap parts first, to get used to the speed of the chemical action. Be careful not to dip non-ferrous metal parts (brass or aluminum) in the acid derusting bath because they dissolve quickly.

Acid derusting will not work on painted or grease-coated surfaces, so it is necessary to first make sure that the parts are stripped to bare metal. For larger metal parts such as fenders that won't fit in an acid derusting bath, acid jells can be used to clean surface rust or even areas of heavier rusting. These jells are available as Naval Jelly which can be purchased in hardware stores, and more concentrated acid jells available from restoration suppliers. As the jell dries, it leaves a dark gray coating. If any traces of corrosion remain, a second acid treatment can be applied (the acid jell is wiped onto the metal with a paint brush). Benzoil peroxide in body filler can react with excess acid to stain topcoats. It's best to remove access acid and use an epoxy primer to seal any acid residue and isolate it from topcoats.

Paint and rust can be removed mechanically with a sanding disc or wire brush, but the process is tedious and time consuming.

49

rust, converting active corrosion to a more stable magnetite. POR-15 and Corroless also serve as a base paint coating to sealing the metal against moisture. A difference in the two products, besides color (POR-15 is available in either black or aluminum; Corroless looks like red oxide primer), Corroless does not need to be recoated—either with primer or a finish paint. However, it is compatible with most automotive paints and can be top coated if desired. POR-15 can deteriorate when exposed to ultraviolet light and needs to be top coated.

Rust Ender and ChemSafe CSM 66 also convert rust into an inert coating; however, their application is different than POR-15 and Corroless (which simply apply like paint) and both need to be top coated soon after application. Following application, both Rust Ender and CSM 66 are washed with water. As the metal dries, a rust inhibiting coating forms that helps with paint adhesion. Application should be done in a well ventilated area, wearing gloves and eye protection. A wash coating of The Destroyer and CSM 66 improves conductivity for welding.

Areas where the rust conversion treatment works particularly well are inner door surfaces, much of which can't be reached by sandblasting, or chassis parts that you don't want to sandblast and shouldn't derust with acid. As with other derusting processes, it is necessary that the surface be clean of grease and paint. If you are treating the inside surfaces of the doors, it helps to have the doors off the vehicle and placed horizontally (outside skin down). Then you can simply pour

Clean metal makes the best starting point for rust repair. The Surburban's sheet metal has been stripped by bead blasting, a media that stresses the metal less than sand. John Hart

enough rust stabilizer through openings in the inner door panel. You can spread the stabilizer over the inside surface of the outer door skin by picking up the door (its good to have help with this) and tipping it up and down and side to side. This movement will also let the stabilizer penetrate into seams. When you feel that the outer skin is completely coated, flip the door over to coat the inner panel. Some of the liquid will spill out through openings in the panel, so it's a good idea to spread out newspapers on the shop floor in the area where you are doing this.

Since the rust stabilizer products penetrate pits and seams where other derusting methods are unlikely to reach, it may be desirable to use these products in combination with other rust removing methods. No single rust removing process is ideally suited for all conditions. More likely, you will use a combination of degreasing, paint stripping, and rust removing processes to bring your truck to the point where it is ready for metal work, refinishing and mechanical rebuilding.

Organic Derusting

A new process, organic derusting chemically deoxidizes rust, leaving a black, powdery coating, which is easily removed by wiping, brushing, or pressure washing. What makes organic derusting unique is that the active ingredients are manufactured primarily from plants and are not harmful, either to the user or the environment. Rusteco, the only product in this category, is available either as a liquid or gel—enabling it to be used on vertical as well as horizontal surfaces. This product works with any metal, removing oxidation from aluminum or copper as well as steel. Parts cleaned with this product can be prepared for temporary storage by brushing or wiping on another light coating. Rusteco's supplier maintains that product residue need not be treated as hazardous waste and requires no special disposal.

End of the Undoing Process

Completion of cleaning and derusting marks the turning point in your truck's restoration or repair sequence. Up to this stage, you have been undoing. From this point on (with the exception of mechanical assemblies) you will be redoing. With sheet metal, the next steps will be to remove dents, repair rust damage and tears, and prepare the truck for its new paint finish. Now that the dirty work is behind, you'll be seeing much more progress toward your goal—a truck you can take out on the highway with pride.

If you've already begun working on your truck you may have discovered one of the most useful for restoring or overhauling an old truck is a gas welding outfit. Mechanics often refer to their welding torch as a gas wrench, and for good reason. Rust-frozen exhaust manifold studs, king pins, chassis and body bolts are often impossible to remove without heat. If you do manage to turn the bolt, more than likely it will break off—and in the case of a manifold stud this means drilling out what remains of the stud and retapping the hole, a frustrating, time consuming and thankless task. In the case of rust frozen king pins, the only way to remove the pins without heat from a pre-1960 straight axle front end may be to disassemble the front end assembly as much as possible and take it to a machine shop where the pins can be forced out with a hydraulic press. Using a gas welding torch to heat the axle ends is a much easier and quicker approach. Of course a gas welding outfit isn't used just for disassembly; it is one of the tools used for repairing metal. Once you purchase a gas welding outfit, you will wonder how you worked on older vehicles (and newer ones, too, for that matter) without it.

As mentioned in the Tools chapter, you purchase the of gauges, hoses, and welding and cutting torches, plus several size torch tips. The tanks (one for oxygen and the other for the fuel gas) are typically rented. This equipment, plus a cart to move the tanks outfit around in your shop, is available in welding shops, auto supply stores, and a variety of tool retailers.

Most gas welding outfits use acetylene as the fuel gas. When burned in pure oxygen (from the oxygen tank) acetylene yields temperatures in the 1,800 degree Fahrenheit range required to heat metal to a cherry-red state. MAPP is an alternative fuel gas that has a couple of advantages for the hobbyist.

1

After opening the valves on the tanks and torch, striking the igniter produces a flame.

2

As you open the oxygen valve at the torch the flame will change shape and color.

First, it rates superior to acetylene in safety and ease of handling. Second, since it is distributed in liquid form, a MAPP canister provides more fuel pound for pound than an equivalent tank of acetylene. Finally, MAPP has nearly acetylene's heat value, making it effective for both welding and cutting.

Safety

When gas welding, it is essential that you carefully follow several safety rules. If you enroll in a welding class at a vo-tech center or technical college, these will be taught at the outset of the class. If you learn to use a gas welding outfit from a book and practice, or are taught by a friend, you may overlook important safety steps. The principal safety rules to follow are listed below.

Never weld near flammable vapors or a gas tank.

Never place the oxygen and fuel gas tanks in a position when they might fall over—a tank with a broken valve is lethal.

Never run over the welding hoses with the welding cart or damage the hoses in any other way. Keep the hoses coiled up when not in use.

Never oil the regulators, hoses, torches, or fittings. The combination of oil and oxygen can produce a deadly explosion.

Never use the oxygen jet to blow away dust and never allow the oxygen jet to strike oily or greasy surfaces.

Always wear welding goggles when looking at the flame.

Always wear welding gloves and protective clothing.

Do not carry a butane lighter in a pants or shirt pocket when welding. A spark from the welding operation could explode the lighter with deadly consequences.

Gas Welding Techniques

Although welding metal takes skill and practice, very little skill is needed to use a gas welding torch to heat-rust frozen parts. Since you will not be cutting metal, you do not need to use a cutting torch. Rather, you will use a welding torch with a medium to large tip. If you have purchased, but have not received instruction in how to use a gas welding outfit, then learning how set the dials on the tanks and light the torch should be your first step. Instruction in welding (both gas and arc) is available at low cost from technical colleges and adult

3

With the flame burning oxygen from the torch, it needs to be adjusted so that correct proportions of fuel and oxygen are emerging from the tip.

4

As you adjust the torch you will see the flame separate into three different parts.

education programs sponsored by skill centers or vocational high schools. The classes are typically held evenings for working adults' convenience. Enrolling in a welding class will thoroughly acquaint you with safety principles as well as instruct you in the theory of welding technology and provide sufficient practice to make you a moderately skilled welder. These steps for using a gas welding torch to heat rust frozen bolts that are given below are not intended to replace formal instruction. Instead they are intended as a quick reminder or review.

Step One—Opening the Tanks

Before heating a rust-frozen bolt or nut, make sure that you will not be directing the torch in the direction of any flammable material (the gas tank, gas line, undercoating and so on). Before lighting the welding torch, you need to open the regulator valves on both the oxygen and fuel tanks. Make sure that both valves on the torch handle are closed before opening the regulator valves. Now you will open (turn counterclockwise) the valve on the oxygen cylinder (always painted green). Turn the valve slowly until the regulator pressure gauge reaches its maximum reading. Then turn the valve all the way open. The fuel tank valve is opened next, and only after the oxygen valve has been opened. Open the fuel tank valve a quarter turn, so the fuel cylinder can be shut off quickly in an emergency. Now adjust the oxygen pressure at the torch by opening the torch valve on the oxygen line (also green) and adjusting the oxygen regulator so that the low pressure gauge (which registers the flow of oxygen to the torch) reads between 8 and 20 pounds per square inch (psi). When this setting is achieved, close the torch valve on the oxygen line.

Adjust the fuel pressure by repeating these steps with the torch valve on the fuel line. Set the fuel regulator so that the pressure reading is between 8 and 9 psi. (This is the pressure setting for a medium to large tip; a small to medium tip would require a pressure setting of 4 to 5 psi.)

Step Two—Lighting the Torch

Before lighting the torch, it is important to purge the lines. This is done by briefly opening both torch valves. As soon as you hear the hiss of gas escaping from the torch, close the

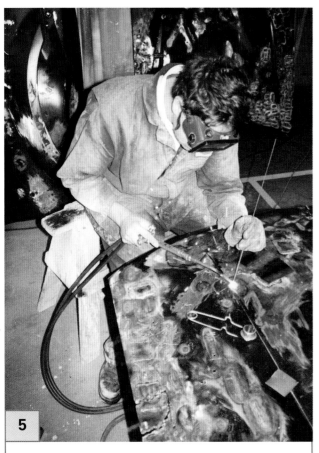

5

Welding is done by heating the metal and filler rod until the rod melts and puddles.

6

Draw the torch and filler rod along the weld, keeping the puddle moving.

valves. Now you will light the torch. As the first step, open the fuel valve slightly (approximately one-half turn). As soon as the valve is opened, strike a spark at the tip with a torch lighter. Do not use matches and *never* use a cigarette lighter to ignite a welding torch. If you have opened the fuel valve too far, the flame will ignite, then blow out. If the setting is correct, a sooty, yellowish flame will lick out of the torch tip.

Open the oxygen valve at the torch slowly and gently. As you do so, the flame will change in shape and color. If you open the oxygen valve too far or too fast, the flame will blow out with a pop. If this happens, don't be alarmed. Just close the oxygen valve and relight the flame.

Step Three—Adjusting the Torch

Once the flame is burning in the oxygen supplied through the torch (rather than in the air) the oxygen and fuel gas need to be mixed for maximum heat. This is done by adjusting both valves until the correct proportions of fuel and oxygen are emerging from the tip. To achieve this setting, put on your welder's goggles and slowly open the oxygen valve. You will see the flame separate into three distinct parts: a small, light-colored cone at the tip, surrounded by a darker colored cone, and the flame's outer halo. A flame with a larger outer cone has too much fuel and too little oxygen. Continue to open the oxygen valve until the outer cone disappears and the inner cone has a smooth, round shape. When you have adjusted the flame to this description, you may need to increase the flow of both fuel and oxygen (in equal proportions) to achieve a hotter flame. As you increase the flame's strength, you will probably also need to readjust the oxygen and fuel settings to bring the flame back to the correct shape cone.

Step Four—Heating and Welding

When heating metal to loosen rust frozen-bolts or king pins, always apply the heat to the nut or fastener that holds the bolt you are trying to turn, or to the area around the pin—never to the bolt or pin itself. Heat enables you to loosen a rust-frozen bolt by expanding the metal into which the bolt is threaded, thereby breaking the rust's grip. If possible, play the flame all the way around the nut or housing into which the bolt is threaded, keeping the torch moving, until the entire area begins to glow a cherry red. If you are heating a casting, like an exhaust manifold, and fail to keep the torch moving, heat will build in one spot and may crack the part.

When the metal begins to show that reddish glow, you can turn off the torch, grip the bolt with a socket or combination wrench, and turn it loose. The bolt should turn fairly easily. If it doesn't, apply more heat—making sure to direct the torch toward the surrounding metal.

After removing the bolt, do not touch it with your bare hands and don't let the bolt drop or lie on a wooden floor. The bolt will have reached a temperature of several hundred degrees from the heat transferred through the adjoining metal and will take quite a while to cool.

When welding, move the torch tip over the metal in a circular motion until it begins to glow and puddle. Keep the torch tip about 1/8 in. from the metal; don't let it actually touch the metal. Hold the filler rod ahead of the torch letting the puddle—not the torch—melt the filler rod. The puddle will solidify behind the torch. It's important to keep the filler rod, torch and puddle moving because you do not want to overheat and stretch the metal. Welding patches onto an old fender or hood as shown in the accompany photos will help you practice holding the torch at the proper angle while keeping the torch and filler rod moving smoothly so that you don't burn through the metal.

Step Five—Shutting Down

When you are finished using the welding torch, always close the valves on both the oxygen and fuel tanks, then purge the lines by opening both valves at the torch. You will hear a momentary hiss as the gas in the lines escapes. Now close the valves at the torch, roll up the hose and hang it on the tanks so that it will not drape on the floor. Then roll the welding cart to a space in the shop where it will be out of the way.

A gas welding outfit is one of the handiest tools in an old truck restorer or rebuilder's shop. Not only does it make disassembling parts far easier, but it also prevents parts from being damaged beyond reuse during the disassembly process. As we proceed through the chapters that follow, we'll be using the gas wrench in many stages of the repair and rebuilding process.

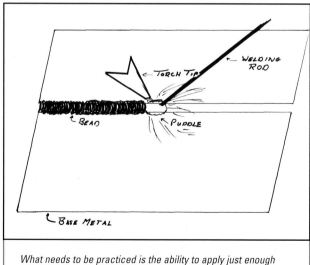

What needs to be practiced is the ability to apply just enough heat to puddle the filler rod without overheating and stretching the panel being welded.

From 1918 until 1960, Chevy light trucks used essentially the same design for the front suspension—namely a solid axle attached to the front of the frame by two semi-elliptical leaf springs. This simple design is very rugged and gives a moderately comfortable ride. But like any mechanical system, a straight-axle front end is also subject to wear and on most older trucks, both the suspension and steering linkage are well enough worn to require a complete rebuild. In the steps that follow , you will find a description of the basic procedures for overhauling any pre-1960 Chevrolet light truck front end. Certain specifics may differ on your truck, so you are also recommended to refer to a service manual for your year and model truck. The intent of these instructions is to give you an overview of the rebuilding sequence and to point out some of the difficulties you are likely to encounter in working on parts that may be nearly as old, or older than you are.

From 1960 onward, Chevrolet has used independent front suspension on its two-wheel drive trucks. The suspension design for 1960 through 1962 uses torsion bars. Starting in 1963 and continuing through modern trucks, the front suspension uses coil springs. In the overhaul discussion for trucks with independent front suspension, it will be assumed that you are working from a service manual. Rather than detail the overhaul procedure for various years and models, the portion of this chapter addressing trucks with independent front suspension will identify parts that are vulnerable to wear and outline the steps for their replacement.

From 1918 to 1960 the front suspension on light and medium duty Chevrolet trucks consisted of a beam axle and longitudinal leaf springs.

Straight-Axle Front End, 1918-1959

The straight-axle front end, also used on four-wheel drive trucks through 1987, gets its name from the beam axle that connects both wheels and supports the springs that form the suspension system and hold the axle in place. Each end of the axle has a hole through which short, rugged steel shafts—called king pins—are inserted to hold the spindle arms to the axle. These king pins allow the spindle arms, on which are mounted the brakes and wheels, to rotate laterally on the axle and in so doing enable steering movement for the front wheels. Attached to the spindle arms is a steering linkage consisting of a tie-rod and drag link. This linkage connects both spindle arms so that when the steering wheel is turned in one direction, both front wheels track together in the same direction.

Rugged and durable though it is, this front suspension and steering system has several wear points which show up in sloppy steering that may become loose enough for the front wheels chatter and shimmy after hitting a bump. Sloppy steering has a number of causes: worn king pins or bushings, worn tie rod ends, loose wheel bearings, wear or incorrect adjustment in the steering box, or a combination of these conditions. Along with loose steering, other front end problems include a slouching front stance (the truck tips to one side or seems to settle lower than normal in the front) and rapid tire wear. A slouching front end traces to sagging or broken springs or worn spring shackles. Rapid tire wear can be caused by a bent axle or incorrect tie rod adjustment that pitches the tires toward each other (called toe-in) or away from each other (called toe-out).

Tools

Rebulding a straight-axle front end is within a handyman mechanic's skills, but requires a rather complete tool set, plus a few specialty items and shop manual. At a minimum, the tool set would consist of: a 1/2 in. socket set, hefty ball peen hammer, assorted chisels, pliers, screwdrivers, punch set, bushing drivers, bushing reamer (optional), gas torch (optional, but recommended), puller, tie-rod separator (optional, but recommended), sturdy bench vise and shop manual. The shop manual will detail various repair sequences and is needed for toe-in and other settings.

Assessing Wear

A front-end overhauling should begin by checking its overall condition and diagnosing its problems. To do this, you will perform three simple tests. For the first test, grip the steering wheel and turn it back and forth slightly. As you do so, look for movement of the front wheels. If the steering wheel has a noticeable amount of free movement (called play) through which the front wheels are stationary, the tie-rod ends and

The expression "rides like a truck" refers not only to the stiffness of the springs but also on the beam axle's tendency to transfer road shocks from one wheel to the other.

steering linkage may be worn, the steering box may need adjusting or have internal wear or damage, or these conditions may exist in combination.

The second test requires that you park the truck on a level surface—which in most cases can be the garage floor. Here you will check for sagging or broken front springs and worn shackle bushings. This is done both visually and by measurement. For the visual check, sight along the springs. Are the springs curved in an arc, or are they essentially flat? Most front springs had some arc when new. Now closely inspect the individual leaves for breaks. Misalignment is another clue of a broken leaf. Often broken leaves can't be spotted until the spring is disassembled, but if one spring is flatter than the other (has more sag), you'll probably decide to remove and overhaul both springs. If you are taking the repair approach and the springs seem to have more or less normal arc and don't show any broken leaves, you will probably let well enough alone.

On a frame-up restoration, you will remove and disassemble both front springs, have leaves re-arced, then paint, lubricate and reassemble the spring assemblies. While inspecting the front suspension, also look for worn shackles (these are the brackets that attach the ends of the springs to the frame). Wear can usually be detected by elongated sockets at the spring eyes. As a sure test for spring sag and worn shackles, measure the distance from the floor (for this measurement to have meaning it is very important that the floor be level) to each frame horn. (The horn is the portion of the frame that protrudes ahead of the front axle.) The difference in the measurements is the amount of spring sag and possible shackle wear.

The third test checks for looseness anywhere in the front-end assembly. To do this test, you will need to jack the front

end off the ground and place jack stands under either end of the front axle. Now lower the truck onto the jack stands, making sure the stands are supporting the truck's weight. Block the back wheels to keep the truck from rolling. You can begin checking for looseness by inspecting the U-bolts that hold the springs to the axle. Sometimes a U-bolt is broken or loose. A broken U-bolt can actually cause the front axle to move as the truck is going down the road. Also inspect the bolts holding the steering box to the frame. If the steering box is loose you can expect to feel play in the steering.

Next check the wheel bearings and king pins for play by gripping the tire with one hand on the top and the other on the bottom. Now attempt to rock the tire by jerking one hand toward you while pushing the other away. More than the smallest amount of free movement (about 3/16 in. is tolerable) indicates that either the wheel bearings or king pins, or both, need service.

To make a final check for looseness in the steering assembly, grab hold of the ends of the tie rod (the long rod that connects the two wheels) and pull forcefully up and down to check for play. If the tie rod end moves up and down there is wear in the sockets and the socket ends will need to be serviced or replaced. If you twist the tie rod you may feel some rotating movement; this is normal. Make the same checks for looseness on the ends of the steering connecting rod.

After making these checks, you should write down all of the areas where you have noticed looseness. Front end assemblies on older trucks typically show extensive wear due to infrequent lubrication and hard use over rough, unpaved roads. If your goal is restoration, you will probably decide to completely overhaul the front end. If your goal is to make the truck serviceable, you now know the areas that need attention. The next section describes how to bring a straight axle front end back to safe operating standards.

Front End Disassembly

For restoration you will completely disassemble and rebuild your truck's the front-end suspension and steering system. This is the approach that will be described here. If you are upgrading your truck by repairs, you can begin your overhaul at whatever point is necessary, depending on your truck's problems, and follow the sequence from there.

Typically this is the point in a frame up restoration where the body and other sheet metal have been removed from the chassis. The engine and transmission have also been pulled, leaving the frame sitting on the front and rear axle assemblies. To remove the front axle and its attached suspension/steering components, you will start by disconnecting the shock absorber arm on lever-style shocks, or the nut from the lower section on double-acting shocks. If the truck is equipped with a stabilizer bar, remove this next. Now you can disconnect the brake flex hoses (on trucks with hydraulic

In a frame up restoration, front end overhaul occurs as part of the chassis rebuild when suspension parts are most easily accessible.

The medium duty truck front suspension shown here is the same design as a light duty truck.

brakes) from the front wheel cylinders. In most cases these hoses will have dried out and cracked and will need to be replaced later during brake overhaul. If the condition of the hoses appears deteriorated, the simplest way to get them out of the way is just to cut them. On an earlier truck with a mechanical brake system, you will disconnect the front brake rods or cables.

Now the steering connecting rod needs to be removed. (This is the short rod on the driver's side of the chassis that attaches to the pitman arm from the steering box; it is also commonly referred to as a drag link.) The steering connecting rod attaches to the pitman arm at the steering box and to the left steering arm by tapered bolts, nuts and cotter keys. This

rod is removed by pulling out the cotter keys, loosening the nuts, then prying or driving the connecting rod studs out of the pitman and steering arms. Since the studs are tapered and will have become tightly wedged into the likewise tapered holes in the pitman and steering arms, you'll find that attempting to separate the parts with a hammer isn't very effective and will probably ruin the connecting rod for reuse.

A better approach is to use a special tool called a tie-rod separator, which should pry out the studs with a minimum of effort. Another alternative is to lift the stud out of the pitman and steering arm with the puller. Although the tie-rod separator and puller are effective on newer vehicles, on an older truck the connecting rod studs have probably been wedged in the sockets for a long time and the two are likely to be rust frozen together. In this case you will need to heat the ends of the pitman and steering arms with an acetylene or MAPP gas torch. With some heat to expand the metal surrounding the connecting rod studs, the tapered studs should drive out of the pitman and steering arms easily. Since the ends of the steering connecting rod are not repairable, the entire rod will need to be replaced if the studs in the ends are worn or if the threads on the ends of the stud are ruined during disassembly. Fortunately, replacement steering connecting rods are readily available from vintage Chevy truck parts suppliers.

The final step in removing the front end assembly from the frame is to detach springs by taking apart the spring shackles. If the shackle bolts are rusted, they can be heated or cut with a torch. You will be replacing the spring shackles so any damage to these parts is of no consequence. With the spring shackles apart, the front axle assembly can be removed away from the frame to an area of the shop where it can be worked on further.

Front Axle Disassembly

In the next series of steps you will break down the front-end assembly into its individual components. When this is done, you can clean and degrease the parts, sandblast items as needed, then begin the rebuilding, refinishing process.

Spring Removal

You will start the disassembly steps by removing the springs. This is done by loosening the U-bolts that hold the springs to the axle. Typically the nuts to these bolts will be rust frozen. Squirt plenty of penetrating oil on the nuts before attempting to loosen them. If you have access to a torch, heating the nuts will assure they come off easily. Whenever possible, avoid damaging or destroying original nuts and bolts because modern replacements rarely match the originals in bolt-head size and appearance. When the U-bolts have been removed, you can further disassemble the springs by loosening the center bolt. Also, you need remove the bushings from the spring eyes. This is best done with a bushing driver.

Keep the spring sets separate by tying together the leaves from each spring, or placing each set of leaves in a separate box. Label the springs left or right side as appropriate. Later, when the front axle system is completely disassembled, you will clean and sandblast the spring leaves and have them re-arched. For now you just want to make sure they don't get misplaced or mixed up with other parts.

Tie-Rod Removal

Now you can remove the tie-rod (the long rod running parallel to and just behind the front axle). On trucks up through 1959, the tie-rod attaches to a steering knuckle arm at either end through an adjustable end assembly. In 1960 and later light duty Chevy trucks, the end assemblies (called tie-rod ends) are threaded into the tie-rod and are replaceable.

On 1959 and earlier trucks, to loosen the tie-rod, remove the cotter keys that fit through the end plug in the tie-rod sockets. If the truck has been kept well lubricated, the end plug should be able to be loosened quite easily. A wide-bladed screwdriver is be used to turn the plug. Lacking this, you can insert a chisel in the slot on the plug and turn the chisel with a crescent wrench. If the plug doesn't loosen, spray penetrating oil around the outline of the plug, let the oil soak in and try again. If the plug still won't budge, you will have to heat the metal around the plug with a torch. Once the plug turns freely, you will need to work the steering knuckle arm out from the

To access the front wheel spindles, the brakes have to be removed. Chevrolet trucks prior to 1971 came factory-equipped with drum brakes. Disc brakes shown here are found on 1971 model year light duty trucks and newer. Disc rotors remove essentially the same way as drums.

tie-rod socket. When you have repeated this procedure at the other tie-rod end, the rod can be pulled free. Be sure to label and save all parts.

With 1960 and later trucks, the tie-rod end is a tapered fit and is removed using the tie-rod separator tool mentioned earlier.

Brake Removal

To get at the wheel spindles (which attach to the axle ends), you first have to take off the brake drums, disassemble the brakes and remove the backing plates. The brake drums should slide off easily after you loosen the spindle nut and remove the outer wheel bearing. Sometimes, however, the brake shoe contact area has worn so that there is a lip on the edge of the drum and this lip catches against the linings. If this is the case, you will have to loosen the brakes (back off the shoes) before the drum will pull loose. Be sure to use a wrench to turn the spindle nut, not pliers. The serrated jaws on a set of pliers will cut into the nut, making it difficult to fit on a wrench when you or someone else decides to use the right tool. Also, be sure to separate right- and left-side bearings and other parts.

Once the brake drum is removed, you should pull the inner wheel bearing out of the drum. This is best done by using a special bearing puller. You can also remove the bearing by prying the bearing seal out of its groove and driving the bearing out of the race by gently tapping on the bearing cage with a punch. Another easier method for removing the inner wheel bearing is to replace the nut and washer on the spindle, then slip the brake drum over the nut and let the hub rest on the spindle. Now pull the drum toward you with a swift, sharp tug that strikes the inner bearing against the spindle nut. This will pop the bearing free without damage to the cage nearly every time.

Before removing the brake shoes and related parts, take photos of the brake assembly. These photos may be useful in reassembling the brakes later. Now you can remove the springs and clips holding the brake shoes in place. Be sure to save all parts. The service manual for your truck should explain the sequence for removing the brake shoes, but in most cases you should be able to work through this mechanical puzzle fairly easily. With the brake shoes out of the way, you will see the bolts holding the backing plates to the wheel spindles. Remove the cotter keys from the bolts at the nut end and loosen the nuts. The backing plates will then slide off the spindles. Set the bolts and nuts aside for plating. At this point you are ready to drive out the king pins and remove the wheel spindles from the axle.

King Pin Removal

The king pins fit through holes in the spindle yoke and axle ends. They are held in place by wedge-shaped locking pins that are driven through a small hole near the end of the axle and

King pins holding the wheel spindles to the axle ends can sometimes be removed by driving them out with a hefty hammer and steel shaft. Often, king pins are rust frozen to the axle ends, which have to be heated with a torch. Even then, the axle may need to be placed in a hydraulic press at a machine shop to force the king pins to move.

kept from working loose by a nut that is usually found on the back side of the axle. To remove these locking pins, loosen the nut and drive the pins out of their holes with a punch. You may also find dust seals at the top and bottom of both king pins. These are metal discs that have been wedged into the holes in the spindle yoke. It is not uncommon for these seals to be missing, either because they were not installed on an earlier overhaul, or because they have worked loose and fallen out. The dust seals are made of soft metal and can be removed easily by forcing a small, sharp chisel into the seal and prying it out of the hole. With the seals removed, you can attack the king pins.

Sometimes king pins will slide out of the axle as easily as pushing a knife through butter, but more often the pins are rusted to the axle and move about as willingly as boulder being pushed by a toy truck. Before attempting to drive out the king pins, spray penetrating oil into the openings at the top and bottom of the spindle yoke, the locking pin hole and into the junctures where the axle and spindle meet. It's difficult to get the penetrating oil directly into the hole in the axle end where the king pin is likely to be rust- frozen, but efforts should be made. After letting the oil penetrate, place the end of the axle on a concrete block, anvil, or other solid object that will not absorb the force directed against the king pin and attempt to drive the pin out of the axle using a hefty 24 oz. hammer and a punch that is slightly smaller in diameter than the pins. If the pin moves after several sharp blows, apply more penetrating oil.

If fortune is smiling, by alternating hammer blows on the pin with squirting penetrating oil into the openings, you will soon have the king pins out and the axle assembly completely apart. More likely, however, the king pins won't move in the least. If this happens you have two alternatives. Assuming the front axle is out of the truck (as has been described in the preceding steps, but may not be the case if you are using a repair approach), you can take the axle to a machine shop and have the pins pressed out on a hydraulic press.

The other alternative (which you will have to use if the axle is still in the truck) is to heat the axle ends with a torch until the metal glows red. A propane torch won't apply enough heat; you will have to use oxy-acetylene or Mapp gas welding torch. Once the metal around the pins has been heated, you should be able to drive them out using strong, sharp blows as described earlier. You won't be reusing the king pins from your truck, so you can discard them, along with their related hardware.

Cleaning, Derusting and Inspecting Parts

Now the axle assembly should be completely apart. Either at this point or after you have cleaned the spindles you will need to remove the king pin bushings from the spindle yokes. This is best done with a bushing driver. An alkaline degreasing bath (described previously in the Cleaning, Sandblasting and Derusting chapter) will make short order of the accumulated grease and dirt commonly found on the front axle and its associated parts. Rust, which is likely to be found on the axle and brake drums, can be removed by sandblasting. Front end parts should not be derusted using acid because of the danger of embrittling the metal.

After the axle has been cleaned, you should check it for trueness. In the rough use most trucks have experienced, it is not unusual to find that the front axle has been bent or twisted. You can check for twisting by laying the axle on its side on the shop floor and looking to see if both axle ends touch the floor (this assumes that the floor is smooth and level). You can check for bends by sighting along the axle. If evidence of twisting or bends exists, you need to take the axle to a machine shop and have it straightened.

The tie rod should also be checked for straightness. If this long rod is bent or kinked, you may want to consider finding another that is straight and true. The other option is to straighten the rod that you have. This should be done "cold". Heating the rod to straighten it will cause the metal to lose its temper or strength and allow it to bend more easily in the future. While inspecting the tie rod, also check the condition of the steering arm balls that fit into the sockets on the ends of the tie rod.

Few trucks are maintained as conscientiously as cars and if lubrication has been neglected, the steering arm balls have probably worn into an egg shape. Out-of-round steering balls will cause the truck will be hard to steer and can also be a

59

factor producing play in the steering. You have the choice of replacing the steering arms or having new balls welded onto the arms. These steering balls are available from vintage Chevrolet truck parts suppliers.

You should have the work of cutting off the old steering arm balls and welding on the new balls done at a machine shop. Strong welds here are critical. If a weld should fail and a steering ball break off on the road, the truck would go out of control.

If you haven't taken the springs apart, this needs to be done next. Removing the center bolt is all that's necessary to separate the leaves. The leaves can then be cleaned and derusted (either by sandblasting or wire brushing). Before reassembling, the springs should be re-arched. This is done by a spring shop. After re-arching, the leaves should be primed and painted.

Before assembling the springs, either place strips of teflon or a liberal coating of grease between the leaves. This is done to enable the leaves to slide freely on one another and greatly improves the ride. After replacing and tightening the center bolt and installing new bushings in the eyes at the ends of each main leaf, the springs are ready to be installed on the axle.

Front End Assembly

All front-end parts should be primed and painted in preparation for reassembly. While refinishing is going on you can send the hardware (nuts and bolts) out for zinc plating; any commercial plating shop should be able to provide this service. You should also draw up a parts list and begin gathering the items you will need to reassemble the front end. The parts will include a king pin set, new steering connecting rod (if the ball studs on the old rod show wear or if the studs have battered ends), tie rod end assembly kits, replacement steering balls (if the old balls are worn out-of-round), new or relined brake shoes, brake return springs, wheel cylinders, spring shackles and wheel bearings (these should be replaced if the old bearings show signs of wear or spackling—chips in the rollers—or if the inner wheel bearings have broken apart in the process of removing them from the brake drums). You will also need new inner wheel bearing seals.

Although you can get all these items from vintage Chevy parts suppliers, you may also be able to purchase some of the items on the list at a nearby auto parts store. Buying parts locally has the advantage of saving shipping costs and delays, and if the items aren't right you can easily return them. National auto parts chains like NAPA have enormous warehouse inventories, so parts listed but not in stock locally can usually be shipped to a nearby store within one or two days.

Once the chassis and other front-end parts have been refinished, you will start reassembling the front end in the reverse order from that in which you took it apart. This means that the new king pins will be installed first.

Reinstalling King Pins

There are basically three things to remember when installing king pins: first, make sure the grease holes in the bushings are in line with the grease fittings; second, place the thrust bearing in the correct location (between the axle and lower spindle yoke); and third, shim the space between the axle end and spindle yokes so that there is no more than .005 in. gap and no free movement. If you follow these guidelines, you will have accomplished the first step in assuring your truck steers easily and runs down the road straight and true.

The procedure of replacing the kings pins begins by installing new bushings in the spindle yokes. This is best done with a bushing driver, available from a specialty supplier like The Eastwood Company and an arbor or hydraulic press. Most hobbyists don't have a press and if that's your case you may choose to have these bushings installed at a machine shop.

If you'd rather install the bushings yourself, you can press the bushings in place using a bench vise. When using a vise to press the bushings, you first need to start the bushings in the holes in the spindle yoke. To start the bushings, round the edges of the bushings slightly with a file, lubricate the hole in the spindle yoke, then tap the bushing into the hole with a plastic hammer. You should place a large washer over the end of the bushing you are tapping to make sure that no damage is done to the bushing's soft metal. Be sure that the hole in the bushing lines up with the grease-fitting hole in the spindle yoke. Once the bushing is started, you can place the spindle yoke in the bench vise (insert a block of wood between the bushing and vise jaw to prevent the jaw from cutting into the soft metal of the bushing) and slowly press the bushing into its hole by tightening the vise.

When all four bushings have been installed (remember to make sure they are all correctly aligned with the grease fitting holes), the new bushings need to be reamed to the diameter of the king pins. You can do this yourself if you have a reamer of the correct diameter (this tool can be purchased from an auto parts store or specialty tool supplier), or you can have the bearings reamed at a machine shop. The cost of having a machine shop do this work will be approximately the same as the expense of the tool, so whether you do the work yourself or hire it done may depend on whether or not you want to add a bushing reamer to your tool inventory. If you decide to buy the reamer, note that you will need a tool that is long enough to ream both bushings at once. This is necessary to establish proper alignment for the king pins.

Now you can begin to assemble the king pins by fitting a spindle yoke over one end of the axle. Place a thrust bearing (or washers on three-quarter-ton and larger trucks) between the axle and the lower yoke. Note that a thrust washer is supplied only with king pin bolt kits for 1/2 ton trucks. Make sure that the closed side of the thrust bearing is at the top. Now check the clearance between the upper face of the axle

This view shows the restored straight axle front end. Notice that the steering box has not yet been installed. John Lilga

end and the upper yoke. This clearance should not exceed 0.005 in. If greater clearance exists, insert shims in this space until the required clearance is met. As you install the shims, check the gap with a feeler gauge. Too loose a fit will cause sloppy steering, but too tight a fit will make for hard steering. As you fit the shims, make sure the holes in the spindle ends line up with the hole in the end of the axle.

With the shims in place you can fit the king pin into the hole. Make sure that the notch for the locking pin faces toward the locking-pin hole in the axle. With the king pin in place, drive the locking pin through its hole in the axle until the pin is wedged tightly against the king pin. Now install a lock washer and nut on the locking pin's threaded end and tighten. To seal the king pin against dust and moisture, place a soft metal plug, rounded side up, in the hole above the king pin on one end of the spindle yoke and wedge the plug into place by giving it a sharp tap on the crest of the bulge with a ball-peen hammer. Do the same with the other spindle end. Now repeat this procedure with the other spindle, and task of installing the king pins will be completed.

Reinstalling the Tie Rod

If the tie-rod ends have been replaced, the new ends need to be threaded into the tie rod. Be sure the threads are cleaned and well lubricated, as it is important that the rod be able to turn easily in order to set the front wheel toe-in. Before threading on the ends, slide the clamps that lock the ends in place onto the tie rods. Do not turn the ends fully into the tie rod, but leave

about one third of the threads showing. Position the ends so that roughly the same number of threads are showing in front of each. Now you need to replace the end assemblies, consisting of a spring seat, spring, two ball seats and end plug. Assemble these parts in the sequence shown in the service manual with the steering arm ball sandwiched between the two ball seats. When all the parts are assembled, tighten the end plug until the spring is fully compressed, then back off to the first cotter pin hole. Insert and lock the cotter pin by bending back the ends. If the grease fitting has been removed it needs to be replaced so that you can lubricate the end assembly. Now repeat the same procedure at the other tie-rod end.

Final Assembly

If a stabilizer bar is included in the front-end assembly, reinstall this component. Now you are ready to mount the front springs. This is done by centering the springs over the axle and clamping them in place with U-bolts. If the frame is ready (cleaned, primed, and painted) you can attach the front-axle assembly by replacing the spring shackles. If the steering box is also in place, you will also hook up the steering connecting rod. Remember that if the ends of this rod are worn (show excessive free movement) or damaged, then this part needs to be replaced. The shock arms also need to be connected to their mounts on the frame. The remaining steps—replacing the backing plates and brake assemblies and adjusting the tie rod for correct front wheel toe-in—are covered in later chapters.

With the front end reinstalled in the chassis, the next steps are to replace the drivetrain. Often the transmission and differential do not need to be overhauled. Procedures to follow for rebuilding these assemblies, if you suspect of know of mechanical problems, are described in the shop manual for your series truck.

Independent Front Suspension, 1960 to Present

In 1960, Chevrolet made one of the biggest advances in light truck development by replacing the beam front axle with independent front suspension (IFS). While Chevy cars had acquired IFS in the1930s, beam axles had been retained in trucks due to their simpler, more rugged design. However, a beam axle gives a much inferior ride to IFS—hence the expression "rides like a truck." In designing an independent front suspension system for their division's and GMC's trucks, Chevrolet engineers faced the challenge of how to build a suspension that would take hard use without coming out of alignment and causing premature front tire wear. The resulting Long-and-Short-Arm suspension adapted the design used successfully for over 25 years on Chevrolet cars to trucks. However, in the truck setting, all the parts were significantly strengthened. From 1960 through 1962, both Chevrolet's light and medium duty trucks used torsion bars for springs. In

With the adoption of independent front suspension in 1960 (first torsion bars, then coil springs), Chevrolet switched from king pins to ball joints as the swivel mechanism for the wheel spindles. This photo shows the upper and lower ball joints with the wheel spindle removed.

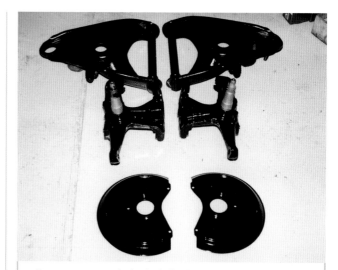

Here we see a set of wheel spindles for an independent front suspension (center) as well as the upper A-arms (top, so-called because their triangle shape suggests the letter A), which replaced the beam axle. The semi-circular objects at the bottom of the photo are a set of dust shields for the brake caliper. Parts like this can be given a durable, attractive finish by powder coating.

1963, Chevrolet re-engineered its truck front ends, reverting to the former I-beam system on its heavy duty trucks and replacing torsion bars with coil springs on its light duty C-10 through C-30 models. Four-wheel drive K series trucks never adopted IFS. The coil spring IFS has the same basic design as the torsion bar system, but costs less to build.

Almost no similarities exist between a beam-axle front end and independent front suspension. A beam axle suspension has essentially no adjustments except toe-in. With independent front suspension, adjustments are also made for caster (the angle of the steering axis from vertical) and camber (the inclination of the wheels from vertical). Both of these adjustments need to be made at a front-end shop, although toe-in can be set at home. When Chevrolet adopted independent front suspension on its trucks, king pins were replaced more advanced ball-joints for securing the steering spindles the ball and socket tie-rod ends were replaced with sealed units.

Wear points on the independent front suspension are the ball joints and the control arms shafts, plus the tie-rod ends. In addition, torsion bars on 1960-1962 models and coil springs on 1963 and later Chevrolet and GMC trucks can become fatigued, causing the front end to sag. If the independent front suspension shows wear (as evidenced by steering wander and premature or uneven tire wear) it should be rebuilt. If the

truck has front-end sag (which may be noticeable visually or can be checked by measuring the height from a level surface like a shop floor to the frame horns), the torsion bars or coil springs should be replaced. Instructions for installing and removing the torsion bars are shown in Chevrolet's 1960 truck shop manual. The 1961 manual is a supplement.

Overhauling Independent Front Suspension

An IFS front end is really no more difficult to rebuild than a beam axle system and can be done by a handyman mechanic using a tool set described at the front of this chapter. The overhaul process is much the same for torsion bar and coil spring suspension, except that a spring compressor is needed to remove the coil springs. After rebuilding, the IFS suspension needs to be adjusted for proper caster and camber settings and aligned for toe-in at a front-end shop.

As mentioned, typical service items on an Chevrolet or GMC truck IFS are the control arm shafts on which the upper and lower A-Arms (also called control arms) pivot and the ball joints that attach the wheel spindles to the outboard ends of these same control arms. On some trucks of collector interest, Chevrolet used grease fittings to lubricate the control arm shafts. If owners of these trucks kept these shafts lubricated, west was unlikely to result. However, due to a variety of causes including clogged grease fittings and the awkwardness of the location of the fittings behind the front tires, proper lubrication of these shafts is rare. When the pivot points on the

Typical service items on Chevrolet and GMC light duty trucks with independent front suspension are the control arms on shafts on the upper and lower A-arms as well as the ball joints that attach to the apex of those the A-arms. Control arm shafts are seen at the base of the A-arm and wear from lack of lubrication.

A top view of the independent front suspension.

control arm shafts aren't lubricated, unwanted movement or play occurs in the upper or lower control arms (or both) and steering wander results. Worn ball joints can also produce steering wander and sometimes a cupping wear pattern on the front tires.

Checking for worn pivot points in the control arm shafts and loose ball joints is the same as the check for worn king pins. Jack up one side of the truck at the front so that the tire is off the ground, which unloads the torsion bar or spring on that side, grip the top and bottom of the tire and attempt to rock the tire in an in and out motion. If any movement is found, there's wear in the control arm shafts or ball joints, or possibly both. The source of the wear or play can usually be detected visually. That is, if the control arms will move slightly

at their pivot points or the spindles will move at the ball joints. The suspension is designed for zero movement at these points.

Disassembly

While it's not necessary to remove the front brake assemblies, which from 1971 on means disc brakes, to service the ball joints, the process is much easier with the brakes and backing plates out of the way. Of course, if you're working on a chassis with the body structure removed, the entire front suspension assembly will be in open view. Servicing the control arm shafts is a bench job, so the entire suspension system is disassembled to remove these parts.

Initially, disassembly proceeds much like a straight axle front end by removing the front brake assemblies. Unbolting the backing plates for drum brakes or the dust shield for disk brakes exposes the wheel spindles and the front suspension components, including the upper and lower control arms and the torsion bar or coil spring. The spring sits in a cupped groove stamped into the upper and lower control arms and is wedged in place by its expansive force.

If there's no torsion bar or spring sag or evident wear in the pivot points on the control arm shafts or upper or lower ball joints, you may just want to clean the suspension members (steam cleaning works especially well here), then repaint the suspension pieces and proceed to overhaul the brakes. But if the torsion bars or coil springs show signs of fatigue and sagging and/or the control arm shafts or ball joints show wear, you'll want to disassemble both front end assemblies and replace all worn parts.

Independent front suspension with the lower A-arm and wheel spindle removed. The steering arm also hangs disconnected.

The front suspension layout for a four-wheel drive truck closely resembles a two-wheel drive, beam axle setup.

The rebuilt and reassembled front suspension.

The A-arm front suspension comes apart by installing a spring compressor tool on the coil spring, tightening the tool to remove spring tension, then removing the nut at the lower end of the upper ball joint, which connects the upper portion of the wheel spindle to the upper A-arm. The ball joint has a tapered shank that is wedged tightly into the wheel spindle. The tool for prying the ball joint shank out of the spindle is a pickle fork, also used to separate tie-rod ends. But if the ball joint shank is rusted into the spindle, a C-clamp puller may have to be used. *Do not* apply heat from a torch to the spindle end to free the ball joint shank. Heat will weaken this critical suspension component. The same process is used to free the lower ball joint.

Once the spindle is free from the upper ball joint, the compressed spring can be removed from between the control arms. To service the control arm pivots or to remove the control arms for cleaning and painting, detach the upper control arm shaft by removing the bolts that attach the upper shaft to the frame. Note that camber has been set by placing shims between the upper control arm shaft and the frame. Be sure to observe the number of shims behind each bolt. There may be as many as eight or nine shims and the shims may be of different thickness. If you place the shims in a plastic food-saver bag and mark the bag with the location of shims on the truck, you won't forget how many to install and which bolt they're with on reassembly. Even replacing the shims exactly as they were removed, you will still need to have the suspension

adjusted at a front end shop. The lower control arm shafts are held in place against the front frame cross member by U-bolts.

On half-ton trucks, the control arm shafts use rubber bushings. Steel bushings are used on three-quarter and one-ton trucks. Steps for replacing the bushings are listed in the shop manual for your year and model truck.

Cleaning and Painting

If the suspension pieces are rusted, the pressed steel control (A) arms can cleaned to bare metal by sandblasting or bead blasting. *Do not* sandblast the wheel spindles. Sandblasting these parts can embrittle the metal weakening these critical suspension parts and possibly causing them to fail while the truck is on the highway. Powder coating is an ideal finish for these suspension parts. That process is described in a later chapter.

Reassembly

Everything assembles in reverse order, with a few cautions. At the factory, Chevrolet attached the housing portion of the ball joint to the control arms with rivets. In most cases, the ball joints will have been replaced, in which case they will be secured by bolts. If the ball joints are original, the rivets can be drilled then cut with a chisel. If spring sag was noticed, both torsion bars or both coil springs must to be replaced. Finally, remember take the truck to a front end alignment shop to make sure the settings for caster, camber and toe-in are correct once the truck is back on the road.

From 1941 onward, Chevrolet trucks used a ball bearing steering gear developed by GM's Saginaw division. This steering system, called recirculating ball, is superior to the worm and sector steering box design used earlier because moving balls provide a rolling, rather than a sliding, contact between the worm gear on the steering shaft and sector shaft, which turns the wheels. The result is easier steering action and less wear between the parts.

While the Saginaw recirculating-ball steering box is a rugged unit, wear does occur and the steering mechanism can get out of adjustment. When loose steering is noticed, it is important to determine whether the cause is in the front end (loose king pins and tie rod ends) or in the steering box, or a combination. Play in the steering box can be detected by having an assistant hold the pitman arm at the bottom of the steering box while you turn the steering wheel. If free movement is noticed while the pitman arm is held rigid, you may be able to take up the slack by adjustments, or the steering box may need to be rebuilt or replaced by a tighter unit.

In some cases, the steering box may be free of play, but excessively high effort may be required to turn the wheels. Causes here may be a low or dry lubricant level in the steering box, improper steering adjustment, or over tightened tie rod ends (on pre 1960 trucks with adjustable type tie rod sockets). Another cause of hard steering is under-inflated tires.

Correcting Loose Steering

After making sure the steering play is not caused by wear in other front-end parts, the steering gear should be adjusted to make its action as responsive as possible. Specific instructions for adjusting the steering on your year and model Chevrolet truck are given in the service manual. The steps presented here are offered as an overview of the general procedure for adjusting a Chevrolet recirculating-ball steering box, and are not intended to replace the instructions in the service manual.

Adjusting steering play begins by disconnecting the steering connecting rod from the pitman arm. It is important to note the relative position of the two parts before disconnecting them so as to get them back in the same position. The rest of the procedure will be done at the steering box.

Two adjustments will be made. One corrects for slop that has developed between the worm gear and the roller bearings that support the worm gear and its attached steering shaft. The second adjustment reestablishes proper alignment between the sector and ball nut. (The sector is the shaft and crescent-shaped gear that turn the pitman arm and steering linkage. The ball nut is a block-shaped gear that moves with the

The steering mechanism on older Chevrolet trucks has numerous wear points that can cause sloppy steering. A four-wheel drive steering setup is shown here.

steering worm via the recirculating-ball bearings and in so doing turns the sector gear.) When both of these adjustments are set correctly, the steering should have the correct pull (between 2 and 2 1/2 pounds) and no play should be felt in the steering box. Of course it is possible for these adjustments to be set correctly and the steering still be excessively hard, and for play still to exist. With a truck that has seen hard service and little maintenance, other causes of steering box problems include worn sector bushings and/or steering shaft bearings, a worn sector gear and ball nut, worn roller balls, or a bent sector shaft.

Adjusting Bearing Tension

To adjust bearing tension, loosen the lock nut at the end of the sector shaft (on the side of the steering box toward the engine) and turn the adjuster screw—the screw has a slot head and is turned with a screwdriver—a few turns counterclockwise. This unmeshes the contact between the sector gear and ball nut and in so doing removes the tension or load from the worm bearings. Now turn the steering wheel slowly and gently in one direction to the stop, then back one turn. Be careful not to turn the steering wheel hard against the stop or damage to the ball guides can occur. Since the first adjustment you will be making affects steering effort, you need to determine how much pull is required to turn the steering wheel. Although there are professional tools (usually found only in a service garage) to test the pull needed to turn the steering wheel, you can also check the pull with a fishing scale—the small hand-scale fishermen use to weigh their catch. To do this, attach the fishing scale to the steering wheel rim above the cross spoke and pull directly down on the spoke. The force required to turn the wheel should be between 1 and 1 1/2 lb.

To set the worm bearings to the correct tension (bearing tightness against the races on the steering worm) loosen the lock nut at the bottom of the steering box and turn the worm bearing thrust screw until no movement can be felt between the worm gear and its bearings. This movement can be detected by pushing or pulling on the steering wheel. To make sure you have not over tightened these bearings, test the pull on the steering wheel. It should be within the limits mentioned. If, when the worm bearing tension is set correctly, the steering box feels lumpy as you turn the steering wheel, then the bearings are probably worn and will need to be replaced. This is a more complex job that requires removing the steering column from the truck and disassembling the steering box. After making this bearing adjustment, check to make sure that the bolts holding the steering box to the frame are tight.

Now you will adjust the mesh between the sector gear and ball nut. The first step in this procedure is to move the steering wheel to its centered position. To do this, you will gently turn the wheel all the way in one direction to the stop, then in the other direction to stop, counting the turns between stops. When the steering wheel has reached the second stop, turn back half the number of turns. This is the center position. In the event that the steering wheel is mounted so that in spokes are not in a horizontal position at the center position, mark the wheel at the centers of the rim with masking tape.

With the steering wheel in centered position, turn the adjuster screw on the engine side of the steering box (at the end of the sector shaft). This adjustor should be turned clockwise until all looseness (lash) has been taken out of the mesh

between the gear teeth. To tell when the lash has been removed, measure the amount of force needed to turn the steering wheel. A pull of 2 to 2 1/2 lb. is correct. When that amount pull is reached, tighten the adjusting screw lock nut and again check the steering pull. If it has changed, loosen the lock nut and reset the adjusting screw.

After adjusting the steering box, reattach the steering connecting rod to the pitman arm and check for play in the steering. This is best done by jacking the front end off the ground, having a helper hold a front wheel while you turn the steering wheel, and noticing any free movement in the steering wheel that is not felt at the front wheel. If the tie-rod ends and king pins are tight, the steering box either needs to be rebuilt or replaced. Instructions for removing and rebuilding a Saginaw recirculating ball bearing steering box are found in the service manual for your year and model Chevrolet truck. Rebuilt steering boxes are available for many years of Chevy light trucks and unless you are an experienced mechanic or desire to rebuild a recirculating ball steering box as a challenge, you will find installing a rebuilt box to be a much simpler (and typically more satisfactory) approach.

If adjusting the steering box appears to have eliminated excess play, make sure that the box is filled with lubricant before operating the truck on the highway. Chevrolet owner's manuals call for filling the steering box with chassis lube. The lube is pumped into the steering box through the opening on the upper side of the box which is sealed with a pipe plug. Do not install a grease fitting in this hole. Grease should not be put into the steering box under pressure. When these trucks were in regular use, mechanics often added a small amount of 90 wt. gear oil to the grease in the steering box to help lubricate the upper bearing and to reduce steering effort in cold weather. Although the manuals do not call for doing this, you may want to fill the box nearly full with chassis lube and top it off with 90 weight gear oil.

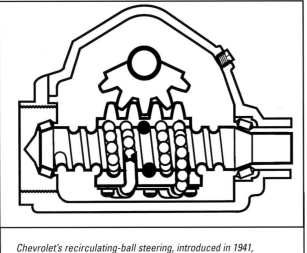

Chevrolet's recirculating-ball steering, introduced in 1941, required less effort than the previous worm and sector design.

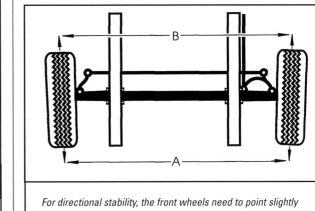

For directional stability, the front wheels need to point slightly toward each other in the front. The degree of this angle is called toe-in.

Alignment

For directional stability, it is desirable that the front wheels point toward each other slightly in the front. The degree to which the front wheels are angled inward is called toe-in. If the wheels point out, the condition is called toe-out and results in very rapid tire wear. At least two methods, not requiring special tools, can be used to set the front wheels of your truck to the correct toe.

The first of these shade tree mechanic techniques for setting toe-in begins by jacking up the truck so that the front wheels are slightly off the shop floor. Now, spin the wheels and spray a thin line of paint (use a light-colored aerosol spray) along the center of the tire. When the paint has dried, spin the wheel and scribe a line in the center of the tire using a nail, Phillips screwdriver, or similar pointed tool. Lower the truck so that the front tires rest on the floor. Now measure to the midpoint of the tires and mark and X across the line at the same height on the front of both tires. Also do this on the back of both front tires.

Using a carpenter's tape, measure the distance between the Xs at the front and back of the tires. The measurement from X to X across the back should be slighter greater than across the front. Typically, the correct toe-in has the measurement at the back of the tires between 1/16 and 1/8 in. greater than the measurement at the front. Toe-in is adjusted by loosening the tie rod ends and turning the tie rod. Note: the wheels need to be raised in order to make this adjustment.

The second do-it-yourself tie-in check is made using a gauge comprised of two sticks of wood clamped together (1 in. stock works well for this). As an alternative to making this gauge The Eastwood Company sells an inexpensive, yet precision toe in gauge. With the front tires resting on the shop floor, loosen the clamps and extend the sticks (or the metal rods of the toe-in tool) until they touch the outermost tread about halfway up the back of the tires. Tighten the clamps so that the gauge is set to this length. (Using the toe-in tool, this measurement is made to the outer edge of the tire.) Now move the gauge to the front of the tires and check the amount of toe-in. As in the previous procedure, the correct toe-in is a difference of 1/16 to 1/8 in. greater distance at the back of the tires than at the front. After the toe-in has been set, torque the bolts on the tie-rod end clamps to 100-120 ft. lb. Be sure to install cotter pins to ensure that the bolts don't work loose.

Upgrading to Power Steering

To some, the real enjoyment of owning a vintage truck is in driving it on a regular basis. In this setting, preserving the truck's originality becomes less important than modifying it for safety and comfort. A popular upgrade is to replace the original steering box with a modern power steering setup.

Adding steering to a truck for which this accessory was originally available is an easy upgrade that requires only the

To upgrade to power steering, you will need both the power steering box and pump. Manual and power steering units interchange.

Here the steering shaft has been disconnected and removed.

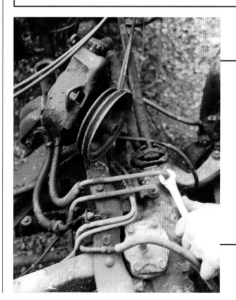

Now the hydraulic lines from the pump are being removed at the steering box. It's not always necessary to loosen these lines.

power steering pump and brackets, plus the hoses and the power assisted steering gearbox. If you getting the parts, as I did, at a salvage yard, you'll want to make sure of their compatibility on your truck. Usually you're safe if you stay within the same styling and engineering series. (GM's 1967-1972 styling series is an example where most mechanical parts interchange between Chevrolet and GMC on all light duty models through all five years.) However, even on these highly compatible trucks, differences can occur between the different load ratings.

If you're uncertain about parts compatibility with your truck, the sure-fire way to find whether or not the parts will fit is to consult a Hollanders Interchange manual. Some salvage yard operators keep copies of this interchange resource in their offices, so it's a good idea to ask. The Interchange manuals are also still available from this publisher. When using the Interchange manual, you will often discover that even car parts will interchange with your truck.

If you're purchasing the power steering components from a salvage yard, it's best to locate the power steering pump on a truck with the same engine as the one in your truck. Otherwise, you may find the hardest part of the installation to be locating the right mounting bracket for the power steering pump and matching up the pump's pulley to the engine's V-belt arrangement. Still, there's no reason to shy away from a power steering setup on a different engine as a wide variety of mounting brackets are available both from aftermarket sources. It's also helpful to have an idea of the donor truck's accumulated mileage. Even the low-friction recirculating ball steering mechanism used in GM cars and trucks since 1941 wears with high mileage, resulting in loose steering. Rather than buy a worn-out power steering box with the thought to rebuilding it, it's a much better approach to use parts from a low mileage truck, or new. The same applies to the power steering pump, which may leak fluid if taken from a high-mileage vehicle. It's easier and cheaper to buy a new or good condition pump than to repair a leaking unit.

Red powder coating on much of this truck's steering mechanism makes the parts highly visible.

On this truck each connecting point in the steering linkage has a grease fitting. If the truck was not faithfully lubricated, wear and loose steering would result.

Although the procedure outlined here describes a power steering conversion for the 1967-1972 styling series Chevy and GMC pickup, trucks from a far wider range of years are candidates for the upgrade. Several parts suppliers for vintage Chevrolet trucks offers power steering conversion kits for the 1955-1959 as well as the 1960-1966 series GM pickup models. These kits consist of adapter brackets, plus instructions for using a later GM truck power steering box and pump.

On a 1967-1972 GM light duty trucks (including Suburbans and Blazers) the steering box and the steering column bolt together as separate units, so removing a power steering box from a donor truck (if one is available) is a relatively easy matter of loosening the mounting bolts holding the box to the frame, removing the nut on the pitman arm, sliding the arm off the splined shaft (here you may need a puller), and removing the bolts that connect to the box to the steering shaft. If salvaging the power steering setup from a bare chassis, try to kept the hoses intact. If you're removing the pump and power steering box from a truck that still has its sheet metal, you'll need to cut the hoses, which will be replaced later.

Since parts purchased from a salvage yard are typically coated with a thick layer of grease and grime, the first thing you'll do when you get the parts home is give them a thorough cleaning. If the hoses have been cut or removed, be very careful when degreasing the power steering box and pump that no dirt or grit gets inside either of the units through the hoses or connectors, as even the slightest contamination can damage the power steering system.

Once you've assembled the needed parts, the power steering upgrade begins by removing the manual steering box from your truck. This step accomplished, the power steering box is remounted in its place. There's nothing complicated about this procedure. Just be sure that all bolts and nuts are thoroughly tightened. GM located the power steering pump in the 5 o'clock position as you face the engine. With the correct mounting bracket it's an equally simple job to attach the bracket and pump. The only tricky part of this step is aligning the pulleys. If in addition to the water pump and alternator, the engine will be driving another device, such as an air pump, in addition to the power steering pump, you should convert to a two-belt setup (if the engine is only using a single V-belt). Adding the second V-belt means replacing the single-groove crank pulley with a dual-groove pulley and either installing a dual groove pulley on the power steering pump or adjusting the mounting bracket so that the pulley aligns with the secondary belt.

If the rubber hoses are deteriorated or have been cut, new hoses need to be made up to connect the pump with the power steering box (you can purchase hose for this purpose from most any auto parts store). The upgrade to power steering is now complete, but before operating the truck, be sure that the fluid in the power steering pump is filled to the correct level.

The steering box on later model Chevrolet trucks can easily be seen in left front wheel well with the tire and wheel removed. The box sits at the end of the steering shaft.

Here the steering box has been removed.

Disassembling the truck to this point makes working on the steering easy.

Installing a Tilt Steering Column

GM's light duty trucks from the 1967-72 styling series have captured the interest of collectors largely because of their styling, but also because virtually all the amenities offered on today's trucks became available during that five-year styling run. GM made front disc brakes standard equipment through out its light duty line in 1971. Floor carpeting and styling cloth seats became available on the Cheyenne model, also introduced in 1971. Buyers could option an AM-FM radio and in-cab air conditioning. Also offered was a tilt steering column. However, like the AM-FM radio or the factory-installed tachometer, few buyers thought this comfort/convenience item worth the extra money. But, a tilt column really is a comfort and convenience plus, especially if you want to change your driving posture on a long trip or friends of larger or slimmer girth slide behind the wheel of your truck.

Installing a tilt steering column on a '67-72 GM truck is not a complicated process, thanks largely to the fact that the column unbolts easily from the steering box. The process begins by removing the steering wheel. Pop off the horn button and loosen the wheel with a steering wheel puller, then remove the existing column by unbolting it from the steering box. You also need to disconnect the transmission shift linkage, and loosen the mounting bracket on the dash. The old column pulls up from the floor and the tilt column replaces it in reverse sequence.

For some reason, GM used a different horn ring for the tilt steering column than the regular column. If the horn ring was missing the part is available from parts suppliers catering to this vintage Chevrolet and GMC trucks. It is also important to get the detents aligned correctly on the shift selector. Otherwise the engine may start with the transmission in gear—a potentially dangerous condition.

CHAPTER 8
ENGINE AND MECHANICAL REBUILD

Restoring an old truck is more than having it look nice; you also want it to run like a well-oiled watch. Given the mileage many older trucks have traveled and the hard work they've seen, engine overhaul is likely to be in order and will almost certainly be done if restoration is the goal. The transmission and differential may also require rebuilding or replacement with tighter units. In some cases, either for ease of operation or for physical disability, you may wish to replace the stock manual transmission with a later-model automatic. Conversions of this sort fall into the mechanical category as well.

Smaller mechanical assemblies—the carburetor, generator and alternator are likely candidates for overhaul as well. The question with these mechanical repairs is whether you feel capable of doing the work yourself. If you're adventuresome enough to tackle rebuilding your truck's steering and front end, overhauling a carburetor or the generator and starter will easily be within your skills.

Rebuilding an engine requires extreme attention to detail and knowledge of how to assess the condition of the internal parts, as well as a basic understanding on how to put everything back together. This isn't to say that overhauling an engine is beyond the skills of a hobbyist restorer; it can be done, but you're likely to need some expert help—or at least

advice—along the way. To get you started, this chapter presents an overview of how to check the engine's condition and gives guidelines on having needed machining done. The step-by-step instructions for rebuilding and assembling an engine are found in the Chevrolet shop manual for your truck.

Depending on your truck's intended use, you may want to modify or upgrade your truck's engine. Prior to 1954, Chevrolet's six cylinder engines had an antiquated oiling system that traced back to the Model T Ford days and even earlier. A specialty shop in California is now modifying these engines internally (with no change in the engine's exterior appearance) to bring the lubrication system up to modern standards. If your pre-1954 Chevy truck will be driven with any rigor (meaning you'll attempt to keep up with traffic), you may want to consider this company's lubrication system modification.

In other settings, it may be desirable to replace a pre-1954 six-cylinder engine with a later unit that has the lubrication upgrades from the factory. Chevrolet built the last edition of its Stovebolt six, now displacing 235 ci. and featuring full-pressure oiling, through 1962. These later engines exchange quite easily in earlier trucks. In 1963, Chevrolet introduced a completely new line of six cylinder engines with displacements ranging from 194 ci. to 292 ci.

Chevrolet's venerable 216 ci. six was nicknamed Stovebolt due to the use of quarter-inch bolts found on old-fashioned stoves

The 235 ci. version of this engine, especially, responds well to performance modifications such as the Edmunds dual carburetor set up shown here.

Lighter in weight and featuring 7 main bearings for smoothness and durability these later engines are far more plentiful than the full-pressure oiling 235s and can quite easily be substituted for an earlier engine.

The Stovebolt nickname for Chevrolet's 216 and 235 ci. engines comes, by the way, from the use by the factory of quarter-inch bolts identical to those found on early 20th Century kitchen stoves to attach the side plates to the engine.

In the process of rebuilding an engine, it is convenient to make modifications that will enable the engine to deliver more power to improve both the truck's performance and fuel economy, and also to extend engine life. These modifications include hardened valve seats to prevent engine damage from burning today's unleaded fuel well as hop-up techniques like installing multiple carburetors and dual exhaust. While the actual how-to of these medications is outside the scope of this book, this chapter will help you decide which upgrades would be most suitable to the purposes you intend for your truck.

Mechanical work is much less pressure-some if you can draw on experience and expertise of a seasoned mechanic when needed. There are several ways to plug into expert help. The easiest, most enjoyable way is to join a local club where you can meet others who have an interest on older vehicles. In this group will be those with strong mechanical skills who will take an interest in your project and be willing to lend advice, if not help. Another avenue is to sign up for an auto mechanics course taught at a local vocational-technical center. You won't become a master mechanics in ten to twelve weeks, but the course will give you a good foundation and you will be able to draw upon the instructor's skills for questions you may have with your

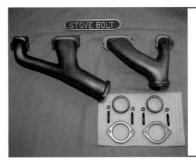

Split exhaust manifolds give inline six cylinder engines a unique sound character totally different from a V8. Langdon's Stovebolt Engine Parts Co.

restoration project. Still another way to get help when your mechanical projects have you shaking your head is to cultivate a friendship with a retired mechanic. More than likely, assisting you with your questions will be as pleasurable to the mechanic as the answers are to you. The experience of overhauling your truck's mechanical components can be richly satisfying in the people it leads you to meet.

Beyond the inclination to do the work and access to help when needed, to rebuild mechanical assemblies you will need a mechanic's tool set, plus some specialty items such as pullers that will be listed as called for. The other essential resource for mechanical work is a collection of shop manuals. Besides the service manual for your truck, it also helps to have a *Chilton* or *Motor* manual that covers your year truck. Instruction manuals on engines, drivetrain components and electrical systems are also helpful. You can sometimes find these instruction manuals at used book stores or swap meets. One benefit of instruction manuals is that they give you the theory behind the component's operation that is missing from a service manual. The reason for gathering several service manuals (a *Motor* plus the Chevrolet shop manual, for example) is that you're likely to have more photos of the disassembly, repair and reassembly steps. Also, different manuals are likely to approach the repair sequence somewhat differently, giving you a more thorough understanding of what you are setting out to do.

Engine Rebuild

If you're driving your old truck, you've probably noticed that it doesn't run like it used to. You may have noticed a puff of light blue smoke wafting from the tail pipe when you accelerate—especially if the engine has been idling for a few moments just before takeoff—and the oil level drops on the dip stick after a few short trips. These are signs that an engine overhaul is in order. The question you may be asking is whether you can tackle the engine rebuild yourself or if it's better to hire the work done. If you're game for the challenge, you may be wondering what's involved. If rebuilding an engine seems too big a stretch for your skills, you'll still need to know the major steps in order to talk knowingly with the engine rebuilder, to judge the fairness of the prices you're quoted and to make sure the rebuild is a quality job.

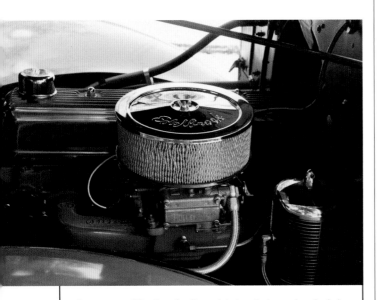

Dress-up modifications for Chevrolet six cylinder engines include chromed valve covers and "bee hive" oil filters. Larry Hurst

Whether or not the engine needs a complete overhaul will be determined in part by your purpose for the truck.

You may also be wondering how to tell whether an engine needs a complete rebuild or if the engine's health can be restored by a partial overhaul. This question can be answered in part by your goal and purpose for the truck. If your goal is to fix up a truck that will be driven, maybe used for some light work, you may be satisfied with an engine that runs strong, perhaps uses a little oil and is free from worrysome noises. If your goal is restoration and you want the work to be permanent—so that you can drive the truck will perform at its best for many years to come—you're not likely to be not be satisfied with anything less than a completely rebuilt engine.

Engine Inspection

Performing a few simple tests can give you a good indication of the engine's condition. The starting point is to check the compression. From this test you will have a good indication of condition of the valves (whether or not they are seating well or burned) and piston rings (whether or not the cylinders are worn or scored and if the rings are seating snugly against the cylinder walls). This check is made with a compression tester, available from auto parts supply stores. The engine section of the shop manual should indicate "in spec" compression readings. Chevy 235 ci six-cylinder engines, for example, should show a compression reading of 130 lb. or better and all cylinders should be within 5 to 10 lb. of each other for satisfactory engine performance. If the compression readings are substantially lower, chances are you've already observed the engine to burn oil, idle roughly, and perhaps even heard a sucking sound at the tail pipe (an indication of burned valves). Be sure to write down the compression readings because they will help a rebuilder, or the machinist if you decide to do the rebuilding yourself, to determine the engine's condition.

Other indications that an engine is in poor health are knocks (indicating worn bearings), low oil pressure (below 10 psi once the engine has been warmed up) and oil blow-by (seen as a heavy oil film around the crankcase breather cap) Blow-by is a sign of poorly seating rings or tapered cylinders. Chevy's long stroke six cylinder engines, used until the modern short-stroke six appeared in 1962, have a relatively rapid wear cycle—particularly in pickup trucks where they are coupled with low-geared rear ends. This means that by 70 or 80,000 miles, enough cylinder and bearing wear will have occurred so that a major overhaul is in order.

If the engine is not running—either because it has been removed from its chassis or you're not able to get it running and therefore you are unable to perform the tests described above, you should assume the worst. In this case the worst is that the engine needs a complete rebuild with major internal parts replaced. If, when you take the engine apart, very little wear is evident, you'll be pleasantly surprised and money ahead. Assuming the worst with a non-running engine is an important bargaining chip in a truck you propose to buy. The owner may say, "Well, it ran when I parked it." But that statement really doesn't mean anything because internal damage may have occurred during the period that the truck has been sitting and you have no way of performing tests that would indicate the engine's real health. With any non-running engine, try to turn the engine over. It may be possible to turn the engine with the starter and a freshly charged battery or by putting a 3/4 in. drive socket on the crank pulley. If the engine is stuck (won't turn), a total rebuild is almost certainly in order—and that's assuming the engine is salvageable.

Unlike new vehicles, the engine is easily accessible on older trucks.

An engine can be stuck for a number of reasons. The most common is that the piston rings have corroded to the cylinder walls. Sometimes it is possible to free a stuck engine by removing the spark plugs, pouring penetrating oil (automatic transmission fluid also works well) into the cylinders. Letting the oil work for several days and then trying to break the engine loose—by towing the truck and popping the clutch, by using a very large wrench on the crank pulley or a pry bar on the ring gear (which can be accessed by removing the starter). Occasionally, a stuck engine will show no signs of damage: compression will be strong and it won't burn oil. But such outcomes are rare. An engine can also seize because the bearings have corroded or rings are so rusted so firmly to the cylinders that the pistons have to be driven out with a hammer. In either of these settings, the engine is either junk or will need costly machining.

Engine Removal

Although the cylinder head can be removed to overhaul the valves and crankshaft and rod bearing work can be done with the engine in the truck, in most situations, and certainly for restoration, the engine will be removed from the truck. On older vehicles this is a pleasantly straightforward job that begins by removing the hood and radiator. If the truck is coming apart for restoration, it also helps to remove the grille assembly. Next all wiring leads to the engine's electrical components are disconnected. If new wiring will be installed, it isn't necessary to label the leads, but if the existing harness will be reconnected you should tag all leads so that you can put them back correctly later. You will also disconnect the fuel line, carburetor linkage, and choke cable. The exhaust pipe needs to be disconnected at the manifold (often these bolts are rust

frozen and have to be heated with a torch to prevent breaking). You will typically remove the starter at this stage, too.

Now the motor mount bolts can be loosened and the bolts removed that attach the transmission to the engine bell housing. This done, you are ready to pull the engine. The best way to lift the engine is by a sling that attaches to the head bolts. Rigging a sling from a length of heavy chain is not recommended because it does not ensure stable control of the engine during lifting. A cherry-picker engine hoist, available at most rent-all stores, is the safest tool for lifting the engine out of the truck.

Engine Cleaning

With the engine removed, the next step is a thorough cleaning. The easiest way to clean of years of accumulated grease and grime is with a steam cleaner—a tool that can be rented from most rent-all stores. Another option is to clean the engine the using Gunk (a commercial degreasing cleanser), or GreaseMaster (the environmentally friendly degreasing

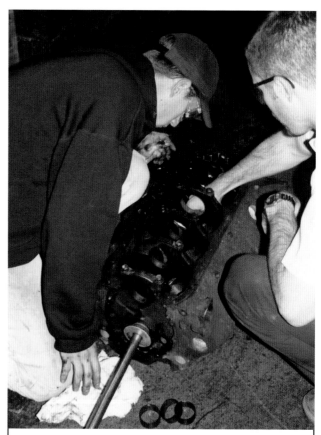

For most major repairs, the engine will be removed.

Working on an engine on the shop floor is not a good idea. First, the floor makes an awkward position and second it's hard to keep out dust and dirt. For assembling, the engine should be mounted on a stand.

product mentioned in the Cleaning and Derusting chapter), hot water, a putty knife and scrub brush. This manual cleaning approach is tedious and time consuming, but it does work.

Once the engine is cleaned, it is ready to be disassembled. The shop manual for your year truck will outline the sequence to follow in disassembling and rebuilding the engine. It's also helpful to have a *Motor* or *Chilton* manual covering your truck as well. To overhaul an engine you will need a moderate level of mechanical skill, and if you are tackling an engine rebuild for the first time, you should also have someone with experience that you can call on for help or advice. Although rebuilding an engine sounds like a major mechanical challenge—and it does require great attention to detail—older engines, particularly the venerable Chevy 216 and 235, are the essence of mechanical simplicity. One thing is certain, if you rebuild your truck's engine yourself you will receive great satisfaction every time the engine spins to life.

Parts Organization

In preparation for the engine's disassembly you should purchase plastic kitchen storage bags in various sizes as well as gather assorted small storage containers like empty coffee cans or plastic milk cartons with the necks cut off, or plastic food storage containers, plus cardboard boxes in assorted sizes to hold pistons and other large parts. The storage bags can be used to hold bolts for different applications like the oil pan, timing cover, and other assemblies so that when you are ready to put the engine back together you will be able to quickly find the right bolts for each step. You will want to wash the bolts in solvent and dry them before placing them in the bags. Be sure

to label each bag using a dark felt marker. It is also important to identify the location of many of the engine's internal parts. The pistons and connecting rods, for example, should be clearly marked as to which cylinder they came from. This can be done with a file, punch, or marker. If the valves will be reused, they too need to be marked with their location. An easy way to do this is to place the valves in sequence in a rack consisting of a length of wood with holes drilled large enough for the valve stem to fit through. Be sure to mark which end

When rebuilding an engine, it's important to replace the freeze plugs that are prone to rusting.

One way to keep track of internal engine parts is with this engine organizer tray available from The Eastwood Co.

Crankshafts always stand on end to prevent bending.

begins the sequence. The Eastwood Co. markets an inexpensive parts organizing tray that stores pistons, connecting rods, pushrods and valves in locations that match their placement within the engine.

Tools

You'll need a few specialty tools to take engine apart and a few more to put it back together. Some of these tools can be rented, or possibly borrowed, if you want to hold the line on tool investments. For convenience working with the engine, and so that you won't be wrestling it around the shop floor where it is likely to pick up dust, you should plan on buying an engine stand. Sturdy engine stands are available from specialty tool suppliers, auto parts stores, and discount marts. For disassembly, you will need a puller to remove the harmonic balancer and a valve spring compressor to remove (and remount) the valves. For reassembly you will need a ring compressor, a brass drift, and a torque wrench. This tool list assumes that you will have a machine shop fit the wrist pins in the pistons and other specialized assembly steps of that nature. Prior to starting the engine you will want to buy or make an oil pump primer. This tool is used to spin the oil pump and fill the oil lines and galleys. As an alternative to purchasing this tool, you can make a primer rod by welding an extension on a spare distributor shaft.

Engine stands are inexpensive or can be home-built.

Replacement Engines

For more modern trucks, specifically those from the 1960s and newer, rebuilt engines are available either in short block (this is the block assembly and internals only, without the oil pan or heads) or long block (complete engine). Buying a short block is typically less expensive than the cost of machining work and purchasing new internal parts separately. The advantage of a long block unit is cost savings over hiring someone else to assemble the engine. The disadvantage of this approach is that the truck now has a non-original engine. Also, depending on the camshaft and compression ratio, the rebuilt may either be a stronger or less powerful engine than original.

For reliability and to compete with modern traffic, some owners of 1950s and older Chevrolet trucks, whose primary concern is the truck's driveability, are installing 1963 and later 194, 230, 250, or 292 ci inline six cylinder engines to replace the original 216 or 235 Stovebolt six. These newer inline six cylinder engines were used in Chevrolet cars as well as trucks and are readily available at low cost. Their other main advantage is the stonger lower end as a result of a seven main bearing crankshaft. Kits for installing these later six cylinder engines in earlier model Chevrolet trucks are available from Langdon's Stovebolt Engine Parts Co., which also makes performance equipment, including dual exhaust cast iron headers, for these engines.

For Chevrolet trucks with V-8 engines, low mileage modern versions of this engine are available at reasonable cost from salvage vehicles.

Machine Shop Selection

Regardless of whether or not you decide to rebuild your truck's engine, the machining work will be done at a machine shop. Selecting the shop to do the machining involves more than just opening the phone book to the Yellow Pages. It helps to make inquiries on the shop's reputation for quality and get recommendations from friends who have had engine machine work done at rebuilding shops in your area. Most machining facilities are small, so satisfied customers are their primary advertising.

The best approach will be to disassemble and clean the parts needing machining before taking them to the machine shop. Once they are delivered, you will get a price estimate on the work and a time frame in which you can expect the work to be done. Sometimes this time frame is met and sometimes it isn't.

Crankshaft journals can be build up by welding, but usually they are cut down to the next smaller bearing size.

Beck's Machine and Tool upgrades Chevrolet six cylinder engines with quieter hydraulic lifters and better performing Iskendarian camshafts. Gene Beck

To understand why the shop is not always as prompt on its work schedule as you would like, it helps to understand how items progress through the shop. In most machine shops, jobs are done in such a way to provide the machinist with a step-by-step work flow. Each operation takes an unspecified amount of time because of individual problems or unique situations that may occur during a particular process. For example, getting a crankshaft ground takes one to three hours depending on the amount of preparatory work that is needed and how many other crankshafts are ahead of yours. The preparatory work would be any further cleaning, magnafluxing (for detecting cracks or potential failure points in the metal) checking straightness and measuring of each bearing surface. If the crankshaft needs repairs, the time involved increases, as does the price.

When the parts are ready for pickup, be sure to check them against the work order to ensure all the parts are there. The work order also gives you a breakdown of each machining process and its individual cost. You should look over each machined part to make sure that the things you wanted done have been done. It's important to realize that this visual check does not guarantee your parts were machined correctly. As an example, a crankshaft that has been ground with a dull grinding wheel can have a slight curvature at the ends of each journal instead of a straight cut. The curvature can grip the bearings causing the crank to seize. Unfortunately, an improperly ground crankshaft can not be touched up. When a flaw like this is discovered, the crank will have to be reground to the next smaller size under and new bearings ordered. The final test of the machine work will be when the engine is being assembled, and this should be done carefully as outlined below. An ample amount of time and money will have been spent by this time and short cuts can undo work that has been done.

Engine Machining

Typically, a rebuild begins by boiling out the block. This is done to remove sediment that may be clogging the oil passages and rust scale and other debris from the water passages. In a Babbitt bearing engine like the 216 ci six used until 1953, hot tanking (as the boiling process is called) can soften or destroy the bearings. Usually in a rebuild, the bearings will be re-poured (or replaced if insert style bearings are used) so no real damage is done.

After the block is cleaned inside and out, the cylinders are checked for taper (a larger diameter at the top than the bottom) and elongation (an egg-shape wear pattern). Cylinder taper occurs as the rings rub on the cylinder walls. If you are restoring your truck taper in excess of 0.005 in. indicates a need to re-bore the cylinders and install oversize pistons. (Honing the cylinders will remove taper to 0.005 in.) Since pistons are sized in increments of 0.015 in. over standard, the cylinders will be enlarged to match the closest piston size.

77

Cylinder taper often exceeds 0.005 in. If the cylinder taper in your truck's engine is in the 0.010 to 0.012 in. range and your purpose is to overhaul the truck to make it serviceable (with cost being a consideration), you could have the cylinders honed and the pistons knurled. This will avoid the cost of having the block bored and buying new pistons (most likely you will replace the rings). The combination of honing and knurling will eliminate half of the taper and expand the pistons slightly. A good machine shop will have advice on the seriousness of the taper and whether the block needs to be re-bored. Problems resulting from cylinder wall taper are premature ring failure and power stroke gasses blowing into the crankcase. When cylinder taper allows combustion gasses to escape past the rings, a condition called "blow-by" can be seen. You may have noticed this in seriously worn engines where the crankcase breather cap "exhales" an oily smoke.

The block receives one other machining operation called "decking", which consists of grinding the surface at the top of the cylinders that mates with the head so that it's perfectly flat.

Although machining work on the block is now complete, other machining operations remain before the lower end of the engine can be reassembled. These include grinding the crankshaft to make sure that the journals for the connecting rod and main bearings are perfectly round and without any surface irregularities that would cut into the bearing surface. The camshaft must also be inspected for wear on the lobes (the triangular extensions off the center of the shaft). A worn camshaft can result in the valves only partially opening.

If the original connecting rods are to be reused, they should be checked at the machine shop for trueness. As it revolves in the engine, bent rod will bind on the crank journal, making the engine difficult to turn over initially and if it is possible to start the engine, that rod's bearing will be short-lived.

If the engine is of the older Babbitt bearing type, new bearings will also need to be poured and bored to size before the engine is brought home for assembly.

Sources of Parts for the Rebuild

With the machining completed, you can make a list of the parts that are needed to complete the rebuild and begin ordering them. The first place to shop for parts is a local auto parts store. Chevrolet is such a popular make and used the same engines for many years in both cars and light trucks that many mechanical parts are still in production. For those items not available at the auto parts store your next source is the one of the many specialty suppliers for vintage Chevrolet trucks. Presumably you have already ordered their catalogs.

Along with the needed mechanical items (new pistons, rings, bearings, etc.) You will need a set of engine overhaul gaskets. You will also want to order the correct paint for your truck's engine and decals for the valve covers. When Chevrolet painted its engines at the factory, everything (except the carburetor and accessories like the generator and starter, which had not bee mounted yet) got a coating of engine paint. This means that the exhaust manifolds were painted, too, but that the paint quickly burned off. However, if you look carefully around the manifold flanges, where the metal does not get as hot, you are likely to see traces of the original paint. If you're a stickler for authenticity, you will apply a touch of paint to the manifolds in these cooler locations.

Engine Block Rebuild

Refitting the internal parts into the block is a high precision job that requires extreme attention to detail. The steps for this sequence can be found in a Chevrolet shop manual.

A major precaution to observe during reassembly is to oil everything well. This is especially critical on engine bearing surfaces. A low-friction oil like STP will give good protection against metal-to-metal contact for the bearings and other rotating parts until the engine is pre-oiled by spinning the oil pump prior to start-up. Also, STP won't evaporate as quickly as regular oil, an important consideration if the engine will be stored for a length of time before being installed and started.

If you attempt to rebuild the engine from an older gasket set (which are sometimes available at swap meets), you may find that the cork gaskets have dried and shrunk. When this is the case, the gaskets should be soaked in water for an hour or so before using to allow them to stretch back to shape. Don't soak paper gaskets, though. Many engine rebuilders advise laying a thin bead of Permatex Blue gasket sealer on all gasket surfaces (both sides of the gaskets) to assure a leak-free engine.

Pressure Oiling for the Chevy 216 "Stovebolt" Six

Over its 34 year life, the Chevy "Stovebolt" six saw two major redesigns. The first occurred in 1937. Changes included raising the displacement from 208 to 216.5, increasing the number of main bearings to four (the initial design had three main bearings), shortening the stroke from 4 inches to 3.75 in., and increasing the bore from 3 5/16 to 3.5 inches. The new block casting was two inches shorter than previously and the increased bearing surface plus shorter stroke helped improve the engine's reliability, particularly since Chevrolet continued to use a low pressure oiling system and poured babbit bearings. The second major change occurred in 1954 when the "Stovebolt" six, now with a displacement of 235 cubic inches, received a full-pressure lubrication system.

Restorers of Chevy cars and light duty trucks with the 216 engine face a quandary: to keep the original engine and be "forced" to travel at poke-along speeds so as not to overstress the engine's primitive splash-feed lubrication system, or to install a pressure-oiling 235 or other more modern engine. For those wanting to preserve their vintage Chevy's authenticity, keeping the 216 has also meant limiting their driving pleasure.

This view shows tubing added to a 216 ci. Chevrolet six to provide full-flow, pressurized lubrication. Gene Beck

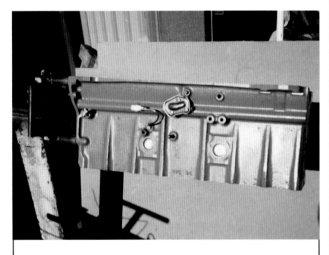

The short length of tubing is the only externally visible sign that the engine has been upgraded to pressure oiling. Gene Beck

Gene Beck at Beck's Machine & Tool also faced this dilemma while restoring a 1936 and 1939 Chevy pickup, but decided to do something about the oil flow problem of the 216 engine. Gene notes, "We did not want to install a 350, 235, or even a 270 GMC engine because it would not be original and [we] may be faced with the problem of smogging at a later date." Instead, Gene set aside part of the family's machine shop business to rework original splash oiler 216 engines into full-flow oiling 216s, complete with quiet-operation hydraulic lifters and long-life insert bearings for the connecting rods. In the process the engine is rebuilt as needed to return it to like-new condition. The result is a modern-technology engine that's dependable for modern driving, including interstate highway travel. Upon completion, Beck's "full flow" Chevrolet

216 engines carry a three-year/50,000 mile (whichever comes first) guarantee.

In addition to the full-flow oiling upgrade, Beck's can rebuild a customer's 216 with any combination of speed equipment. A popular item is an Isky Racing Cam. Oil filters, "split" manifolds, and chromed "dress-up" valve covers are among other desirable options.

Externally, the full-flow oiling 216 will appear identical to original. Beck's even paints rebuilt engines the original gray. However, since the engine will now produce between 25 and 35 psi of oil pressure, the original oil pressure gauge will "peg" at its 30 psi maximum reading. This problem has a rather simple fix.

Upgrading the Oil Pressure Gauge

Beginning in 1939 GMC light-duty trucks used an OHV six cylinder engine of 228 ci displacement. While similar to Chevrolet's OHV six, the GMC engine was larger in both bore and stroke and had full pressure oiling with insert bearings. For this reason, the oil pressure gauge on the GMC dash has a maximum reading of 60 pounds, versus 30 pounds on the Chevy oil pressure gauge. This variance in oil pressure gauges continues until the introduction of Chevy's high pressure oiling 235 cubic inch six in 1954. Since the GMC oil gauges will fit in the Chevy dash, it makes a good swap into a Chevrolet pickup that either has its "splash oiler" 216 replaced with a full pressure 235 engine, or has its 216 upgraded to a pressure oil system.

For restorers wishing to install a full-flow oiling 216 in a show truck, Beck's has developed a by-pass regulator that delivers 15 pounds of pressure to the oil gauge and 45 pounds to the engine. The full pressure is there, but "for show" it doesn't show.

How to tell whether the engine is a 216

Although a 216 engine can be distinguished from a pressure-oiling 235 by the tall pushrod cover which goes all the way to the oil pan and surrounds the spark plug holes, the older non-pressure oiling 235s also used this tall pushrod cover. So the surest way to tell a 216 is by the engine serial numbers and/or block casting numbers. Serial numbers are located on the right side of the cylinder block behind the fuel pump and/or stamped on a milled pad to the right side of the engine at the rear of the distributor.

Cylinder Head Rebuild

All Chevrolet engines ever built use the valve-in-head design. This means that the valves and valvetrain are serviced with the cylinder heads. As with the block, the cylinder head (two on a V-8

Chevrolet Stovebolt Renovation

By Gene Beck
Beck's Machine and Tool

The three most common problems associated with the Chevrolet 216, 235 and 261s. are rear seals, hydraulic lifters, and oil pumps.

Rear Main Oil Seals

Throughout the years GM, Ford, Chrysler as well as other car manufactures have used a composite type rope seal to prevent oil leakage from the real main to the clutch housing area. The rope seal was introduced to replace the centrifugal slinger designed to dissipate the oil away from crankshaft and into a trough, which returned the oil to the pan. The rope seal provided a simple means of preventing oil leakage and reduced the necessary labor for machining slingers into the crankshafts. Unfortunately, the rope seal often provide little to no sealing and the oil began to flow everywhere. To make situations worse, gearheads and hot rodders started making oil pump modifications to increase oil pressure and volumetric flow. These changes literally forced the oil out past the seal and into the clutch housing. Many ideas have been developed over the years in attempt to solve this problem. One attempt in particular is the idea of knurling the seals riding surface area. The knurl would fluff the rope seal as it rotated and prevent the seal from becoming flat. As material technology improved, new materials were developed to replace the original rope type material.

A new fluoroelastomer rear main seal was developed for the late 1950s Chevrolets. This seal was similar to the idea of the rope seal in the fact that it rode on a smooth surface and was of two-piece design. These types of seal drastically improved the oil retention of the rear main. These types were not only applied to the Chevrolet sixes, they were also used in the legendary small and big block Chevrolet. But as we all know, nothing is ever perfect. The two-piece seal design was flawed in the fact that it was comprised of two halves and often, the seals would tend to leak at those two adjoining halves. So to fix this, people would rotate the two halves in the bores and somewhat eliminate the gap. Other times, the seal would be joined together with a small dab of silicone at the edges.

After all of this fooling around with two-piece design, many engine manufactures finally went to a full circle seal that provided oil retention at its best. Unfortunately the early Chevrolet sixes never made it to this point and was laid to

Beck's also installs modern neoprene seals to prevent rear main bearing oil leaks. Gene Beck

rest around the early 1990s. Small and big block Chevrolets continue to this day to use these types of full circle seals, as well as many imports and even the new 4.2L Chevrolet inline six. So why did the early 1937-1962 inline six get left behind? From everything that I have read, it seems that the early Chevrolets are still lost in the 1960s. But there is a solution to every problem. The solution for the 1937-1962 inline six is a full circle seal made by Chicago Rawhide (CR). This seal fits the outer diameter of the crankshaft on all 1941-1962 Chevrolet sixes. Unfortunately, the 1937-1940 sixes need to swap their crankshafts for the later 1941-1952 crankshafts to have the necessary surface area for the seal to ride upon.

The new seal is also made of fluoroelastomer, much like the 1960s two-piece seal. The fluoroelastomer material will hold up to high temperature applications, petroleum based fluids and many cycles. The CR part number for this seal is 38649-V and can be purchased through most any seal distributor. The dimensions of the seal are 3.875 in. by 4.751 in. by .375 in., and it will fit nicely on the crankshaft surface.

The only trouble with this seal is that it is not a direct replacement. The real cost will be in the machining of the block to accept this new seal. The rear area of the block will need to be counter bored or stepped to provide a shelf for the seal to be placed. Cutting this step will take out the outside retaining lip, leaving the inner lip that needs a drain hole drilled through it. In addition, the seal's riding surface on the crankshaft will need to be checked for the proper diameter and proper surface finish. This may not necessarily be the best idea to attempt if your motor has already been rebuilt or is in fine shape. But, for those who are in the process of building their dream motor, this is a good step in the right direction. Any competent machinists with the proper tools and understanding of engine modifications can accomplish this type of installation.

Hydraulics

There are also problems with the 1in. hydraulic lifters and the oil pump that are used in these Chevy sixes. The hydraulic lifter needs good oil pressure and volume to perform properly. There has to be an adjoining oil gallery that runs the full length of the lifter bores that is fed by the oil pump of 30 to 45 lbs. The 216 Stovebolt does not have either one from the factory. The block needs to be drilled

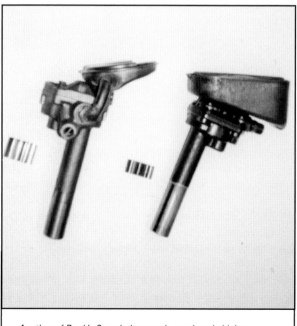

Another of Beck's Stovebolt upgrade services is higher pressure oil pumps. Gene Beck

from one end of the block to the other end through the lifter bores at a certain height to insert steel tubing to create an oil gallery for the lifters. This oil gallery needs to be feed by the main oil gallery that is located on the opposite side of the block. The path of the oil to feed these lifters should be very direct.

These lifters will perform very well if these points are understood. The first condition that needs to be met is good oil pressure and volume. When this is accomplished, the next issue is not to adjust them down not more than 1/2 to 3/4 of a turn from zero lash. The reason is that when you speed up the engine, these lifters like to pump up causing the valve to float. This causes a hammering effect of the valve retainer against the valve guide. The standard head specifications seem to be a little over a 1/4 of an inch clearance between the guide and the valve retainer. We recommend that this distance should be measured and make the change to 1/2 of an inch of clearance for those heavy footed people. Watch your cam specifications for valve lift and make sure that the clearance is adequate. Make sure the cups of the push rods don't bind on the balls of the rockers. The clearance of the guides and this type of binding can give you bent push rods.

Oil Pumps

The Stovebolt Six was known for the 7 to 14 lb oil pressure system with the squirt gun trough oiling system. The rods were Babbitt and had the scoop for oil pickup on the end cap. Drilling the crank did not come into play until 1954 unless you did the job yourself and cut the rods for inserts. Some companies in the earlier years cut the rods for inserts that worked fine even with the low oil pressure or the squirt gun system.

The early oil pump had a valve on the pump for over-pressure and was not for regulating the pressure. On the side of the block was the regulator of 7 to 14 lbs that kept the pump from pumping too much to the oil system. When Chevrolet started pressure feeding the rockers, it saved from oiling them manually and created a cooler for the oil through the line that went through the water jacket. This posed another problem when the oil pressure regulator malfunctioned and pumped all the oil to the top end. Beck's uses this side-of-the-block regulator to give our rockers and the original oil pressure gauge the lower pressure. The best oil pump to fit the 216 is the 1953 - 235 oil pump that was the first 45 lb recirculation pump that Chevrolet used. The pickup tube needs to be reworked with some engineering to fit and to clear the crankshaft.

Chevrolet 6 cylinder Casting Numbers

Cylinder head

Year	Number	Application
1929	835503	All
1930-31	836273	
	836275	All
1932	836718	All
1933	836961	CA Master
1933	600569	CC Master
1934	837230	DA Master
1934	473740	DC Master
1935	837230	Early
1935-36	837981	All
1937	838355	Early
1937-40	838773	All
1941-48	839401	All 216, 235
1949	3835409	All 216, 235
1950-53	3835517	All 216
1950-52	3835499	
	3835909	235
1953	3701887	235
1954-55	3835913	235
1954	3835499	261 truck
1955	3708570	261 truck
1956	3836848	235
1954-55	3836241	Corvette 6

Year	Number	Application
1935-36	836010	All
1937-38	838710	All
1939	838941	All
1940	839132	All
1941	839400	216 car, truck
1941	3660439	235 truck
1942-47	839770	
	838810	216 car, truck
1942-49	839931	235 truck
1942-49	3897715	235 truck
1942-53	3835794	216 car, truck
1948-49	3835253	216 car, truck
1948-49	3835309	235 truck
1950-52	3629708	235 truck
1950-51	3692703	car w/Powerglide
1950-51	3835497	216 car, truck
1950-51	3692713	235 truck
1952	3835692	235 car w/Powerglide, truck
1952-53	3835849	216 car, truck
1953	3701946	
	3835946	235 exc. Powerglide
1953	3701481	235 w/Powerglide
1953-54	3843363	235 car,truck
1953-55	3835911	235 Corvette
1954	3701481	
	3835363	
	3835911	235 w/Powerglide
1954-55	3702436	
	37333950	

Year	Number	Application
	3703414	261 truck
1955	3835911	
	3836386	
	3733949	235 exc. Powerglide
1955	3836233	235 w/Powerglide
1955-56	3836340	261 truck
1955-57	3837004	235 truck
1955-57	3733414	
	3837012	
	3833340	261 truck
1955-63	3738813	261 truck
1958	3733813	
	378881	261 truck
1958-62	3738307	235 car, truck
1958-62	3739716	235 car, truck
1958-62	3764476	235 car, truck
1959-62	3739365	
	3769717	
	3769925	261 truck
1960-62	3738365	261 truck

Engine casting numbers are found on the lower right (distributor side) front of the engine.

Source: Generator and Distributor, publication of the Vintage Chevrolet Club of America.
Additional engine casting numbers by Joe Persoon

Cylinder block

Year	Number	Application
1929	835501	All
1930-31	836409	All
1932	836573	All
1933-34	837231	CA, DA, truck
1933	473180	CC Standard
1934	473741	DC Standard

Further tips for identifying Chevy engines
By J. Daniel Groman

The 235 ci. engine can be distinguished from the 216 by the engine serial number prefix as follows:

1941	AG or AL		1949	GDA, GDM, GEA, GEM
1942	BG or BL		1950	HDA, HDM, HEA, HEM
1946	BG or BL (1st design)		1951	JDA, JDM, JEA, JEM
1946	DDA, DDM, DEA, DEM (2nd design)		1952	KDA, KDM, KEA, KEM
1947	EDA, EDM, EEA, EEM		1953	LDA, LDM, LEA, LEM
1948	FDA, FDM, FEA, FEM			

engine) will also be taken to a machine shop. The cylinder head should be cleaned first; otherwise the machine shop will charge you for this preparatory step. You should ask the machine shop to magnaflux the head for cracks. Cracks that develop across valve seats are sometimes visible, sometimes not. It is very important that all cracks, visible and invisible be detected and repaired. Otherwise, the engine may leak coolant into the cylinders quickly resulting in a ruined engine. The head will also be machined to make sure it rests flat against the block—a process called decking. The machine shop can press out the old valve guides and install new ones and also seat the valves.

Besides these standard machining steps, on pre-1969 engines, this is an opportune time to have the valve seats cut out and hardened seats installed. The question as to whether hardened valve seats are needed by older engines in collector vehicles is still being debated. The reasoning for hardened valve seats is that tetraethyl lead, which was added to gasoline during the era when these older engines were built, provided lubrication that prevented valve seat wear. Since today's gasoline no longer contains lead, the reasoning follows that rapid valve seat wear will now occur. Others argue that thousands of agricultural engines built during the leaded gasoline period have shown no signs of engine damage, including valve seat wear from burning unleaded fuel. The decision is yours, but having the machine shop install hardened valve seats is an easy way to end the debate on the safe side and the process will never be less expensive than at this stage of the engine rebuild.

After following instructions in the shop manual for installing and adjusting the valves, a fresh head gasket is placed on the block and the head bolted in place. Be sure to follow the tightening sequence for the head bolts that is shown in the shop manual and tighten the bolts to the specified torque.

When you have finished assembling the block, you can install the oil pan and manifolds and set this unit aside. Be sure to cover the engine to keep it clean and dust free and seal or plug openings to prevent dust from sifting inside and settling on moving parts.

Details

Besides painting the engine and accessories to match the original color scheme, engine detailing consists of running the spark plug wires through the proper guides or tying the wires together with retainers, replacing the decals on the valve covers, and placing the fuel and vacuum lines in their proper path and securing these lines with the correct clips installed at the original positions on the engine. For the perfectionist who is preparing a truck for show competition, illustrations in the Factory Assembly Manuals show the factory routing of the spark plug wires, the orientation of the bolts holding the generator to its mounting bracket, and other details of this sort.

You may want to dress up the engine with accessories that were available during the period. These options for making

Detailing an engine requires following the factory color scheme as well as correctly routing wires, hoses and fuel lines.

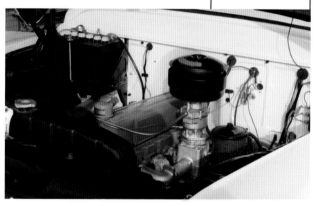

Detailing also extends to the engine compartment.

Detailing the accessory-laden engine compartment of a more modern Chevrolet truck tests the restorer's patience.
Rod Bergum

1955-56 Chevrolet Truck Engine Colors
by Robert Hensel,
Chevrolet Truck Technical Advisor
Vintage Chevrolet Club of America (VCCA)

There is very little information on the First Series '55 truck, but we do have some. The 235 light duty truck engine is gray and has a decal on the rocker cover that states "Thriftmaster 235" on the 3100, 3600, 3800, and 4000 series. On the 5000, 6000 and Forward Control models, this decal states "Loadmaster 235". The "Loadmaster 235" was optional for the 4000 series. The optional engine for the 5000 and 6000 series was a 261 which was painted green with a decal stating "Jobmaster 261" on the rocker cover. This engine information is for the 1954 trucks and we are assuming it carries over to the '55 First Series models.

For the 1955 Second Series Chevrolet trucks, the standard 235 on the 3000 and 4000 series was painted gray and the rocker cover decal states "New Thriftmaster". The heavy duty 235 that was optional on the 4000 series and standard on the 6000 was painted green. The engine in the Forward Control model was gray and had a "New Loadmaster" decal on the rocker cover. The optional engine for the 6000 series was a 261 painted yellow with a "New Jobmaster" decal. The 265 V8 that was used only with the 5000 series was painted yellow with the words "Chevrolet" in black on both rocker covers. Later in the year, the 265 V8 became available in the light duty trucks and was painted gray in that application. This information comes from the Truck Engineering Features books for 1954 and 1955, except for the note on the gray 265 which comes from a bulletin.

Correct color engine paints and replacement decals are available from vintage Chevrolet pickup parts suppliers.

your truck a livelier performer, as well as giving the engine a performance look include polished aluminum, finned valve covers, multiple carburetor intake manifolds, hotter camshafts, and cast iron dual exhaust headers. Dual exhaust gives Chevrolet six cylinder engine a very distinctive and appealing exhaust note. These dress-up and performance accessories are available from Patrick's Chevy Pickup Restorations and Langdon's Stovebolt Engine Parts Co.

Start the Engine
During a frame-up restoration, the engine may be stored while work proceeds in other areas. If you are rebuilding the truck, the engine will probably reinstalled and gotten running as promptly as possible. In either case, preparation steps for getting the engine running include re-mounting the carburetor and distributor as well as the starter and generator, fuel pump and other external components, connecting the fuel lines and attaching the engine's electrical connections. New spark plugs will be installed, along with new spark plug wires run from the distributor cap to the spark plugs. Be sure to follow an electrical diagram for the engine to make sure that the wires to each spark plug are inserted in the correct sockets in the distributor cap. Also make sure the distributor timing is correct. The shop manual will have instructions that for replacing the distributor and setting the timing.

Before starting the engine, it's essential to prime the oil pump to pre-lubricate the engine. This is done either by purchasing an oil system primer that is inserted through the distributor hole and spun by an electric drill or making a primer by removing the cap. rotor and any other internals from a scrap distributor. Next braze a bolt to the top of the distributor shaft (with the threads sticking up). If the distributor shaft

Success of an engine overhaul comes when the engine is first cranked over and started.

meshes with the camshaft, grind off the teeth on the distributor using a bench grinder. Insert the distributor into its hole and spin the bolt by hand to check for any binding that would not allow the shaft to turn freely. Now use an electric drill to spin the shaft and prime the pump. This will take a few minutes. Air must be expelled from the pump for the lubrication system to become functional. You will feel when the system becomes active by a greater load on the drill.

Priming the carburetor with gasoline avoids a heavy load on the starter and battery while cranking the engine to fill the fuel line. If the engine has been rebuilt and installed correctly, and the timing is properly set, it should start right up. If the engine refuses to start, check the ignition timing and other trouble shooting steps to make sure the cylinders are receiving fuel and the spark plugs are delivering hot spark.

Carburetor Overhaul

Single-throat carburetors, used on Chevy six cylinder trucks into the 1970s, are the essence of simplicity. But, as is common with low-tech designs, these simple fuel-metering devices can appear to operate just fine while actually disguising problems warranting a rebuild. Usually engine performance deteriorates gradually: the points wear, the ignition timing shifts, the carburetor operates a little rich, the engine may become hard to start and fuel economy drops off.

If you are overhauling your truck's engine, or doing a complete restoration, rebuilding the carburetor is part of the process. Although this discussion focuses on a simple one-barrel carburetor, rebuilding a two- or four-barrel carburetor follows the same pattern. In this section you will get an overview of the rebuilding process and an insight into how a carburetor works. Regardless of the carburetor you're rebuilding, you'll want to open the Chevy Shop Manual for your truck and follow the step-by-step instructions.

Carburetor Removal

In order to overhaul the carburetor you've got to remove it from the engine. This is a straight-forward process that starts by taking off the air cleaner, disconnecting the gas line, accelerator linkage and choke cable (where a manual choke is used), then unbolting the carburetor from the intake manifold. To remove the gas line, you will need two open-end wrenches. The wrench sizes are usually 1/2 and 9/16 in. One wrench will be used to hold the carburetor inlet fitting while you loosen the gas line fitting with the other. Adjustable wrenches should not be used because they can easily slip off the soft brass fittings, rounding the edges. The throttle linkage may be held in place by tiny clips. If so, be careful not to break or lose these fasteners. The choke cable usually pulls free after loosening a clamp and set screw.

When removing the carburetor, be very careful not to drop the carburetor nuts or lock washers down the hole in the intake manifold. As soon as the carburetor is off the engine, plug the inlet hole in the manifold with a clean rag to prevent dust or stray parts from entering. If the engine has been operated recently, the float bowl will still contain gasoline, most of which can be poured into a suitable container by turning the carburetor on its side.

Rebuild Kits

Before taking the carburetor apart you need to locate a new set of gaskets.

Carburetor gaskets are included in what is called a carburetor kit. Actually, there are two types of carburetor kits. One is intended for a complete rebuild and, in addition to gaskets, will contain a new needle and seat, accelerator pump, and numerous small parts such as the check ball, springs, clips and fasteners. The other, called a jiffy kit, will include gaskets plus a few basic

Single-throat carburetors can be rebuilt using few more tools than a screwdriver.

The carburetor disassembles into a handful of parts.

tune-up parts. For a carburetor rebuild you should have the complete kit.

In order to cover a broad range of carburetor applications, some rebuild kits include extra gaskets and small parts not needed for your repair job. To make sure you use the right parts, you will sometimes need to compare old parts from the carburetor with new parts from the kit. Often, the rebuild kit will include an instruction sheet for servicing the carburetor. This sheet is useful, but should be considered a supplement to the carburetor overhaul instructions in the service manual.

Just because the carburetor is sitting atop a fifty-year-old engine is no reason to think that the rebuild kit will be hard to find. The first place to look is a nearby auto parts store

When the auto parts store does not have, and cannot order a carburetor kit for your truck, the next step is to contact a specialty supplier or a vendor who specializes in carburetor repair. Before contacting the supplier, you should know the make of carburetor and model number. This information is usually contained on the metal tag that may still be attached the float bowl or is embossed on the carburetor casting. If the tag is missing (probably discarded in an earlier rebuild), and no information ran be read from the casting, the make and model information for the carburetor for your truck will be listed in the service manual.

Carburetor Disassembly

Taking a single barrel carburetor apart is very easy. Basically, the carburetor casting consists of three parts: the air horn assembly at the top, the body which contains the float bowl, and the flange base which holds the throttle valve and is sometimes cast integral with the body. Screws hold the air horn and the flange base to the body.

The choke linkage, which runs up the side of the carburetor, will have to be disconnected in order to separate the casting elements. Before undoing the linkage, take a close look at how it functions and fits together. If you have a service manual, you may be able to refer to photos or illustrations showing the linkage when reassembly time comes. Lacking a manual or a clear view of the linkage, it is a good idea to take several photos of the carburetor with linkage intact, or draw a schematic of how the pieces fit together for future reference.

While the carburetor is still in one piece, the choke and throttle shafts should be checked for wear, felt as slop or play where the shaft passes through the casting. The choke is the large valve at the top of the air horn. The throttle is located in the flange base casting. On some early carburetors the choke and throttle shafts are made of brass. More commonly, though, the shafts are made of soft steel. Both the choke and throttle shafts turn in holes drilled through the carburetor casting, another soft metal. In normal operation, wear occurs on both the shaft and casting. The shaft wears undersize where it passes through the carburetor casting and the holes in the casting wear oval-shaped. Because the throttle moves almost constantly while the truck is in operation, wear is far more likely to be found on the throttle shaft than on the choke shaft, which moves mainly when the engine is being started. Signs of a worn throttle shaft are erratic idling and a whistling sound sometimes heard on acceleration. If the throttle shaft or housing shows wear to the degree that the shaft slops around in its holes, a less worn carburetor should be used.

If the throttle shaft is loose, and a carburetor body with less wear cannot be located, you'll need to consider resizing the shaft. The simplest approach is to locate a slightly oversize shaft and re-bore the holes in the carburetor base to fit. Although this repair is relatively simple, this solution is usually impractical because finding a new shaft for most older

Cleaning the float bowl and internal fuel passages is an important rebuild step.

Clean debris from jets and fuel passages with an air hose.

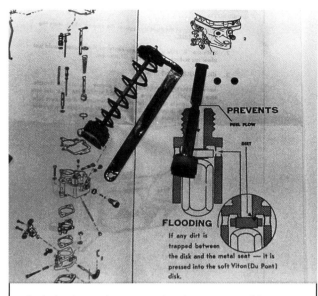

Replacing the accelerator pump is an important part of the carburetor rebuild. An exploded parts diagram that may be included in the parts kit is helpful for seeing the assembly sequence.

Though slightly more complex, four-barrel carburetors follow the same rebuild principles.

carburetors is nearly impossible. As a result, if throttle shaft wear is severe enough to require repair, you'll probably have to send the carburetor away to a repair service.

To take the carburetor apart, simply remove the screws holding the air horn and flange base to the body. As these components are separated, you'll also have to detach portions of the choke linkage—a process that can be something like working a Chinese puzzle. When the air horn is removed, you will see the float and nearby (in what appears to be a narrow well) another mechanism that looks like a plunger. This is the accelerator pump that provides the engine's fuel needs when you tromp down on the throttle. At the bottom of the float bowl you'll also see what appears to be a copper screw. This is a jet that passes a metered amount of gasoline into the air stream that is drawn down through the carburetor and into the engine.

Carburetor Cleaning

The carburetor should be cleaned of the grease and grime is has accumulated from its years of service, but first you should remove the float, accelerator pump, and other internal parts. The float is removed by slipping out the thin copper pin that acts as a hinge. Always check the float for leaks by shaking it beside your ear. If a slight sloshing noise is heard, the float may have a pinhole in a seam or other spot that is letting gasoline leak into the hollow interior. A leaking float will fail to keep the gasoline level in the float bowl at the proper height, resulting in a richer mixture as well as possible flooding. If the leak is severe and the float becomes filled with gasoline, the carburetor could overflow, sending a stream of gasoline down onto the intake manifold.

The accelerator pump is removed by disengaging the plunger from its linkage. Other parts, the main jet, check ball, fuel metering rod, and idle adjusting screw (located in the flange base) should also be removed prior to cleaning. Instructions in the carburetor kit should show these parts; if not they will be identified in an exploded diagram of the carburetor found in the service manual.

Several methods can be used to clean a dirty carburetor. A good non-caustic cleaner is an industrial strength detergent such as Trisodium Phosphate (TSP), which can be purchased at home supply stores. The detergent is mixed with hot water and carburetor left to soak for several hours. After soaking, the parts are washed with clear water. At this stage any remaining grime can be scoured off with a vegetable brush or toothbrush.

Another cleaning method is to soak the castings in mineral spirits to remove grease and grime, then clean the outer and inner surfaces with carburetor cleaner. You will probably purchase the carburetor cleaner in a spray can since a quantity of carburetor cleaner sufficient to soak the castings is moderately expensive. If the spray can approach is used, you can give the castings a good soaking with cleaner, allow the solvent to work a few minutes, then scrub any caked-on grime

87

with a parts cleaning brush. Rubber gloves should be worn for this operation.

When the carburetor is thoroughly cleaned, blow carburetor cleaner through all holes and openings, then visually inspect these passages to assure that all are free of build-up and residue. Blow all passages clean with an aerosol air gun of the type used to clean photographic equipment (available in photo supply stores) or a needle-tip blow gun from an air compressor to make sure that no obstructions or residue remain.

Throttle and Choke Shaft Problems

Before starting to reassemble the carburetor, check the throttle and choke assemblies for bent shafts. Bent shafts are not all that unusual on a carburetor that has seen much use and some abuse. A bent choke shaft can be caused by a mechanic sticking a screwdriver down the air horn to hold the choke open. A bent throttle shaft is likely to be caused by a severe backfire or someone jamming the gas pedal to the floor, causing the linkage to kink the shaft on the end. Signs of a bent choke or throttle shaft are failure of the butterfly valve to seat properly against the housing or a visible kink in the portion of the shaft that sticks out of the housing.

Often a bent choke or throttle shaft can be straightened without removing the shaft from the carburetor housing. This operation is delicate and requires care. If the shaft is bent inside the housing, tap against the bend with a light hammer and brass drift until the butterfly valve seats evenly. If the bend is outside the housing, the shaft may be straightened with pliers. Be sure to wrap a piece of cloth or paper towel around the end of the shaft to prevent the plier teeth from chewing into the shaft.

If the shaft has to be removed to be straightened, the first step is to turn out the screws holding the butterfly valve to the shaft. Sometimes the ends of these screws have been peened over to prevent their loosening. If that is the case, remove the

peened area with a small file, then turn out the screws. Before removing the butterfly valve, note that the lip that closes down on the housing is beveled on the bottom side while the lip that closes up on the housing is beveled on the side facing you. In order to seat properly, the valve will have to be reinstalled with the bevels in this same orientation. So that you do not mistakenly reverse the orientation of the valve (with the result that both bevels would face the wrong way and the valve would not shut off the air flow), you should mark the top of the valve with a piece of chalk or a marker. Sometimes the valve will slip out of the slot in the shaft by hand. If not it can be pulled loose with pliers. With the valve removed, the shaft will slide out of the housing. Now the bent shaft can be straightened by rolling it on a flat surface and tapping against the bend with a brass drift.

When the shaft is ready to be reinstalled, coat it with light grease (lVaseline works well) so that it will slip easily through the holes in the carburetor. Likewise coat the butterfly valve so that it will slide easily into the slot in the shaft. It may be necessary to shift the valve in the shaft until it seats evenly on the carburetor housing. Remember to reinstall the valve with the beveled edges facing the housing. To check for proper fit, close the valve and hold the carburetor housing to the light. If no light can be seen around the edges of the valve, it is seating correctly. Continue to hold the valve closed and replace the screws that attach the valve to the shaft. Place a drop of Loctite on the threads to prevent the screws from loosening and dropping into the intake manifold.

Proper float height is critical and is set by bending the hinge on the float.

Carburetor Rebuild

Clean, smooth surfaces on the needle and seat are critical to a carburetor's operation. Because these tight-fitting parts can become worn, the carburetor kit typically contains replacements. The needle and seat control fuel flow and are located behind the float. The seat threads into the outlet hole on the float bowl and becomes the attaching point for the fuel line. Since the needle (the cone-shaped part) is held in place by the float on many carburetors, you won't slip it into the seat until just before replacing the float.

On most carburetors that have been sitting for years on an older vehicle, the accelerator pump will have dried out, causing the engine to sputter and spit when the gas pedal is tromped for fast acceleration. To remedy this problem, the repair kit also includes a new accelerator pump (this is the plunger that fits into the well beside the float bowl), as well as a replacement for the check valve at the bottom of the well. The check valve, which is often nothing more than a tiny steel ball about the size of a B-B and a clip, prevents fuel from running back out of the well—causing a hesitation on acceleration and raising the gasoline level in the float bowl. In replacing the accelerator pump, the spring and arm will have to be removed from the old pump and fitted to the new. Then the pump can be slipped back into the well and the arm fed down through the hole that exits through the bottom of the casting. Later this arm will be connected to the throttle linkage.

A carburetor rebuild kit should show the procedure for replacing the check valve and accelerator pump as well as the main jet, metering rod, and other internal parts. If new springs and gaskets are supplied with the kit, substitute these for the originals. Some adjustment may be called for in replacing the metering rod. If so, these instructions should also be contained in the kit's procedure sheet or the service manual.

The last step inside the carburetor is to replace and set the float. This procedure is critical to the carburetor's proper operation and must be done accurately. Remember that if the needle fits into the seat from the bowl side, it must be inserted before replacing the float. Wipe the needle with dry, soft paper towel before slipping it into the seat.

It is essential that the float be installed right-side-up. Looking at the float, no side may appear to be the top, but the orientation of the hinge gives the float a top and a bottom. Normally, the loops for the hinge face the bottom of the float bowl. If in doubt, the instruction sheet from the kit or parts diagram from the service manual should show the proper float orientation. Now the float can be slipped into the float bowl and held in place by inserting the pin through the hinge.

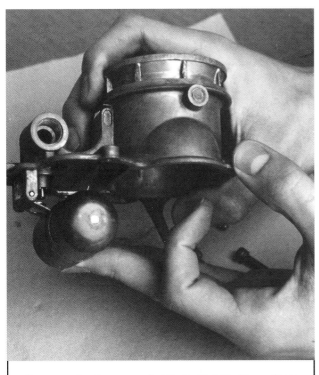

On some carburetors you can test the float height with your finger.

It's important to reassemble the carburetor with new gaskets.

89

The float must be set to the ride at the correct level. Most carburetor kits will supply a paper gauge to be used to set the float. If a gauge is not included, measurements for the proper float setting can be found in the specification sheet with the kit or the service manual. Typically, the gauge with the carburetor kit will look like a short ruler with two tabs protruding on one side. This type of gauge is placed across the top of the float chamber so that the tabs hang down toward the float. In raised position, the float should just touch the tabs.

The float's purpose is to control the fuel level in the float bowl. As the fuel is drawn into the carburetor's air stream, the float drops and when the float falls low enough to release the needle, more gasoline flows into the bowl. This raises the float and cuts off the fuel supply. The float is adjusted to the correct height by bending the arm or tab on the hinge slightly until the top of the float reaches the required level. This is a simple procedure, but one that demands accuracy.

Before reassembling the carburetor, make sure the float drops easily and does not bind on either the hinge or the needle. To check the float action, tip the bowl assembly back and forth in your hand, watching the movement of the float. Old gaskets, found in carburetor kits that have sat on a supplier's shelf for many years, usually have shrunk from their correct size. Assembling the carburetor with these undersized gaskets can also bind the float. To make the bowl gasket pliable so that it can be stretched to its original shape, soak the gasket in water for an hour or so before installing.

In addition to making sure the gasket between the body and air horn fits the outline of the float bowl and does not interfere with the operation of the float, also check the gaskets between the body and flange base to be sure that all holes align properly. Now you will insert and tighten the screws holding the air horn and flange base (or base and spacer) to the body. With the carburetor reassembled, you're faced with putting together that Chinese puzzle—the linkage. Chances are you'll need to refer to the photos or diagrams you made before disassembly, or to an illustration in the service manual as a guide in putting the linkage together.

With the carburetor reassembled and ready to mount back on the engine, you should make one more inspection to be sure that the float moves easily, that the linkage works correctly and engages the accelerator pump when the throttle is opened, and that the throttle and choke shafts turn smoothly without binding. To check movement of the float, listen for the clicking sound of the float releasing and closing the needle as you rock the carburetor back and forth in your hand. If everything appears to work correctly, the carburetor is ready to be reinstalled on the engine. To do this, fit the base gasket over the studs on the intake manifold, slide the carburetor flange down on the studs, and replace the lock washers and nuts. Next you can reconnect the throttle linkage and choke cable (assuming

Now the rebuilt and reassembled carburetor is ready to be installed on the engine.

the carburetor has a manual choke). When connecting the throttle linkage, make sure that the throttle closes all the way with the accelerator pedal released. If needed, readjust the linkage where it connects to the throttle shaft.

Carburetor Adjustment

Since the idle screw was removed for cleaning, it will have to be adjusted. Specifications call for rough-adjusting the idle screw between a half and one-and-a-half turns off the seat. If the throttle screw has not been tampered with in the rebuild, it can be left where it is and the engine should run. If the throttle screw has been removed and replaced, turn it in enough to keep the engine running. Final adjustments can be made under the hood. What you're aiming for in fine-tuning the carburetor is the highest vacuum or rpm at idle. To achieve this, you will adjust the throttle and idle settings in tandem, often turning in the throttle screw slightly, backing off the idle and so forth until the optimum setting is reached.

Carburetor overhaul can make a dramatic difference in an engine's responsiveness, economy, and overall performance. The process is simple enough for any old truck owner to perform successfully and applies with very little increase in complexity to two- and four-barrel carburetors as well.

Few hobbyist mechanics possess the skills and specialized tools needed to rebuild an automatic or manual transmission or a light-duty truck rear end. However, thee units need to be inspected for wear and problems like worn bearings and leaking gaskets that could cause a breakdown on the road. In the first part of this chapter you'll learn about noises and other indications of transmission and rear drive problems, as well as guidelines that may save you money and prevent headaches that can occur when you're trying to find a reliable shop to rebuilt major mechanical assemblies from an older truck. There'll also be tips for removing the transmission and driveline from the truck. For step-by-step instructions on these removal procedures, you'll want to refer to the Chevrolet shop manual for your year and series of truck.

Later in this chapter, you will find instructions on how to raise the rear end gearing, either by installing the higher gearing ring and pinion set from Patrick Dykes' Antique Cars and Trucks or by installing an overdrive transmission. BorgWarner overdrive transmissions were an option most years between 1955 Second Series and the mid 1960s. Both the higher gearing ring and pinion and an overdrive transmission offer advantages in fuel economy, reduced engine wear and higher cruising speeds.

Toward the end of the chapter there is information on the extremely rugged four-wheel-drive conversions for 1950s and 1960s Chevrolet and GMC trucks supplied by NAPCO. Until 1958, the NAPCO 4x4 driveline assemblies were retrofitted to two-wheel-drive trucks, which means that if you own an early to mid 1950s Chevrolet truck and come across a NAPCO setup, you could swap the parts to your truck. That's what Chevrolet dealers did for customers who ordered four-wheel-drive when the trucks ere new.

Automatic Transmission Problems

By the nature of their design, automatic transmissions—available on Chevrolet and GMC trucks beginning in 1954—are subject to different kinds of wear and failure than manual transmissions. If your truck is equipped with an automatic, three quick checks (be sure you do these checks if you're purchasing an automatic transmission truck) are to look underneath for any sign that the transmission is leaking fluid, notice whether the truck slips in gear or slams into gear, and inspect the color of the transmission fluid.

Leaking fluid can be seen in puddles on the ground or garage floor, or in traces of dripping fluid at the end of the transmission case or front of the drive shaft; leakage at the rear of the transmission is more likely to occur when the truck is parked on an incline. Leakage around the pan at the bottom of the transmission or the rear seal is relatively easy to fix with the transmission in the truck. Slippage and hard shifting can be signs that the transmission needs to be rebuilt.

Chevrolet used General Motors' Hydra-Matic transmission in its trucks and the Division's own Powerglide transmission in cars. Powerglides of mid-50s vintage leaked transmission fluid when parked for prolonged periods and the leakage is not a sign of mechanical problem. The Hydra-Matic transmission may leak fluid over long storage periods, again without indicating mechanical trouble, but the incidence of leakage is far less common.

Fluid is checked in an automatic transmission with the engine running and warmed up. In this setting, the fluid should reach the full mark on the dipstick. The transmission fluid should appear a dark red. A brownish color, typically coupled with a burnt smell, means that the transmission is slipping and is a sign that the automatic transmission is in need of a rebuild.

Manual Transmission Problems

Manual transmission problems are identified by noises. A rumbling noise coming from the location of the transmission under year feet with the engine idling and the clutch out is probably coming from a worn front transmission bearing. A similar noise from the same location when the truck is being

Manual transmission problems are identified by noises.

A hobbyist mechanic can overhaul a manual transmission, but some specialized tools will be needed.

If the truck is being disassembled for restoration, the transmission will be removed after the engine. If you are taking the rebuilding approach—and the transmission shows signs of needing to be rebuilt—it can be removed without disturbing the engine by uncoupling the drive shaft on mid 1955 and later Chevrolet trucks or by sliding back the rear end and torque tube on light-duty Chevrolet trucks built through early 1955.

When selecting a transmission rebuilder, look for a shop or repairman with experience on transmissions of your truck's vintage. Gasket sets and bearings for Chevrolet manual transmissions are readily available from restoration suppliers. Replacement gear sets may be expensive and difficult to find. For this reason, it's probably wiser to replace a worn, high-mileage manual transmission with a better condition unit. In later model trucks with automatic transmission, truck and car units interchange, making parts and service quite plentiful.

Clutch and Pressure Plate Problems

The clutch provides a coupling that is used to disrupt the power flow from the engine through the transmission to the rear end. When the clutch is engaged and the pedal released, power from the engine flows through the driveline. When the clutch is disengaged, by depressing the pedal, the engine is disconnected from the driveline. The clutch itself consists of a disc-shaped plate containing friction material. When engaged, the clutch's friction surfaces are pressed tightly against the flywheel by the pressure plate. This allows the input shaft of the transmission to turn at the same speed as the engine.

Basically three types of problems can occur at the clutch coupling. The first is clutch wear, which leads to slippage. The second is clutch chatter, an annoying jumping motion as the clutch is engaged. The third is wearing of the clutch mechanism rather than the clutch itself.

Clutch wear and slippage are easy to recognize. When slippage occurs, the engine's power isn't being transmitted to the rear wheels. If the truck is operated in this condition you may notice a burning smell. Slippage is a sure sign that the clutch needs to be replaced.

Chatter can be caused by several factors. If the engine has an oil leak through the rear main bearing seal, the clutch facing could be picking up oil, which can cause the friction material to slip, then grab several times before seating tightly against the flywheel. If the clutch has worn so that its friction disc has developed hard spots, this can also cause chatter. In addition, chatter can be caused by a flywheel that has high spots on its face, or is not squarely seated on the end of the crankshaft.

Wear in the clutch mechanism is most readily noticed as a high pitch vibration or chatter heard when the clutch is disengaged that indicates a dry or worn pilot bushing or throw out bearing. Any of these conditions will require removing the engine and/or transmission to access the clutch mechanism.

driven in third gear and that isn't heard with the transmission in neutral probably indicates a worn rear bearing. A chipped or missing tooth on first or second gear often can be heard as gear noise when the truck is operated in either of these gears, although you can expect to hear gear noise from any high-mileage transmission.

Besides worn bearings and worn or chipped gears, manual transmissions can develop excessive end play (movement of the gears and shafts inside the case) due to normal wear of the thrust washers and synchronizer clutches, and possible broken snap rings that are used to hold the bearings in place. End play becomes most noticeable when the transmission jumps out of gear. What happens here is that you are driving along and let up on the gas momentarily and the transmission shifts itself into neutral.

Although abusive driving and running the transmission low on gear oil can cause the problems described above, these are also natural signs of wear that result from high mileage. If the truck you are restoring or overhauling has worked a long, hard life, you should plan on a transmission rebuild or look for a low mileage replacement unit.

On a Second Series 1955 to present day manual transmission truck with Hotchkiss drive, it's easiest to reach the clutch by disconnecting the universal joints and removing the drive shaft and transmission.

While servicing a worn clutch, it's advisable to remove the flywheel and have the face checked for trueness and surface condition at a machine shop. If problems are noted, the flywheel should be machined to a true, smooth surface. The pressure plate should also be inspected for worn fingers (the prongs that contact the throw out bearing when the clutch is disengaged), grooves and other signs of wear on the contact surface, or warped or broken springs (a sign of severe use). The pilot bushing should also be checked for wear and replaced if necessary. It is important to remember to lubricate the pilot bushing before installing a new clutch.

Replacing a clutch is within the skills of most hobbyist mechanics. The only specialized tools required are a torque wrench and an alignment shaft to center the clutch disc on the pressure plate. The service manual for your year of Chevrolet truck gives a good step-by-step guide to follow if you're replacing a clutch for the first time.

Coupling an Automatic to a Stovebolt Six

Numerous GM automatics, including aluminum case Powerglide, Turbo-Hydramatic 350, 400, or 700R4 and 2004R overdrive automatic transmissions, can be bolted to Chevrolet's 1937 to 1953 Stovebolt 216 engine as well as 235 six from 1941 to 1963, the 1954 to 1963 large truck 261 engine or a GMC 228, 248, 270, or 302 engine from 1939-1962.

You will need a 5/8 in. steel plate adapter from the Stovebolt Engine Co. The adapter is precision-cut with all holes drilled and tapped for easy installation. The automatic transmission conversion requires the use of a common Chevrolet starter from a 1970 Nova six-cylinder automatic that bolts to the bottom of the adapter plate.

Universal Joint and Driveshaft Problems

Universal joints are inserted into the driveline to change the angle of the powerflow from the transmission to the differential rear end. When kept properly lubricated, universal joints will last indefinitely. When lubrication is overlooked these constantly moving parts can wear rapidly. The first sign of universal joint wear is usually driveline vibration. This occurs because the needle bearings in the universal joints wear sufficiently to throw the drive shaft slightly out of balance. When the universal joints wear to the point that they are making noise, some of the bearings are gone and you are not going to be driving your truck many miles before the universal joints fail.

Universal joints are used in the coupling between the driveshaft and differential and between two-piece driveshafts to change the driveline angle.

It's possible to replace the universal joints and still experience driveline vibration. The cause in this case would be an out-of-balance, bent, or improperly installed drive shaft. You can have the drive shaft balanced at a machine shop. When installing the drive shaft in the truck, the sliding yoke goes at the upper end, behind the transmission.

Differential Problems

Like other parts or the driveline, wear in the differential rear end is also signaled by noises. Basically, there are three kinds of noises that indicate rear-end problems. A howling sound (not a scream, but a noise that sounds like poorly meshing gears) indicates gear wear in the differential. This noise will normally change as you accelerate and decelerate, thereby altering the load on the ring gear and drive pinion. A rumble or rougher sound points to worn bearings. A clunk, heard when starting to back the truck up, is a sign of backlash or wear, which may

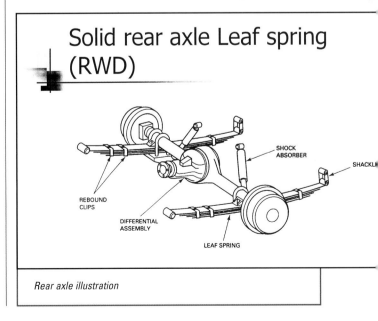

Rear axle illustration

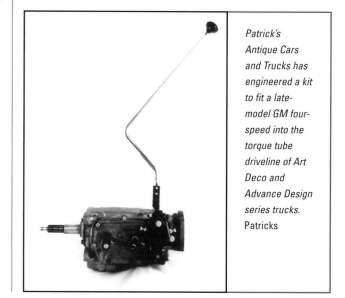

be occurring anywhere in the driveline, but is often located in the rear end.

The other problem to look for is oil leakage. This may be seen around the differential gear housing in the center of the rear axle where the cause is either loose bolts around the differential cover or a bad gasket. Drive pinion seal leakage will sometimes cause oil to be thrown from the rear universal joint yoke when the truck is running. This can cause the oil level to drop below the drive pinion in the differential. Oil can also leak past the seals at the ends of the axles. When this happens, the leakage is sometimes seen on the rear wheel backing plates or can be seen when the rear brake drums are pulled. Along with looking for signs of oil leakage, always check the oil level in the differential. A low oil level is a good indicator of the need for service to the differential.

Gear noise can often be reduced or eliminated by adjusting the mesh between the ring and drive pinion gears. The lack of care that pickups often receive can cause differential wear that is not normally found in cars. For example, if the truck has been driven extensively with different size rear tires, the differential pinion and side gears are likely to show more wear than would be expected for the truck's mileage.

When listening for bearing noise, don't be confused with normal tire noise. If your truck is fitted with mud and snow tires or if you are driving on rough pavement, the whine you hear from the rear of the truck is probably tire noise. To distinguish bearing noise occurring inside the differential from noise generated by the rear wheel bearings, turn the truck sharply to the left then right on smooth pavement. Wheel bearing noise gets louder as the truck is turning. Any internal bearing or gear noise means that the differential needs to be disassembled for inspection and repair.

The easiest way to tell if looseness or backlash is occurring in the differential is to jack up the rear end and have a friend put the truck in gear and slowly engage the clutch while you watch how far the drive shaft turns before the wheels begin to rotate. Unless you want your truck to be in factory-new condition, some backlash is tolerable as long as the rear end doesn't howl.

Transmission and Rear-End Rebuild

It's possible to overhaul the rear end keeping this assembly in the truck, although if you are doing a frame-up restoration you have probably removed the rear end in preparation for cleaning the frame. Rear-end repair, like transmission overhaul, is work best left for professionals. Since the basic design of light-duty truck rear ends has changed little over the years, any repair shop with experience on Chevrolet trucks should be able to perform this work satisfactorily.

Although gaskets and bearings are readily available—back to the 1940s at least—you may have more difficulty locating replacement gears. One approach is to substitute a rear-end from a lower mileage truck. A better alternative is described next.

Higher Rear-end Gearing

For 1940–1955 First Series trucks, a 3.55:1 ring and pinion, available from Patrick Dykes (Patrick's Antique Cars and Trucks, Casa Grande, AZ), provides the higher (lower numeric) rear end gear ratio that many owners of these trucks have been seeking in order to drive at today's highway speeds. The 4.11:1 original rear axle ratio on these trucks elevates engine RPM to such a high pitch that it's both annoying and mechanically destructive to drive a truck of this vintage for long periods at 55 mph or higher. Since these trucks are no longer used in their hauling roles, the engine has ample torque to take advantage of the higher gearing.

The higher rear end gear set retains the original torque tube driveline—making it a suitable upgrade for those who are restoring their trucks for show competition and are concerned about originality. Retaining the torque tube drive also preserves to driveline stability. Before availability of this higher rear end gearing set, owners of Advance Design and earlier trucks would often substitute drivelines and differentials from Blazers and other later-model vehicles. In those substitutions, the suspension also needed to be changes and there were other problems with wider wheel track and different bolt patterns on the wheels. Patrick Dykes 3.55:1 ring and pinion avoids all these difficulties and can be purchased as the gears alone in combination with the bushings, bearings, shims and gaskets for a complete rear end overhaul.

Swapping a ring and pinion set can be done by the hobbyist mechanic using Patrick's. illustrated instruction guide that walks through the process step-by-step. Patrick also sells a took kit with the few specialty items you'll need. If working inside the differential seems too daunting, you can pull the rear end from your truck and ship it to Patrick who'll have his mechanics put in the new gears for you.

Patrick's Antique Cars and Trucks has engineered a kit to fit a late-model GM four-speed into the torque tube driveline of Art Deco and Advance Design series trucks. Patricks

While higher rear end gearing brings down the engine rpms, making an older truck enjoyable as a driver, there's still a problem with the ratios in the original three-speed manual transmission. Since Chevrolet designed these trucks as working vehicles on farms, in construction and other settings, the first gear ratio is very low—allowing the truck to creep along or start out under a heavy load. To take fuller advantage of the higher rear end gearing in under the driving conditions owners of these trucks are likely to encounter today, Patrick has engineered a kit to fit a late-model GM four-speed into the torque tube driveline. Patrick Dykes likens the ratios of an original three-speed transmission to a ladder with every other rung missing. The four-speed, he says, fills in these steps and puts the shifts at comfortable increments. There's also a well-illustrated manual for installing the 4-speed transmission, but the job is more complicated than the higher rear end gearing because it requires at least one machining step. A late-model four-speed transmission will not pass the authenticity muster and should not be considered for a truck that will travel the show circuit, but it is highly desirable for a truck that will be driven and entered, perhaps, in local competition.

Higher Gearing Using an Overdrive Transmission

For Second Series 1955 and later Chevrolet trucks, there's another, often more suitable higher gearing alternative that doesn't require changing transmission and differential. The gearing solution in this case is an overdrive transmission.

Overdrive uses a step-up sun and cluster gear arrangement to spin the drive shaft and differential gears faster than the engine crankshaft speed. The typical step-up ratio is 30 percent or nearly one-third. With a normal manual or automatic transmission, the drive shaft turns at the same speed as the engine. So, an overdrive's step-up of engine revolutions means that for the same highway speed, the engine turns nearly one-third slower, saving fuel and prolonging engine life plus making the engine quieter for the driver. Expressed numerically, on a truck with a rear end ratio of 3.90:1 (the standard half-ton Chevrolet rear end ratio in 1957), the final gearing ratio with overdrive becomes 2.61 and comfortable highway speed increases from 45-50 to 60-65 mph.

Although overdrive became available in the 1930s, Chevrolet didn't offer the step-up transmission in its cars and light trucks until 1955 with the switch to Hotchkiss (open) drive. At that point overdrive served primarily as a fuel economy option and was not an especially popular Chevrolet truck accessory. One of the reasons may be that Chevrolet had an extremely loyal following, and since Chevrolet cars didn't offer overdrive in the pre-1955 era, most Chevrolet truck customers weren't familiar with the benefits of overdrive. On Studebaker, where overdrive had been an option from the 1930s, new truck buyers favored the step-up transmission.

For trucks with open drivelines, higher gearing can be achieved quite easily by installing a BorgWarner overdrive transmission. Overdrive was an option on Chevrolet half-ton pickups from 2nd Series 1955 through the mid-1960s, but few buyers selected that option.

When installed, the overdrive transmission sits behind the standard three-speed and is activated by a combination electrical and mechanical control system. Like other domestic manufacturers Chevrolet purchased its overdrive units from BorgWarner. Because car and light truck engine and transmission combinations are so similar, overdrive can be retrofitted to a 1955 and later pickup (Chevrolet made the option available through the mid-Sixties) without a great deal of difficulty. If a truck overdrive isn't available, the same unit from a car will work, but you can't just find an overdrive transmission and bolt it to the back of your truck's three-speed. The two transmissions were designed as an integrated pair with the companion three-speed gearbox having a longer output shaft that extends into the second box and turns the overdrive gear cluster. To retrofit overdrive on a late-Fifties, early-Sixties Chevrolet truck, you'll need locate the combination three speed and overdrive transmission. Scrap yards have a good source of these transmissions, as are swap meets and the internet.

What keeps every owner of Chevrolet light trucks where overdrive was available from installing this cure for low rear end gearing and opportunity for better fuel economy in his truck? Several things. Borg Warner overdrives were electrically controlled and the prospect of finding a working set of electrical components—a solenoid, relay, wiring harness and kickdown switch—discourages many from taking an overdrive swap seriously. The mechanical controls, kickdown switch, etc, are even harder to locate than the electrical parts since the mechanical controls must come from a truck, whereas electrical parts from a car electrical will work in a truck as well. Far fewer Chevy trucks were fitted with overdrive than cars.

BorgWarner overdrives couple directly to the primary transmission.

Overdrive gains its step-up gearing by a cluster gear set shown here engaging a sun gear.

However, the parts are available and electrical controls for 12-volt electrical systems (used on Chevrolet trucks were overdrive was available) are far more plentiful than 6-volt controls.

Installing or servicing an overdrive transmission on trucks where this option was originally available is relatively simple. The standard three-speed will come out by removing the drive shaft at the universal joints, disconnecting the speedometer cable and shift linkage, and unbolting the transmission at the bell housing. Installing the three-speed and overdrive unit is a matter of reversing these steps, although in some cases the transmission mounts may be different. Unless you also locate a drive shaft from an overdrive-equipped truck of the same model, you'll need to have drive shaft shortened. This work should be done by a shop that can balance the shortened drive shaft. You'll also need to run a cable from the dash to the overdrive lever to engage and disengage the secondary transmission. It shouldn't be too difficult to find an overdrive lever (stamped OD) and cable in a scrap yard or swap meet, or you can buy a suitable cable control at an auto parts store. The overdrive wiring harness is available from electrical suppliers like Rhode Island Wiring Service or vintage Chevrolet truck parts suppliers. Wiring diagrams for connecting the wiring harness and instructions for hooking up the overdrive are given in service manuals like Motor or the Chevrolet truck shop manual.

How an Overdrive Transmission Works— the FreeWheeling Clutch

An overdrive transmission operates like this. When driving down the road with the overdrive unit disengaged, the transmission main shaft passes directly through the center of the sun and cluster gear so that the overdrive output shaft rotates at the same speed as the main shaft. When overdrive is engaged, the sun gear slides forward to engage a cluster gear set, which turns an surrounding ring gear at a speed 30 percent faster than the transmission main shaft. This step-up rotation passes though the transmission output shaft to the rear end.

On deceleration, a freewheeling clutch disengages the driveline. The freewheeling clutch is located at the rear of the overdrive gear set and consists of a set of 12 clutch rollers which press against an outer ring gear while the mainshaft is receiving torque from the engine. When the engine torque cuts back (by letting up on the accelerator) the clutch rollers disengage, thereby disconnecting the power link between the mainshaft and output shaft. This allows the output shaft to turn with the differential without being restrained by engine braking.

Freewheeling is operative whenever overdrive is engaged and will cause the truck to coast without benefit of engine braking when going down hills. The advantages of freewheeling are greater fuel economy and the possibility of clutchless shifting once the truck is underway. The disadvantages are faster brake wear and the possibility of a run-away if overdrive is left engaged in hilly travel.

Trouble Shooting a BorgWarner Overdrive Transmission

Only rarely does the cause of a non-functioning overdrive lie with the transmission itself. The mechanism is simple and rugged and won't let you down on the road. The likely cause of most overdrive problems is with the electrical control circuitry.

BorgWarner overdrive transmissions use three electrical circuits to operate the controls. One circuit incorporated a governor and allows the overdrive to kick in above 28mph. Another circuit energizes the solenoid to engage the overdrive. A third circuit, activated by the kickdown switch, disengages overdrive. To check for problems in the electrical circuitry and controls, you will need:

Test light or VOM meter

Extra 30amp fuses

A 3-4ft length of 12- or 14-gauge test cable with alligator clips soldered onto the ends

A shop manual for your truck

Optionally, a Chilton's or Motor manual of your truck's vintage that covers overdrives

Patience and perseverance.

With electrical problems, always check the simplest cause first. The relay has a fuse. Be sure the fuse is good; looks don't always tell. If the fuse is blown, replace it and try the overdrive. If the overdrive still doesn't engage, you can proceed manually to troubleshoot the three control circuits.

To check the governor circuit, turn the ignition switch off and on. If the relay or solenoid clicks when the switch is turned on, there's a short in the circuit or the relay is defective. To check which is the problem, remove the wire from the relay to the kickdown switch (refer to a wiring diagram showing overdrive). If the relay clicks, it is defective. If it doesn't, there's a short in the governor circuit.

To determine whether the solenoid is working, apply current to the "hot" terminal while grounding the case of the solenoid. This can be done under the truck or you can remove the solenoid and make a check at the battery. If the solenoid operates, it is obviously OK. If it doesn't, you need a new one

The easiest way to isolate overdrive electrical problems is to check for continuity (current flow) at each connection. If the solenoid is good, but doesn't operate with the ignition switch on, use a test light of VOM to make sure current is passing to the relay. If the relay is "dead," there is a short in the wiring between the ignition switch and the ignition terminal on the relay.

As previously noted, make sure the relay fuse is good. You can check the fuse with a test light or VOM by connecting the test device to the end of the fuse opposite the ignition lead and checking for continuity. When making a current check, be sure to touch the other end of the lead to a good ground.

To test the relay, connect the test device at the solenoid terminal and ground and use the wire with the alligator clips to ground the kickdown terminal. If the test device does not indicate current flow, the relay is defective.

Now check for continuity at the solenoid by grounding the kickdown switch terminal at the relay. If the relay is working properly, the solenoid should click when the kickdown terminal is grounded. If it doesn't, and the solenoid is good (as indicated by the earlier test), there is a break in the wiring between the relay and solenoid.

The kickdown circuit grounds engine ignition momentarily when the accelerator is pressed to the floor. The brief power interruption allows the solenoid to disengage the overdrive. To check the kickdown circuit, first observe whether the wire running from the kickdown switch to the coil is connected to the DIST side of the coil. If the wire is missing or connected to the BATT side of the coil, properly connect the wire. Next, remove the wire from the kickdown switch at the solenoid (refer to the shop manual's wiring diagram for the wire's color code). While the engine is running at fast idle, reach under the accelerator pedal and press the kickdown

For a number of years, an Ohio supplier was modifying BorgWarner overdrives to couple these auxiliary transmissions to torque tube drivelines.

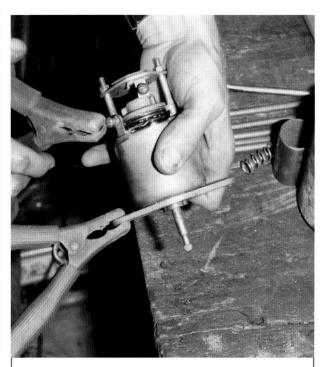

The overdrive solenoid can be tested using battery jumper cables.

switch until it bottoms. The engine should stop. If it doesn't, there is a short in the wire from the distributor to the kick-down switch, or between the switch and the solenoid.

Assuming you have checked everything and the electricals are OK, but there is still no OD, the problem has to be mechanical. An overdrive is quite a lot simpler mechanically than a manual three-speed transmission. If you've done the mechanical work described in this book so far, there's no reason you couldn't overhaul an overdrive transmission. Detailed instructions are found in late 1950s, early 1960s Chevrolet truck and car shop manuals or in a Motor or Chiltons for 1940s through 1960s vintage.

Overdrive's Gear Splitting and Hill Holder Features

The advantages and versatility of overdrive extend beyond fuel economy and higher gearing to gear splitting and holding the truck without keeping pressure on the brakes on a hill. Gear splitting refers to accessing overdrive in first and second as well as third, or high gear. Overdrive's gear splitting feature offers the potential of six forward gears. As mentioned earlier, sometimes the ratios of the three standard gears aren't suitable for the travel conditions. For example, second gear might be too low and third gear too high for in-town traffic. In these situations, ability to select overdrive from a lower gear can be the answer. The problem in overdrive's operation is that the step-up transmission doesn't engage until about 30mph, which would be an excessive speed in first gear and somewhat high revving in second. Using a manual switch to power the overdrive solenoid allows gear splitting by engaging overdrive at any speed in any gear.

The downside to this switch is that overdrive remains engaged until the switch is closed even when the truck is stopped. If the truck is stopped with overdrive engaged, it will not back up. Overdrive has a lock-out feature described below that prevents engaging reverse. Also, when starting out, the truck will be in the overdrive ratio, which may be uncomfortable high for starting. An answer to these problems is to run power to the ignition and to the overdrive solenoid through a normally closed push button switch (that operates similar to a dome light switch). Quickly pushing this switch while accelerating kills the engine and power to the solenoid, allowing the overdrive to shift out.

Since the vehicle can't back up in overdrive, the auxiliary transmission can be used as a hill holder. A switch between the governor circuit and ground can be used to activate the relay and solenoid.

To gain the hill holder effect, just before the stopping the truck, turn on the switch and let the truck roll gently back against the freewheel clutch. Then the switch can be turned off. The truck won't roll backward and the overdrive will stay engaged until the moving forward slightly, at which time it

will shift to direct drive. As to gear noise or damage using reverse, there is no need to worry. The transmission cannot be shifted into reverse when the overdrive is engaged. The lever won't move to the reverse position. It is locked out by a notch on the overdrive engagement pawl. This same lockout prevents the overdrive from engaging while the transmission is in reverse, even if you did get the truck up to 30mph backing up. On a hill, while the overdrive is engaged, you can shift to neutral and relax both feet. If the switch is left on, the truck will move out in overdrive, something like starting out in second gear. Always be careful to let the truck roll back gently against the overdrive to make sure nothing gets broken inside the transmission.

Modern Overdrive

On modern trucks, overdrive gearing is built into the transmission. For Chevrolet and GMC light-duty trucks from late 1960s (when BorgWarner overdrive was no longer available) through the 1970s, a modern aftermarket overdrive can be installed to give these trucks the same driving feel as a new model. The most versatile and ruggedly engineered modern

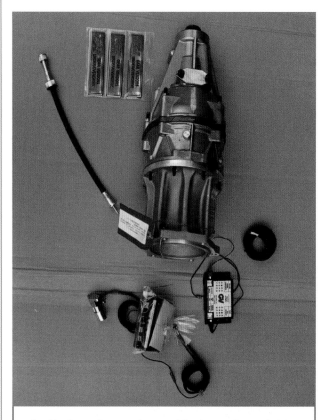

GearVendors makes a modern overdrive that can be coupled to manual three- and four-speed transmission as well as 350 and 400 Turbohydramatics.

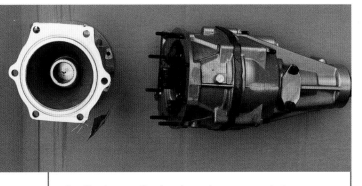

GearVendors supplies the adapter for your transmission.

aftermarket overdrive unit is the under/overdrive transmission from Gear Vendors, which is a popular produce with owners of recreation vehicles. This auxiliary transmission can be coupled to manual three- and four-speed transmissions as well as Turbo-hydramatic 350 and 400 automatics. The transmission also works with four-wheel drive.

Like original equipment overdrives, the Gear Vendors under/overdrive attaches to the back of the primary transmission, but unlike the BorgWarner unit, the Gear Vendors product bolts to the back of the primary transmission's case using a special adapter to eliminate the tail shaft housing.

The Gear Vendors transmission is a sealed unit with its own lubrication and control systems. The separate unit feature

Here the adapter is attached to a Turbohydramatic 400 transmission.

is important. If the overdrive shared the same lubrication as the primary transmission, if either transmission failed, contaminated lubricant would circulate through both, further destroying bearings and other moving parts.

A Gear Vendors transmission can be ordered directly from the manufacturer or from dealers located across the United States who can also install the transmission in your truck. When purchasing the transmission from the manufacturer, you will need to know the your truck's type of transmission and the rear end ratio. The transmission and rear end ratio specifications may be listed on the order sheet pasted to the back side of the glove box door or the build sheet (often stuffed into the seat springs on the seat back). The rear end ratio may also be stamped on a metal tag attached to one of the differential bolts. Lacking all of the above, you can calculate the rear end ratio by jacking up one rear wheel, turning the wheel slowly and noting the number (or fraction thereof) of wheel revolutions to one full revolution of the drive shaft.

With the transmission, Gear Vendors provides an adapter to the primary transmission, an extension for the speedometer cable, a new speedometer gear calibrated to the truck's rear end ratio, a speed sensor that will be coupled to the end of the new extension to the existing speedometer cable, an electronic control box, and a foot switch for locking overdrive in and out plus Gear Vendors stick-on nameplates to advertise the under/overdrive feature on your truck.

Installation

To install the Gear Vendors overdrive transmission, park your truck in the work area, disconnect the battery, raise the truck to a height that allows comfortable working space underneath and place sturdy jack stands under the axles to support the truck at this elevation. It's not necessary to elevate the truck very much. A couple inches' clearance between the tires and the shop floor should give ample space to move freely underneath the truck. Be sure to support the truck with professional-quality jack stands, and never work under a vehicle that is supported stacks of concrete blocks or other makeshift arrangement that can collapse and pin you under the vehicle.

The Gear Vendors installation manual detailed instructions for measuring the drive shaft angle to make sure the extra transmission length doesn't pitch the drive shaft at too steep an angle for the universal joints and gives calculations for making sure the shortened drive shaft will be within acceptable limits. You will need to study these instructions and "engineer" the installation before proceeding.

If your truck has a two-piece drive shaft, it may be necessary to eliminate one of the shafts—going to a one-piece drive shaft with no center bearing. In most cases, the only modification required is having the drive shaft shortened by 14 in., the length of the Gear Vendors auxiliary transmission.

Installing an auxiliary transmission requires shortening and rebalancing the driveshaft.

The installation procedure begins by removing the drive shaft, which is accomplished by loosening the universal joint yokes at the rear axle. This done, you can drop the drive shaft by pulling it out of the slip yoke at the transmission, and put it aside for the time being. Next, you will disconnect the speedometer cable from the transmission, then you will remove the universal joint yoke and tail housing at the transmission. If your truck has an automatic transmission, you will want to put a pan underneath the tail housing to catch any transmission fluid that may seep out as you loosen the tail housing bolts. You won't be draining the fluid from the transmission, and it's likely that only a small amount of fluid will have seeped into the tail housing. This is the extent of the disassembly steps.

After lubricating the coupler in the new tail shaft adapter, installing the under/overdrive is a bolt-up process. First the adapter is bolted onto the back of the primary transmission, in place of the tail shaft housing, and then the overdrive is bolted to the adapter. To keep the bolts from working loose, place a dab of Loctite blue on the bolt threads. It's all a very straightforward process from here. The Gear Vendors castings are machined for precise fits. A gasket is supplied to place between the adapter and overdrive and you'll use the old gasket (or a replacement) between the transmission and adapter.

With accurate measurements, you can have the drive shaft shortened at a shop that performs this service. This is a more critical step than the overdrive's installation, and it's important to find a shop that can also balance the shortened drive shaft. The shortened shaft installs in reverse-order from that in which it was removed.

The remaining steps are to hook up the electronic controls, which consist of a switch unit that mounts in a convenient location under the front edge of the dash, a "black box" that can be mounted to the firewall or kick panel near the fuse box, and a foot control switch that mounts to the floorboard. After topping the under/overdrive with Dextron II automatic transmission fluid and lowering the truck to the shop floor, it's off for a test drive.

If the Gear Vendors under/overdrive is coupled to an automatic transmission, it can be operated in two modes: automatic or manual. In automatic mode, which is set by flicking a rocker switch on the control panel, the vehicle will shift through the gears in normal fashion, then climb into overdrive automatically at about 47 mph. When overdrive engages, the engine speed will drop by 500rpm to 700rpm—yet the vehicle will maintain the same road speed.

In manual mode, overdrive can be engaged between any of the transmission's lower gears. This means that a three-speed transmission now has six-speeds. The extra gear ratios between first and second and second and third are called "underdrives"—hence the transmission's name, under/overdrive. With a manual transmission, the under and overdrive gears are selected by depressing the clutch momentarily and pressing a switch.

Experiencing Overdrive

An overdrive transmission can add substantially to the pleasure of driving a collector- vintage truck. Not only are cruising speeds in the range of today's traffic, but with its gear splitting feature, overdrive can provide the right gear for any driving condition.

With a BorgWarner overdrive, leaving keeping the cable control pulled out in provides constant use of the auxiliary transmission's free wheeling feature, which allows shifting first to second and second to high without using the clutch. It's important to remember to disengage overdrive's freewheeling and apply the emergency brake when parking. When free-wheeling is active, there's no engine compression to hold the truck in gear.

When a BorgWarner overdrive is active through the cable control, the transmission engages automatically above 28 mph. At that point, the engine revs have dropped as though the transmission has shifted into a higher gear (which, effectively, it has done).

It's fun to use the overdrive as a gear splitter for the three-speed transmission (as an over-the-road trucker would use a two-speed rear axle on his 10-speed gearbox.

I like the feel of overdrive and haven't tired of finding the right gear for the driving condition.

NAPCO: Chevrolet's Add-on Four Wheel Drive

Many dyed-in-the-wool Chevrolet truck enthusiasts aren't aware that between 1951 and 1957 GM made four-wheel drive available as an aftermarket add-on. For its four-wheel drive conversions, Chevrolet and GMC used a front-drive axle and two-speed transfer case made by NAPCO, a Minneapolis-based company. The NAPCO 4x4 conversion consisted of a short drive shaft from the existing four-speed transmission to a two-speed transfer case, which split power between the front and rear drive axles. The front drive consisted of a Chevrolet rear axle modified with Bendix-Weiss constant velocity joints to allow the wheels to turn for steering. A shortened rear drive shaft, front drive shaft, and support bracket for the transfer case completed the package. When the buyer specified a NAPCO conversion for his new Chevy truck, installation was done either at NAPCO plants in Minneapolis or Detroit, or by a distributor (usually a Chevrolet dealer).

NAPCO sales brochures suggested that the buyer save the beam front axle and reinstall it on the truck at trade-in time, removing the 4x4 setup and using it on the new truck. That advice speaks highly for the unit's durability. These NAPCO 4x4 units are reported to be among the most rugged ever built, which means that if you find a NAPCO assembly your chances of its still being usable are good.

Installation of the four-wheel drive components is straight-forward and requires no welding or major modification. This means that if you own a three-quarter or one-ton Chevrolet or GMC Advance Design or early Task Force truck (pickup, Panel or Suburban) and you would like the versatility and novelty of four-wheel drive (and you can find a chassis or parts truck that has the 4x4 setup) you can make the conversion to your truck fairly easily. It's important when gathering parts that the gear ratios for the front and rear differentials match.

Installing NAPCO Four-Wheel Drive

If you wish to convert your Advance Design or early Task Force Chevrolet pickup, Panel, or Suburban to four-wheel drive, you will need to start with a three-quarter or one-ton chassis. NAPCO units were not designed to use on a 1/2-ton truck. Next, you will need to find a NAPCO setup matching

This NAPCO front drive axle sits under a 1954 Chevrolet pickup chassis. Greg Carson

This photo shows the complete NAPCO conversion kit except for the front axle. Greg Carson

your truck's year and series. Conversion units for Task Force trucks are different from those installed in the Advance Design series. Two different-style front axles are used: one referred to as six bolt and the other as eight bolt. On the six-bolt axle, so called for the number of lug bolts on the brake drums, the differential is located on the right side of the truck. This axle was used on Advance Design series trucks through 1955. The eight-bolt axle has the differential on the left side of the truck. This axle was used in 1955 and later Task Force trucks. Part numbers are stamped on the right side of the differential.

The third requirement is that the gear ratio be the same for both the front and rear axles. This means you will need to check the ratio on the NAPCO front differential and make sure the rear axle ratio matches. The standard NAPCO three-quarter ton front axle in the Advance Design series had a 4.57:1 ratio, with 5.14:1 optional. On a 1 ton, the 5.14 was standard. You should be able to find ratio tags on the axle. If not, turn the drive shaft and count the turns at the wheel hub. When the 4x4 setup is installed, you also need to use the same tire size front and rear. On GMC trucks, some modification to the oil pan may be required to clear the front drive axle.

The NAPCO four-wheel drive assembly installs as follows: First, elevate the truck and support the frame on jack stands. Then remove the I-beam front axle. Now install the NAPCO front axle. A different pitman arm is used and needs to be installed in place of the Chevrolet arm. The shocks can now be connected to the special mounting plates on the NAPCO front axle and brake hoses attached to the wheel cylinders.

To mount the transfer case, you'll need to install a new cross-member. (This piece may be on the 4x4 parts truck.) First, though, you need to drop the drive shaft, remove the muffler and tail pipe and disconnect the parking brake rod. The two upper rivets on the running board bracket need to be sheared off and the holes enlarged to 15/32 in. diameter. The cross-member bolts through these holes. With the cross-member bolted in place through the running board bracket holes, you will see where the remaining holes need to be drilled. As you will see on the parts truck, rubber cushions are used where the cross-member attaches to the frame mounts. In most cases these cushions will have hardened and you will have to locate or make replacements. Body cushions or engine mounts may make suitable substitutes.

With the cross-member in place, the transfer case can be installed. The NAPCO 4x4 setup includes a different bracket for the muffler, which moves the exhaust system farther outboard toward the fame. Other modifications also occur at the rear axle. To mount the springs, a 4 in. spacer is placed between the axle and springs. This spacer requires longer U-bolts. Extensions are also welded to the shock absorber bracket, raising the mounting position 4 in. Inside the cab, a hole is cut in the floor for the transfer-case shift lever.

Final steps include installing the drive shafts (with the slip yokes at the transfer case end), bleeding and adjusting the brakes, setting the front wheel tow-in between 1/16 and 1/8 in., installing chrome NAPCO plates on the cowl and placing the shift diagram on the glovebox door.

Parts such as the dash decal are available in reproduction form, as are the NAPCO shop and parts manuals. Mechanical parts are less easy to find and NAPCO has long been out of business. Some original NAPCO parts can still be purchased from vintage Chevrolet parts sources, and Dodge Power-Wagon authority David Butler says that some NAPCO front-drive parts interchange with Power-Wagon items.

NAPCO literature and emblems are available from vintage Chevrolet parts suppliers.

In 1957, GM brought 4wd in-house. Early Chevrolet 4x4 trucks have a tall stance because the transfer case was mounted separately from the transmission, but by the 1960s, 4wd was as we see it today. This front drive axel view is from a 1966 Chevrolet K series 4wd pickup. Daniel Doehr

CHAPTER 10

BRAKE OVERHAUL AND UPGRADE

However sound a truck's mechanical systems appear to be, one that should be inspected and almost always overhauled and rebuilt is the brakes. On a frame-up restoration, the brake system would be rebuilt as a matter of course. Brake systems on older trucks need attention for the simple reason that an original brake system on a twenty-year-old, or older, truck is very prone to failure—a dangerous proposition. The primary cause of brake failure is leaking hydraulic fluid, but worn linings, scored drums, and improper adjustment can all contribute to poor braking response, which can be nearly as dangerous as no brakes at all.

Rebuilding your truck's brake system shouldn't be approached in patchwork fashion. Rather, the entire braking mechanism should be inspected and overhauled, which leads to the question of where to begin. Before answering this question, let's visualize what happens when we press on brake pedal. As the foot pedal is depressed, it presses a plunger in the master cylinder, mounted under the floorboard on Chevrolet trucks through the Advance Design series and on the firewall of Task Force and later trucks. This plunger compresses a small amount of hydraulic fluid in the cylinder and in so doing sends a pulse of pressure through the brake lines to the four wheels. Here the pressure expands in the wheel cylinders, forcing the brake shoes out against the brake drums, slowing the vehicle. This is what is *supposed* to happen.

Now let's look at what can go wrong on a worn and out-of-repair brake system. First, the brake pedal can have worn on its shaft so that it binds when pressed, requiring extra pedal pressure. Then, corrosion inside the master cylinder (caused by moisture trapped in the hydraulic fluid) can allow some of the fluid to leak past the plunger, reducing pressure to the lines and causing brake fluid to be lost from the system. As the fluid in the lines receives pressure from the master cylinder, a corroded line could spring a leak, causing the pressure to normalize and preventing brake action.

Assuming the lines are intact and braking pressure is passed to the wheel cylinders, here too corrosion on the cylinder linings can cause fluid to leak past the pistons reducing braking action or old gummed-up fluid that has collected in the wheel cylinders can result in very little braking movement. If the pedal pressure is transferred through the system, worn linings or grooved, out-of-round brake drums can also hamper braking efficiency. Where a combination of problems occur, as is more likely the case in a deteriorated brake system, braking action will be seriously reduced at each stage between the brake pedal and the wheels.

Overhauling a brake system typically starts by removing the wheels. If this is your first experience with brake overhaul, and you're not doing a frame-up restoration where every part will be stripped, cleaned, and refinished, it's a good idea to redo the brakes on one side of the vehicle at a time. This way you can look at the other side for a guide to fitting all the parts back together correctly.

Brake Removal

Loosen the lug nuts with the wheels on the ground, then jack up the truck and support it on professional-quality jack stands, not a makeshift stack of blocks. With the truck elevated on secure supports, remove the lug nuts and slip the wheels off the brake drums. To remove the brake drums, first loosen the brake adjustment. This is done by popping out the adjusting hole cover in the lower area of the backing plates (in many cases this cover will probably be missing), reaching into the hole with a brake adjusting tool or screwdriver and backing off the star wheel that moves the brake shoes toward the drums. If the star wheel turns, you will know whether you are tightening or loosening the brakes by whether or not you feel the shoes drag as you rotate the drum. In many cases the star wheel will be rust-frozen. Where this is the case, proceed with the steps for removing the brake drum. With luck, the shoes will be worn enough so that the drum will slip off without having to back off the shoes.

On the front drums, you will pop off the dust cups that cover the spindle nuts (if these covers are still in place) by inserting a screwdriver between the cap lip and the brake drum hub and prying while working the screwdriver around the hub. Mechanics usually remove these caps by grabbing them

To remove the brake drums, the adjusting mechanism first has to be loosened.

Flex hoses to the front wheels are usually deteriorated and should be replaced.

Be sure to secure the new flex hoses in their clamps on the frame.

with channel-lock pliers and flipping them loose, but this method leaves the caps with dents that look like the creases in a highway patrolman's hat. With the cap out of the way, you will pull the cotter key from the spindle nut and turn the nut loose with an adjustable wrench, open-end wrench, or socket. Don't use pliers to loosen the spindle nut. Their serrated edges will cut into the nut, making it difficult to fit the right tool onto the nut the next time you need to tighten or loosen it.

With the spindle nut removed, the drum should pull toward you easily. If it seems stuck on the brake shoes, grab the edges of the drum and work it back and forth, over the shoes. The difficulty sometimes encountered here is that the brake shoes can wear the drum so that a lip forms at the outer edge of the brake sweep area. If the drums are not turned to cut away this lip when new linings are installed, the lip can become quite deep. Where a lip has been allowed to form, and the brake adjustment star wheel is rust-bound and refuses to turn, the drums may catch on the shoes and refuse to pull loose. When this happens the only way to get the drums off may be to cut the ends of anchor pins that hold the shoes to the backing plate with side cutter pliers or a torch. Cutting the anchor pins will enable you to pull the drums loose, but the shoes will probably pop free of the wheel cylinder which may also cause the wheel cylinder to come apart. This method for freeing the drums should only be used as a last resort.

As you slide a front drum off the spindle shaft, the large washer that sits behind the spindle nut and outer wheel bearing will usually slide off the spindle. The washer and bearing should be picked off the spindle before they fall onto the shop floor and placed in a container for safe keeping. It is important not to mix bearings from one wheel to another, so a good idea is to place a container (clean, empty coffee cans work well) at each wheel to hold parts as they are removed. Now you can slide the drum free and place it on the floor in a nearby, but out-of-the-way location.

Rear wheel drums on Chevrolet half- and three-quarter ton trucks remove easier than on many other makes because they bolt to a flange at the end of the axle rather than being wedge-fit onto the axle shaft. Here, too, the brake adjuster should be loosened as the first step. Then, with the lug nuts removed, the brake drums can be pulled loose. If the drums have rusted to the axle flange and lug bolts, spray penetrating oil around the base of the lugs and hole in the center of the drum. Then tap the drum a couple of times around the flange area (the flat surface beside the lugs) and the drum should pull free. With the drums off, you can now see what's been happening when you mashed down on the stop pedal.

Brake Inspection

Typically, what you'll see as you look at the brake mechanism of an older truck are worn linings (often just a thin layer of friction material will cover the metal brake shoes), scored

Typically what you'll see as you look at the brake mechanism with the drums removed is worn linings and a great deal of dusty residue covering other internal parts

drums (with deep scratches in the drum's contact surface), a great deal of dusty material (residue from the worn off lining material) coating the backing plates, brake shoes, and other internal surfaces, and possibly darker sediment (a mixture of leaking brake fluid and lining dust) around the wheel cylinder. It's possible that you may also see other problem signs such as broken return springs, or cracked linings.

The parking brake on half and three-quarter ton trucks with 3-speed transmissions is provided by a cable, which activates the rear brake shoes. Other models use a propeller shaft parking brake. Remember to check the condition of the parking brake cable. Replacement cables and handles are available from several suppliers.

Brake Rebuilding

Since the performance of your truck's brakes is crucial to its safe operation, the overhaul procedure will be essentially the same whether you are restoring or rebuilding. The only difference may be in whether or not you refinish the parts that will be visible when everything is reassembled.

Fortunately, brake parts for vintage Chevrolet trucks are in good supply. You may even be able to purchase new brake springs, shoes, and wheel cylinders from a local auto supply

Chevrolet light duty trucks 1971 and newer are factory-equipped with front disc brakes that have fewer parts than drum brakes and are easier to rebuild.

store. The other alternative is a vintage Chevrolet truck parts supplier. When rebuilding a brake system the best policy is to replace all the operational parts. Before any new parts are installed, however, you will remove the brake mechanism and backing plate at each wheel, then clean and refinish the brake drums and backing plates. In a ground-up restoration, brake overhaul usually occurs as the last stage of redoing the chassis. When taking a rebuilding approach, the brakes should be overhauled as the first step to making the truck operational. While the front drums are off, you should also inspect and replace worn king pins (on trucks with straight-axle front ends), as well as refinish other chassis parts the front axle and springs.

Disassembling the brake mechanism at the wheels is a simple matter of removing the springs that place tension on the shoes, unhooking the clips and pulling off the shoes. The wheel cylinders attach to the backing plates with bolts that are reached from the back side of the plates. Once these bolts are removed, the brake line has to be disconnected from the wheel cylinder. At the front, the brake line connection is through a rubber flex hose that is usually hardened and cracked. If this is the flex hose's condition on your truck, it can simply be cut and removed later. At the rear, the brake tubing will be connected directly to the wheel cylinder. If the fitting has become rust frozen to the wheel cylinder, the line will have to be cut.

The backing plates are held in place by four bolts. Loosening these bolts allows you to remove this last part of the brake assembly. The next step is to clean the backing plates and prepare them for refinishing. Next, you will clean and inspect the drums.

Wheel Bearing Removal

The front brake drums ride on two bearings. The outer bearing is held in place by the spindle nut and washer and

comes out when you remove the drum. The inner bearing is located at the rear (inside) of the drum's center opening. These inner bearings can be removed using a special wheel bearing puller (this is a hook-shaped tool that looks like a miniature crowbar) or by tapping on the perimeter of the inner race with a long punch inserted through the hub. A speedier method for removing the inner bearing, and one commonly used by mechanics, is to replace the nut and washer on the spindle, then slip the brake drum over the nut so that the hub rests on the spindle and pull the drum toward you in a sharp, downward jerk that forces the bearing cage against the spindle washer. This sharp tug will pop the bearing free nearly every time.

Occasionally it may be necessary to rotate the drum 180 degrees and jerk the drum against the spindle nut again. Although this method usually doesn't damage the seal, on a twenty- to fifty-year-old vehicle these seals are usually dried out and should be replaced.

Brake Drum Refinishing

Rather than assume that the brake drums can simply be cleaned, refinished and reused, the drums need to be inspected for cracks, warpage and adequate wall thickness. If the drum has become cracked from excess heat build-up, the crack will usually show on the lining sweep area. Warpage can be checked by laying the drums face down on a flat surface. Drum wall thickness should not be less than twenty percent of original. On an Advance Design half-ton pickup, this calculates to a maximum inside diameter of 11.1 in., an increase of 0.1 inch over the original 11 in. inside diameter. Measurements this fine should be taken with brake drum gauge. A brake shop should have this tool and will be able to tell you if the drums have enough metal to be turned, or if they need to be replaced. You should also inspect the drums for cracks or warpage and look for replacements if either of these conditions is present.

Brake drums can be prepared for painting by sandblasting or treating the surface rust with a oxidation neutralizer. Acid derusting should never be used on brake drums because dipping the brake drum in an acid bath can make the metal brittle, possibly causing the drum to crack.

Wheel Cylinder Disassembly

Since brake parts for most Chevrolet light trucks are readily available from auto parts stores and specialty suppliers, it is advisable to rebuild the brake system with new parts. As an alternative to replacing the wheel cylinders with new units, the old cylinders can be rebuilt.

Wheel cylinders fail, that is, they leak fluid or become gummed-up and sluggish, due to contamination of the hydraulic fluid. Unlike newer cars and trucks, the hydraulic brake systems of older trucks are not sealed to outside moisture. This fact can be observed by looking closely at the cap on

the master cylinder. On Chevrolet trucks built prior to the late 1960s, you will be able to spot a small vent hole in the cap. This hole allows air to enter the hydraulic brake system in order to prevent a vacuum from forming as the fluid drops in the brake reservoir. The fluid level drops as the brake linings wear because more the wheel cylinders require more fluid to press the linings against the drum.

As air enters the brake system, so does moisture. The standard brake fluid used in cars and trucks is a polyglycol product that carries a DOT 3 designation. (Brake standards are set by the Department of Transportation.) This fluid attracts moisture like a sponge. For this reason, service manuals call for flushing and replacing the brake fluid every few years. In actuality, this is seldom done and the result is moisture-laden brake fluid residing in an older truck's brake system year after year. Eventually, the moisture corrodes the wheel and master cylinder linings and rusts the brake lines from the inside. The moisture also attracts other contaminants, which gum up the wheel cylinders. When the wheel cylinders on an older truck are disassembled, they will typically show this damage.

Once the wheel cylinders have been removed from the backing plates, their disassembly is a simple process that begins by peeling the rubber dust boots back from the casting lips. The grooved pins that hold with the brake shoes are inserted through the dust boots and will usually pull out of the wheel cylinders with the boots. Inside the wheel cylinder you will see two small metal cylinders. These are the pistons that move outward in the wheel cylinder to force the brake shoes against the drums when the brake pedal is pressed. If the pistons move freely, they may be removed from the casting by pushing both pistons out one end of the cylinder. I have seen cases where the internal parts of a wheel cylinder were so encrusted with a

This photo shows the location of the master cylinder on the chassis where it was located on trucks before mid-1955

mixture of old brake fluid, moisture, and rust that they have to be driven out with a punch and hammer.

When you have taken the wheel cylinders apart and cleaned the castings, you can hold them up to the light and inspect the condition of the bores. Quite typically the cylinder lining will be scarred with pits. If the pits are shallow, a smooth lining surface can be restored by honing. In this process, the bore is enlarged a few thousandths of an inch with a grinding stone. Honing isn't something you would do at home, but would be done by a machine shop. On an older truck, pits in the brake cylinder linings are likely to be too deep to be removed from honing. My advice is to ignore honing and if any pitting is present, either purchase new wheel cylinders or have the old cylinders relined. This will assure no fluid leakage at the wheel cylinders.

Master Cylinder Disassembly

Typically, if pitting is found in the wheel cylinders, the master cylinder bore will also be corroded. On Chevrolet light trucks through the Advance Design series (up to mid-year 1955), the master cylinder is mounted under the floorboard behind the brake pedal on the driver's side. On Task Force trucks (starting mid-1955) and later trucks, the master cylinder is mounted on the firewall inside the engine compartment.

Once the master cylinder is removed from the truck, its disassembly is a simple process of prying off the piston boot and removing the retaining clip that holds the piston, seals, and compression spring inside the casting. While working off the clip, you should press on the piston to prevent the piston and spring from flying out of the housing when the clip is released. Wiping the master cylinder bore with a clean cloth and holding it up to the light will allow you to see whether or not the bore is pitted. If pitting is visible, you should add the master cylinder to your parts needed list.

Rebuild Parts

The brake system parts list will consist of front and rear brake shoes, brake shoe clips, brake shoe retainer springs, flex hoses, wheel cylinder rebuild kits or new wheel cylinders, brake lines, and, depending on their condition, replacement master cylinder and brake drums. Many of these parts may be available from a local auto parts store.

Whether or not the cylinder bores of the wheel cylinders are pitted, you will need to renew the seals. This can be done by installing a rebuild kit, a slightly less expensive option than buying new wheel cylinders. If the cylinder bores are pitted, you can have the bores sleeved and install the rebuild kit. This alternative will be at least as costly as buying new wheel cylinders but has the advantage that the cylinder bore sleeves will be a non-corrosive metal. Both stainless steel and brass sleeves are available. Either metal is non-corrosive, but stainless has the advantage of being very hard and therefore highly resistant to scratching.

Pre-bent brake lines, either steel or stainless steel, are available from several suppliers.

On a frame-up restoration you would replace all brake tubing, typically with pre-bent stainless steel lines. Stainless is preferred, especially on restorations, because the metal won't corrode. Since on trucks built prior to 1968 a rupture anywhere in the lines will cause the loss of all brake action, the only wise approach is to replace old brake tubing whether you are restoring or rebuilding the hydraulic brake system.

Wheel Cylinder Rebuilding

If you are installing new wheel cylinders, you can skip this step. The assumption here is that you either have had the wheel cylinders relined or are working with used wheel cylinders that have absolutely clean, smooth bores. Before proceeding to install the rebuild kits, you should clean and paint the castings. Some relining services will bead blast the castings and send them back in ready-to-paint condition. The castings can also be prepared for painting by wire brushing and treating the metal with rust neutralizer. Aerosol cans work well or painting these small parts. When spraying the casting, be sure to mask off the ends of the cylinder to keep paint out of the cylinder bores.

Wheel cylinder rebuild kits typically consist of new springs, seals, and boots, but require that you reuse the old pistons . To make sure that the pistons are smooth and free from scratches, clean them first in solvent, then scrub the outer cylinder area with super- fine #0000 steel wool. Follow this with 240 grit sandpaper to smooth any scratches, and then polish the surface with 600 grit automotive sandpaper. After sanding, wash the pistons in soapy water to remove all sanding residue. If the pistons are badly pitted, they will need to be replaced.

The cylinder walls should be lubricated before installing the pistons and seals. Petroleum-based lubricants must *never* be used on any of the hydraulic brake system's internal parts. Wheel cylinder rebuild kits will typically contain small vials of special lubricant to be used for this purpose. If not, special brake system lubricant can be purchased at an auto parts store.

Before reassembling the wheel cylinder, the bore should be wiped clean with a lint free cloth, then coated with the special lubricant. The spring is inserted into the cylinder next. Then the seals are moistened with lubricant and fitted against the tightly wound coils at each end of the spring. The pistons should also be lubricated before sliding them into the cylinder. You will need to press the pistons against the spring slightly to keep them inside the cylinder while installing the dust boots. A few drops of the special lubricant on the lips of the dust boots will make it easier to slide the boots over the ends of the casting. The last steps are to install new bleeder screws (available from most auto supply stores) and to seal the brake line openings with tape or plug them with a lint-free cloth to prevent dust from entering the cylinders as they are stored before installation.

Brake Line Replacement

You can cut and bend replacement brake lines, purchasing straight steel lines in various lengths at an auto parts store, but bending the lines requires special tools and re-flaring the connections at the ends of the lines is a step that requires both precision and special tools. If the connections are not made correctly, the lines will leak, causing the brake system to fail. Most people who are restoring or rebuilding an older truck, purchase pre-bent lines that match the originals on the truck. Several suppliers sell replacement brake lines either steel or stainless steel. Steel lines match the originals from the factory, but will rust unless treated with a clear coating. Stainless steel is impervious to rust. The difference in price is not significant.

Here's a trick to use if you are rebuilding one set of wheels before the other. This restorer has finished the front wheels and brake lines, but not the rears. Adding the small section of kinked hose at the end of the line to the rear brakes has enabled him to fill the master cylinder with brake fluid and bled the front lines, making that portion of the braking system operable.

Brake Assembly

On a frame up restoration, the front suspension will have been checked and rebuilt, and all components cleaned and painted. The rear axle assembly will have undergone the same thorough examination and been rebuilt as needed. On repair work, the brakes may be overhauled separately. In either case, the assumption here is that the backing plates are in place on the axles. The next steps are to mount the wheel cylinders, connect the brake tubes (front) or lines (rear) to the cylinders and install the brake shoes. Before mounting the brake shoes, it is important to wipe a coating of light lubricant on the anchor pins and to oil the adjusting mechanism. Skipping this step can result in squeaky brakes that become hard to adjust. On the rear brakes you should also lubricate the parking brake cables.

Next, connect one set of shoes to the adjuster by installing the spring at the bottom of the shoes. If one of the linings is shorter, this is the primary shoe and goes toward the front.

If you decide to bend and flare the brake lines yourself, you will need to purchase special brake line flaring tools. Be very careful that the flares are correct and that the lines don't leak. You will also need bending tools and old lines to use as a pattern.

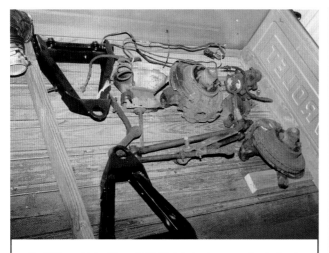

On 1960s and later Chevrolet light duty trucks, upgrading to front disc brakes can be done with parts salvaged from a later truck.

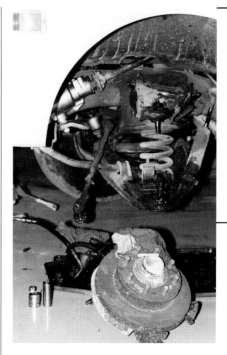

On a drum-to-disc conversion the spindles will have to be changed, which provides a good opportunity to rebuild other front suspension parts.

Note that the star wheel on the adjuster should be near the primary (front) shoe on the left side of the truck and adjacent to the secondary (rear) shoe on right side brakes. Now attach the shoes to the backing plates with the anchor pins and hold-down springs and position the tops of the shoes in the slots in the wheel cylinder connecting links. On rear brakes, connect the parking brake cable.

To finish the job, hook the brake return springs through the holes on the shoes, clip the spring from the primary shoe over the anchor pin, then pull the spring from the secondary shoe over this same pin. You will find this job much easier to do if you use a special brake tools than if you attempt to spread the springs with pliers or a screwdriver. Now pull the shoes away from the backing plates and tap them a couple of times to make sure they are seated on the wheel cylinder and adjuster. Check to make sure that adjusters are turned all the way in and install the brake drums on the rear wheels.

Wheel Bearing Packing

Before installing the front drums, you will need to repack and replace the wheel bearings. Packing wheel bearings can be like playing in the mud as a kid. When you're finished, your hands are completely gooped and there's likely to be a liberal coating on your clothes as well. The packing method I learned from my father is to scoop up a gob of wheel bearing grease and place it in the palm of one hand, then stroke the bearing (which has been cleaned in solvent and allowed to air dry—do not dry bearings with an air gun) through the grease with the other hand. After two or three passes, Dad would tap the bearing against the heal of his hand to pack the grease, then he would repeat the scooping and tapping steps until grease oozed out around the bearing rollers. This process isn't complicated, but it is messy. Fortunately, there is an easier method.

Aerosol wheel bearing packers that pump grease into the bearing—eliminating the messy hand packing steps—are available at most auto supply stores and discount marts. To use the aerosol packer, just place the bearing in a funnel-shaped clamp supplied with the packer, insert the aerosol nozzle into the packer and press down on the grease container. In less time than it takes to say "Peter Piper packed a pair of bearings," grease will be oozing out the clamp and the bearing is packed and ready for installation.

The inner wheel bearings are installed first and are held in place by a seal ring that presses into the brake drum. (When not available from a local auto supply store, replacement seals are available from specialty Chevrolet truck parts suppliers.) The seals are seated by tapping them into the hub with a plastic hammer. Now the front brake drums can be slipped onto the spindle and over the linings. If the drums won't fit, pull them back off, tap the shoes with the heel of your hand to seat them tightly against the wheel cylinder, check the star wheel to make sure the shoes are fully retracted and try again. With new linings, the fit may be snug, but the drums should slide over the shoes, though perhaps with some turning and tapping.

Now the outer wheel bearings can be packed. This done, the bearings are slipped onto the spindle and pushed into the bearing cone in the brake drum hub. A washer fits between the bearing and spindle nut. In tightening the spindle nut, draw up the nut against the bearing until the bearing drags as the drum is turned, then back off the nut until that the drum spins freely. Lock the spindle nut in this position with a cotter key and spread the key to hold the nut in place.

Brake Adjustment

Adjustments are made by reaching through the access hole in the bottom of the backing plates and turning the star wheel. While a screwdriver can be used for this operation, a special brake-adjusting tool, shaped like a lazy Z, works best. The brakes should be adjusted by moving the shoes toward the drums until slight drag is felt, then the adjustment is backed off until the drums turn easily. Adjustments at all four wheels need to be as uniform as possible to prevent one or more of the wheels from locking under panic braking and to keep the shoes from dragging.

Brake Fluid

Although original braking systems used DOT 3 polyglycol fluid, many old car and truck owners are switching to DOT 5 silicone brake fluid. Unlike polyglycol fluid, silicone brake fluid does not attract moisture. As another benefit, silicone fluid lubricates and helps preserve rubber brake system parts like wheel cylinder seals and flex lines. The disadvantage of silicone fluid is that it has a tendency to destroy hydraulically-actuated stop light switches—the type used on Chevy trucks with master cylinders mounted under the floor. Since these switches are inexpensive items and installed quite easily, it seems preferable to replace the stop light switch (as required) rather than go through an annual flushing of the brake system to remove contaminated brake fluid, which should be done when polyglycol fluid is used.

Bleeding the Hydraulic Brake System

Whichever fluid you use, before the truck can be driven, trapped air needs to be bled or purged from the brake lines. There are several ways to bleed the brakes, but the simplest calls for two people and takes little more than a half hour—assuming all goes well. The helper will pump the brake pedal to build up pressure while you will bleed the air from the lines by loosening the bleeder screws at each of the wheels.

Begin by filling the master cylinder with brake fluid. When the fluid reservoir is full, screw the cap on tight and have the helper pump up the brakes (push the brake pedal down several times in quick succession until braking action is felt). While the assistant holds his or her foot on the pedal, you will proceed to the wheel farthest from the master cylinder (the right rear) and loosen the bleeder screw to the wheel cylinder. (The bleeder screw inserts into the backside of the wheel cylinder and is accessible on the rear side of the backing plate.) To keep brake fluid from squirting on the chassis and running down the backing plate (polyglycol fluid will eat off paint; silicone fluid is harmless), you should fit one end of a length of plastic or rubber tubing over the tip of the bleeder screw. Place the other end of the tube in a can or jar to catch escaping fluid.

As the bleeder screw is opened, air will escape from the brake lines. As this happens, your assistant will feel the brake pedal sink slowly toward the floor. When the fluid runs clear and free of bubbles, turn the bleeder screw shut. Now ask the assistant to pump up the pedal again and keep pressure on the pedal. Open the same bleeder screw again to make sure fluid from that line runs clear, without bubbles. Be sure to warn your assistant not to release the brake pedal once it sinks to the floor until you tell him or her to do so. Releasing the brake pedal before the bleeder screw is closed will suck air into the lines, requiring that the bleeding process be done all over again.

Once air is purged for the line to one wheel, refill the master cylinder, then move to the next and repeat the bleeding process. Less than a quart of fluid should be required to fill and bleed a rebuilt brake system. Before finishing, check all line connections to make sure there is no leakage.

Maintaining the System

Maintenance to a hydraulic brake system consists of checking the fluid level of the master cylinder periodically, watching for leaks at the brake line connections and wheel cylinders (severe wheel cylinder leaks can be seen as streaks on the insides of the tires), and if polyglycol fluid is used flushing and refilling the brake system on an annual basis. On more modern trucks with self-adjusting brakes, the only other maintenance step would be pulling the brake drums and checking for lining wear at 30,000 mile (or thereabouts) intervals. On truck without self-adjusting brakes, the fall or spring cleanup and maintenance session should include adjusting the brakes.

A properly rebuilt and maintained hydraulic braking system will ensure safe driving for you and your passengers.

At this stage, the drum brakes and suspension for one wheel have been removed and their disc brake replacements collected.

Upgrading to disc brakes

The realization that a brake system designed for the traffic pattern of a quarter-century ago is hazardous in the face of today's "cut in and cut 'em off" drivers came as I was driving a partially loaded 1969 Chevrolet pickup home from a day spent vending old car parts at an area swap meet. The road was clear ahead as I approached an intersection. Then suddenly a car darted out of a fast food restaurant directly in my path. An instant later, as the traffic light at the intersection ahead turned to yellow, the car suddenly stopped. The moment I saw the flash of brake lights I had slammed my right foot hard against the truck's brake pedal, but rather than feel the truck shudder to a stop, I watched the gap between the truck's hood and the car's trunk close rapidly with little noticeable change in the truck's forward speed. I pressed harder against the brake pedal wondering if I'd suddenly feel the pedal drop to the floor, a brake line burst. The truck slowed, finally stopping just inches from the car's rear bumper.

Bad brakes? Not really, just a system designed for far different traffic and driving situations than those most of us are likely to encounter every day. Like most collectible trucks, the 1969 Chevrolet came from the factory with hydraulically-operated drum brakes on all four wheels—a system adequate for leisurely stopping in a less congested and less erratic traffic, but clearly inadequate for the panic stops of the type I encountered returning from the swap meet that day.

Realizing that regardless of how defensively I drove, the old truck really wasn't safe, led me to the choice of either limiting the collector truck to parades and tours in the company of other collector vehicles or upgrading the brakes to a system that would bring the truck to a swift halt, whenever the occasion arose.

The remedy I looked at first was to install a power brake booster. Chevrolet offered this option in 1969, but after discussing my objective with a technician specializing on power train and chassis upgrades to collectible vehicles, I realized that to achieve braking parity with today's traffic, the real solution was to upgrade from drum to disc brakes. Of course a power booster would also increase the performance of a disc brake system.

While front disc brakes began to appear as standard or optional equipment on American cars in the mid-1960s, they weren't adopted by light duty trucks until the early 1970s. Ford was the first to offer front disc brakes on its F-250 and F-350 light duty models beginning in 1968. On the F-100 series front disc brakes were not available until 1973. Chevrolet made front disc brakes standard on all its light duty models (C-10 through C-30) in 1971. Dodge first offered front disc brakes as an option on its restyled 1972 truck models. Today, front and rear disc brakes are standard equipment on all full-size pickups.

At least three reasons have led manufacturers to supply disc brakes as standard equipment: 1) discs are nearly fade

After sandblasting and powder coating, the disc brake spindles, dust shields, and upper control arms look like new.

In this application, the upper control arm for the drum brakes had to be replaced with a similar unit for disc brakes.

resistant; 2) they offer a very noticeable improvement in braking action over drum brakes; and 3) service is simpler with disc, as opposed to drum brakes. It should also be noted that with the universal adoption of disc brakes, power brake boosters have also become standard equipment.

Upgrade Options

In upgrading a drum brake equipped collectible truck to front disc brakes there are three approaches one can take. The first is to retrofit later disc brake components to an earlier truck. This option is not always available as the newer truck components only interchange on a limited number of years. The second approach is to install a disc brake conversion kit. The kit approach is the mostly widely applicable with disc brakes now available for Chevrolet trucks, using the stock front suspension, back to 1928. A third way to improve an older truck's stopping power is to install an independent front suspension setup that also includes disc brakes. This option is used more widely by builders of street rods than it is by rebuilders and is shunned by restorers. I chose the first approach factory parts could be refitted to my year Chevrolet.

With either the retrofitting or kit approach, converting from drum to front disc brakes is a relatively straight-forward process that consists mainly of installing disc rotors and dust shields in place of the brake drums, either swapping spindles or adding brackets to hold the disc brake calipers, installing the calipers and brake pads, replacing the front flex hoses and installing a disc brake master cylinder and proportioning valve in place of the existing master cylinder. As in any brake overhaul, working in the vicinity of the front suspension also invites inspecting and replacing worn steering and suspension parts such as the tie rod ends and ball joints or king pins.

On a retrofit conversion, the upgrade parts such as the rotors, dust shields, and spindles can come from a donor truck (as a cost saving alternative to purchasing new parts from an aftermarket source or the manufacturer's dealer) while items such as disc brake calipers and master cylinder are available in remanufactured form from most any auto parts store. A cost saving can be realized here too by using remanufactured as opposed to new parts. Used rotors from a donor vehicle typically need to be turned by a brake shop to remove any rust or scoring. The brake shop will also determine how much serviceable life remains in the rotors by comparing their thickness with factory specifications. If the donor vehicle's disc brake rotors are warped, badly worn or scored, replacements are available from nearly any auto parts store or a Chevrolet dealership.

On a Chevrolet light duty truck with independent front suspension, swapping the disc brake spindles also necessitates replacing the ball joints. Naturally, the disc brake parts need to come from the same series (load rating) truck. In other words, a 1970 or earlier drum brake half-ton C-10 Chevrolet would use 1971 later C-10 ball joints, spindles, rotors and associated disc brake components while a three-quarter ton C-20 Chevrolet would use disc brake parts designed for that truck's heavier load rating.

Installation

The disc brake upgrade begins by elevating and placing the truck on jack stands, removing the front wheels and front brake drums, then disassembling the brake shoes and related brake hardware. Unless a conversion kit is used that mounts the disc calipers to the drum-style backing plates, the backing plates also need to come off.

On a coil spring front suspension truck, removing the spindles requires compressing and removing the coil springs using a special tool called a spring compressor (as discussed in the front end chapter), then pressing the ball joints out of their locating holes at the top and bottom of each spindle. When compressing the coil springs it's extremely important to be alert to the danger of a spring under compression. The spring should be compressed (shortened) only enough to remove it from its perch between the upper and lower A arms. If your tool inventory doesn't include a coil spring compressor, and you can't borrow one from a friend, this tool can be rented from most any rent-all store or can be purchased from most auto parts stores. Once the spring is removed, the compression tool should be released and removed. Usually it is not necessary to compress the front coil springs for re-installation.

If you're retrofitting disc brakes from a later model and are using disc brake spindles, rotors and dust shields from a donor truck, you'll probably want to degrease and sandblast these

The disc brake conversion is now complete.

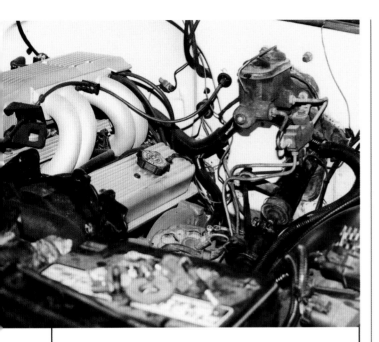

The original drum brake setup lacked a power booster, which would be a last piece in the brake system upgrade.

Disc brakes require a proportioning valve seen in front of the master cylinder. With the addition of the booster unit, the brake system upgrade is now complete.

items. Refinishing can be done with a spray can using Eastwood's Chassis Black, or by adding a "dash" of flattener (check the mixing proportions supplied with the product) to a gloss black automotive finish applied by a spray painting system. If you've set up your shop for powder coating or there's a powder coating service nearby, you may want to coat the parts with this process. (Powder painting is an easy at home process, which is treated in a later chapter.) powder painted. The powder coating is an extremely durable coating and ideal for chassis components.

On an independent front suspension truck, once the springs out of the way you can set about replacing the ball joints, which are factory riveted to the upper and lower A arms. Replacement ball joints are secured with bolts, so you can tell at a glance by the type of fasteners—rivets or bolts— whether or not the ball joints have been replaced. With the front suspension this far apart it makes good sense to remove the A arms and inspect the bushings at either end of the control arm shaft for wear. Worn control arm shaft bushings are a cause of steering wander. When removing the upper A arms, be sure to keep each shim pack intact and note the location of each set of shims. Reinstalling these shim packs in the location from which they were removed will return the front suspension to its existing caster setting. On straight axle trucks, you're advised to inspect the king pins for wear and replace as needed.

From this point the disc brake conversion should be a simple matter of reassembling and adding the new parts. But if you're using parts from different year GM trucks, you may encounter compatibility problems. On the 1969 C-20 Chevrolet that serves as our project truck the lower ball joints for the newer spindle wouldn't fit into the retaining cups stamped into the truck's lower A arms. This incompatibility came as a surprise because upper ball joints fit the truck's original upper A arms perfectly. In other applications this incompatibility may not exist, but if it does the solution is an easy one—just replace the incompatible suspension pieces with their counterparts from the disc brake donor truck.

Consequently, if you're using a later model disc brake donor truck as your parts source, it's good insurance to get the upper and lower A arms, disc brake master cylinder, and proportioning valve as well. If the suspension parts aren't needed, you have only added to your scrap metal collection at little cost. But if some of the suspension pieces are required to make the conversion, you've spared yourself a trip back to the salvage yard with the possibility that the needed pieces have gone to someone else—or worse that the truck has been scrapped. The master cylinder can be used as a core exchange on a rebuilt replacement.

When working with used parts, it's good policy to chase tapped threads (such as those for in the spindles to mount the dust shields) with a tap from a tap and die set to remove any

Front disc brakes are also available for Advance Design and earlier Chevrolet trucks.

rust or debris and to use stainless steel bolts (so that parts such as the dust shields can be removed, should that be needed, in the future). Whether independent front suspension or a straight front axle, disc brake rotors install on the spindles just like brake drums. First new bearing races are pressed in place, then the inner wheel bearing is packed with grease, dropped into its race and the bearing retainer tapped in place. Next, the outer wheel bearing is packed with grease, the rotor slipped onto the spindle and the bearing pushed into its race. As with brake drums, the retaining nut is seated, then loosened slightly to allow the rotor to turn freely, yet without "play", and cotter-pinned in position.

With the rotors installed you're ready to mount new pads on the disc calipers and bolt the calipers onto the spindles. On 1955-1966 disc brake conversion kits, the calipers bolt to brackets that are attached to the drum brake backing plates. One of the advantages of disc brakes is the ease with which new pads are installed — a much easier job than replacing drum brake shoes. The final step in this location (aside from bleeding the hydraulic system and remounting the front wheels) is connecting the calipers to the hydraulic system with new flex hoses.

Before cleaning up your tools, it's important to check the tie rod ends on other steering linkages for wear, replacing parts as needed. This is also a good time to lubricate all front-end grease fittings, especially those on the freshly-installed control arm bushings.

Master Cylinder

With the upgrade work completed at the front wheels, the action now moves underneath the hood. Here we'll replace the drum brake master cylinder with a unit designed for disc brakes, add a proportioning valve to the system (and a vacuum booster if power brakes are desired) then reconnect the brake lines to the master cylinder.

A disc brake master cylinder differs from the drum brake unit it replaces. On trucks older than 1967, the new master cylinder will have two chambers: one supplying hydraulic fluid to the front wheels and one to the rear wheels. These are called dual master cylinders and were made universal on all cars and trucks sold in the U.S. in the late 1960s. Trucks newer than 1967 will already have the dual master cylinder, but will need a different unit with a larger front fluid chamber for disc brakes. (With a drum brake dual master cylinder both chambers are basically the same size.) The greater stopping power of the front discs and amount of fluid needed to move the disc brake caliper piston are the reasons for the larger front chamber. To prevent all the stopping force from being exerted at the front of the vehicle, front disc brake systems also include a proportioning valve that diverts part of the braking action to the rear wheels.

On trucks newer than 1967, which already have dual master cylinder, the new disc brake unit installs the same way as the master cylinder it replaces. On older trucks, it is necessary to purchase an adapter, from Engineered Components,

Inc. of Vernon, Connecticut. On these trucks, it is also necessary to replace and re-route the brake lines to create a dual braking system.

Upgrading to disc brakes also invites adding a power brake booster (a process described next), so rather than simply replace the master cylinder, you may also be installing both the disc brake master cylinder and a power assist unit. With the new master cylinder (and booster unit), plus the proportioning valve in place, it's time to reconnect the brake lines.

Before filling the master cylinder and bleeding the lines, it's a smart idea to check the condition of the rear brakes. This requires elevating the rear of the truck to remove the rear wheels and brake drums. On our project truck we discovered a leaking axle seal on the driver's side, which had allowed grease from the differential to soak the brake linings. Grease sodden linings usually grab and lock against the drum under heavy braking and are not helpful in bringing the truck to a swift, smooth stop. In inspecting the condition of the rear brakes, you'll check the drums for scoring, evaluate the amount of lining remaining on the brake shoes and inspect the condition of the wheel cylinders as well as the brake shoe return springs and related hardware.

Bleed the New Disc Brake System

With new front disc brakes installed and the rear drum brakes in A-1 condition, it's time to flush, fill and bleed the hydraulic system. The old brake fluid is purged or flushed from the lines by blowing compressed air into the lines at the master cylinder end with an air hose (you'll need to do this before connecting to the master cylinder, rear wheel cylinders, and front flex lines). To remove all traces of old fluid, inject several ounces of pure isopropyl alcohol (available at pharmacies) into the line openings with a syringe and blow until no trace of the old brake fluid emerges from the lines. Now all brake line connections can be secured and the fresh fluid added to the master cylinder.

Filling a hydraulic brake system causes air to become trapped in the lines. The process of purging this entrapped air is called "bleeding". It's best to have a helper when bleeding the brakes. After your assistant "pumps up" the brake pedal, you will release the bleeder screw at each wheel cylinder, one at a time until all air is bled from the system. With all entrapped air purged from the hydraulic system, the truck is ready to drive, but with independent front suspension, before heading out on the highway, the truck should be taken to a front end alignment shop to check the caster and camber settings on the front wheels.

This upgrade has mounted the master cylinder on the firewall and used a dual reservoir master cylinder for safety.

Brake Upgrade for Art Deco and Early Advance Design Trucks

By John Hart

When restoring 1950 or earlier GM truck, it's good to remember that GM dramatically improved the design of the brake system on half-ton trucks in 1951. Before 1951, brakes were Huck style. The 1951 and newer Bendix design is far superior in stopping power and efficiency.

The shoes in Huck style brakes adjust at the top and pivot on a rigid pin at the bottom. As a result, only about 60 percent of the face of the shoe actually comes into contact with the inside of the drum. This isn't an efficient way to get the job done.

With Bendix brakes, the shoes adjust at the bottom and float on springs. More of the shoe surface meets the drum and, even better, the floating shoes have a rotating motion causing a jamming effect. This is a good way to stop a truck.

On my 1946 Suburban, I wanted to retain as much originality as possible, so I restored the original brakes. This was a mistake. They wouldn't stop the truck efficiently.

At a swap meet, I found a full set of front brake components from a mid-1950s GM truck. With these, I upgraded the front brakes on the Suburban as a straight bolt-in operation. At the rear the job is more complex because the face plates chanced in 1951, so Suburban's my rear brakes are still original. Most of the stopping action occurs at the front, however, so now my truck stops—a big improvement and much safer.

Power Brakes

While upgrading to disc brakes, adding power to the braking system makes sense. If your truck was built prior to 1967, you should purchase a power brake unit engineered for your truck. Brake booster systems for vintage Chevrolet trucks are available from Engineered Concepts, Inc. and other suppliers. On a 1967 and later truck here are the steps to install the power brake unit

1) Install a T fitting in the manifold with the large opening pointing in the direction of the left fender.
2) Guide the assembly onto the four mounting studs and after checking to see that the push rod clevis mates with the brake pedal arm (under the dash) you may tighten the four nuts tightly.
3) Underneath the dash install the pin through the clevis and brake pedal, then secure these parts using a new cotter key.
4) If there is a little bit of free play between the clevis and brake pedal arm, then you are finished under the dash. (The brake light switch may also need adjusting.) If not, you will have to obtain that free-play by adjusting the clevis either in or out then locking the nut on the rod to prevent the shaft from turning.
5) Retighten the four nuts holding the assembly onto the firewall.
6) Connect the lines leading from the proportioning valve to the connector blocks on the left side behind the front suspension cross member.
7) Reconnect the brake light warning switch wire to the proportioning valve.
8) Bleed the brakes using new brake fluid with the recommended DOT rating.

Do not attempt to install an original power brake unit from a 1967-1970 truck on a 1971-1972. Earlier trucks, up to 1970, have drum brakes on all four wheels (some 1970 trucks had disc brakes, but these are very rare indeed). Trucks built in 1971 and 1972 have disc brakes on the front and drums on the rear. The power brake unit (master cylinder and booster) from a disc brake equipped truck is not compatible with the earlier trucks with four-wheel drums. Don't install the earlier unit on the disc brake truck as the same rule applies. They are not the same. Don't let looks fool you; the units are different.

The easy way to tell if the donor truck's load rating is by the number of lugs on the axle flange.

Three-quarter ton trucks have 8 wheel studs
1967-70 half tons have 6 wheel studs
1971-72 half tons have 5 wheel studs

The large drum-shaped object behind this dual reservoir master cylinder is the power booster. On brake systems showing internal corrosion, these parts will be replaced.

nless you own an exceptionally rust free truck that has led a pampered life, a major phase in the process of restoring or rebuilding your Chevy truck will be repairing rusted and dented metal. In restoration the truck is typically disassembled for the derusting/stripping process. When the rebuilding approach is followed, the fenders and doors may be removed, but the cab is left on the frame.

In most cases, the rust and dent damage should be visible, but you may need to probe with a small bladed screwdriver or ice pick at suspicious spots, such as where the paint has bubbled, to determine the full extent of rust damage. On Chevrolet trucks, rust-prone areas include the bottoms of doors, cab corners, and the cowl panels just past the rear of the front fenders, as well as the bottoms of the pickup box supports. If the screwdriver or ice pick punctures the metal, you've done no harm. Solid metal would not be penetrated and the fact that you've jabbed a hole only shows that the metal in this area needs to be replaced. You may also discover

Dents are worked out using an assortment of body hammers and dollies. The dent should be worked from the outside in.

dents that were covered with filler either by having the pick stick in a hardened filler or by running a magnet across wavy surfaces that suggest amateur repairs.

If the rust damage is extensive, you may want to consider finding better parts. For Advance Design series and later Chevrolet trucks, rust free cabs and doors are still in plentiful in states south and west of the rust belt. For repairing the common rust areas (bottoms of doors and cab corners) patch panels are available for Advance Design, Task Force, and other model Chevrolet trucks. Instructions for installing patch panels follow in this chapter.

Dent Repair

Since trucks are working vehicles, dent damage is common. Although dents can occur anywhere, the most typical places are in the fenders and cab rear panel and roof. Dents can be worked out of fenders most easily if the fenders are taken off the truck. Dents in the cab can usually be reached from the inside once the seats and headliner (on trucks that have this fiberboard covering) have been removed.

When possible, dents should be worked out with the metal at air temperature. Sometimes, however, extensive dent damage in the heavy gauge sheet metal of older trucks will require applying heat to straighten the metal. Although warming the dented area with a torch makes the metal easier to straighten, it also increases the chances that the metal will become stretched. The problem with stretching is that when you have smoothed the dent you will have an extra bulge with no recess to fill. This bulge will have to be shrunk in order to finish the dent repair.

Skill in straightening dents comes with developing a feel for the metal and the best way to acquire this is through practice. Instead of starting out by attempting to smooth the dents on your truck, begin with beat up panels from a parts truck or buy a fender from a scrap yard with the same gauge metal as that on your truck and pound in some dents if need be. Then practice working out these dents on the scrap parts. After a few sessions of practice "metal bumping," as the skill is called, you will be equipped to start working out the dents on your truck.

Dent repair requires a special set of bumping hammers and dollies. You can buy body hammers and dollies (metal weights that are pressed against the top of the dent to prevent hammer marks and spread the hammer blow over a wide area) from specialty tool suppliers including The Eastwood Company, which advertises in major hobby publications. You won't need all the hammers and dollies shown in the catalog, but you will need an assortment to work out various shaped dents.

The first step in straightening a dent is to rough out the depression with a bumping hammer and dolly. Rather than try to force the metal back into shape with a few hard blows, work the dent out gradually, usually beginning at the outside of the depression and working toward the center. Your goal here is not just to straighten the metal, but also to keep it from stretching. When the metal becomes stretched, you will end up with a bulge that won't lie flat no matter who much you work it. There are basically two ways to get rid of these stretch bulges. One is to shrink the metal with a special serrated shrinking hammer and dolly. The other is to heat the bulge with a torch, then quickly cool the metal with water. This heating and quenching method works well on older, heavy gauge metal body panels but should not be used on modern high-strength steel panels.

When the dent is close to the correct contour, you will use a finishing hammer and dolly to smooth the surface as much as possible. The technique here is to hold the dolly against the metal on the opposite side that the hammer will be hitting. Dollies have contoured surfaces and it is important to find a contour on the dolly that matches the shape of the smoothed dent. It is sometimes possible to smooth the dented area so that only very fine surface imperfections remain. When this is the case, the small hammer marks can be eliminated with a file and any remaining blemishes covered with primer. More likely, however, a skim coat of body filler will needed to cover hammer marks and other small traces of the dent repair.

Rust Repair

Mending rusted metal requires welding skills and some additional specialized tools in addition to a welding outfit. While the rusted area can be cut out using tin snips or a hack saw, a metal nibbler or cut-off tool makes the job much easier. The patch panel will need to be cut to fit the rusted area and a panel nibbler also makes this job easier. Other tools that are highly useful to the metal repair process include

Panel flangers—used to form an offset flange so that replacement panels can be flush fit

Crimping pliers—used to pinch replacement skins to the door frame

Carbide burr—used to grind weld beads

Panel holding clamps—used to secure panels for welding. Sheet metal screws can also be used for this purpose.

Heat sink putty—used to prevent heat warpage.

Panels can be welded in place using both gas and arc welding methods, but as the next section will explain, wire welding (a form of arc welding) is the superior method for attaching patch panels with the least risk of heat damage to the surrounding metal.

Perforations on the lower passenger side section of this Chevrolet Suburban show metal that has been weakened by rust. You can test the integrity of the metal by poking it with a narrow bladed screwdriver or ice pick. If the tool punctures the metal, there's rust damage that needs to be repaired. Here an exploratory section has been cut to determine the soundness of the inside panel, which, fortunately, is rust free.

Wire Welding

Both gas welding and standard arc welding that uses a flux-coated rod for the electrode present problems as methods for welding in patch panels. Gas welding creates intense heat that will almost invariably warp the panel. Fusing body metal with the standard type of arc welding is difficult for the amateur to do. But these problems with the more common welding technologies do not mean that the hobbyist can't do his or her own body repair. Wire welding equipment, designed with the handyman and hobbyist in mind, has become available at

Rust repair begins by cutting out the bad metal. Rotary cutoff tools make this job easy, but eye protection must be worn.

prices that are little higher than a standard arc or gas welding outfit. The advantage of wire welding is that with a little practice you'll be laying down professional-looking welds and the localized heat of this welding method means that it can be used with minimal risk of warping the surrounding metal.

The basic difference between wire welding and "stick" welding (stick refers to the use of a filler rod that also serves as an electrode in standard arc welding operations) is that with wire welding the filler material is very thin (0.030 in.) and is fed automatically into the weld area. The thin filler material of wire welding is ideally suited to sheet metal repair and the fact that the filler wire is fed out automatically means that the welder only needs to concentrate on moving the electrode holder along the work surface. With standard arc (stick) welding, the welder also needs to concentrate on maintaining the correct gap between the electrode and work surface, a somewhat complicated matter since the electrode is continually being consumed in the weld.

Welding Equipment

Two types of wire welding equipment are available to the hobbyist One uses wire with a flux core as the electrode and filler metal. The flux core shields the weld in the same way as the flux coating does on an arc stick welder. The advantage of this wire welder is its relatively low cost. The disadvantage is a generally thicker wire due to the flux core. Thicker wire increases the possibility of burn through on thin body metal.

The other type of wire welder uses an inert gas to shield the weld. This MIG (short for Metal Inert Gas) welder has the advantage of using wire as thin as 0.024 in. and because the weld is shielded with gas rather than flux, the welding process creates very little smoke and splatter. Professionals prefer MIG to flux core wire welders and the difference in price between the two types is not so one-sided as to make the lower cost equipment the hobbyist's choice.

Because of its ease of use, wire welding equipment allows a hobbyist to become a proficient welder in a short time. Further, wire welding works equally well in horizontal or vertical positions. This means that welding patch panels in place on the truck body requires no special skills beyond familiarity with the wire welder. Once the equipment is set up, the procedure for wire welding is to attach the ground clamp to the truck body near the work area, turn on the welder, set the wire speed control and heat dial, then strike the electrode to the work surface and proceed across the seam that you are joining with the weld.

Welding Technique

To get used to the rate at which the wire feeds out of the gun and laying down a smooth bead, you should practice on automotive-gauge sheet metal. A common practice exercise used in welding classes is to weld rectangular patches to a piece of auto

body metal. If scrap metal, like an old hood, is used, the areas where the patches will be attached needs to be sanded or stripped to bare metal. The patches are first tack welded in place at the corners then finish welded along the sides. This pattern of joining a series of short welds is also used when attaching patch panels to the truck itself.

When welding in patch panels, you will work the bead a couple of inches across a seam, then release the feed button on the gun and move to another point on the seam or to the opposite end of the seam you are welding and lay down another two or so inches of weld. Then you can go back and continue the first weld for a short distance, skip back to the other weld and so forth. This way, you will keep heat from building up in one area and warping the metal. On very large flat panels, such as doors, heat can also be contained by using a heat dam made of asbestos putty sold through specialty suppliers like The Eastwood Company.

Typically, the biggest problem novice welders experience when first practicing with wire welding is having several inches of wire feed out of the gun before finding the starting location on the seam and striking an arc. The extra wire will melt once the arc is struck, but will become a glob of metal at the start of the weld. A technique for easily striking the arc without the problem of excess wire feeding out of the gun is to touch

Filler mixes with a small amount of hardener.

119

Filler is applied with a plastic squeegee to the repair area and allowed to harden.

additional beads as needed for thicker metal. The special feature of MIG welding is that a shielding gas, usually carbon dioxide, is blown around arc to keep oxygen away from weld. With flux-core wire welding, the slag serves to shield the weld. The purpose for keeping oxygen from the weld is to prevent oxidation (rusting) from occurring as the weld is formed.

After the patch is welded in place, the seam should be ground smooth. Since these welds are hard, this is best done with a carbide grinder. If the patch was joined in a butt joint, grinding the weld may be the only finishing step required before priming and painting. More commonly, however, some filler, either lead or plastic, will be needed to smooth the seam.

Wire welders designed for light duty auto body work are available from specialty tool suppliers. Someone with a basic background in arc welding should be comfortably proficient

the electrode to the seam where you intend to begin welding with your helmet lifted and the welder turned off. Then when you lower the helmet over your face and press the feed button on the gun you can begin to move the gun along the seam as soon as the arc appears. A steady cracking and hissing sound is a sign that you are holding the gun the correct distance from the work surface and moving the gun at the proper rate.

On thicker metal, multiple passes may be needed to build up the weld to the full depth of the metal. With flux core wire welders, the slag that forms on the weld will have to be chipped off between passes in order to get a sound weld. With MIG welding there is no slag, so you can simply apply

Filler should be used very sparingly to cover minor irregularities in the metal.

Then the filler is scraped and sanded smooth.

After the repair is primed, any very small imperfections can be filled with glazing putty, which, as shown here, is also mixed with hardener.

Rusted door hinge boxes are a must repair.

Here the bottom hinge box has been cut out and a replacement box has been welded in.

with wire welding after a little practice. Instructions with the welder will provide a guide to setting the wire feed and heat controls on the welder.

If you are a newcomer to welding, the best way to learn is to enroll in an evening welding class at a vocational-technical center or technical college. These classes typically cover gas, stick arc, and wire feed welding and will give you practice on all three methods. In addition, you will learn and practice good safety rules—the most important of which it to wear proper eye protection.

Always be sure to wear a welding helmet when doing wire welding. The bright flashes from the weld, looked at with the naked eye, can burn the retina. This condition is not correctable and can lead to blindness. Also, if you are welding in the presence of others, be sure to caution them not to look at the weld. This is particularly important when children are in

the work area. Their natural curiosity will draw their eyes to the bright arc flashes. Always make sure that children are out of the area before starting to weld.

Cab Repair

Just as cars have their rust-prone areas, so do trucks. Spots most susceptible to metal rot include the rear cab corners, bottoms of the doors, front cowl section (behind the front fenders), the cab floor, and pickup box supports. Fender eyebrows on late 1950s Task Force series trucks trap dirt and road salt and the caulking sometimes leaks at the roof peak on 1967-1972 trucks, adding to the rust-prone areas. On Fleetside trucks, the area around the rear wheel wells is especially rust prone. The section that follows explains the process

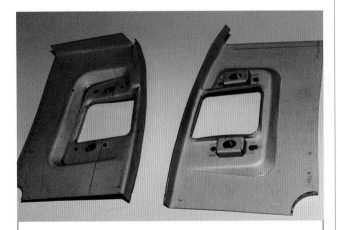

Hinge boxes stamped to match the original contours with cage nuts for the hinges are available from parts suppliers.

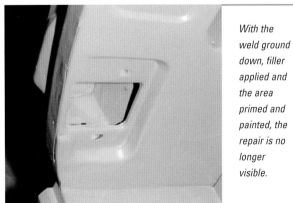

With the weld ground down, filler applied and the area primed and painted, the repair is no longer visible.

of repairing rust damage using patch panels. For the common rust-out areas repair panels are available for most years of Chevrolet trucks.

The repair sequence being described is common with trucks that have been driven in areas where highway departments use salt to keep roads free of ice in winter. For a Southern or Western truck, rust damage to the extent shown in the accompanying photos would be extreme, but even on these trucks some repair in the moisture catching is likely.

Among the most rust prone areas on any pickup are the along the floor in the area adjoining the firewall, the rear corners and under the doors. Die stamped repair panels (also called patch panels) that match the contours and have the same thickness as the original metal can be purchased to rebuild a cab as severely rust damaged as that shown in the accompanying photos.

Assessing Rust Damage

The first step in any metal repair process is to assess the extent of the damage. Quite typically, a rusted section will look more solid than it is. The only signs of rust may be blisters in the paint. As mentioned earlier, jabbing a thin-bladed screw driver or pick into a paint blister is a quick way of checking the condition of the metal. Don't worry about doing damage. If the metal is sound, the tool won't penetrate. If the point stabs through you can proceed with the steps described here. The rust may also manifest itself in gaping holes as shown in these photos. Whether the rust is hidden or evident, the next step is to find where sound metal begins because you can't weld the patch to rust.

Once you've established the limits of the damage, you can draw an line to show where the metal is to be cut away. A pencil line will make a clear marking. It is important is to make the line as straight as possible (use a ruler or some sort of straight edge). The cut away area doesn't need to match the size and shape of the patch (which should be larger than the rust out). You will size the patch to match the hole, not visa-versa.

Cutting Out Rusted Metal

Before cutting away rusted metal, it may be necessary to brace the cab. The cab becomes very flexible when rocker panels or step boards, lower door pillars, and parts of the floor are removed. If the repairs are made with the cab in a distorted or misaligned position, the doors will not fit. Braces can be temporarily welded in place and removed later after the patch panels are installed.

An air driven cutter wheel is the best tool to use for cutting away the rusted metal. The cutter can be guided easily along the pencil line and will slice out the damaged area in seconds. Be sure to wear safety glasses or goggles to protect your eyes against flying sparks and metal chips. If you don't

With the bad metal cut away, the repair process can begin.

Patch panels should be trimmed to match as closely as possible to the contours of the cut-out metal.

own a cutter wheel, a hacksaw or tin snips can be used, but these leave jagged edges which will have to be smoothed before installing the patch.

In some areas you may need to cut the tack welds that hold portions of the cab together. An easy way to remove the tack welds is with a spot weld cutter. Now that you have removed rusted metal and opened up the areas needing to be repaired, you will either fabricate a patch or cut a pre-formed patch to fit the hole. If you are making a patch, usually for a non-contoured, flat area, laying a sheet of cardboard over the hole and cutting the cardboard to the dimensions of the patch is the easiest way to make a pattern from which to cut the metal. If you are using repair panels, the panel can be held up to the hole and marked for cutting.

The tack welds are spaced several inches apart to avoid localized heat build-up. Some of the spaces between these tack welds have already been joined.

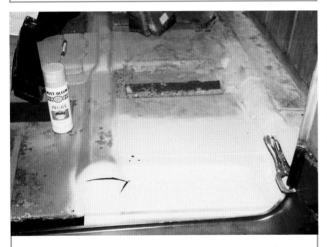

Now the patch has been temporarily primed to prevent rusting.

Welding in Patch Panels

Two methods can be used to weld in the patch. One is called a lap joint. Using this method, you will form a lip along the edges of the patch where it joins the body metal. When the patch is installed this lip will fit behind the sound body metal and the panel will be welded along this seam. The other approach is to cut the patch so that it fits perfectly to the contours of the hole and use the weld to fill the tiny gap between the patch and surrounding body metal. This is called a butt joint, as it gives a smooth seam, and reflects superior workmanship. A butt joint is harder to do since the patch panel fit with the hole it fills has to be nearly perfect.

To form a lap joint you will cut the patch panel about 1/2 in. larger than the hole. Then you will bend the edges of the patch with a special lip-forming tool. Next you will fit the patch in place. For welding, the patch has to be clamped tightly to the body metal. This can be done with pop rivets or sheet metal screws, which can be removed and the holes filled later, or with panel holders. Various welding methods can be used to fuse the patch to the body metal, but wire welding is preferred because, as previously discussed, this method creates less heat—thereby lessening the risk of warping the body panel. As an alternative, a stick welder can be used. But with stick welding care has to be taken to avoid heat buildup. Oxyacetylene welding can also be used, but utmost care must be exercised to prevent heat buildup and metal warpage. One way to control heat build up it to use a heat dam around the joint.

To make a weld a butt joint, the patch needs to make a precise fit and then is tack welded in place in several locations. Again, this is best done with a wire welding apparatus. If the joint fits closely enough, the patch can be welded into the hole so cleanly that it may be possible to grind the weld, prime, and paint. If you achieve this quality seam, you are doing professional work indeed. More likely, the seam will need some filler.

The patch will guide where the cutoff line should be.

Note that patch panels cover fairly small sections. Here two patches are clamped together for a test fit prior to welding.

A new cab corner has been welded in place on this side of the truck.

On Advance Design cabs, when installing cab corner patches, before welding, the patch needs to be fitted around the edge of the door pillar. This fit is made by tapping along the edge of the patch with a body hammer until a tiny lip curls around the edge of the pillar. You will also see this lip in the original metal. Chevrolet Advance Design cabs were not one-piece welded construction seen on light trucks today. Instead they were formed from numerous panels, some with unfinished seams—as is the case at the door pillars.

Again on an Advance Design cab, with a cowl patch, it is necessary to recreate the tack welds that were made at the factory to attach the cab's rear panel to the door pillars. This is can be done in two ways. One is to drill a series of holes in the patch at the approximate locations of the spot welds, then weld the two layers of metal together through the holes. The other is to drill holes through both layers of metal and weld the holes closed. Either method will assure that the weld penetrates both layers. When the welds are ground smooth they will look like the original factory spot welds.

With the patch welded in place attention can now be given to smoothing the seam. As mentioned earlier, if the patch has been butt welded, the only finishing work may be to grind the seam, prime and fill remaining blemishes with body putty, then wet sand, add another primer layer, and finish paint. More likely, whether the patch is attached by the lap or butt weld method, some filler will be needed to smooth the seam. Since no moisture should be able to penetrate the seam, plastic filler can be used. Some purists feel that only body lead should be used as filler, but this material can present paint blistering problems. If the solder flux becomes trapped under the metal, it may work to the surface blistering the paint. When this occurs, the only remedy may be to remove the paint, melt out the lead filler, clean the metal and rework the seam—a complicated, tedious, thankless process that also requires expensive repainting.

If the patch was installed using the lap joint method, it is advisable to weld or caulk the lap joint on the inside of the cab. If this seam is left open, moisture may collect and blister the paint or rerust the metal. After the inside seam has been filled or caulked, and the outside seam smoothed by grinding and applying a skim coat of filler as needed, the repair should be invisible.

Hammer Welding

This process is used in conjunction with a butt joint to produce a nearly invisible repair that can often be finished with just priming and painting. The steps are as follows: After cutting out the rusty section, fitting the new patch, coat the seam with a rust-prevention product The Eastwood Company's Cold Galvanizing compound. Now tack weld the patch about every inch, then go back and fill between the welds 1/2 in. at a time. Alternate from one area of the patch to another to prevent or minimize warpage. Placing a heat dam around the welding area with heat sink putty helps control heat from the welding spreading across the panel. As you finish each 1/2 in. of weld, set the torch down and quickly hammer and dolly the weld flat before it has a chance to cool. This technique requires that you can get access to the back of the weld for the dolly.

Replacing Floor Panels

It's not uncommon for an otherwise rust-free truck to have rusted floors. Road salt isn't the only rust culprit. Dirt, sand, and debris that is tracked into the cab and builds up under the floor mat is an ideal moisture collector, especially in seams and recesses. The result is a rusted floor that need to be repaired or replaced.

The repair sequence being shown is on a 1967-1972 cab, but the basics of the repair apply to year Chevrolet truck. The steps are as follows:

- Determine the extent of the rust; is the damage just on the floors or do the cab mounts also need to be repaired. Repair panels are available from Chevrolet parts vendors specializing in your year truck.

- Cut out the floor panel to remove rusted metal. Leave as much sound metal as possible and cut the repair panel to fit.
- Note: The cab support braces underneath the floor may also be rusted. If so, cut away the damaged metal. These braces can be repaired much more easily if the cab is off the truck.
- Replace or patch the cab support braces. These supports are typically welded in place.
- Fit and weld the replacement floor panels. Grind the welds and finish the seams as needed.

Now a template is made for the patch. Richard Matott

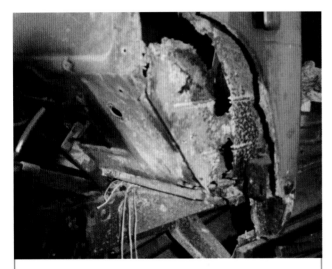

Where patch panels don't exist, repair patches have to be fabricated. Richard Matott

The first step is to cut out the rusted metal. Richard Matott

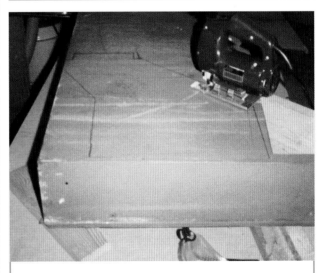

The template is then transferred to a sheet of metal. Richard Matott

Note the bracing welded onto the cab to maintain dimensions while repairs are being made.

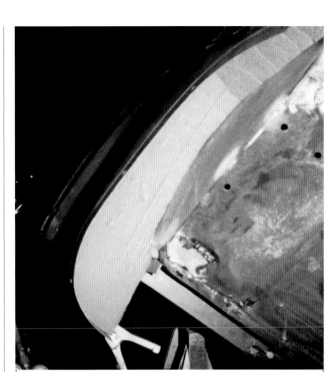

Above, below, and opposite: *A more complex patch is being made the same way. Suppliers continue to expand their line of patch panels, making most fabrication unnecessary.*

In this case the patch has been secured by brazing, which acts more like a solder and therefore requires less heat, but lacks the strength of welding.

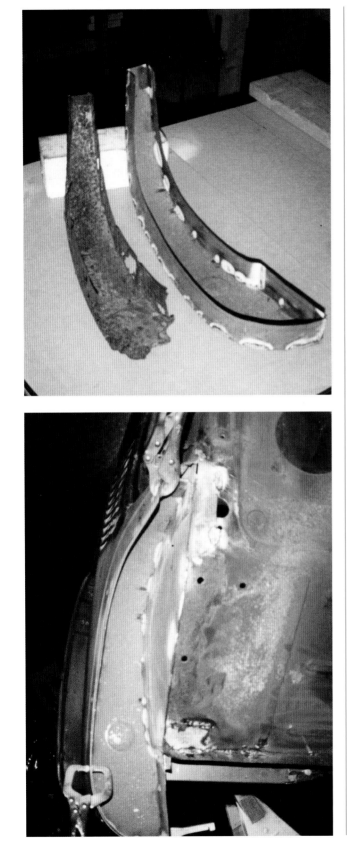

Five-Window Cab Conversion
by Ric Hall

Metal work on an older truck sometimes goes beyond welding in patch panels or putting on a door skin. One of example of this would be when entire side panels on a Fleetside box are replaced because the existing panels are rusted beyond repair. Another example where a large panel may be replaced is in the conversion of a three-window Advance Design pickup cab to a deluxe five-window cab. To many collectors, the nearly panoramic view of the five window cab makes these much more desirable. If your truck has the more common three-window cab (the three windows consist of the two door windows and back light; the five window cab also has corner windows), you may want to follow this relatively simple procedure to convert your truck to a five-window cab.

Although the specifics will vary, the instructions given here are similar to those followed when replacing any large panel. Tack welds will need to be cut, seams cut open, the panel positioned correctly, then welded in place and metal finished. The method shown requires a minimum amount of metal finishing. The only body filler needed will be at the windshield posts and only a very thin coat is used even there.

Why would you want to cut-up your perfectly good three-window cab? One reason is you need not remove your truck's cab from the frame, which is a monumental a labor savings over the time required to remove all the front sheet metal, electricals, and other steps involved in swapping cabs. If the cab is rust free in the floor and front lower corners, but the five-window cab you have found is not, then you have another reason for using this method to give your truck a deluxe cab. Door gaps can also be improved greatly when joining the two cabs—and this is a *big* bonus. In the process of this conversion, you will improve the door fit and gaps that have deteriorated over the years, or were never very good from the factory in the first place. Doors only adjust so much, but now the door openings can be made to fit the doors.

To make this conversion, first remove the front and rear glass and remove or mask the door windows and gauges with heavy paper to prevent pitting during grinding and welding operations. Also removed are the seats, weather stripping and most importantly the gas tank. Next, adjust the doors for fit at the cowl and top. Don't worry too much about the fit at the back edge since this is where the new cab can be fitted to the door later.

The door striker should be unbolted from the cab door-jamb to prevent any preload from a poorly adjusted striker. Most of the door adjustment on this model truck is obtained where the hinges bolt to the door. More likely than not, you will have to remove the doors and hinges to free them from rust so they can be adjusted. Reinstall the hinges and doors, adjusting one hinge at a time until you are happy with the door gap. A block of wood and a floor jack are invaluable in this process, which may take some time—several hours per door is not uncommon.

Cutting Windshield Posts and Spot Welds

Carefully measure a midway point on the windshield posts for cutting. The window opening has too many curves to get a good measurement, so a template works well and enables the marks to be made at exactly the same spot on each post and on each cab. (Remember, you are cutting the roof and back cab sections from two cabs and will use the section from one cab on the other, so it is very important that the cuts be made at exactly the same location.) Now cut through the posts on both cabs using a hacksaw. The center windshield support can be drilled or twisted out easily since it is attached only with spot welds.

The rear of the cab has spot welds along the lower edge. Drill these out on both cabs. A couple types of spot weld cutters are available at specialty suppliers. Be careful to drill only through the rear panel, since the other cab's spot welds are in the same place. If you drill out the spot welds in the floor metal too, there will be little to weld the new cab onto.

The most secure welds to contend with are in the doorjamb area: one is down low and the other at the seat support. Use a cutting torch here to cut as close to the weld as possible, being careful not to cut into the part you want to save. Once the cab is apart the remaining metal and weld can be ground off. Inside the cab are five braces to be cut. Three are behind where the gas tank mounts and two are down inside the corners. Cut the braces in each cab so that they will overlap. A flush splice is not needed here.

The part of the three-window cab that is not being saved can most easily be removed by pushing it onto its back. This action should pop loose any spot welds not fully drilled out. Be more careful with the five-window cab, prying it loose and lifting it off to prevent bending. When the five-window cab section is removed, lay it down onto padded saw horses.

Using grinding wheel on a body grinder, remove all burrs, rust and paint from areas to be welded. If you want to clean the metal with sandblasting or use chemical stripping method there is no better time to work on the inside of the cab then now. Before welding, seal blind areas against rust by using a cold galvanizing compound like that sold by The Eastwood Company. Unlike paint, this product has weld-through capabilities.

Welding Windshield Posts and Replacing Spot Welds

After positioning the five-window cab piece by lifting it onto your truck's cab platform, you can hold the two cab parts together with vice grips. Now adjust the position of the back panel to give the doors a proper fit—not too tight, not too loose. Then weld the windshield posts, rain gutter and all. To make the strongest possible splice, the metal on the inside of the post should also be welded together. To accomplish this, cut and remove about a 2 in. x 3 in. section on the doorjamb for access. This section can be welded back into place after making the welds on the insides of the posts.

A wire-feed welder is best suited for making this cab conversion because it creates less heat and warpage, but a gas welder can also be used. Take it easy no matter what welding method you use, especially when making the spot welds on the back panel. If you are doing gas welding, use a heat sink putty to prevent warpage of the surrounding metal.

After welding the windshield posts, replace the spot welds. Leave the lower rear doorjamb until last to assure proper door alignment. The doorjamb should be welded in the same place as the factory welds. The five braces inside the cab can be welded or bolted together since they will not show once the gas tank is in place. With very little metal finishing, no one should be able to tell that the truck didn't come from the factory with a five-window cab—unless you tell them why the doors fit so well!

Fabricating a Spare Tire Mount
by David Bush

For some reason lots of people who originally had 1941-1946 Chevrolet pickups removed the under-bed spare tire carrier and lost it. This was the case with my 1946. All of the hardware was missing. After some research I decided that Chevrolet didn't offer a side-mount tire carrier for these trucks.

Since I couldn't find the hardware for the original carrier, and because I really wanted the side-mount, I decided to design one myself. I took measurements, built a scale model from cardboard, drew up the plans on graph paper to scale, and took them to a local welding fabrication shop. One week later I got my side-mount. Although the rear fender is not welled (fitted with a cutout for the tire), I think the result looks reasonably original. The mount is made of five pieces of sheet steel, the basic frame being built of 1/8 in. plate, and the tire mounting flange being 1/4 in. plate. It attaches by five stainless steel 3/8 in. bolts to the bed side and the forward stake pocket. I've done some preliminary testing for strength (it's strong enough for me to stand on and hasn't fallen off when I've driven down some bumpy dirt roads), and now it's at the powder coater's getting a gloss black finish.

Nearly every older pickup will need repainting. If the truck is undergoing restoration, its various components and assemblies will go through the painting process at different times. If you are overhauling the truck, chances are you will repaint the entire truck at one time. Whichever approach you take, the steps in the painting process are essentially the same.

Repainting your truck starts in researching original colors and selecting the color of your choice from this list. Here you probably have two concerns: what was my truck's original color; and what other colors were available. If your truck has been repainted, and odds are that it has, you can find the original color quite easily by checking locations that aren't likely to be repainted—like the firewall. The colors Chevrolet made available on your make and model truck can be found on Paint Sheet, available from Chevrolet truck parts suppliers and are listed in some of the Chevrolet truck reference books. Unfortunately, these are only color listings and paint chips

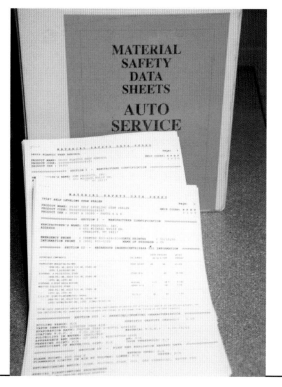

To understand the hazards associated with modern automotive refinishing products, it's important to obtain and read the Material Safety Data Sheets (MSDS).

showing what the color looks like are not included in these sources. You can get a sense of what these colors looked like from original Chevrolet sales brochures. These brochures can be purchased from antique car literature dealers at large flea markets. The brochures give likeness of the color because in most cases the colors they are not printed with exact hues.

As you select the exterior color, keep your truck's interior color in mind. Until 1954, Chevrolet offered basically one interior color, which more or less matched with the limited range of exterior colors. In 1951, for example, the interior color was a deep maroon on the seat upholstery and door panels with silver on the dashboard. Whatever the exterior color, this was the interior scheme. On more modern Chevy trucks, particularly those from the mid-sixties and later when choices in seat covering material became available, you should select the exterior color to harmonize with the interior. For example, let's say that your truck's original seat covering is blue and the upholstery looks fresh enough to keep as is, you would not want to select a conflicting exterior color (such as green). If you are replacing interior coverings, you can select a color to match the exterior paint color, but be aware that you will also need to paint the interior of the cab a matching or harmonizing color.

Once you have selected the color, the next decision is what type of paint to use.

Modern paints are "systems" products, meaning all the different paint, solvent, hardener and additives used in the entire

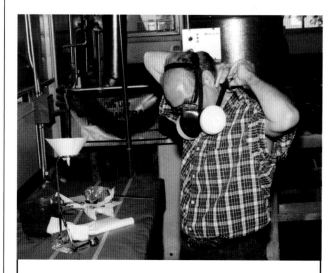

Be sure to wear a proper respirator when mixing or spraying painting products.

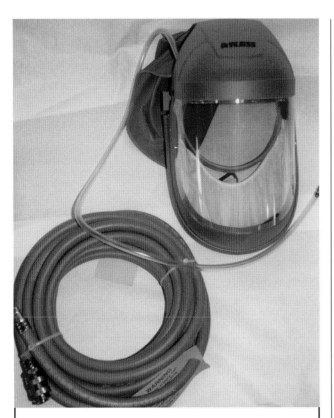

For maximum safety when spraying paint products containing isocyanates the painter should wear a hooded suit and full face mask with external air supply.

refinishing process should come from the same manufacturer. Blending different manufacturers' products not only risks blemishes, hardening problems, lifting and other painting disasters, but you'll find you've voided the product's warranty. This same system concept applies within a manufacturer's various product lines and assures compatibility for the entire product range from primer to finish coating.

Selecting a Finish System

Once you've picked a paint manufacturer you're going to be pretty well locked into its products, so the choice of paint line is important. Factors to consider include service and technical assistance available from the stores selling the different brands, color availability and specialty finishes. The next decision is the type of final coating you plan to use (yes, this decision needs to be made at the start of the process), whether single coat enamel, enamel with hardener, basecoat/clearcoat, tricoat or multistage finish, or a specialty coating. Knowing the finish coating, you work backward through the paint system select compatible undercoat products. One of the automotive paint product manufacturers, Sikkens, makes selecting the finish system easy what it calls the "Sikkens

Simple System." Sikkens begins by asking why the new finish is being applied: is it covering an existing finish, a repair coating or a fresh finish over bare metal? Once that question is answered, a compatible undercoat and color finish can be selected. Even fillers should be chemically compatible with their refinishing products. Straying from the systems path invites problems.

Color Systems

Easy to spray lacquer paints have disappeared due to the ozone-producing effects of their solvents. Today the simplest, easiest type of finish coating for the hobbyist to apply, is a single-stage color using acrylic enamel. This can either be a relatively simple and relatively safe non-catalyzed acrylic coating or a more hazardous and complex catalyzed urethane coating with or without a clear coat. More complicated yet are the basecoat/clearcoat finishes where a very thin color layer (the base coat) is covered by a protective clear coat that enlivens the color and adds gloss.

Undercoat Systems

The topcoat system must be applied over a corresponding set of undercoat products. The typical undercoat consists three products: primer, which makes a bond for the finish over the underlying surface whether bare metal or an old finish; primer surfacer, which adds thickness to the primer coating and can be sanded to give a smooth base for the color finish; and sealer, which bonds the new finish.

The system approach interlocks these products to provide a stable base. These undercoat products can be designed for a variety of functions. Primer can be formulated to bonding over bare metal, galvanized metal, or an existing finish. Primer surfacer, which some manufacturers are now calling primer-filler, can be formulated to spray on thick for fast build-up. Painters used to spray and sand as many as a dozen filler layers, but with today's high-build primer surfacers this process is cut to as few as two or three coatings. Sealer can be tinted to match the color of topcoat so that those inevitable stone chips won't be as noticeable a blemish.

Some undercoat products can even cross categories. By changing the mixing ratio, some primers can be turned into primer surfacers and make a thick bonding coat that can be sanded. They may even do triple-duty and also act as a sealer. Combining the functions of several products in one not only saves money, but also time.

By assuring compatibility between the various coatings, the systems approach has improved quality. Yesterday's general purpose primers were often mixed with reducers or thinners of lower quality than those used with the color coating. Today the same reducers are used across the system to assure that the final finish won't fail due to an inferior product being used at some point in the painting sequence.

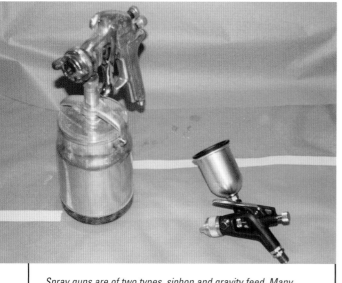

Spray guns are of two types, siphon and gravity feed. Many painters favor the gravity feed gun shown on the right for its compactness and light weight.

Siphon spray guns are also of two types, high pressure and high volume/low pressure (HVLP).

System Peripherals

Just as computers gain versatility through added devices, or peripherals, painting systems gain versatility through products that add to or enhance the paint's capability. Examples include accelerators to speed drying time, fisheye preventer to counter the effects of silicone in the spray area, and flattener to produce a semi gloss coating. Keep in mind that a manufacturer may list several peripheral products with each tailored to a different system. It's essential to select product that's compatible with the painting system you're using.

Using Painting Products Safely

Health and safety hazards exist during each stage in the painting process presents. Toxic chemicals used to strip off an old finish can be both a health and fire hazard. Mixing painting products invites skin contact as well as inhalation of vapors. Spraying concentrates flammable and toxic vapors while improper storage and disposal add the risk of fire and contamination. Although some painting products are only mildly irritating, others, namely the two-part products that require a catalyst to set, containing isocyanates are a serious health risks to the point of being potentially lethal.

To use these products safely:

Keep a clean shop. Clutter invites accidents as well as spilled paint or solvent. Clean thoroughly after sanding or painting.

Store painting products in locked, fireproof cabinets. Locking the cabinet prevents access by children.

Don't smoke inside the shop. Painting products are flammable. Post no-smoking signs to alert others of shop policy.

Mount foam or dry powder fire extinguishers in easy reach. Do not try to put out paint product fires with water.

Have a first aid kit in the shop. Post a list of emergency procedures for exposure to painting products, which can irregular or halted breathing.

If the shop does not have a sink or other washing facility, such as a hose, post directions for the nearest source of fresh water.

Do not bring food or beverage into the shop. Always wash hands after handling painting products.

Wear protective clothing while working with painting products. Clothing should include lint free coveralls with elastic wrist and ankles, a painter's cap with elastic or adjustable band, rubber gloves offering chemical resistance to solvents and hardeners

Wear an approved paint spray respirator. When spraying two-part paints with hardeners, it's safest to wear a full face piece respirator or preferably an hood with air supplied by an oilless compressor.

Paint in a spray booths or enclosure with a filtered ventilation system. Make sure air is exhausted away from buildings and/or people.

Properly dispose of all leftover painting product that has been mixed with hardener. Don't store expired and non-usable product. Never pour coating products or solvents into drains or dump them into the soil.

Isocyanates

Although they're not found in all automotive refinishing products, two-part coatings where the paint is mixed with hardener are likely to contain reactive isocyanates that are both a short term and long term health risk. You'll know if isocyanates are present by the Hazard Rating on the Material Safety Data Sheet (MSDS) for the painting product. Many hobbyists believe the MSDS is only for professionals, but the hazard information on these sheets are probably more important to us since we are likely to be more casual in our handling and use of toxic products. The Material Safety Data Sheets are available from the painting products supplier; however, you'll probably have to ask for them.

Anyone using automotive painting products is required by law have proper MSDS sheets in a readily available location. When purchasing painting products and supplies be sure to ask for the MSDS package and read the hazard information as well as what to do about spills and disposing of left-over painting product. The MSDS also lists first aid treatment and protective information

Health Risks of Isocyanates

Exposure to isocyanates produces reactions ranges from coughing, dryness of the throat, or a burning sensation of the nose, throat and lungs, to chronic and sometimes long-term, respiratory difficulty. A severe reaction may resemble an asthma attack or flu-like symptoms of fever and chills. The reactions do not necessarily result from a single exposure. If one becomes sensitized to isocyanates by repeated exposures over a period of time, severe responses could result from mild exposure. Sensitization to isocyanates may be temporary or permanent.

Isocyanates don't have a detectable odor, so you're not going to smell the toxic chemicals. For a margin of safety, a painter should to wear a hood or full facepiece with air supplied from an external source when applying two-part paints.

The easiest way to avoid contact with isocyanates is not to use products containing the chemical. However, this means spraying primarily non-catalysed refinishing products A full range of primer products and color coatings can be selected that do not mix with hardener. For hobbyists, these isocyanate-free products may be the wisest choice.

Alternatively, the hobbyist might apply only the base coatings, leaving the color finish for the professional. This approach makes sense for financial as well as health reasons. The high cost of the paint itself removes much of the financial incentive for a hobbyist's attempting to spray a quality finish without proper the proper equipment.

Paint Preparation

In large measure the quality of the final finish lies in the amount of effort and attention given to the primer coat.

Arriving at a smooth primer finish involves a multi-step process that begins by making sure that the surface to be painted is clean and rust-free. If you will be painting over an older finish, make sure that rust isn't bleeding through from underneath and that the paint isn't cracked. The best assurance of a smooth finish is to remove the old paint layers. However, if the existing finish is sound and limited to the factory coating, you may decide to paint over it. If so the old paint must first be sanded to assure a good primer bond.

To scuff up the old finish for repainting you should use a dual action (D/A) sander. A rotary sander will leave circular marks and gouges that will show up in the finish and trying to sand the old finish by hand is not only extremely tedious and time consuming, but will also result in an uneven base. A dual action sander is an air powered tool that operates in slow motion and is ideal for surface preparation. Before approaching the old finish with the D/A sander, be sure to wipe down the truck's exterior with a wax remover solvent available at the automotive paint supply store. If you used paint remover to strip off the old finish, you will still likely use the D/A sander to clean off paint and primer residue.

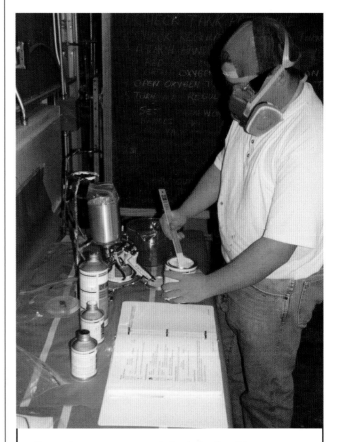

Be sure to wear a proper respirator during the mixing process.

Use a beaker or scales for precise measurements.

Paint should be poured into the gun cup through a filter.

Professional painters record to quantity of painting product they use.

Primer Coat

The primer coating is applied with a pressurized spray gun. Its purpose is to provide adhesion with the underlying surface, whether bare metal or an old finish and a bonding coat for the final finish. The primer layer is also used to smooth any minor irregularities in the underlying surface.

Successful painting lies as much in knowing what products to use in what sequence as in knowing the application technique. Some primers also contain corrosion resistant properties. These are used on inner body panels and chassis parts where moisture condensation can cause rust. These base primers are not sanded.

On surfaces that will be seen, primer surfacer is typically applied over the primer layer. Primer surfacers give fast build-up for filling minor surface imperfections. This coating is sanded and often several primer surfacer coatings are applied with sanding between each. Rough surface areas where rust has been removed by sandblasting will require high-build product for an extra thick primer build up. When you've achieved a smooth surface, apply a primer sealer coating. The sealer layer prevents solvents from penetrating and lifting the underlying finish and keeps sand scratches in the primer from opening up and ruining the final finish. When tinted, it also enhances the color in the finish coat.

Spraying Primer

Before applying any automotive refinishing product, you must read the manufacturer's Product Information sheet. This sheet tells you what you need to know to apply the product correctly and with the desired results. It begins with a short description of the product's characteristics and intended use followed by required preparation steps as well as compatible base and topcoatings. The sheet also gives application instructions that include the mixing ratio, pot life, spraying technique, the recommended drying times, time frame by which overcoats must be applied and any incompatibility that might arise with additives. These sheets also give safety instructions. More

Painting should be done in a ventilated booth or curtained enclosure.

Catalyzed products have a pot life after which they must be discarded. In the case of our Self-Etching Primer, let's say the pot life is 8 hours at 70 degrees F. Pot life will vary by temperature, decreasing when warmer and increasing when colder.

Wearing a Respirator

An approved respirator is a must when working with any professional painting product. The respirator should be worn whenever the product's lid is removed—mixing as well as spraying. With a mask-type of respirator, be sure to adjust the facepiece for a tight seal and change the filters at recommended intervals or when paint vapors are detected through the filters. Disposable respirators are available for use when sanding.

Respirators with charcoal-activated, rather than paper filters are essential when you work with paints containing isocyonates. A better respirator for these paints is the type that draws the air supply from outside the painting area.

Tinting

It's common to add a color tint to the primer coating both as a guide for sanding and to make sure no primer is visible underneath the finish. To use as a sanding guide, a thin coat of tinted or contrasting color primer (gray over red or visa versa) is applied. When sanded, the contrasting color shows spots that are low and need more filling. Often the guide coat, sanding and building up process needs to be repeated several times produce a uniformly smooth surface. Without this guide coat step, the small surface indentations are difficult to detect, although they will show up under the gloss of the final color finish.

detailed safety instructions are printed on the product label and the Material Safety Date Sheet (MSDS), which is required by law for all harmful substances.

You need to obtain and read the Product Information sheets because the specifics vary for each product. Let's say you are preparing to spray a primer coat over bare metal that has had the old finish removed by chemical stripping and sanding. Your painting products retailer recommends a Self-Etching Primer, which is supposed to save the step of acid etching the metal (wiping the surface to be primed with a mild phosphoric acid solution). The Product Information sheet will confirm that this step is not necessary, or in the case of a non self-etching primer, remind you that preparing the metal is necessary.

Of vital importance is the mixing ratio, which may call for a catalyst as well as a solvent. When automotive paints were only mixed with solvent, painters were often haphazard, dumping painting product into the gun cup and adding solvent until the mix had the consistency of milk. These crude mixing methods worked with lacquer but are a recipe for disaster with modern painting products, especially those that add a catalyst. If the proportion of catalyst is even minutely wrong, a whole range of problems from shrinkage, to cracking, to the primer staying gummy and not drying are likely to result and none is easy to correct. The mixing ratio has to be exactly what is specified on the Product Information Sheet. Products should be carefully measured by volume (an inexpensive chemist's measuring bowl, available from photographic supply stores, can be used).

Many painters color tint the primer to help with the finish coat.

Masking

Surfaces you don't primed need to be masked. Some people use newspaper because it's free but can cause overspray at the perforations along the edges of the sheets can cause overspray and oils from the inks can transfer to the surface. Though more costly, painter's masking paper should be used.. If you are priming an assembled truck, you will need to loosen the box from the frame and slide it back or take it off the frame to paint the rear of the cab and front of the box.

Before priming or finish painting, surfaces not being coated need to be masked.

When painting the interior, the steering wheel and column, gear shift and emergency brake lever also need masking.

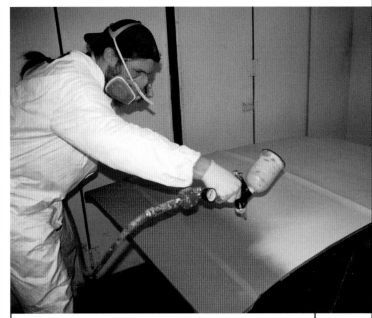

Whenever possible, parts should be placed and sprayed flat.

Spraying Technique

With primer painting, the quality (and expense) of the spray gun is not significant, since most primer layers will be sanded. With finish coats, however, a professional-quality spray gun is essential to achieve a professional grade finish. Let's say the Product Information Sheet for our Self-Etching primer specifies an air pressure setting between 35 and 40 psi for conventional spraying and 5 to 10 psi at the gun for less wasteful high volume low pressure (HVLP) application. If our coating shows sags or drips we have added too much solvent, are holding the gun too close to the metal or are moving the gun across the surface too slowly.

Applying the primer coating is the right time to learn spray gun technique, which consists of holding the spray gun at an even distance (about 8-10 inches) from the work surface, pointing the painting nozzle directly at the surface being painted and overlapping each pass by about 1/3. After making a pass, bring the gun back across the panel in the opposite direction overlapping approximately a third of the previous spraying sweep. Continue overlapping the bottom third of the previous sweep and reversing the direction.

Most novice painters sweep the spray gun in an arc over the work surface. Instead, move the spray gun directly parallel to the surface. Sweeping the gun in an arc builds up more paint in the center than at the start and finish of the pass.

If the mixture is right, air line pressure is within the accepted range, the spray gun is properly adjusted, temperature is within the allowed range (typically between 70-85 degrees F), the gun is held the right distance and pointed directly at the surface, not a lot of skill or experience is needed to apply a primer coating. If runs or sags occur, they're removed during sanding. The main purpose of the primer stage is getting product on the vehicle.

With older products, painters thought about drying as the necessary waiting time for recoating and sanding. Most of today's automotive refinishing products use a catalyst for drying, which really means curing or hardening. Now painters have to be concerned with not just when the paint is firm enough to sand or recoat without dripping, but when the paint has hardened so much another coating will no longer bond. If the recoat time elapses, the only options are to sand a surface that probably has the hardness of granite and recoat with same product. For this reason, it's very important to note and adhere to the recoat window provided on the Product Information Sheet. Since the recoat window is relatively short, it's important to schedule both primer and finish coats so that the entire painting sequence is finished within the allowed time.

In the past with lacquer and enamel paints, a truck might sit in its primer coating for years with no damage except the possibility of rust. Today, a passage of even a few months could require repeating almost all the priming preparation stages to assure a suitable bond for the finish coat.

Sanding the Primer Coat

Before it can be sanded, the primer coat needs to cure. The curing time and temperatures will be listed on the Product Information Sheet and possibly on the can label. Sanding before the primer coating has cured may result in the paint rolling up in little balls on the sandpaper. Usually primer coatings are wet-sanded using special wet/dry automotive sandpaper. The sand paper is dipped in water frequently during sanding to wash off paint residue. You can also spray water (from a household spray bottle) onto the sanding surface to lubricate it.

It's not advisable to wet-sand water-porous paints. Old style lacquer and enamel paints were porous and allowed moisture from wet-sanding to penetrate, which in turn allowed rust to form on the underlying metal eventually blistering and lifting the paint. The same result occurred with primed metal that had been stored outside where dew or rain settled on the primer finish. Most lacquer and enamel primers should not have been wet-sanded, though often they were because dry sanding is a much dustier and unpleasant job that also calls for wearing a dust mask or painting respirator. Most of today's catalyzed primers have a moisture barrier allowing them to be wet sanded.

A coarser 220 grit sandpaper is used to smooth filler coats, but this will leave scratch marks that need to be filled and smoothed by additional primer build-up sanded that is with increasingly fine 360, 400, and 600 grit papers. You'll go

Primer coatings are sanded to a smooth surface.

When sanding cuts through the primer, these spots will need to be re-coated.

136

through a lot of sandpaper, but can stretch the paper's life by folding the fresh sheet in half (on the long direction) then tearing or cutting the paper at the fold. Folding the half sheet in thirds (as you would fold a business letter) gives three sanding surfaces. As one side of the tri-folded sheet loses its grit, you can flip or refold the sheet to expose an unused surface. When dry sanding, sandpaper life can be extended by periodically tapping the folded sheet against a board or other hard object to clear the sanding dust.

Since primer has a dull surface, the most difficult part of the sanding process is knowing when the primer coating is smooth. It is very difficult to see scratch marks, grooves or ripples that will show up in the shiny finish. Painters eliminate scratch marks in the primer by using progressively finer grit sandpaper. Topping the primer coatings with a sealer helps prevent sand scratches from opening up when you spray the color finish. The best way to prevent grooves or ripples is to use a sanding block rather than holding the sandpaper in your hand. With a sanding block, the paper lies flat against the surface. Hand held sandpaper cuts grooves where the paper rubs harder at the knuckles and palm. Using color tinted or contrasting color guide coats also helps you see imperfections in the primer surface.

Putty-like fillers can be used to smooth nicks or small gouges in the primer surface. But only very thin coats of filler should be applied. When dry, the filler can be sanded using the block sanding technique.

Sealing the Primer Coat

Although the finish coat can be applied directly over primer (assuming compatible base and finish paints have been selected), for best results it is advisable to apply a sealer coating before the final finish. Sealer is available either as a clear coating that serves only to prevent moisture and painting solvents from penetrating the primer layer or as a combination primer and sealer that can be sanded, but forms a hard coating as it cures. Primer/sealer is often preferable because this product consolidates two steps into one. Remember, if you seal the undercoat and wait an extended period of time to apply the finish coating, the sealer will continue to cure and develop an almost granite hard surface. It this happens, you'll have great difficult sanding out any blemishes that may occur from handling and the coating's hardness offers a poorer surface for the final finish to bond to than the softer surface of fresh sealer.

Preparing the Finish Coat

The surface should be completely free of dust before painting. To remove sanding dust, first blow off the areas to be painted with an air nozzle. Be sure to blow into seams and crevices on the vehicle, as well as into seams and folds on the masking paper that might hold trapped dust. Then wipe down the

Plastic sheeting protects this chassis from sanding residue and paint overspray.

entire surface with tack cloths, available at automotive paint supply stores.

If you are doing a ground-up restoration, the painting process will occur in stages. Typically the chassis is painted first, then the cab interior followed by the insides of the fenders and hood, next the cab assembly with front fenders and hood attached and finally the box. With this approach, unless you are careful as you handle the various assemblies preparation and painting work at the next stage can damage finish work that is already completed. One way to protect a refinished chassis while doing painting preparation work on the cab is to cover the chassis with a large sheet of plastic (available from building and farm-supply stores), then attach the cab and front end assembly through the plastic. The plastic will protect the chassis from sanding dust, water and primer residue from wet-sanding and paint overspray that are collect in preparing and painting the parts at the next stage. After the all phases of the painting process are completed, the plastic can be pulled off and discarded. Everything underneath will still look freshly finished.

If you are painting an assembled truck, you should cover the engine and accessories to protect against sanding dust and painting overspray. Tires can be covered with trash bags to prevent their being coated with paint overspray or the wheels can be removed and the truck supported on jack stands. The new finish will look much more professional if you take the time to remove model markings and other trim.

Finish Painting

To apply the color finish you need a dust free environment. Sealing up the shop by taping seams around windows and doors won't work because dust inside the shop will still be blown onto the finish. Sealing the shop also exposes occupants to health risks from the paint vapors. The solution is to find access to or construct a spray enclosure that filters incoming air and exhausts the fumes, including overspray.

One way to gain access to a professional spray booth would be to enroll in an auto body course at a vocational-technical college. If you're allowed to use your truck as a project, you can probably paint it in the school's spray booth. The alternative is to construct a spray enclosure in your shop by partitioning off a section large enough to enclose the truck with sheets of vinyl. The incoming air can be filtered using furnace filters and an exhaust fan can suck out solvent vapors and overspray. Before building such an enclosure be sure to check local building and fire codes. To eliminate the possibility of a spark from the fan igniting solvent vapors, the exhaust fan should not be the type with steel blades and should not be mounted in a steel housing. Also, the exhaust fan should be placed so that the air flow pulls vapors away from both the painting area and the painter.

If plan to paint more than one vehicle, you should consider investing in a professional spray booth. These items are not as expensive as one might think. On hobbyist purchased a paint booth from a school that was closing its automotive program. Possibly a club or friends might share the cost of a painting facility which all could use.

Color Finish Spraying Technique

As you apply the color finish you need to be concerned with the spray gun angle, the distance from surface, and the gun travel speed.

Spray gun angle—move the gun across the metal surface horizontally, pointing it directly at the surface you are painting and keeping it parallel to the surface throughout the paint stroke.

Painting Tips

Cast iron parts on Advance Design and earlier models were sometimes painted, sometimes not, depending on the production pace. In restoration these parts can be painted with a "cast blast" coating that gives the look of fresh cast metal.

To paint the letters on the hood name plates, rather than trying to mask the individual letters, paint the lettering and compound the excess off the plate using a piece of leather to work the compound.

The division point between interior/exterior colors is where the exterior skin ends.

When painting the engine, don't put too much paint on the block. Paint hinders heat transfer.

Color tint the top primer layer for the undercarriage black and chips in the final finish won't show a drastic color change. Color tinting also works for the truck's surface finish.

When painting trim and other smaller parts, hang the parts from wire strung between step ladders. (Avoid this approach with body panels whose weight can cause them to warp.)

When fitting painted parts during reassembly, tape off the edges with 2-inch masking tape and pull off the tape after the parts have been fitted, just before bolting up.

Tailgate lettering for 1955 and earlier models is painted the same color as the tailgate, not contrasting.

On 1947-48 Advance Design Series trucks, the grille bars and back splash bars are painted body color. The leading edge of each outer bar has a horizontal stripe matching the cab stripe.

From 1947-53, cabs and fenders are the same color. Two-tone cabs were first available in 1954. Then the top is white as an option only on deluxe five-window models.

On 1949-53 Advance Design trucks with the painted grille, the back splash is painted light gray or white. On chrome grilles the outer bar is plated and the back splash is Waldorf White

On 1952 and 53 Advance Design trucks, many formerly chrome plated items are painted. These include hub caps, bumpers, grille, radio speaker trim, glovebox door.

Dark green is the standard exterior paint prior to 1955 Second Series

With cabs, the interior color is applied before the exterior.

Likewise, the door jambs are color painted before the rest of the outside surface.

Distance from the surface—the "rule of thumb" is to hold the gun 8 to 10 inches from the surface. A closer position interferes with atomization of the painting product and lays down a coating that may be excessively wet. Farther away allows too much atomization and a dry paint film. You can familiarize yourself with your gun's optimal distance by spraying against a sheet of cardboard or scrap metal. Start first with the recommended distance and increase or decrease for an even pattern. The closer you hold the gun to the painting surface, the faster you should move the gun.

Gun travel speed—the gun should move fast enough to provide a uniform build with 50 percent overlap on each sweep. Slowing the rate of travel will lay on more paint. Increasing the speed will decrease the amount of paint. To get the speed "right," watch the area you are spraying very closely to make sure you are "wetting" the surface and that about half of your sweep overlaps the previous pass.

Don't be afraid to "wet" the panel. If you move too quickly or apply the paint too dry, the finish will either lack gloss or have lots of "orange peel." Getting the paint too "wet" could cause a run, but in undercoats these can be sanded out. Never pass directly over the same spot twice. Wait for the paint to "flash" (begin to set) before returning.

Atomizing the Painting Product

A spray gun does more than blow paint onto a surface; it atomizes, or breaks paint into tiny droplets that fog the surface in a "mist." Controlling this atomization is the nozzle set, consisting of the air cap, fluid tip, and paint needle. Spray gun manufacturers offer a multitude of nozzle set combinations or "gun setups," each designed for different types of refinishing products—such as undercoats, single stage color, or basecoat/clearcoat. Changing the "gun setup" (the air cap, fluid tip, and paint needle combination) alters the "fluid to air ratio," that is the amount of paint coming through the fluid tip compared to the amount of air flowing through the air cap.

The fluid-to-air ratio can go out of balance on the side of either fluid or air. With too much fluid, the paint will lay on wet, causing runs and sags. The build (or thickness) may be more than desired, and the paint will dry more slowly. With too much air, the paint will be dry, have very little "flow" and likely produce an "orange peel" texture. The build will be thinner than desired and a fast "flash dry" on the surface may not allow solvents trapped underneath to escape. While either condition could probably be corrected in a basecoat by sanding, with a finish coat heavy runs or severe orange peel

139

Color is applied starting at the top and working down.

coating for durability and appearance. Too thin a paint layer may cause the finish to peel or fade. A thin color coating is also easily rubbed through in the buffing/polishing process. The recommended thickness for a single stage color finish is 2 1/2 mils. One mil is 1/1000 or .001 inch, about the thickness of a sheet of plastic food wrap. To build a paint layer of the desired 2 1/2 mil thickness, you will need to apply 2 to 3 wet coats.

The typical mixing ratio for acrylic enamel is 2 parts color to 1 part reducer. Adding hardener changes the mixing ratio as do additives such as fisheye reducers and gloss enhancers. Always check the mixing instructions for the products you are using. Allow 15 to 20 minutes drying time after each coat. Refer to the Product Information sheet for the recommended number of coats.

Single stage finishes can be micro sanded using very fine 1000 to 1500 grit sandpaper followed by compounding to remove any minor imperfections and to bring out gloss. Be very careful not to sand along sharp curves or ridges—like the letter reveals on the tailgate. These edges have less paint buildup and will sand off and expose the primer very quickly. To prevent accidentally sanding into low paint buildup areas, place masking tape over any sharp edges (like the ridge around the hood on 1967-1972 Chevy and GMC trucks and any sharp curves like the tailgate letters.

Micro sanding will leave the finish somewhat dull, so to restore the gloss the paint needs to be buffed with polishing

could result in sanding down the finish and starting over again—an expensive, time-consuming process that's better avoided by understanding how to select and adjust the gun setup to best suit the paint product you're spraying.

The first step in setting a proper fluid-to-air ratio is to request the setup chart for your make and model spray gun from your paint supplier. Product manufacturers print these charts showing fluid tip and air cap combinations recommended for various paints and primers. Now you can adjust the spray gun for proper atomization.

Adjust the air regulator (at the air line drop) to the appropriate psi range. As a rule of thumb, use the lowest pressure required to achieve full atomization and a good spray pattern. Set the regulator near the bottom end of the range and adjust upward if needed.

Hold the gun stationary at a 90 degree angle, horizontal to a test surface and the appropriate distance for the drying speed of the paint (typically 8 to 10 inches).

Squeeze the trigger on the gun to full open. Gradually adjust the air/fan control on the gun.

Repeat the triggering/adjusting operation until you have a smooth elliptical spray pattern 8 to 12 inches in width.

Applying a Single Stage Color Finish

All older color coatings were single stage, meaning that the color was not overcoated with a clear paint film. Today single stage finishes are still available in acrylic enamel. These are the easiest paints for the amateur to apply. Besides runs and drips, the painter's main concern is laying on a sufficiently thick

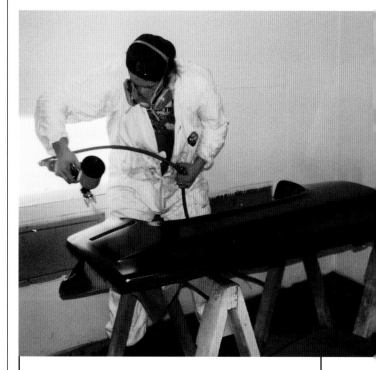

Fenders should be painted from the same batch of paint as the cab to avoid color shifts.

Masking tape should be used to prevent chipping when assembling forward sheet metal.

Small parts are also painted and carefully stored for assembly.

compound. This will bring out the gloss. It is very difficult and time consuming to polish a finish effectively by hand so a power buffer should be used.

Applying Basecoat/Clearcoat

These newer two-part finishes offer the rich gloss formerly found only in hand-rubbed lacquer. However, lacquer finishes are very fragile and the solvents are outlawed in many areas, making this paint largely a relic of the past. Although more difficult to spray than a single stage finish, basecoat/clearcoat color systems can be successfully applied by an amateur who precisely follows every detail of the paint product manufacturer's mixing and spraying instructions.

Thickness or build is also critical in two stage finish systems; however, now you have to gauge the thickness of both the basecoat *and* the clearcoat. The basecoat is typically kept thin, about one mil. Recommended basecoat thickness is two medium coats with an additional coating or two sometimes required to achieve consistent color. The coatings are applied medium dry as opposed to wet and require only 5 to 10 minutes flash time before recoating. The typical mixing ratio is 1 part paint to 1 1/2 parts reducer as basecoats are not designed to dry glossy. The flat finish you see as the basecoat dries will remain until the clearcoat is applied at which point the true color will also appear.

Any runs or sags can be sanded out using 500 grit sandpaper after 30 minutes drying time. After sanding, trouble spots need to be recoated. The basecoat should dry (cure) 10

minutes times the number of coats or 20 to 30 minutes depending on whether 2 or 3 coats were applied). If the clearcoat isn't applied at immediately after this cure time, you'll need to make sure the waiting period doesn't exceed the basecoat's recoat window—24 hours is the typical. If the recoat window expires, you'll need to scuff sand and add another coating of basecoat before spraying the clear. The clearcoat should be twice as thick (2 to 2 1/2† mils) as the basecoat—two to three full coats (with some products four coats may be recommended if the finish is to be polished). Be sure to wait the recommended on dry time between coats. Follow mixing instructions and spray gun settings exactly as they are printed on the product information sheets. If drips or sags occur, the damage can be sanded after the clearcoating has cured, but the repair will have to be recoated.

Cleaning the Spray Gun

To avoid problems in the future, the spray gun should be properly and cleaned after each use. As soon as the painting session is finished, the gun should be back flushed by placing a cloth over the nozzle and triggering the gun for a blast or two. Triggering the gun against the tight cloth seal forces painting material back into the cup. Next, remove the cup and pour out the paint. Now pour in about a quarter-cup of solvent compatible with the paint product. Tighten the air nozzle and trigger the gun until it sprays clear solvent. Loosen the air nozzle, cover with a cloth, and repeat the back flush step.

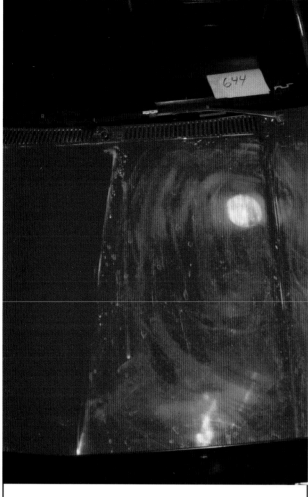

Micro-sanding should not be deep, but leaves a dull finish.

Polishing restores the finish's gloss.

If the spray gun is a siphon type, hold the gun vertical and shake it up and down while triggering against the cloth. This motion jiggles solvent out the pressure hole in the cup lid, helping keep the hole clean and open.

Now tighten the air nozzle and then remove the cup. Dip the cloth in solvent and wipe both the outside of the gun and the cup until completely clean. Replace the cup and return the gun to storage. Observing this procedure after each use will keep the gun clean and working properly.

Changes in Spraying Technology

Along with paints, the spraying technology is changing. Automotive finishes have been applied with high pressure (35 to 80 psi) spraying that results in only 25 to 30 percent of the paint product coating the vehicle. The other two-thirds of the paint and solvents are blasted off the vehicle's surface as overspray and are either exhausted into the atmosphere or settle on nearby objects (including the painter). The

painter who is not wearing a proper respirator, inhales large amounts of this overspray—with grave health consequences. The hobbyist concerned with painting only one vehicle may not consider the cost of paint and solvents lost in overspray a significant waste, but to the professional painter, losing 70 to 75 percent of product means a sizeable financial waste. Painting overspray also damages the air we breathe.

To address both of these concerns, professional refinishers are switching to low pressure paint spraying equipment called HVLP (high volume, low pressure). Hobbyists are well advised to follow the professional's lead. The new HVLP technology creates little overspray and applies up to 90% of the paint to the vehicle. The major change in technique with HVLP is holding the gun closer to the surface and using a slightly faster painting stroke.

Unlike conventional paint spraying, which requires a high pressure, HVLP requires a high rate of air delivery (15 cfm at 39 psi.). With the compressor supplying a high volume of air, moisture is a hazard. The air supply should be run through piping so that moisture can be drained (through drain taps in the piping). Painters should also use moisture filters and dryers placed in the air supply and an in-line filter at the spray gun.

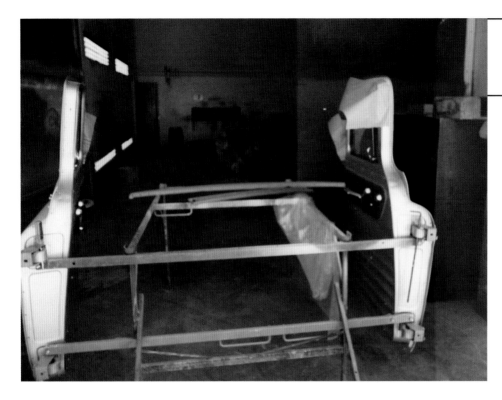

Correcting Problems with the Color Finish

Unlike primer coatings where problems can be sanded out and covered in the next coating, errors in the color finish can be a major setback, possibly requiring that the finish be sanded and re-sprayed. By knowing about and avoiding these problems the added time and expense to correct them can be avoided. Likely problems include

Dust or dirt particles in the paint as well as insects if spraying is done in an open shop. Don't try to pick out dust or dirt particles (or an errant insect) while the finish is still wet. Wait until the finish dries (typically 24 hours). With solid colors or clear coat, wet sand with 1200 to 1500 sandpaper then polish. Wax and grease remover works well as a sanding lubricant.

Sags or runs on vertical surfaces occur because the paint was applied too thick and too fast. Depending on how bad they are and their location, sags and runs may be removed by microsanding and polishing. Runs or sags in the basecoat mus be removed before you apply the clearcoat.

Orange peel, a rough finish texture, resembling the skin of an orange, occurs when the spray gun air pressure setting is too low, the gun held at the wrong distance from the surface, or the paint is improperly mixed with reducer.

Lack of gloss so that the finish looks dull or dry is caused when the air pressure at the spray gun is set too high or paint buildup is too thin. A dull finish can also result from too much solvent added to the paint or solvent that evaporates too fast.

Fisheyes—tiny bubble in the paint that look like fish eyes—are caused by the presence of silicone, either from a wax coating that wasn't properly removed or from silicone-based products, such as Armor All, that are present in the air and settle on vehicle surfaces in the shop. Where silicone is present on the panel surface, it resists the paint, which then forms a circle around the affected area. Oil in the air supply line is another cause. Silicone is the painter's curse. Fortunately, fisheyes can be prevented with painting additives.

Advanced Design Pin Striping

On Chevrolet trucks of the Advance Design series, the pinstriping consisted of two stripes on the wheel rims and one stripe around the cab. The stripes were 1/8 of an inch wide. The cab stripe was located right in the middle of the two creases, which formed what is referred to as the cab belt. Standard wheel color on the Advance Design series was black. Deluxe wheels were painted body color and pin striped. The stripes are 1/4 inch wide and the outer stripe is located dead center on the valve stem hole. There is a 3 3/2 space between the inner and outer stripes. The inner stripe is not covered by the hubcap, but is near the hubcap's outer edge.

143

A major advantage to powder coating and the primary reason for its increased use in industrial applications, is its essential safety and ease of application. But for the hobbyist, the attraction of powder coating is how much fun you'll have doing it. As added benefits, powder coating eliminates complicated mixing formulas with solvents, catalysts, and hardeners, exposure to toxic chemicals, and the need for a ventilated painting area, or even a high level of skill. When applying the powder coating you should wear a respirator with a charcoal-activated filter, but for mixing and cleanup, a dust mask is all that's needed.

Powder coating isn't a painting, at least not in the traditional sense of a liquid coating. The powder is finely ground plastic that requires heat to melt and flow. The finish is tougher and more chemically resistant than paint. Should a wrench slip and strike a powder coated surface you're not even likely to see a scratch. Spill solvent or a corrosive chemical like DOT 3 brake fluid on powder coating and you may see temporary wet look but no lifting or other permanent damage.

Although powder coating isn't practical for the truck itself, it's ideal for many suspension and engine parts as well as metal trim pieces. The coating doesn't work for most sheet metal items because the coatings aren't formulated to the manufacturers' finish colors and because most sheet metal pieces would require a very large oven to melt the powder.

The Equipment

Until rather recently, powder coating equipment was too expensive for most hobbyists and required an industrial baking oven. The breakthrough in do-it-yourself powder coating came in 1998 when The Eastwood Company released its HotCoat powder coating system. Although the HotCoat applicator gun works comparably to professional equipment at a very low price, for the hobbyist, the breakthrough wasn't the gun but a solution to baking the plastic. Few hobbyists could be expected to purchase the HotCoat applicator system if they also had to buy and install an expensive baking oven. But for most hobbyist powder coating uses, a regular kitchen oven will suffice. However, you can't use the same over for power coating that you use for cooking food.

You'll need to purchase (from GoodWill Industries or other used appliance outlet) a kitchen range with a working oven and install the appliance in your shop.

The HotCoat® system consists of the applicator gun, powder cup and disposable filter, aswell as the power supply unit and activator switch. The gun requires both a 110-120 volt AC power source and an air supply. The air requirements are so low that a portable regulated air tank would be adequate for powder coating one or two parts; however for coating a batch of parts you'll need an air compressor whose air supply can be regulated to less than 10 psi. The gun requires less than .5 cfm at 8 psi, so a small hobbyist compressor will suffice. Along with the gun and air supply, you will need to purchase small quantities of the desired shades of powder. Popular colors include Semi-Gloss Black (for chassis parts), Stamped Steel or Cast Iron (for underbody and chassis parts that left the factory unpainted), Chevy Orange (for Chevrolet engine parts), and Satin or Gloss Clear (for protecting and enhancing the appearance of polished items). Some of the textured and translucent specialty colors may also be desirable. Since powder coating eliminates virtually all material waste, an 8 oz. container will coat numerous parts.

Three additional items are highly desirable and should be included on an initial order. The first is the High Performance Deflector, a low cost tip for the gun that improves transfer efficiency. The second is a roll of high temperature masking tape, which is needed if only some of the surfaces on the parts are to be coated. The third is a set of extra gun cups with lids. Although cleanup takes little time and is done mostly with compressed air, having a supply of extra gun cups eliminates the need to clean the cup—either at the end of the powder coating session or when changing powder colors. Labeled

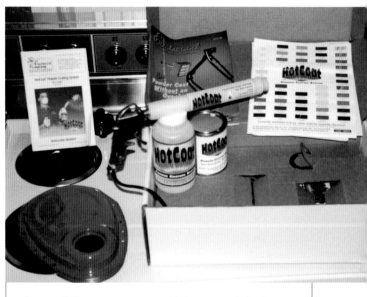

Eastwood's Hotcoat system uses a kitchen oven to bake the powder. The same oven can't be used to prepare food.

with a marker, the cups can be used to store the various colors of powder.

Depending on the condition of the parts being powder coated, you may need to purchase high temperature filler to use in smoothing pits or other flaws in the metal. While powder coating is intended as a one-step finish over bare metal, the coating can also be used over primer and filler if these products are designed to withstand baking temperatures of up to 500 degrees F. For filler, Eastwood sells a product called Lab Metal. An assortment of high temperature plugs is also useful to fill holes in parts. Unless threaded holes are plugged or covered, the powder will coat the threads and make bolts difficult to thread into the holes.

With the equipment and supplies in place, you'll also need a baking oven. For small items, a toaster oven that plugs into 110v AC household current can be used. For larger pieces, you'll need an electric kitchen oven. Eastwood cautions against using gas ovens to bake its powder coating. Note that a kitchen oven requires 220v AC. With a second hand kitchen oven installed in your shop, you'll be able to powder coat such items as, valve covers, wheels and most suspension items, along with a variety of smaller parts.

How Powder Coating Works

Powder coating using the HotCoat system is actually simpler than painting from an aerosol can because there's no danger of runs from too much powder (if the coating seems a little thick, you blow or wipe it off and start over). The object being coated receives an electrical charge, which attracts the powder to the part and even draws the powder around curved edges. The risk of failure with this system is just about zero, even for someone who has never tried the powder coating process before.

As with liquid painting, the first step is preparing the parts. The metal needs to be clean and rust free; however, it's possible to powder coat over chrome or painted finishes,

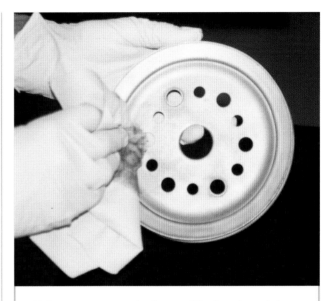

It's important to remove dust from sandblasting using a cloth dipped in a acid etch solution. Note the plastic gloves to keep skin oils from contaminating the metal.

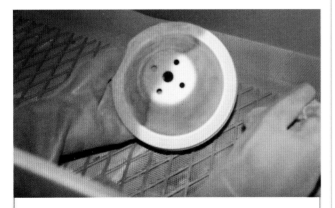

Sandblasting removed the rust from the crank pulley and gave a smooth surface for the powder.

Powder is simply poured into the gun dispenser.

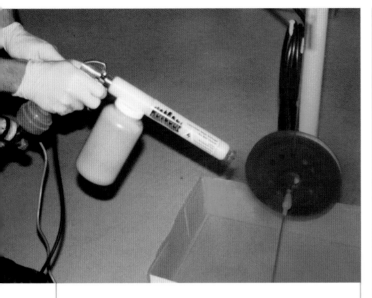

A grounding clip to the gun is attached to the part to provide an electrostatic attraction for the powder.

Before spraying on the coating, you may need to rig some sort of hanger to hold the part so that all surfaces can be coated. To catch any stray powder, which can be reused, box lid or similar container can be placed under the fixture from which parts are being suspended.

To start the actual coating process, clamp the ground lead from the gun is clamped to the part in some location where its mark won't be seen in the finished coating, or to the wire suspending the part. After adding powder to the gun cup and setting the air supply to 8 psi, you're ready to begin. It's also important that the air supply be moisture free. An air compressor that has been working hard for abrasive blasting should have the moisture bled from its tank before powder coating begins. Eastwood supplies a disposable moisture separator with the HotCoat gun, but a water extractor or dryer in the air line is also desirable. If the powder gets wet, it turns to unsprayable goo.

You'll be surprised at what happens when you trigger the gun. The powder isn't expelled under pressure, like conventional spray painting. Instead, it drifts toward the part in slow motion like leaves falling down from trees on an autumn day. Because the grounding clip from the gun has given the part an attracting electrostatic charge. The powder blows in only onto the part. In my first powder coating experience, I held the gun steady, sweeping it across the part as I do when spraying solvent-based paints. My instructor told me to loosen my wrist, shake the gun slightly as though I'd just finished a cup of strong coffee. A slight shaking motion agitates the powder and helps assure a constant feed. The powder coating process is so simple, it's just about impossible to goof.

When you've finished coating the part with powder, you need to momentarily touch the emitter (metal rod protruding from the tip of the gun) against the grounding clip attached to

providing the underlying finish will not blister or lift under powder coat's 400 degree F. baking temperature.

Rusted parts should be abrasive blasted to bare steel. After blowing off any sand residue, the metal should be wiped clean with metal prep and allowed to air dry. Be sure to wear vinyl gloves while washing and handling the parts, both to protect your skin from the metal prep's mild acid solution and to avoid contaminating the metal with oil from your skin.

If the object being coated has surfaces that should remain bare, these surfaces have to be masked with a high-temperature tape.

The freshly coated pulleys are now suspended in the baking oven.

Baking melts the powder, forming an attractive, durable coating.

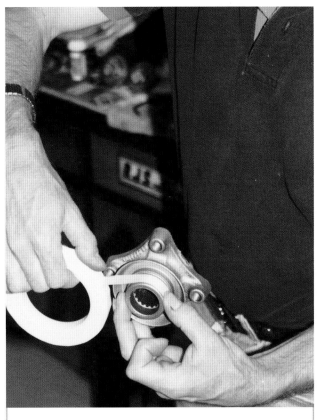

Surfaces that should not be powder coated need to be masked. Eastwood sells a high temperature masking tape to be used for this purpose.

When all the surfaces have turned glossy, the coating needs to cure for another 10 minutes, at which point you can turn off the heat, open the oven door slightly, and let the part gradually cool. Cooling the part too quickly, as in taking it out of the oven immediately after curing, can dull the finish.

While you'll nearly always be pleased with the quality of the finish, if the gloss isn't quite as sharp as you want or the finish has a little too much orange peel texture, the cured coating can be smoothed by wet sanding with 400 grit wet/dry sandpaper and then compounded to a higher luster with a paint polishing compound or buffed using white rouge on a loose section buffing wheel.

Safety

A dust mask provides sufficient respiratory protection from the powder when applying the powder coating. Though not toxic, the powder could be a respiratory irritant and should not be inhaled. Eastwood recommends wearing an activated charcoal respirator when checking on the powder as it cures because at this stage the powder gives off mildly toxic fumes. You may also detect a slight odor.

The biggest safety risk with powder coating is the potential flammability of powder dust suspended in air. Adequate ventilation in the spraying area, a clean shop, and being careful to eliminate all possible sources of ignition are the necessary precautions to counter this risk. Never smoke or allow someone who is smoking to enter the powder coating area. Make sure the electric oven is in good repair with no dangling wires and that all shop wiring conforms to code. Because of possible sparks from the motor, do not use a shop vacuum to clean up powder coating residue. Also, because of the powder's potential flammability, do not use a gas oven to cure powder-coated parts.

Clean Up

The spray gun and powder cup are cleaned with a few quick shots of compressed air. You'll save cleanup time for yourself by wearing disposable vinyl gloves and you should wear a dust mask throughout the powder coating process. Any powder that gets on your skin or clothing should first be blown off with compressed air and can be washed off with soap and water. Very little powder is likely to be lost in the coating process. Laying a box, flat sheet of cardboard, or a tarp under the spraying area allows any stray powder can be collected and reused. To be sure that any powder collected in this way is free of contaminants, the residue should be filtered though a paint strainer as it is poured back into the container.

One of power coating's biggest advantages is that any unusable residue can be disposed of as household waste. Since the powder consists primarily of pulverized plastic, spillage does not create an environmental hazard and cleanup requires only the precautions mentioned above.

the part. You'll hear a click and see a small spark. This action discharges the gun. If you fail to do this, you may receive the gun's electrical discharge. Now you can set down the gun and unplug the power unit. If the part is coated evenly and completely, it can be placed in the oven for heating.

Eastwood's instructions call for preheating the oven to 400 degrees F. and checking the temperature with an oven thermometer or an infrared thermometer. However, if you've checked the accuracy of the oven's temperature settings, you can just turn the dial to 400 and wait for the preheat light to go off. The problem with these instructions is that you're placing parts in a hot oven where you could burn yourself and possibly drop the part. So, before heating the oven, it's a good idea figure out how you're going to place or suspend the part(s) in the oven. You might hang suspending wires from the oven racks or you might purchase racks from Eastwood to suspend parts in the oven.

Once the powder reaches its curing temperature (about 400 degrees F; 204 degrees C) you'll see the coating begin to melt. If you watch the process through the oven window, you'll see the dull, flat powder melt into to a smooth, glossy finish.

147

Powder Coating Die Cast Parts

From the 1930s to the 1950s, Chevrolet trucks used die cast stampings for trim pieces. Also called pot metal, die cast is porous and can present problems for both chrome plating (which is typically the original coating) and powder coating. In the plating process, the metal is immersed in chemical vats and the liquid often seeps into the porous metal. Since die cast that might be powder coated has previously been plated, liquid absorbed during the plating process may still reside inside the metal.

When a trim piece that has been powder coated is heated, contaminants may boil out of the metal producing bubbles or pits in the finish. To prevent this from happening, heat die cast and other porous parts such as cast aluminum or magnesium to between 200 and 400 degrees F. Then the parts are allowed to cool. This process should remove trapped contaminants prior to powder coating.

The main reason for powder coating die cast trim is to avoid having to replate these items. The plating process not only traps contaminants, but can also release contaminants that were absorbed earlier. When this happens the plating will be marked with bubbles or pits, just as might occur with powder coating. However, in plating, there's no way to boil out contaminants ahead of time, so when replating die cast, the outcome is always uncertain. Having to replate a part to get rid of the bubbles generally makes things worse. For this reason, if plating isn't needed for authenticity, powder coating makes a desirable alternative for die cast trim.

Special Effects

While you wouldn't normally coat a die cast trim piece with standard color, a specialty or hi-tech color, such as a translucent or a reflective, can be eye catching. Reflective Chrome is a popular coating for die cast trim because it's the closest to real chrome plating that you'll ever get from a spray gun. Creative, original colors can be created by applying a translucent or reflective powder over a chrome or silver base. Powder coating offers many options for dramatic effects or for keeping bare metal parts looking like new.

Brighten Parts with Reflective Chrome

Applications for Reflective Chrome powder coating include numerous smaller engine, suspension, and trim parts that might otherwise be chrome plated. On suspension pieces, especially, the bright powder coating is superior to chrome plating because the electroplating process can cause hydrogen embrittlement, which weaken steel parts. Of all the parts you don't want weakened, suspension and steering pieces are at the top of the list. Also, elecroplating is dangerous and environmentally hostile, whereas powder coating is safe and environmentally friendly. Additionally, chrome plating is expensive whereas powder coating using the HotCoat system is cheap.

An air cleaner cover is another good candidate for powder coating. With smaller parts, several items can be baked at the same time.

On a show truck or street rod, the wheels could be another candidate for Reflective Chrome. Keep in mind that Reflective Chrome isn't real chrome plating, so you wouldn't want to powder coat diecast trim, or coat the wheels with Reflective Chrome on truck you are restoring for show, It works fine for a truck you are refurbishing to drive, or for a custom truck.

Reflective Chrome turns distressed trim and some otherwise painted parts into one of the truck's most embellishing features without the exhorbitant expense of restorative chrome plating.

Add Color Tints with Translucents

If the plating on a diecast trim piece is still sound, you can color tint the part with a translucent powder coating. You'll find that the baked and melted powder adheres to chrome much better than paint. And you're certainly not limited to coating diecast; infact, the opposite is the case as diecast is often an undesirable base for reasons discussed above.

Metal interior pieces such as door handles and window cranks make good candidates for Translucent, Reflective Chrome, or straight color powder coating as long as the parts are free of plastic knobs or springs that might be harmed by baking. As previously mentioned, for maximum effect, the translucent coatings should be applied over chrome, but polished metal also provides a reflective base as does an Argent Silver powder coating base. If you want to preserve a polished

Since valve covers are a prime part to powder coat, we experimented with this cast aluminum set from a Corvette.

Now, Rich Jensen, whose shop we were using for the powder coating, wipes the powder off the valve cover ridges and lettering. If he makes a mistake, no problem. We'll simply spray on more powder.

Wiping the powder off the ridges and lettering gives this cover a factory appearance.

finish as is, you can coat the metal with Super Gloss Clear powder. Possible candidates for polishing and clear coating include aluminum under hood parts like water inlets and performance intake manifolds.

Metal nameplate scripts and emblems can also be customized and dressed up with powder coating. For example, if the nameplate script overlays a metal plate, you could powder coat the plate, wipe the powder off the script and have a two-tone chrome and translucent nameplate. Just be sure you're working with metal, not plastic as is used on more modern nameplates.

Wrinkle Texture for a Performance Look

Engine valve covers take on a whole different personality when powder coated with a Wrinkle finish. To give the cover a more professional look, you can wrap a shop towel around an index finger and carefully wipe the powder coating from the Chevrolet lettering (the name is stamped into Chevrolet V-8 valve covers of the 1950s and 1960s). Wiping off the finish from selected areas is one of the abilities of powder coating that is difficult if not impossible with liquid paints.

149

This wipe-off treatment—virtually impossible with liquid paints—works with other parts too.

Wrinkle texture makes a muscular-appearing backdrop for custom instrument panels as well. Just be sure the panel material is metal. Plastic won't withstand powder coating's 400 degree F. melting and curing temperatures.

Preserve Original Appearance of Cast Iron and Stamped Steel Parts

Many under hood and suspension parts aren't coated at the factory. Here the challenge for the restorer is keeping these parts looking factory-new without adding a non-original clear finish. A good example is the brake master cylinder reservoir, which will not retain paint if filled with DOT 3 brake fluid and will quickly rust if left uncoated. Coating the master cylinder with

Cast Iron powder prevents corrosion and preserves the part's new-from-the factory appearance. Stamped Steel powder coating can be used on many suspension and driveline pieces.

Brake drums and disc brake hubs are other candidates for these coatings. Assuming the drums have been cleaned and sandblasted, and that the linings will be turned, it's not necessary to mask, except to prevent powder from entering the hub or coating the bearing race. On disc brakes the hub can be powder coated and the rotors area kept bare by wiping off any stray powder.

High Temperature Exhaust Manifold Coating

Most paints and coatings won't withstand the high temperatures (1000 degrees F or higher) that engine exhaust manifolds

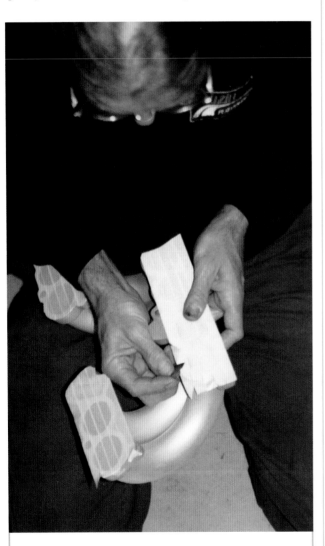

Rich Jensen carefully trims the masking tape with an X-acto knife.

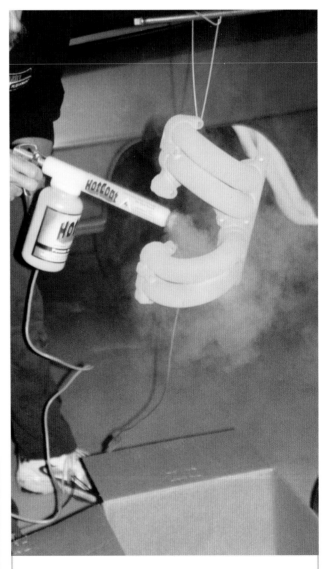

Again, the powder is sprayed on.

Notice the use of welder's gloves when handling hot parts.

can experience. Special high temperature powder coating for these parts can preserve a cast iron manifold's original appearance and can also protect exhaust headers.

Mixing and Tinting

While powder doesn't mix and tint like paint, it is possible to mix small amounts of powder of a darker or lighter color with a standard color to alter the standard color's hue. You'll want to mix the powder well and test the color on a scrap part. For example, you might add a small quantity of Black to Medium Green to achieve produce a shade of Hunter Green, but it's also possible that the mix will produce a variegated (streaked or spotted) color. In some instances, the variegated finish may be desirable for a custom effect. Still, it's best to mix a small amount and see what it produces rather than waste material and effort on a finish that isn't what you wanted and isn't easily removed.

Powder Coating has more color flexibility than you might think. However, this flexibility doesn't extend to mixing opaque or translucent colors unless you're looking for a speckled "salt and pepper" effect.

Smoked Chrome

A tint of black adds another twist to powder's bright coatings. Smoked Chrome can add an interesting contrast with reflective bright work. Since the tint gives brightness without glitter, Smoked Chrome may be a desirable coating for bumper guards and similar trim pieces.

Prism Finishes

If you want a multi-colored prism finish, you can add a small amount of Prism powder (the mixing ratio is 1 part Prism additive to 40 parts powder). The Prism additive contains multi-colored flecks, not just aluminum, so it gives a combination pearlescent and metallic effect, which is especially dramatic when added to dark colors—especially black.

Powder Coating Shop Tools

If your wrenches are hardware store variety, rather than professional tools, you could try the powder mixes out on them. Most generic wrenches have adequate tolerances to accommodate the 0.003 inch to 0.004 inch powder build without affecting the size.

Powder coating's uses and special effects are virtually endless, limited only by the size of the baking oven and your ingenuity. Keep in mind that if the powder coating surface isn't as mirror smooth as you'd like, you can always compound and buff the finish.

Non-Powder Detailing Paints

While powder coating has many applications for detailing engine compartment and chassis parts, not all engine and chassis items can be powder coated, usually because they can't be baked. In restorations also, you're often challenged with detailing parts that were originally cadmium plated, a coating no longer available. With these parts you can use specialized detailing paints, usually provided in aerosol (rattle) cans. These include, Eastwood's Gold Cadmium system of four tints that overlay to create the reflective, multi¬hued look of cadmium. Brake boosters and calipers are another common application.

Carb Renew, available in either silver and bronze, is detailing paint formulated to imitate the factory plating on carburetors.

If you're wondering whether or not your truck's wiring needs replacing, the simplest way to make that decision is to take a close look at the condition of the wiring. If the insulation is cracked or maybe even missing in places, or new wiring has been spliced in and old wires wrapped with electrical tape, a new wiring harness is definitely in order. Failure to replace deteriorated wiring invites problems on the road, burned-out electrical equipment, or an electrical fire that can destroy the vehicle and the truck as well as the building in which it is stored. If you have any doubt about your truck's wiring, replace it. As you will discover in this chapter, the procedure is not difficult and does not require electrical expertise. On a frame-up restoration, you will install a new wiring harness as a matter of course.

On a frame-up restoration, the harness will have been removed when the truck is disassembled so a wiring diagram plus the instructions provided with the harness will be used to show the correct connections. For a guide as to where to route the harness, you will need to refer to photos you took of your truck before disassembly, the factory assembly manual, or other original or correctly restored trucks.

Tools and Supplies

Regardless of the truck you are rewiring you will need essentially the same tools and supplies, including a new wiring harness, a shop manual with wiring diagram, pliers, wire stripper, butt connectors, assorted screwdrivers—regular and Phillips—a socket set, vise grips, test light (a VOM meter is also desirable), and in some cases a steering wheel puller.

Be sure to order the harness only from a reputable vintage Chevy parts dealer or wiring harness manufacturer. I've had Chevy truck owners tell me that the"bargain" harnesses they ordered from a discount mail order auto parts outfits was so far from original standards in color coding, wire size, and lengths, that they had to discard it and order another from a quality wiring harness supplier. A quality harness will be constructed of the correct gauge wire and covering (although some harness manufacturers offer plastic coated wiring as an optional replacement for older original fabric insulation) and have the original color coding. All these details contribute to the ease of installation.

Preparation

With the harnesses you should receive written and illustrated instructions showing hookup connections. Even so, you should also have a service manual with a wiring diagram for your year and model truck to refer to as you install the harness.

(Wiring diagrams can also be purchased separately.) The wiring diagram will help you understand your truck's electrical system and will be used to troubleshoot any problem circuits. Before replacing the wiring, spend enough time studying the wiring diagram so that you are recognize the major circuits and understand the color coding scheme. The wiring diagram will identify each wire by its color (and sometimes by gauge as well). You should practice tracing various color wires from a component, the tail light for example, to their power source or ground. This way, if you have questions about which wire from the harness attaches to which terminal on a component, you can find the answer in the wiring diagram. As you study the wiring diagram you will also realize why it is so important to have a correctly color coded harness.

Wiring diagrams for trucks built before the mid to late 1950s won't show signal lights due to the fact that until this time signal lights were considered an aftermarket add-on, installed either by the dealer or owner. Lights used for signaling during this period were typically mounted on the front fenders and at the corners of the box and were turned on or off by a switch that clamped to the steering column. If you are restoring your truck for show competition, you will probably choose to omit signal lights on trucks where they were after market items, but if you plan to drive your truck, signal lights are important for safety in today's traffic where other drivers will probably mistake hand signals as gestures.

You can usually tell if the wiring needs replacing by looking at it. Cracked or frayed insulation, spots of bare wire, dangling connectors are the tell-tale signs.

In addition to the instructions with the new harness, a wiring diagram for your truck is very useful.

Where signal lights were not factory equipment, the tail lights and parking lights can be wired to use for this purpose. The harness manufacturer may even offer a supplementary signal light harness using these lights. In many instances, though, using the tail lights as signals will mean that a second tail light has to be installed.

Where signal lights were not factory equipment, many restorers converted the parking and tail lights on their trucks to serve this function as well. You will find the signal light conversion especially easy to do if you specify the signal light option (for earlier trucks without factory-wired signal lights) when you order the wiring harness. To make the conversion, it will still be necessary to change the parking and tail lights to double filament bulbs and add a signal light switch, but with this addition to the new harness you won't be splicing in new-style plastic coated and odd-colored wires for the signal lights.

It's a good idea to consider other options that may be available with the harness as well. As mentioned earlier, some manufacturers build older-style fabric insulated harnesses either with the original cotton insulation or with modern plastic coated wiring. The cotton wrapping is required for originality, but it you are restoring or rebuilding your truck to drive, plastic coated wire will be more durable.

During Chevy's Advance Design styling period, two different fuel tank sending units were used: one with a separate ground wire and one where the sending unit grounded to the tank. You'll need to check your truck's original wiring or a wiring diagram for your truck to order the right harness. If you plan to equip your truck with an original heater, and this accessory also ties into the electrical system, you also need a

heater harness. Accessories such as overdrive (not available on Chevrolet trucks until the mid 1950s) also required a separate harness, as does the optional tachometer on late 1960s and 1970s trucks.

Besides making sure that the wires on the new harness are connected to the correct terminals on the gauges and other electrical components, it is also important that the contacts be clean, and circuits like the lights that ground through the body sheet metal are making a good grounding connection. Electrical systems in older cars and trucks used a rather primitive grounding method whereby most circuits ground through the body metal and frame. On urestored vehicles, this ground path is easily broken by rust buildup while on restored trucks a heavy coating of paint can break the ground path. You can help assure a good ground by using new or derusted and replated bolts to attach the electrical components (like the lights, for example) and to scrape away paint or surface rust at some of the mounting points to make provide that a good ground path.

Another preparation step, buy new grommets and junction blocks before installing the new harness. On Advanced Design pickups, the junction blocks are mounted on the front inner fender and are made from fiberboard. The grommets are used to plug holes where the wiring passes through the firewall and other locations in the sheet metal. Both junction blocks and grommets are available from most vintage Chevrolet pickup parts suppliers.

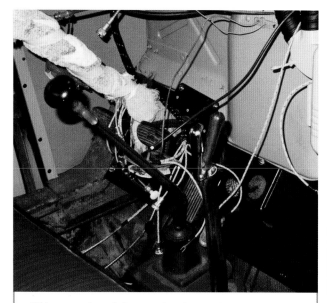

With a properly made harness, the wires will be color-coded to match the wiring diagram.

To be original, older wiring harnesses used a fabric wrapping. The harness manufacturer may give the option of fabric or plastic wrapping and the choice will depend on your purpose for the truck.

Here, the rebuilder is using wiring salvaged from another truck.

Replacing the Old Harness

The first step in installing the new wiring is to lay out the new harness on the ground along the driver's side of the truck. The portion of the harness that runs under the hood and to the lights can be installed by disconnecting the old wires and replacing them with new, one terminal at a time. This process is very easy and straight forward, providing the wiring has not been modified greatly. It also works, obviously, only when the original wiring is still in the truck. With a frame-up restoration, the old wiring will have been removed long ago. In these cases, you will have to rely on a wiring diagram (found in a service manual for your year and model truck) and the harness manufacturer's instructions.

Wiring the Dashboard

As you lay out the new harness alongside the old, you may find that the hole through the firewall is not large enough to accommodate both harnesses. You can cut the old harness at the firewall and then disconnect the entire dash wiring as a unit. When doing this, either make a note of the connections or make sure your shop manual is clear on the connections for the headlight switch and gauges. If you plan to repair or replace the gauges or headlight switch, it's a good idea to do this before taking the trouble to hook up the new wiring.

You'll find that removing the seat cushions and sliding the seat all the way back makes the job of lying on your back and working above your head underneath the dash slightly more pleasant. Banging your head on the clutch or brake pedal is something you will not want to do more than once or twice. You will find that it's necessary to have the cushions out to

This restorer has gotten access to the back of the dashboard by loosening the entire dash assembly. David Bush

On older trucks with uncluttered engine compartments, under-hood wiring connections are easy to make.

connect the gas tank wires, so you might as well take them out before working on the cab wiring.

With the old harness out of the way, you can feed the new harness through the firewall. A quality wiring harness will have instructions and a schematic showing wire connectioins that, when combined the Chevrolet Shop Manual, make the task of hooking up the dash wiring as simple as a paint-by-number set. The main problem is the cramped work space and the contortionist position needed to reach most everything under the dash.

Wiring the Cab

If you are installing new wiring in a well-preserved or original truck, you may have to remove the headliner in order to run the dome light wire. This was not necessary in my truck, as there is no headliner left. In a frame-up restoration, the dome light wiring should be run before the headliner is installed. If that is done, the headliner is not a problem. To feed the dome light wire up through the windshield pillar simply tie the new wire to the end of the old wire and pulling it through. You may have to feed a fairly stiff wire down through the puller to use

for pulling the new wire if the wiring has been stripped out of the cab in an earlier disassembly step.

Wiring the Engine Compartment

With the dash and cab wiring connected, you can turn your attention to the engine compartment. All connections here were very easy to make; it's simply a matter of disconnecting one wire and connecting its replacement on the new harness. If you plan on painting or detailing under the hood, this should be done before installing the new wiring. When you come to the connections at the junction blocks (on the front

Here new wiring to the engine compartment has been installed before reattaching the front sheet metal. John Lilga

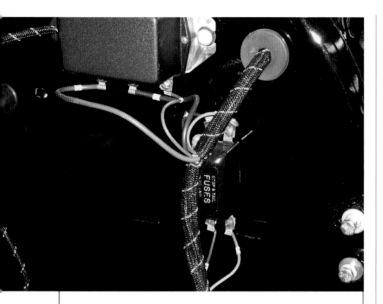

Rubber grommets need to be used where the wiring harness passes through the firewall to prevent chafing and possible short circuits. *John Lilga*

fenders) you will probably also find that the blocks have deteriorated and should be replaced. You will also need a set of grommets to plug the holes where the harness passes through sheet metal. Plugging the holes with grommets gives the new wiring a finished look and prevents chafing which can eventually cut through the harness wrapping and create a short circuit or burn out the electrical system. Most vintage Chevy truck parts suppliers also carry replacement rubber boots to cover the hole where the wiring enters the back of the headlight buckets. In most cases these boots will be deteriorated and should be replaced.

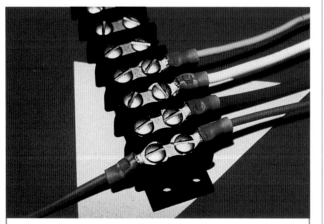

Wiring to the lights may flow through a junction block, somewhat resembling this one.

Wiring the Headlights and Parking Lights

With the driver's side of the new harness wired to its junction block, you can procede to the lights. First, though, remove the headlights and inspect the condition of the buckets. This is a common rust area and in some cases you may have to replace the buckets along with the light sockets.

You may choose to convert the parking lights to serve both as parking lights and turn signals. The first step in this procedure is to run the parking light wire from the junction block through two clips mounted on the front of the fender behind the grille. The second step is to remove the parking light housings. Since you will need to change these lights from single- to double-filament bulbs, it is also necessary to remove the light sockets. Removing the parking lights is very easy. On a 1947-1953 Advance Design series, just two bolts secure each light housing. Another plus is the fact that the light socket is screwed to the housing, not riveted.

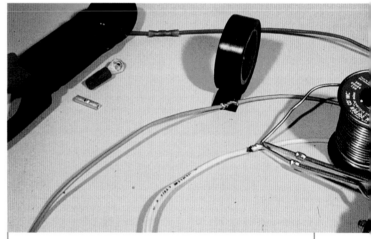

You may want make your own wiring for signal lights and other accessories.

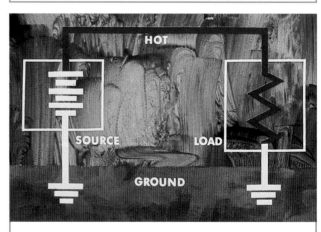

Electrical current always flows from a source to ground.

To add a larger, double filament socket to the light housing, lay the housing on a workbench, back side down. Then, using a small chisel, star the edges of the original hole and bend the new tabs back, insert the larger light socket and bend the tabs tight against it. To make sure the socket don't work loose, drop a bead of solder or braze at several points where the tabs and socket contact. With new sockets installed, replace the parking light housings. The parking light/turn signal conversion is recommended for several reasons: it preserves the truck's original look and is an improvement in appearance over large add-on turn signal lights, and makes driving the truck safer.

Wiring the Coil and Starter

Work continues under the hood connecting the coil and starter If the old harness has been left in place these connections are a simple matter of disconnecting one wire and connecting another. If the harness has been removed, you will carefully follow the instructions with the harness and a wiring diagram. If you plan to replace the ignition switch, now is the time. You will find that making the connections to the ignition switch is easier if attempted from the passenger side.

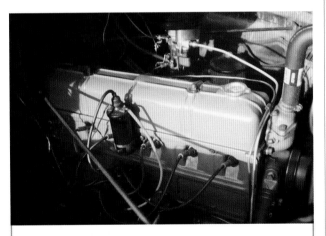

Wiring the coil and starter is a simple process of unhooking the old wire and connecting the new.

Wiring the Dimmer and Brake Light Switches

Now it's down and under to wire the dimmer switch, which is an easy hookup. The brake light switch is a simple connection, but if you plan to replace the switch, now is the time. Besides vintage Chevrolet parts vendors, these switches can be obtained through a local auto parts store.

If the original harness clips were still in place and in good condition, you can reuse them. Otherwise, you can order replacements from one of the vintage Chevrolet truck parts suppliers. These clips hold the harness in place as it runs along the frame.

Wiring to the dimmer and brake light switches can be done from underneath the truck or inside the cab if the floor boards are removed. David Bush

Wiring the Gas Tank

Next, hook up the new wiring to the gas tank. When both single wire and two wire fuel sending unit harnesses were used, as is the case in the Advance Design series, the wiring harness manufacturer will ask you to specify which is correct for your truck. If the old wiring is in place, you can tell easily just by looking at the old harness. If the wiring has been removed, you will have to check the number of connections at the sending unit. Replacing the wiring at the fuel tank was very simple, thanks to YnZ's numbering system and the fact that only the sending unit wire comes from the main loom at this point.

Wiring the Rear Lights

Connecting the rear lights is not overly complicated. Two taillights were an option in 1950, but is seems that over the years most of these trucks have acquired the second light. If the tail lights on your truck have been replaced by after market units and you want to return to the original style light, Jim Carter's Classic Chevrolet Parts has correct replacement lights, as well as mounting brackets.

For running the harness to the rear lights, you may find that the harness provides an extra foot or so of wire to enable you to route the harness in the direction that best suits your needs. I ran the harness to the driver's side light as original and crossed to the passenger side light inside the last frame rail. Two connections are made per light. If you are using the rear lights as turn signals, at this point install the turn signal switch.

Wiring the Horn

Finally, you can hook up the horn. This is a single-wire connection, but the steering wheel must be pulled. There are several ways to remove the steering wheel, but the best with the least chance of damage is using a steering wheel puller. This tool is available from specialty tool suppliers like The Eastwood Company. The new horn wire is pulled up through the steering column by tying it to the old wire.

In addition to making your truck safer to drive, installing a new wiring harness gives the additional bonus of the satisfaction found in a job well done. Replacing the bare and spliced wiring in your truck is an investment you will never regret.

Troubleshooting Electrical Problems

It's not uncommon after installing new wiring that some electrical component will fail to function properly. For potential electrical problems, it's helpful to know some electrical troubleshooting techniques and have an understanding of how an electrical circuit operates.

Check for a Faulty Circuit

Let's start by checking the circuit. If the lights, horn, heater, or some other electrical component won't work, there are three potential causes for the problem. Power is not getting to the

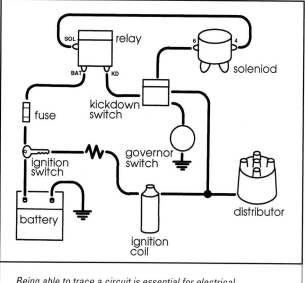

Being able to trace a circuit is essential for electrical troubleshooting.

component, the circuit from the component is open due to a poor ground, or the component itself has failed. Let's use the example of a non-functioning taillight to see how the three potential electrical problems come into play and what trouble shooting approaches are used to solve the problem. We'll assume that when the headlight switch is turned on, the headlights illuminate, but that the taillights don't. If we still had the original wiring, we would probable suspect a break in the wire to the tail lights. With a new harness, we have every reason to

Troubleshooting a faulty circuit means finding the break in the current or identifying the faulty component.

In some cases, the cause of a faulty circuit is in the switch. Different types of switches are shown here.

158

believe that the wiring is intact. Therefore, if the circuit is broken, the break has occurred either though an incorrect or poor connection, or is the result of a poor ground. It is also possible that the tail light bulb is burned out or not properly inserted, though this is not too likely if both lights are out.

Test for Current Flow

The first step when electrical troubleshooting is knowing that the problem has a logical cause. To find the cause, you would begin by removing the tail light lens and bulb. This done, you will check to see if current is flowing to the tail light socket. Two devices can be used to check current flow. One is a simple test light that you can buy for a few dollars in the automotive section of a discount mart or an automotive parts store, or make yourself from an automotive light socket and two short sections of wire (one to bring current to the light and another for ground). The other test device is a VOM meter. A VOM meter is preferred to the test light because it also tells you how much current the circuit is receiving. These meters are available from discount marts and electronics stores.

Whether you are using a test light of VOM meter, the connections will be the same. Place the hot lead (the red wire on the meter or commercial test light) on the contact point in the light socket. Now hold the other lead (which will be black) against the side of the socket. If the test light illuminates, or the meter hand swings into the appropriate current range on its dial (6 volts for a 6 volt electrical system or 12 for a 12 volt system), you know that the problem with the light is a burned our or improperly installed bulb. More likely, the test light or meter will not show current flow. If this is the case, keep the hot lead on the contact point and touch the ground wire to a location on the body or chassis where you are sure to have a good ground. You need to touch the lead to an unpainted

surface, a spot of clean bare metal or a plated bolt should give a good ground. If the light or meter now shows current flow, you know the problem is an improperly grounded tail light.

You can correct for a poor ground in two ways. The first is to remove the light housing, clean the mating surfaces so that some bare metal is exposed, and reattach the housing. If the light socket is dirty or corroded, you will also clean the socket using mild steel wool or emery cloth. Now test the circuit again, this time grounding to the socket. If the test device works, the problem is corrected.

Sometimes it is very difficult to create a good ground through sheet metal. When this happens, you may have to run a ground wire from the component to some point on the chassis. This approach should not be taken when doing a show restoration because the ground lead will be non-original and will cause your truck to lose points. But on a truck that is being overhauled so that it can be enjoyed and driven, running a ground wire is an easy way to assure a properly functioning circuit. You can attach one end of the ground lead either to the component, in this case to the light socket, and the other end to a bolt on the frame.

Test for a Broken Circuit

If current flow didn't result with a good ground, the circuit is broken somewhere ahead of this component. What needs to be done now is to determine the location of the break. You will do this by tracing back along the circuit, following the harness and the referring to a wiring diagram, until you find a switch, junction, or other accessory powered by the same circuit. At this point, you will again test for continuity (power flowing to that point).

When troubleshooting electrical problems, a Volt-ohm meter is very helpful for checking continuity, or current flow.

One common cause of electrical problems is a bad ground due to rusted metal. Likewise, a layer of paint can insulate an electrical component from ground.

With a tail light, tracing back the circuit would take you to the light switch on the dash board (or brake light switch if the problem was with the brake lights). Now you will check to see if the circuit is live to the switch. You will do this by placing the red lead of the test light or VOM meter on the hot lead to the switch (the wiring diagram will show which lead supplies power to the switch). If current is flowing to the switch, the problems may be a corroded or misplaced connection or a faulty switch.

Check first for a poor connection by removing the wire going to the portion of the circuit that is dead (the tail light wire in this case) and cleaning the end of this wire, plus its contact on the switch with a piece of emery cloth. Now replace the wire, turn on the switch, and check the circuit. If the component works, you have solved the problem. If it doesn't, chances are the problem is with the switch. You can test the switch by removing the wire to the component (the tail light in this case) and press it against the hot lead to the switch. The component should work. If this happens, you will need to replace the switch.

This troubleshooting example applies quite commonly to hydraulically operated brake light switches on 1950s and earlier trucks that attach to the back of the master cylinder. Replacements for these switches are still readily available.

By following this step-by-step troubleshooting process, you will be able to trace the source of any electrical problems and make the necessary repairs until all your truck's electrical components are functioning properly. Keep in mind, that its entirely likely that electrical accessories like the horn, clock, heater motor, fuel sending unit, or radio may well have quite working long ago and will have to be rebuilt or replaced..

Other Solutions to Electrical Problems

Some electrical components will simply wear out, others need cleaning, and some need replacement because of exposure to the weather. Because the headlight dimmer switch is located in an area of the cab floor often affected by rust, check the switch for physical damage.

Other electrical items that frequently fail due to rust are the cab courtesy light switches mounted in the doors and cab. These tend to rust and seize up. You can buy generic replacements, but they usually don't work well as they are much larger than the original GM type and require drilling. GM switches can often be obtained from vehicles at salvage yards or may be purchased new from Ron Francis Wire Works. This supplier carries a wide variety of useful electrical components, including complete custom wiring kits.

Dim or flickering lights and headlights do not necessarily indicate major electrical system trouble. Dim lights can be caused by corrosion, faulty grounding, or broken wires. Because the headlamp wiring sits exposed inside the front grille, it is easy for moisture and dirt to accumulate in the lamp sockets and lamp prongs. To fix this problem, take apart the headlight assembly, remove the headlights, and clean the sockets and prongs with contact cleaner or fine sandpaper. Next, check the ground wire from each headlight to the grille. Occasionally the ground wire breaks or comes unscrewed. This connection is often difficult to see and may necessitate removal of the headlight assembly to repair.

Check the headlight control switch and clean it as well. You will be amazed at how much dirt and dust can collect over 25 plus years. The same holds true for the other switches. Clean switches and contacts ensure an uninterrupted electrical flow. If you must replace any switches, they are readily available. In ordering these parts, it is important to know the correct part numbers for your truck—found in a parts book.

If your truck dash came with warning lights (better known as idiot lights), consider adding a set of gauges. Indicator lights simply are not sensitive enough to quickly alert you to any mechanical or electrical problems. A set of below-the-dash mounted gauges is relatively easy to install and will provide a more detailed view of how your engine, lubrication, cooling, and electrical systems are operating. For example, noticing that the amp meter is registering at 16 or 18 instead of 14 can indicate a need to correct a charging system problem before it becomes more serious and expensive to remedy.

Battery Care

The heart of an automotive electrical system is the battery. Unfortunately, in trucks that are stored more than they are driven, batteries often fail even before their warrantee expires. Battery life can be substantially prolonged if these conditions are observed: 1) keep the case clean and dry, 2) make sure the electrolyte stays above the plates and 3) keep the battery fully charged. Dirt and grease on the case form a path for electrical current to follow that can discharge the battery. To keep the case clean, periodically remove the battery from the truck and wash the battery case with a cloth soaked in ammonia or a baking soda and water solution. When washing the case with baking soda, be very careful that none of the solution gets into the cells as it will neutralize the electrolyte. If you are placing the truck in storage, wipe the case dry and place the battery in a location where it won't pick up condensation. (Don't store the battery on a concrete floor where condensation will form under the case, creating a path for electrical discharge).

Before charging always check the level of the electrolyte in the cells. Some electrolyte is lost each time the battery charges and discharges. If the liquid falls below the top of the plates, permanent damage to the battery will result. Distilled water should be used to raise the electrolyte level. On most batteries, the correct electrolyte level (1/4 to 1/2 inch above the plates) is indicated by a ring in the cell port. Because a battery will discharge on its own, periodic charging is required to keep the battery in peak condition. In vehicles that are driven regularly,

The key to long battery life is keeping the battery at or near full charge. One way to do this is with a battery charger whose intelligent circuitry prevents overcharging.

recharging is handled by the generator or alternator. In storage, recharging is done with a battery charger.

The ideal charging rate is 4-6 amps, the output of most home/shop battery chargers. Some old truck owners shorten battery life because they hook up the charger for a short period and think they've brought the battery back to peak energy. Actually brief charging periods raise a battery only slightly from its discharged state.

The most accurate way to tell when a battery is fully charged is to take a reading with a hydrometer. You can also monitor the battery's charge noticing when the amp reading on the battery charger's scale cuts back to one or two amps and stay there. As the battery nears full capacity, its internal voltage rises, causing the charging rate to decrease. Battery chargers are also available that monitor the battery's charge and reduce or stop the charging rate to prevent overcharging. These chargers can be left on a battery indefinitely to maintain full charge.

During recharging, the battery needs to be able to release the hydrogen gas that is created during the charging process. The vent caps contain small holes through which this highly volatile gas can escape. If the vent holes are plugged, pressure will build up inside the battery that can cause an explosion. To prevent any risk of fire or explosion during recharging, remove the cell caps and place a damp cloth over the top of the cells. As the hydrogen gas is released, it will be absorbed into the cloth where it will harmlessly combine with the water molecules. After recharging, the top of the battery case should be wiped dry and the cell caps replaced.

A battery should not stand for more than a couple of weeks without recharging. As a battery discharges, which occurs even in storage, crystals form on the plates that prevent the electrolyte from making contact with the active plate material. These crystals are harmful only when the battery remains discharged for several weeks or if the electrolyte drops below the tops of the plates. When the battery is recharged, these crystals recombine with water in the electrolyte to form sulfuric acid. However, if these crystals are allowed to harden, which will happen if the battery remains in a discharged state, they form a crust that does not fully dissolve during recharging. If this neglect continues, the plate surfaces eventually become coated and the battery must be replaced. Frequent recharging is the secret to long battery life.

Before replacing the battery after storage, be sure to clean the posts and cable clamps, battery hold down frame and bolts. Whenever the battery is been removed, always remember to replace and tighten the case support and hold down clamps.

Maintaining Batteries in Storage

- Charge the battery every two weeks
- Store battery in as cool a place as possible to minimize self discharge
- Keep case clean and dry,
- Don't allow electrolyte level to fall below the tops of the plates
- Install a shut off switch of remove battery cables while vehicle is in storage to prevent possible shorts in the electrical system from discharging the battery or starting a fire.

Electrical Shutoff

Replacing frayed and decayed wiring certainly gives peace of mind, but even so it's wise to disconnect the truck's battery from the electrical system during storage, or even when days or weeks will pass without the truck's being driven. If your truck has an original electric clock, it is imperative to disconnect the battery because the clock will run down the battery in a relatively short period of time and burn itself out in the process. Even on trucks without clocks it's wise to disconnect the battery because of the possibility of an unnoticed trickle discharge somewhere in the system that will not only discharge the battery but could produce a fire.

Rather than loosen and remove a battery terminal each time you store the truck, the easier method is to install a quick disconnect switch on the battery terminal. If you plan to enter your truck in shows, this switch can easily be removed at show time.

All that remains is to get in the habit of using the disconnect switch each time you park your truck. You will also find that the switch provides a small measure of anti-theft protection, since would-be thieves may not notice or want to take time to by-pass the switch.

Although truck interiors are designed for utility, ruggedness, and durability, a vintage Chevy truck would have to be extremely well cared for not to show signs of wear and perhaps some tears on the seat, a sagging headliner, and other signs that the interior needs to be upgraded or replaced. Fortunately, redoing a truck interior is a much simpler and less expensive process than replacing the upholstery in a car. Until the mid-fifties, Chevy truck seat coverings consisted of plain, durable Naugahyde or vinyl, headliners were simple cardboard strips, door panels (when not steel) were vinyl-covered cardboard, and the cowl kick panels were simply painted steel from the Advanced Design series onward (the kick panels are cardboard covered on pre 1947 models). Through the mid-Forties, even the color of the interior was durable. On the Art Deco series (1941-1946) and earlier Chevy trucks, seats and cardboard interior trim were a sort of moose brown color that withstood soiling because dirt and grease blended right in. But that's not to say that a worn, soiled interior will look good in a refinished truck. One of the most dramatic improvements you can make is to recover the seats, refinish the interior, and install new headliner, door, and cowl panels on trucks where these interior coverings apply.

Thanks to seat covering, headliner, and door panel kits, which are available for most Chevrolet light trucks between the years of 1937 to 1972, redoing your truck's upholstery can be a highly satisfying do-it-yourself undertaking. If you'd rather have an upholstery shop redo your truck's interior instead of tacking the job yourself, it still pays to work from a kit for two reasons. First, with a quality interior kit from a reputable Chevrolet light truck parts supplier, you'll come as close to matching the original color and materials as it is possible to get. Second, besides keeping your truck as close to original as possible, a kit enables a professional upholsterer to replace the seat coverings and install the interior panels in a small fraction of the time that would be required to fabricate these items.

A complete pickup interior consists of several items, which may be sold separately or combined in interior packages. These include the seat coverings, new coils with which to rebuild worn spring sets or new foam padding for the wire spring cushions used in Chevrolet pickups since the mid-1960s, the headliner, door panels (for trucks that used fabric panels), kick panels (where used), sun visors (on trucks from the 1940s and earlier, the right-hand visor is optional), arm rests (which may be optional), floor mats in rubber or carpet on later models, dash pads for the 1967-1972 series and related hardware. When ordering a seat covering kit, inquire whether the supplier includes padding. If not, depending on condition of the cushions, you may need to order a seat rebuilding kit. Also inquire whether the kit includes hardware needed for this job and an instruction set. Recovering seat cushions is not complicated, as you will see, but instructions are helpful. You will need to purchase a couple of specialty tools.

Interior Finishing

Year	Interior coverings	Material
1936-1938	Door panels	Steel, painted
	Headliner	Cardboard
	Kick panels	Cardboard
1939-1940	Door panels	Steel, painted
	Headliner	Cardboard
	Kick panels	Cardboard
1941-1946	Door panels	Steel, painted
	Headliner	Cardboard
	Kick panels	Cardboard
1947-1955 1st series	Door panels	Vinyl covered cardboard
	Headliner	Cardboard
	Kick panels	Steel
1955-59 2nd series	Door panels	Steel
	Headliner	Cardboard on deluxe models and Cameo
	Kick panels	Steel, painted
1960-66	Door panels	Steel
	Headliner	Cardboard on deluxe models
	Kick panels	Steel, painted
1967-72	Door panels	Vinyl covered cardboard
	Headliner	Vinyl covered cardboard on Cheyenne
	Kick panels	Steel
	Dash cover	Padded vinyl

The interior of this Art Deco series Suburban awaits attention. John Hart

Here the new door covering material has been installed. Note the matching color arm rest.

Seat coverings began to be fancier in the mid-1950s.

An Advance Design series seat has a plainer cover.

Interior Painting

The interior should be repainted before the seats are replaced or the headliner, door, and kick panels (on trucks where these items were used) are installed. The typical sequence is to paint the truck's interior before the exterior. If the truck has not been completely disassembled, extensive masking will be required to protect the windshield, steering column and wheel, and the dash assembly (if has not been removed) from over spray. If the cab has been completely stripped and removed from the frame, the advised procedure is to paint the bottom and firewall first, then drape plastic sheeting over the frame and mount the cab. Now you can paint the interior, hook up the mechanicals, and run wiring to the dash, etc. The plastic sheeting will protect the frame from over spray when you paint the cab exterior and do the follow-up microsanding process that leads to a smooth, mirror finish.

When repainting the cab interior you will need to pay special attention to detail. In late '30s Chevy trucks, the dash has a special cackle finish. When detailing the cab of Advance

The cab interior is typically painted before the exterior. When restoring, the interior is painted before seats and door coverings are installed.

Design series trucks, the recesses between the ribs on the stainless-steel dash plate are painted the interior cab color. On 1952 models, where this dash plate is plain steel, the recesses are painted interior color and the ribs painted silver. On Task Force and 1960s models, the top of the dash is covered with a nonreflective finish. On whatever year and model truck you are restoring, you should note the interior paint scheme and finish details of this sort before stripping/sandblasting or other preparation steps.

After the cab is painted, you can install the interior coverings—just be very careful not to nick or scratch the paint.

Recovering Seat Cushions

As with other phases of your truck's restoration, interior work calls for a few special tools. These include heavy-duty scissors, hog-ring pliers, a utility or Xacto knife, and a heavy-duty wire cutter. The seats are usually removed from the truck during body repair and painting, so they can be recovered anytime. Installing the headliner and door panels will wait until after exterior and interior painting. If your truck still has the original cardboard headliner and door panels (refer to the chart above to see if your truck had steel or upholstered panels) you should take detailed photos or make sketches of exactly how these pieces fit. It's also a good idea to keep the original pieces to use in checking the authenticity and fit of the new panels. The original headliner can also serve as a guide when bending the replacement to fit the roof contours.

Several preparation steps need to be done before actually recovering the seats. First, the cushions will be removed from the truck and stripped of whatever remains of the old covering,

Seat upholstery kits contain coverings for the seat back and bottom cushions.

Here's the bottom cushion with the covering removed. On more modern trucks, the cushion is molded foam rubber over flat springs. Earlier trucks used cotton padding with a burlap covering over coil springs.

Cracks and tears in seat covering fabric signal that the cushion underneath may also be also be worn or damaged and need repair or replacing.

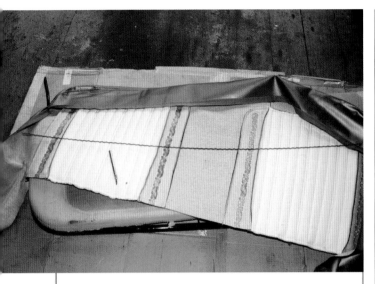

Long wires called listing wires thread through the edges of the covering to prevent the fabric from tearing and pulling loose when clipped to the cushion frame.

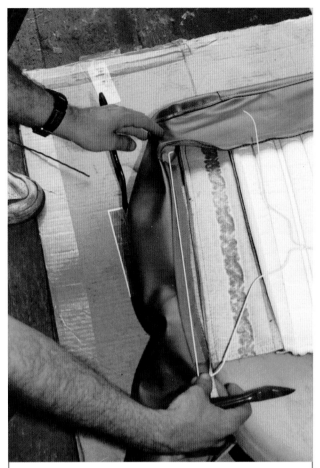

No wire was found at the sides of the original covering, so Ed makes a new wire from a coat hanger.

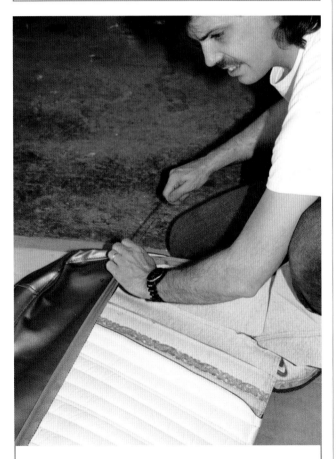

Eddy, my upholsterer friend, is fishing the long wire through the front edge of the new cover.

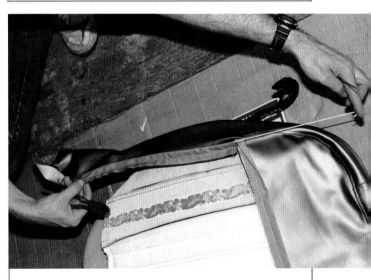

Now the new wire is slipped into the pocket at the bottom of the new cover.

165

Ed pulls the new cover tight over the cushion.

padding, and spring wrapping. When the old covering has been removed, you can inspect the spring set for soundness. It's not uncommon to find breaks in the seat frame as well as broken or badly sagging coils, and a light to heavy coating of surface rust. If the springs are badly worn you have two alternatives: find a better set or rebuild the set you have.

Now he fits the cover before clamping it in place with hog rings.

On Advance Design and newer series Chevy trucks, it should not be difficult to locate a set of sound, recoverable seats at a scrap yard or through want ads placed in a club newsletter or eBay. On earlier trucks, finding replacement seat springs may not be as easy. Spring sets can be rebuilt by welding cracks or breaks in the frame and replacing the broken or sagging coils. New seat spring coils are available from some parts suppliers. Where the spring frames are rusted, you should clean the metal by sandblasting or with a wire brush and spray on a protective coating of rust-resistant paint. If you haven't already done so, this is the time to order the seat covering kit.

Seat springs can be recovered by one person but an extra pair of hands makes the job much easier, especially when stretching the new covering over the repadded springs. Starting with the seat frame, the first step is to replace any weak or broken coils. Once the frame is sound, the seat frame will be wrapped with the burlap covering supplied with the kit. The burlap attaches to the seat and backrest frames with hog rings that are also supplied with the kit. The purpose of the burlap covering is to keep the padding from settling into the coils.

Next you will place cotton padding over the top and around the sides of the springs (here you will work one spring set at a time). In most cases, kits provide the exact amount of padding so don't cut any excess until you are sure everything is installed right. If the kit includes foam rubber, as well as or in place of the cotton padding, the foam is placed over the cotton padding on the top of the cushion. If the kit does not include foam padding, you will probably want to purchase a sheet of inch thick foam rubber to place over the cotton padding.

The deteriorated condition of the foam cushion, visible from the underside of the seat, indicates that the foam may also need replacing.

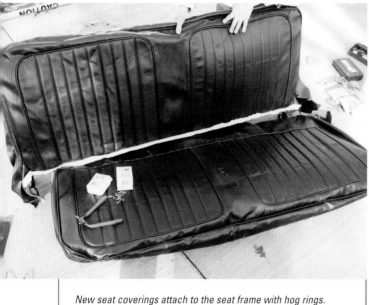

New seat coverings attach to the seat frame with hog rings. Special pliers with grooves in the jaws make clamping shut the rings a fool-proof process.

By the early 1970s, Chevrolet was offering carpet as a floor covering and wood applique dash trim.

Otherwise, as the truck is driven, the cotton will compress, lowering the cushion height and giving the seat a less comfortable feel. Foam rubber is resilient so it will preserve the seat's cushiony feel and maintains the right cushion height for many years. The padding and foam are held in place by the cover, which will be fitted over the cushions next.

On later model trucks with wire (as opposed to coil) springs, the padding is a molded foam cushion. Often this foam has deteriorated to the point that it needs to be replaced, either because the covering is torn and chunks of cushion have broken off or been torn out or because the foam has crumbled and disintegrated. In either case, the answer is to use a new pre-molded replacement cushion, usually available from the supplier of the new seat covering. Attempting to repair your old cushion by gluing strips of foam into damaged areas is not generally satisfactory.

As you pull the cover over the padded spring set, your three goals are to align the seam around the edge of the cushion, work out all wrinkles in the covering and pull the fabric tightly enough so that it won't sag when you sit on the cushion, but not so tight that cushion has no give. Once you have worked the cover over the springs, with the seam forming an even outline for the spring set, smooth out any wrinkles, then turn the cushion over and pull the fabric tight. Now you can begin to attach the covering to the spring frame using hog rings. (If these wire clips are not supplied with the kit they can be purchased from most any upholstery shop, hardware store, or ordered through a restoration supplier such as The Eastwood Company.) The hog rings have sharp ends that allow them to

be pressed easily through the cover fabric. The rings are then squeezed around the seat frame using hog-ring pliers.

The sequence for attaching the seat covering begins at the front. Here you will clip the covering to the seat frame with a few hog rings along the front edge. Next you will pull the fabric snug and attach a few hog rings at the rear. If the covering has too much, or not enough give, you can remove the clips at the rear of the frame and allow a little more slack or pull the covering tighter. By adjusting the tension from the back of the seat, any holes left from refitting the hog rings won't be noticed. When the covering has the desired snugness, it should be pulled slightly tighter to allow for future stretching, then secured to the frame with hog rings spaced about two to three inches apart. Here it helps to have two people, one to stretch the cover and the other to insert the hog rings. Repeating this process on the other spring set (cushion or backrest) finishes the seat upholstering job.

Usually, you can get a firm enough grip on the fabric with your hands to pull the covering sufficiently tight. However, there's also a stretching tool that looks like a very broad nosed pliers that assures a good grip on the fabric and allows it to be pulled to the right snugness. You can purchase these seat cover stretching pliers from The Eastwood Company. If you use these pliers, be careful not to over-stretch and tear the fabric.

Recovering a truck's seat cushions is easy enough so that after one set you'll feel like a pro and can give advice or assistance to friends who are restoring their trucks.

Installing Interior Coverings

As the Interior Descriptions chart above shows, in some years, Chevrolet finished its truck interiors with a cardboard head-

Restored Advance Design cab interior using correct color scheme.

liner and door panels. In other years these the cab interior surfaces are simply painted. From 1936 to 1946, and some earlier years, the **work

interior finishings included kick panels made of cardboard. These interior coverings are available for Chevy trucks through the mid 1950s in easy-to-install kit form. Unlike car interiors where blind tacking and other tricks of the upholsterer's trade are used to conceal door panel and other trim fasteners, trim panels on trucks are held in place in straightforward manner with sheet metal screws. In the 1941-1946 Art Deco series and earlier models, metal strips along the edges of the headliner and kick panels are used to secure these coverings. Metal strips also position the windlace around the doors on Chevy trucks through mid-year 1949.

Although Chevrolet did not use a full headliner in its pickups, as did some of the other manufacturers, the interior roof covering is still somewhat tricky to install—particularly when forming the bends for the roof contour. If you try to bend the headliner dry, you will probably crease the cardboard in attempting to make the bends. The correct procedure is to moisten the backside of the cardboard in the areas where the bends will occur with a mixture of 80 percent household ammonia and 20% water. This mixture can be placed in a Windex bottle and sprayed onto the cardboard (remember, to spray the back side so that stains will not show on the good side). The cardboard should not be soaked, just moistened. You will find that the moistened cardboard will bend easily without crinkling. The ammonia may smell for a day or so until it dries. You'll find that installing a headliner is definitely

a two-person job, so plan to have a helper on hand when you tackle this project.

Pickup door coverings will also fit Suburbans and Panels. Seat coverings and headliners are also available for early 1940s to mid-fifties models of these trucks in kit form. Other interior coverings for these specialty models will need to be fabricated by a trim shop.

Trim items completing an interior restoration include armrests, sun visors, glove box liner, and windlace for the door opening. Quality reproduction armrests are available for Advance Design through early Seventies models. During much of this period, Chevrolet installed only one armrest—on the driver's side—but the passenger side arm rest was an option. Likewise, reproduction sun visors are available for Advance Design and Task Force trucks. Here, too, Chevrolet installed just the driver's side sun visor, making the passenger visor an accessory. Since reproductions of the right hand bracket are available for the most popular models, many restorers choose to install both visors. The original cardboard glove box liners are often torn or missing. Replacement liners are also available for most years.

Through the Advance Design series, Chevy sealed its pickup cabs against air drafts with windlace that installed on the inside of the door frame. This windlace, which looks like oversize fender welting, is placed against the door outline with the round section projecting into the door opening and the flat tacking strip against the door outline. Most commonly, windlace is held in place by tacks or staples, which go into a tack strip. The tack area is then dressed out with metal retainer strips. From mid-year 1949 to the end of the Advance Design series, this door windlace slides into a metal track.

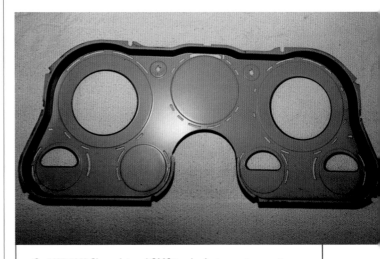

On 1967-1972 Chevrolet and GMC trucks, instruments mount as a unit into this inner casing. Note that this casing lacks a hole for the tachometer. Alvin Shier

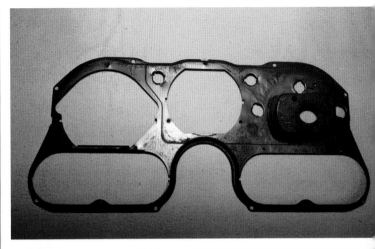

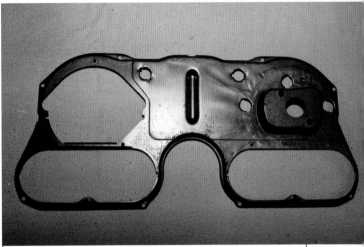

Here's the back side of the same part with the tachometer cutout.
Alvin Shier

Instrument Cluster Restoration

On most older trucks, some of the gauges may have quit working and the gauge faces will be faded and the markings obscured. As part of either a cosmetic upgrade or complete restoration, you will want to refinish the instruments. Services are available that do this work and can guarantee quality results. But you can also redo your truck's instrument cluster yourself.

The job of cosmetically refinishing an instrument cluster begins with disconnecting the wiring and removing the gauge set from the truck, but if some of the gauges are not working you will want to do some electrical trouble shooting first to determine if the problem is faulty wiring, a bad sending unit or the gauge itself. How to trouble shoot a non-working electrical component is described in the wiring. Once you have determined whether or not the gauges are functioning and have the instrument panel out of the truck, you can disassemble the instrument cluster and remove the gauges. Refacing kits that you can apply yourself to give your truck's gauges a like-new look are available for Chevy trucks from 1936 to 1966 from the major vintage parts suppliers like Jim Carter. Where the gauge lettering is applied to the dash face, as is the case with the 1940 to 1946 models and the plastic instrument faces used on the 1955 to 1959 Task Force series, show-quality replacements are available.

The instrument panel face will need to be repainted a flat (non-glossy) finish. Flattening agents are available from automotive paint suppliers. In many cases, the chrome bezel around the instrument cluster (found on Advance Design and earlier series) will also need to be rechromed or replaced. Professionally rebuilt speedometers are available from vintage Chevrolet suppliers for most years or you can send your truck's speedometer to a specialty speedometer rebuilding service. Typically, the speedometer rebuilder will ask if you want the odometer to show the existing mileage or set to all zeros.

The metal outer casing often needs cleaning and refinishing. Note the difference in casings for and without the optional tachometer. Alvin Shier

Redoing your truck's instrument cluster makes an ideal winter project. The process requires more patience than skill and an advantage of making this an off-season project is that any time delays such as sending the speedometer off to the rebuilder won't interfere with driving your truck.

1967-72 Instrument Panel Restoration by Alvin Shier

The instrument panel on this series trucks differs in two important ways from the earlier gauge layouts. First, the gauge housing is plastic with a chrome-plated appearance (this is also true of the 1966 dash facing). Second, rather than being individually connected to the wiring harness, the instruments in this series and later Chevrolet and GMC trucks are wired to a printed circuit that in turn connects to the wiring harness. While these differences do not make an instrument cluster

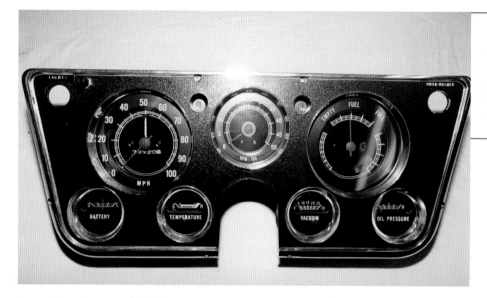

This restored instrument cluster contains the rare vacuum gauge. The speedminder (white needle pointing to 50 mph on the speedometer) was not available in 1971 or 1972. Alvin Shier

from this series more difficult to restore than an earlier gauge set, a few special instructions do apply. Much of the procedure described below for restoring this more modern instrument cluster also applies for the earlier units.

The instrument panel used in 1967-'72 Chevy and GMC trucks is both practical, good looking. On standard models, the cluster consists of two gauge displays with the speedometer on the left and a combination fuel gauge, warning lights for oil and alternator output, plus temperature gauge, in the large circular opening on the right. A center circular opening can be filled with an optional tachometer. The deluxe version of this instrument panel, installed as standard equipment on CST (Custom Sport Truck) and Cheyenne trucks and available as an option on the Custom models, added four small gauge openings along the bottom of the dash panel. Inserted in these openings were the amp, engine temperature, and oil pressure gauges. The fourth opening could house an optional vacuum gauge or clock. On this deluxe instrument panel, the large opening on the right housed only the fuel gauge.

When new, the attraction of this instrument panel came not just from the easy-to-read gauge layout, but also from the appealing combination of the panel's chrome edging (including gauge insets) and black matte finish. On Cheyenne trucks the panel's face had a woodgrain covering. With age these instrument panels become drab and dull looking. The bright chrome wears off and fades away, the plastic gauge coverings scratch and become cloudy, even the instrument needles take on a dull appearance. What was once a highlight of the truck's interior now calls attention to itself by its shabby look. As a result, renewing the instrument panel can be considered a must-do step whether you are restoring or upgrading a 1967-72 truck.

If yours is a standard truck your first step will probably be to purchase a deluxe instrument panel—that is unless you

This back view of a 1967-1972 Chevrolet or GMC instrument cluster shows the printed circuit board that provides the wiring for the instruments receiving electronic signals.

want to keep the truck factory original. The deluxe instrument clusters with their row of smaller individual gauges along the bottom of the panel have a much higher quality appearance than the standard panels. Used instrument panels are still relatively easy to find in swap meets or scrap yards. They are also readily available new and ready to install from specialty suppliers for this vintage Chevrolet truck. Many collectors feel that the deluxe panel isn't complete without a tachometer. This desirable accessory is also relatively available with used examples showing up at swap meets and new units obtainable from specialty suppliers.

Panel Removal

Whether you are renewing your truck's gauge set or a used one you purchased, or are replacing the instrument set with a new unit, you will need to remove the instrument panel from the truck. This job is much easier than you might think because of the printed circuit and its single connector to the main wiring harness. Now that you know the wiring is not a hassle, you might assume that the instrument panel can be removed simply by loosening the screws at the top and sides of the plastic housing. However, the job is not quite that simple. It's really not all that complicated either.

Before starting the actual removal process, disconnect the battery. Then, back inside the cab you will loosen the steering column at the base of the dash (remove two 5/16 in. screws which hold the steering column tight to the dash). This allows the steering column to drop down slightly. Next you will remove the screws holding the panel to the dash. You'll find the panel is still held in place by the light switch and wiper knobs. The wiper knob removes easily by loosening the small set screw. With the knob off the shaft you can unscrew the bezel. The light switch knob is a bit trickier. This knob attaches to a long shaft that inserts into the switch box. The knob doesn't come loose until you reach under the dash and push in a button on the top of the switch box housing. As you hold down on this button, the light switch knob and shaft will slide out easily. Now you can unthread the nut holding the light switch box to the instrument panel.

Before removing the gauge cluster you will need to reach up from underneath the dash and loosen the speedometer cable and oil gauge tube (if your truck is so-equipped—some aren't). The oil line connector takes a 5/16 in. wrench. Some oil may drip from the line. To prevent the oil from dripping onto the floor mat or carpet, tie a plastic bag around the open end of the line. Now you can pull the instrument panel four to six inches away from the dash. This space will enable you to reach behind the panel and disconnect the large electrical connector that inserts into the back. Squeezing the lock tabs on the sides releases the connector. The instrument panel can now be lifted free of the truck and is ready for the restoration process.

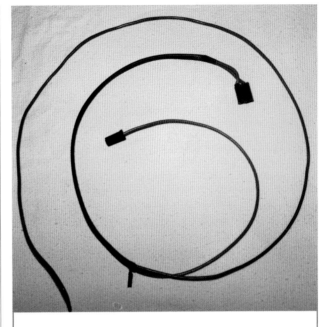

The tachometer requires its own wiring harness.

Note: some trucks may also have throttle and/or choke controls. These controls would also have to be removed before the cluster can be lifted out of the dash.

Panel Disassembly

To prepare the instrument panel for restoration, you will remove the nuts and bolts holding the circuit board to the outer case. All of the twist-turn light sockets are also removed. Then the circuit board lifts free. It is worth noting that printed circuits are very easy to break. Sometimes the break is not even visible so my advice is to replace the printed circuit. This can solve a lot of electrical troubleshooting later on. Now remove the instruments by loosening the screws that hold the metal instrument housing to the plastic housing. Be careful to observe where everything goes so that you will have no trouble at reassembly time. As you lift the metal gauge assembly off the panel facing, you will find the clear plastic gauge covering as well as several small black spacers. Put the spacers with the screws in a container so that you don't have to hunt for these easily misplaced items when reassembly time comes.

Refurbishing the Gauges and Faces

The next step is to send the plastic gauge housing out for replating. For a small additional charge, you can have the plating service repaint the face of the panel (or replace the woodgrain finish if the panel is for a Cheyenne model). If you wish to bypass the plating step, new dash faces are available from 1967-1972 Chevrolet/GMC truck suppliers like

LMC Truck. Cheyenne woodgrain decals are also available from this source.

While the dash cluster is apart, you may want to touch up the gauge needles and send the speedometer for cleaning and reconditioning. Brightening up the gauge needles is an easy process. I use a common florescent paint. You can obtain spray bombs of florescent paint in almost any hobby store. The technique here is to spray some paint into the spray can lid or other suitable container. Allow the paint to "flash off" allowing enough time for the paint to become thicker and brushable. Using a very small camel hair (good quality) brush, practice on a toothpick until you can complete the painting operation in one stroke. For success in this, you will discover that it is important that the paint be the right brushing viscosity. If you have to stop and start again along the needle, you will break the flow and this break will be visible. After you have mastered painting the toothpick, you can graduate to painting the gauge needles. Be very careful not to drop any paint on the gauge face as this will permanently mark the gauge and will spoil its appearance.

The black face of the instrument cluster can be cleaned quite nicely with soft tissue and warm water (go gently as too much pressure on the face will mark the semi-flat black surface). After cleaning the instrument face of dust, I dampen a Kleenex with Armor All and lightly reclean the surface. Then I gently polish the surface with another tissue or very soft cloth. This process is a little tedious but if you do a good job the results are well worth the time spent. After finishing with the instruments you can set them aside in a safe place.

Cleaning the Lenses

The next steps are to clean up the inner and outer cases and polish the lens. If the green paint on the cases needs to be refinished, most well-equipped hobby stores can supply the color you need. Failing this, you can have nearly any auto parts store that sells paint products mix up the paint and package it in a spray can. The black inner case is sprayed a semi-gloss.

The instrument lens is available for these gauge clusters with and without a tachometer. In my experience, purchasing a new lens is no guarantee of a clear face for the instruments. I've purchased many and some come smudged or otherwise imperfect from the factory. I reject these and reorder until I get a lens that's perfect—after all, why pay a new price for a substandard part. If you choose to reuse your original lens and it is not too badly marked up, you can restore it to like new appearance. Here's what to do.

When attempting to refinish the plastic instrument lens, it is very important that the scratches be very superficial—otherwise you will not end up with a clear face. I begin by sanding the front of the lens (this is the side without the numbers) using micro fine 2000 grit wet and dry sandpaper until all the scratches are gone. Now you can

On a 1967-1972 era truck, the easiest access to the radio location is through the glovebox opening.

Radios are a popular accessory on Advance Design trucks.

either power polish the surface or apply a coat of clear paint to the sanded surface. Either will produce a crystal clear lens—though of the two methods clear coating is the easiest. I apply the same clear coat that is used over final finishes. For those desiring a bit of a custom look, you can add a few drops of black paint to tint the clear. This will give the panel facing a slightly cloudy appearance. Don't add too much black or you will make the instruments hard to read. If you don't have access to spray painting equipment, you can polish the face using a very fine grit polishing compound and end with 3M's Imperial Machine Glaze or Hand Glaze.

Tachometer Installation

If you plan to install a tachometer (this is a very popular accessory on these trucks), adding this option is easy because the tachometer parts (the tachometer head, tachometer lens, the tachometer printed circuit board and tachometer harness are readily available. Most larger trucks (one ton and up) had tachometers and many also had the very desirable vacuum gauges and super rare clocks.

Panel Assembly

Now we're ready to reassemble the panel. Start by placing the rechromed or new gauge housing face down on a soft, clean surface. A section of blanket or old towel makes soft surface that will protect the new chrome on the gauge housing from becoming scratched while you assemble the gauge cluster. Next, replace the small soft rubber tubes that act as a buffer between the lens and gauge housing. Now lay the lens in place in the housing, making sure that the locater pin lines up properly. The inner case goes on next followed by the outer case and gauges. Screw these parts together.

The circuit band installs last. Be sure to handle this part very carefully because it is delicate. The circuit band is held to the metal instrument case with cap screws. If you have purchased a tach unit and circuit band at a flea market or salvage yard beware that it is very possible for the printed circuit board to have a short. This will show up if the gauges fail to work properly or if the fusible link at the battery burns out. To test for a short in the circuit board, you must check each circuit for continuity. If any of the circuits fails, you will have to replace the printed circuit. As mentioned above, circuit bands for this series Chevrolet and GMC trucks are still available.

If you installed the tachometer, you will the tachometer wiring harness, which you can either purchase from suppliers like LMC Truck, or make yourself. The tachometer harness consists of a brown 12 gauge pink wire 65 in. long which connects the tach to the coil and a pink 12 gauge wire 35 in. long to connect the tach to the ignition side of the fuse block. The tach head is marked "coil" and "battery" to guide you in attaching these wires. You will need to attach clips to one end of both wires to mate to the tabs on the back of the tachometer. The other end of the brown wire will need an "eye" or "U" connector. The pink wire attaches to the tab on the tachometer marked "battery" (or sometimes "12 Volt") and to a hot location in the fuse block (located under the dash above the driver's left foot). To prevent the tachometer from draining the battery when the truck is in storage, this hot lead

Carpeting has replaced this truck's original rubber floor mat. Besides being non-original, the carpet catches dirt and absorbs moisture, which could rust the cab floor.

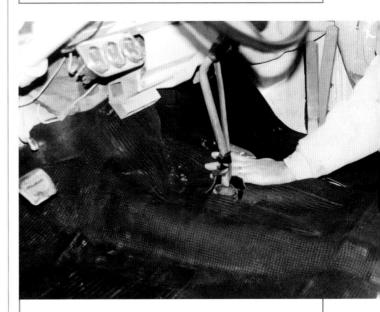

Big trucks, in this case a 1968 C-50, have a lower transmission hump than light duty models. New floor mats are not available for big trucks, so the vendor recommended an automatic transmission mat for a better fit over the low hump. The problem of where to cut the hole for the gearshift lever and dump levers was resolved by using the carpet floor covering as a template.

should attach to a location which is dead when the ignition switch is turned off. The brown wire attaches to the coil lead on the tachometer and the negative pole on the coil.

The correct place to route the tachometer harness through the firewall is slightly down from the fuse block connector and to the right (as viewed from underneath the hood). You will need to drill a hole in this location. To complete the "factory" look, and to protect the wire from abrasion, you can first place a rubber grommet in the hole and run the wire through it. Grommets are available from auto parts stores.

The rebuilt panel goes back in the truck by reversing the order of the steps that you followed to remove it. A restored instrument cluster goes a long way to upgrade a truck's interior.

Radio Installation and Upgrade

Chevrolet first made a radio available in its trucks in 1947. While original radios are available, unless you are preparing your truck for show competition you'll be better served by installing a modern radio than by locating an original. For near authenticity, you can have modern solid state works installed in an original radio case. The radio will look authentic and the difference won't be noted until turning it on.

Not only is the quality of the sound far superior in the modern radio, but you also gain FM and tape playing capability. The radio shown in the accompany photo sequence is specially designed by Custom Autosound for installation in Chevrolet trucks from the Advance Design series forward. This AM/FM stereo radio and auto-reverse tape player has all the features one would expect from a modern sound system and is designed not only to fit the Chevy truck dash, but even has the Chevrolet bow tie emblem on the tape cassette door.

The installation shown here is in a 1969 Chevy C-20 Longhorn pickup. The truck's original radio, a basic AM player, had an annoyingly raspy tone and limited reception. The replacement unit uses high quality stereophonic speakers that are mounted in a compact assembly that installs in the same location under the dash as the original single speaker.

Radio and Speaker Removal

The first steps to installing the new radio are to remove the old radio and speaker, or if the truck is not fitted with a radio to gain access to the area behind the dash where the radio will be mounted. On most Chevrolet trucks, access to the place where the radio mounts in the center of the dash is gained most easily by removing the glove box door and liner. On this 1969 model, taking out the glove box liner (a simple matter of removing eight sheet metal screws and two bolts) is far easier than reaching the radio from underneath, which on this truck would have meant unhooking an after market air conditioning unit, dropping the heater controls, and taking out the ash tray assembly. With the glove box liner out of the way, the speaker

can be reached easily to loosen it from its mounting. In this case, a mounting bolt in the back and lock nuts on the radio controls are all that held the original radio in place.

Radio and Speaker Installation

After taking the old radio and speaker out of the truck, preparations for installing the new radio begin by splicing the new sound system's wiring harness into appropriate power sources. This step looks more complicated than it is because the wiring harness supplied for the radio contains outlets for a power booster as well as speaker wiring. Actually, only two wiring splices need to be made and these are for the power supplies (modern radios require two power supply sources). One power supply needs to be to a constant current source. The other should be wired to a source that will be dead when the ignition switch is turned off. For the constant power source, we tapped into the hot wire to the cigarette lighter. For a power source that turns off with the ignition switch, we used the wire that supplied current to the original radio.

Installing the new double speaker unit was a breeze. The speaker assembly is designed so that it attaches to the original

---

Firewall Cover Preservation
by Russell Emond

After removing an inner firewall cover that is good enough to use again from a 1947-53 Chevrolet, do not store the cover on the floor. To keep the cover from changing its shape and be hard to reuse, hang it on the wall or stand it in a corner. I failed to do this to a firewall cover on one of my trucks and it was so out of shape when I went to reuse it that I had to junk it. Here is the best way to preserve the cover's shape. Do this the same day the cover is removed.

Cut a piece of 3/8 or 1/2 in. plywood to the dimensions 24 in. by 58 in. Cut ten 3 in. by 3 in. squares from 1/8 in. Masonite (or plywood). Gather ten 1 1/4 in. screws (drywall screws work well). Lay the firewall cover on the plywood backing, and using the 3x3 squares. Secure the cover to the plywood through the same holes that it fastened to the firewall. Do not disturb the padding on the back and do not over tighten the screws. Place wadded up newspaper under the hump. Do not pack the hump tight. Hang the cover on the wall upside down.

When I followed this procedure, I took the cover down 20 months later, blew it off, brushed it, wiped it down with paint thinner, gave it three coats of flat black, and installed it. It looks like new.

speaker bracket. The wooden speaker mount could be seen through the speaker grille in the dash, so we covered the speakers with black cheesecloth from a fabric store. The cheesecloth won't distort the sound nor muffle the speakers, but it does camouflage the speaker mount. With the speakers in place and wiring hooked up, we "bench tested" the radio—that is, we attached the antenna lead and tried the radio and tape assembly out before fitting the sound machine in the dash. The instructions call for this bench testing step and it's a wise one. Should the radio be defective, or if the wiring has been hooked up wrong, you'll want to know this before putting in the time to fit the radio in the dash.

Our radio tested out fine so the next step was to disconnect the radio from the wiring harness and tie up the harness so that it wouldn't drape down on the heater controls. Before positioning the radio, we slipped on the plastic face plate. A bright metal plate to line the dash opening is also supplied, but we decided not to use it. The radio fit into place easily with the control knobs lining up perfectly in the holes. Support for the radio comes from the control knob shafts in the front and a bracket, which attaches to the speaker mount in the rear. To get the proper support from the control knob shafts, you will need to thread a set of nuts onto the shafts and adjust their position so that they press-fit against the dash when the radio and its face plate are fit tightly into the hole. A set of washers fits over the control knob shafts from the outside and another set of nuts is threaded onto the shafts and turned finger tight. You'll find that the radio will have a more original look if you paint these washers to match the dash. A set of spacers is now cut to the correct depth and fitted over the control shafts. Then the knobs are pressed in place. With the ignition switch turned on, the radio can be taken through its functions. You'll want to set the digital clock and pre-set stations, adjust the base/treble control, and become familiar with the radio's many features.

The radio went in place as it should with no modification. The only improvement you may want to make would be the addition of a carpet and headliner to help reduce the reverberation created by a metallic box, otherwise known as a cab. If you want all-around sound, under-the-seat speakers are preferable to making the sheet metal alterations required by door mount, armrest or overhead console speakers. You will find that many car stereo companies offer box speakers specifically designed for use in pickups.

Other Interior Upgrades

With its CST (Custom Sport Truck) and Cheyenne models which appeared in the 1967-1972 series, Chevrolet began to dress up its pickup interiors with carpeting and high fashion seat coverings. Bucket seats and center console were also offered as an option. Bucket seats give a superior ride over a bench seat, but the tradeoff is loss of the third passenger seat space. Trucks from this series are plentiful enough in scrap yards that it's not difficult to find the dressier Cheyenne door panels and headliner. Bucket seats were installed in Blazers and so they, too, are fairly plentiful. Typically the vinyl covering will be torn, but new, correctly embossed coverings are available. The coverings on the upper seat support do not simply slip over the cushion, but wrap around the top, sides, and bottom and clip to the springs on the rear of the spring set in the same fashion as bench seats. Bucket seats use fiberglass panels to cover the backs of the upper seat supports. These panels simply attach with screws and if replacements are needed, they are available. So are the fiberglass consoles that sit between the seats.

On trucks through the 1950s, passenger side sun visors and arm rests were options. Now that these items are available from vintage truck suppliers, they are commonly installed during refurbishing or restoration. The original visors are usually badly soiled, their cardboard liners bent and stitching frayed or disintegrated and are very difficult to repair or restore. In most cases, authentic looking replacements are now available from vintage Chevrolet pickup suppliers.

Through the 1967-1972 series, insulating pads were placed under the rubber floor mat or carpet to reduce road noise and insulate the cab floor from heat in summer and cold in winter. Replacement padding is now available. For earlier vintage trucks where the rubber mat lay over the steel floor, padding can be cut and installed, and is a good idea.

Heating and Cooling Systems

In the 1960-1966 series, Chevrolet offered two types of heating systems: deluxe and thrift. The two styles are easy to distinguish. The deluxe system uses outside air and has a three-lever panel to control the heating, ventilating and defrosting cables. This system was continued in subsequent series trucks. The temperature inside the cab can be varied by adjusting the levers to mix cold outside air with heated air. The thrift (recirculating)

Clock Accessory
by Al Shier

I have heard more than once that a clock was available in 1972. It was housed in the right lower inside gauge on trucks equipped with option 253 (amp, oil, and temperature gauges). I have never seen a truck with one, so I installed the clock from a 1973-77 Monte Carlo in this housings and it looks great.

heater warms outside air and blows it into the cab. This is a carryover from a simpler, earlier heating system. There are no adjusting levers on this heater and temperature is controlled by a 3-speed fan switch located on the dash. The same knob attaches to a cable. Pulling the knob out opens the air door. A lever on the defroster unit (located on the passenger side firewall) operates the defrost duct door. This lever can deflect the entire air flow to the defroster ducts or down to the floor ducts. The center position of the lever provides air flow to both ducts. The thrift heater functions well, but is less efficient if door and window weather stripping or air vent seals are in poor condition.

The deluxe heating system, while more convenient to operate, is also prone to lever breakage. New levers, cables and control faceplates are available. In this deluxe system, defroster air is ducted to vents on the dash. These ducts are often missing or worn and dislocated from their connections. Replacements are available, as are the plastic dashboard vents, which came in various colors matching the truck's internal color scheme. The ducts are not difficult to replace, the biggest hurdle being their access under and behind the dash.

On any older truck, entirely likely that the heater core may need attention. Although the truck may be in storage during the winter months, that doesn't mean there won't be a few cool mornings or evenings during the spring and fall. If the heater core develops leaks that are not tended to, water may enter the heating system. This can cause moisture damage to the blower motor and defrost system. Rebuild kits for the heater, which include new heater cores (the miniature radiators that provide a source of heat for the cab), blower motors and replacement seals are available through Chevrolet pickup parts vendors.

Factory air conditioning became available in the 1967-1972 series. The air conditioning system used a different cab dash and a much more complex duct work system. If a non-air truck is being converted to factory air conditioning, an air conditioning dash or cab would have to be located. The duct work and controls are available from restoration suppliers.

Gas Tank

From 1960 to 1972, Chevrolet mounted the gas tank inside the cab and directly behind the seat. The idea of sitting in front of a gas tank is not appealing to many owners and some have gone to great lengths to relocate the tank to the rear of the truck. The gas

The tank is hidden from view by a cardboard gas tank cover. These covers tend to come loose and rip. Replacement covers are available and if the original cover is damaged or missing, it should be replaced.

Seat Belts

It's wise to install seat belts in any vehicle, regardless of age. Because they are a safety feature, the AACA (Antique Automobile Club of America) does not deduct points in show competition on vehicles where seat belts were not original equipment. If the truck was equipped with seat belts, it's likely that the belt webbing is frayed and soiled. The buckles may show wear and the retractor mechanisms may be broken. Services are available that will rebuild seat belts to factory new condition. On 1967-1972 series trucks, shoulder harnesses were available and the upper mounting location is visible under a plug above the driver's left shoulder in the upper portion of the cab. Trucks with these shoulder harnesses are very rare, but the mounting location is there and can be used to install a shoulder harness from a later model vehicle.

On trucks without seatbelts, it's important to build secure mountings on the floor of the cab and not simple bolt the belts through cab floor sheet metal that will allow the mounting bolts to tear loose in the event of a crash. Secure mounts can be made by reinforcing the cab floor at the seat belt mounting points in the center and sides at the rear of the seat.

In upgrading your truck's appearance, it's easy to overlook the need to replace the rubber parts. Window and door seal, the rubber donut around the gas filler pipe, and other rubber items on the truck deteriorate at roughly the same rate as the rest of the vehicle so the rubber's condition doesn't stand out (unless the truck has spent time in the south-western U.S. where the hot sun and dryness seem almost to fossilize the rubber). If you're doing a ground-up restoration where all the rubber items will be removed, the need to replace these items will quickly become obvious because most will be destroyed as you take the vehicle apart. Where rubber parts sometimes get neglected is in the rebuilding approach. Here, deteriorated window rubber or door weather seal may not be noticed until after the truck is painted. The smarter approach is to take inventory of the truck's rubber parts and begin ordering replacements early on in the restoration or rebuilding process. In most cases, your shopping list will soon grow to a respectable order.

Checking Rubber Parts for Wear

Dryness, cracking, and chunks of missing rubber are not the only reasons for replacing a truck's rubber parts. The 1969 Chevrolet Longhorn pickup seen in various chapters thoroughly throughout this book had sound looking door weather, yet air could be heard hissing in around the door openings. As door weather seal ages, the rubber loses its elasticity. It appears to be resilient enough to make good contact with the door, but instead collapses when the door is shut. Windshield rubber deteriorates by drying out and cracking, causing water to seep past the glass and drip onto the dashboard and into the cab. If you are disassembling your truck for a major restoration, you will want to replace all possible rubber parts so everything will have a consistent, like-new appearance. Even where a full-scale restoration isn't planned, replacing rubber parts needs to be on your agenda.

Trucks that have been partially or completely disassembled, or have received an amateur restoration, often lack many of the original rubber items. The problem this presents is figuring out what's missing. One way to determine what rubber items belong on the truck, and their locations, is to order a vintage truck supplier's catalog or buy a copy of the

The pickup cab has numerous weather seal parts that may be missing or decayed. These include the rubber seal around the doors on newer trucks or welting on older trucks such as the Art Deco model shown here, draft seals for the clutch, brake and starter pedals as well as the shift and emergency lever boots.

When removing old rubber weather seal, be sure to note whether the rubber attaches to the door or truck body. Here the weatherstrip attaches to the Suburban rear doors. John Hart

factory assembly manual and compare the rubber items shown in the catalog or assembly sequences with those still on the truck. Likely to be missing are draft seals for the clutch, brake, starter pedal and shift and emergency brake lever (for trucks where these pedals and levers protruded through the floor), hood and tailgate bumpers and seals.

A convenient place to start building your shopping inventory of needed rubber parts is at the cab. If the door weather seal is original, it's probably cracked and chunks may be missing. On newer trucks, this weather seal may be intact, but will have lost its resiliency and should be replaced. While you're checking off the rubber items visible on the outside of the cab, notice the condition of large rubber grommet (often called a donut) around the gas tank filler pipe. Chances are the rubber has hardened, cracked or is missing altogether. The rubber mouldings around the windshield, back light and vent windows are also likely to be cracked and hardened.

Inside the cab you'll add brake and clutch pedal pads, boots for the accelerator, floor shift lever, and hand brake (on trucks where this brake is floor-mounted) to the rubber parts inventory. Even though they're likely to be missing, don't overlook the clutch and brake draft seals that fit over the pedals shafts and rest against the floorboards (on trucks where the clutch and brake pedals depress through the floor board). On Task Force through 1972 models, the kick panel air vent door seals may also need replacing. Add the steering post pad and check for missing firewall grommets as well as the little bumpers behind the glovebox door.

You should check the condition (or absence) of the hood and cowl lacing (used as an anti-rattle buffer on trucks with alligator-style hoods) and hood insulator and cowl seal rubber on trucks with front-opening hoods, door window channels and glass sweepers. If your truck has seen lots of use, the window channels (U-shaped, whisker-lined grooves in which the window glass slides) may be missing. Since these channels prevent drafts and keep the window glass from rattling against the door, replacements should be installed if the originals are missing or worn. In most cases, the sweepers and seals at the bottom of the window openings will also need to be replaced. These sweepers or seals attach to the door at the base of the window frame and keep water from dripping down inside the door. They also clean the window as it is rolled up and down.

From 1947-1955 Chevrolet placed rubber gaskets between the headlight buckets and the front fenders. These are likely to be cracked and should be added to the rubber parts list. Walking around the front of a 1947-1955 first series Advance Design trucks, note the cowl vent and add its seal to the rubber parts inventory. On early Advance Design series (1947-1950) you should also add the rubber seal for the side cowl vent. On 1955 first series and older pickups, fender welt is often used to seal the seam between the rear fenders and the box. Welting is also used on the front fenders through the

Advance Design models. On 1955 Second Series and later stepside pickups, there should be a weather seal between the short "step" and the box. If this seal is missing, moisture can collect in this crevice and cause rust. Later model trucks have a rubber seal at the base of the tailgate.

At the truck's business end, you may notice two important rubber parts—the tailgate chain covers—are missing. These will join the wanted list. The rubber inventory list is growing but isn't complete. How about the shock absorber and suspension bushings or the rubber body mounts? Rubber parts differ with the various model trucks. You may notice other items not mentioned here. In any event, make the list of rubber and weather seal parts as complete as possible. Then you can go shopping.

Sources for Rubber Parts

Parts suppliers specializing your vintage Chevrolet truck are the best source of the rubber items on your list. Two additional sources of rubber items are Metro Moulded Parts, Inc. and Steele Rubber Parts, suppliers of rubber parts for a very wide range of vintage cars and trucks. In the case of universal items like window channel, you can take measurement from the

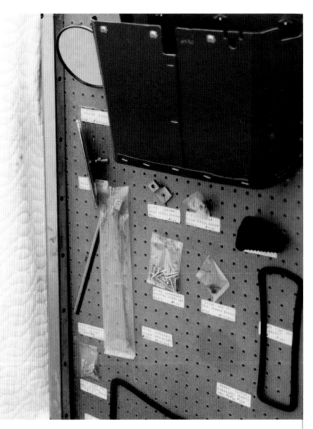

Replacement rubber and weather seal parts are available from vintage Chevrolet parts suppliers.

parts on your truck and order the needed length. Some weather seal items like these were used on many some like window channel, you won't be satisfied with a universal floor mat. Reproduction floor mats meeting OEM standards are available for most year Chevrolet trucks at reasonable prices. Universal floor mats are molded oversized and can be trimmed for your truck, but problems arise in trying to match any pre-cut holes with the actual location of the clutch and brake pedals, floor shift lever, accelerator, and starter control on your truck. Also, universal mats aren't molded to the contour of your truck's transmission hump and you'll be trying to figure out how to work out the lumps.

On 1960 and newer trucks, sill plates mounted on top of the rocker panel box, help hold down the edges of the floor mat. Most original sill plates are badly worn and should be replaced with new factory or reproduction items.

Occasionally, it's possible to find original rubber parts at swap meets. If you're searching for a specific part, it helps to look the part number up in advance, or better yet, bring along a cross section or the complete original part. If you buy any new-old-stock (NOS) rubber parts, make sure they are still pliable, and don't listen to a vendor's story that a stiff rubber part can be softened with a couple of coatings of ArmorAll.

Rubber Parts Installation

Rubber parts are typically installed as part of a larger process (like replacing the windshield) or as a detailing step after repainting the exterior or refinishing the interior. Usually the only difficulty in installing rubber parts is making sure they're not forgotten and in some cases recalling exactly where they go. If your truck is still intact (awaiting a mechanical and cosmetic upgrade or a thorough restoration) be sure to take photos and make notes on the locations of rubber parts before taking the truck apart. If the truck is already apart, you can get this information by taking photos and noting the locations of rubber parts on other original or restored trucks you may find in scrap yards or see at club events. You will also get clear instruction on the proper location of many rubber items from a Factory Assembly Manual.

An example of where the original rubber part or an illustration in the Factory Assembly Manual is helpful is in showing where to glue the door weather seal. The question here is not only the correct placement of the rubber, but also the proper location of seam if the weather seal is not all one piece. The seam location is important on a truck that will be entered in show competition, but even if competition is not your aim, it makes sense to attach the door seal in the original, rather than a haphazard, location.

Cabs from 1960 require one weather seal per door. The seal is mounted on the cab itself and the shop manual provides complete installation instructions. You can buy a complete set of door weather stripping from a variety of vendors. Besides

The rubber gasket holds the glass in place. Where the gasket has leaked, you will often find caulk or sealer that has to be removed to allow the new rubber to make a good seal.

looking fresh, the new weather seal eliminates drafty, leaky doors. This one-piece weather seal glues to the door.

Drafts can also be prevented from entering the cab by leaking air vent seals. On 1960-1966 trucks, the cowl/hood seal mounted on the cab along the rear of the hood deflects engine heat away from the wiper blades, thus extending their life of service.

Two sets of body seals which are rarely discussed (and not even mentioned in the Chevrolet Shop Manual) are the fender welt and rubber running board gasket. The welt between the rear fender and the box seals out water. The rubber running board gasket seals the surface between fender and the "step" on Stepside pickups. Serious damage can occur if water is allowed to accumulate in the area between the fender and the box or step.

In almost every instance, rubber parts are installed after painting. This is the sequence in which they were attached originally, with the result that rubber items left the factory unpainted. On trucks using hood lacing, this should also be attached after painting. the same sequence applies to door window channel and sweepers. In some cases, as with fender welting, the rubber items will be replaced as part of an assembly step. This means that on the older models where welting is used to prevent squeaks and seal the seams between fenders and body or box against moisture, the fenders would be painted separately, then installed with the welting being inserted as the fenders are bolted in place. It requires great care to avoid nicking or scratching the paint when bolting on the fenders. With 1967 and later model stepside trucks that do not use welting on the rear fenders, a bead of sealer (silicone or rubber caulk) should be applied to fender lip where it contacts the box to prevent moisture from penetrating this seam.

Rubber parts that are installed as part of mechanical repair, such as spring, shock absorber or front end bushings, are replaced during the appropriate reassembly step. To replace a steering column floor seal, it's be necessary to remove the steering column from the truck and disassemble the tube from the steering box. This effort is warranted on a frame up restoration where you may be overhauling the steering box and applying a high-gloss finish to the column, but if you're only doing needed mechanical and cosmetic work, removing the steering column to replace the post pad probably isn't worth the effort unless the original pad is completely deteriorated or missing—and then you may want to slit the replacement pad so as to fit it onto the post.

Many rubber items, both inside the cab and on the truck's exterior, are replaced as part of detailing after the truck is painted. Examples inside the cab would include the pedal pads, draft seals, and glove box bumpers; examples on the exterior would be the gas tank filler pipe grommet and tailgate chain rubbers. Most of these items just slip into place. If the fit is snug, as will most likely be the case with the filler pipe grommet and tailgate chain rubbers, a light coating of liquid dish soap to the rubber surface will allow the items to slide easily into place.

Door weather seal attaches with special glue. This process is relatively simple, but does involve several steps. At some point, the old rubber has to be removed. Usually this is done in preparation for rust repair and repainting. Although the old weather seal can often be pulled loose by hand, usually some of the rubber and glue sticks to the metal and has to be scraped clean with a putty knife. If you just want to replace the rubber and aren't planning on repainting, you will need to scrape very cautiously to avoid scratching the paint. Prep solvent, used to remove wax and tar from a finish in preparation for painting, can be used to soften the old glue and should be used to clean the surface before gluing new weather seal in place.

The metal around the old weather seal may look solid, but you're likely to find rust scale behind hardened or decayed rubber. If so, it's essential to clean away the rust before proceeding. When metal work isn't planned, you can clean surface rust with a wire brush or spot sandblaster, then prepare the metal with Naval Jelly, a phosphoric acid jell available in hardware stores. The white residue left by the jelly should be wiped off with a damp cloth before painting. The metal can then be primed and touch-up painted. If refinishing is planned, the weather seal channel can be sandblasted and any rust damage repaired.

Weather seal cement may be available from the rubber parts supplier and can also be purchased at auto parts stores. This glue comes in two types. One is applied to the metal and the rubber is pressed in place before the glue sets. With the other, a bead of glue is applied to both the metal and rubber. With this type, you wait until the glue becomes tacky before pressing the weather seal in place. With either type, you should be careful not to dab the glue on painted areas outside the weather seal channel. Any extra glue can be cleaned up with prep solvent, but it doesn't come off easily. If necessary, the rubber can be held in place on curves and the bottom of the door openings with strips of masking tape while the glue sets. Normally the glue is sticky enough to hold the rubber snugly in place without the tape. Be sure to give the glue time to set before closing the doors. Cowl vent and foot vent seals are attached using the same method.

On most trucks, window channel simply press-fits into the U-shaped channel on the door frame. On some, however, it glues in place against blocks, or is held by screws. If you removed the old channel, then the attaching method should be clear. If you weren't the disassembler, when you buy the replacement channel ask the vendor which attaching method applies to your truck. To install new window channel, first measure the channel distance (sides and upper window frame area), then cut and bend the channel to fit the contour of the window frame. Correct length channel is available from many specialty suppliers.

Installing door glass sweepers is somewhat trickier. On older trucks, the sweeper strips are held in place with clips. On newer models, the sweepers are secured with staples, but clips can be used if holes are drilled for them. When installing the sweeper, make sure the glass is rolled down as far as it will go. If you need even more glass clearance, you can detach the glass frame from the roll-up mechanism and let it rest against the bottom of the door. The sweeper has to be installed after the glass is in the door and the problem here is the risk of breaking the glass while squeezing the clips to secure the sweeper. If the window is made of non-tempered automotive glass (as found on older trucks and commonly used as replacement for side windows and flat windshields), it will crack very easily.

New rubber window seal is installed when the windshield and rear window glass are replaced after painting. Unless you have experience working with the large glass pieces that make up a windshield and side window, it's best to leave this job to professionals. Besides making glass installation look easy, the professionals will also make sure that the rubber is sealed to the window channel to prevent future seepage. Replacing ventilator pane weather strip (on trucks with vent pane windows) requires that the window glass and frame be removed. This procedure is described in the window glass section that follows.

Rubber Parts Preservation

Rubber deteriorates (dulls, hardens, and cracks) when exposed to sunlight, so to keep rubber parts soft and pliable, and to preserve their freshly-installed glossy look, it's a good idea to treat the rubber each time you wash your truck. The product to use is Armor All, a rubber moisturizer and protectorate, available at any discount mart's automotive department. ArmorAll can be sprayed directly onto the rubber, or applied to a rag and wiped on, where it freshens the rubber and leaves a glossy sheen. The product also freshens and helps prevent cracking on tires.

New rubber and other weather seal items change a truck's appearance more than you'll realize until you see the new parts in place. They give a restored or upgraded truck that finished look while making the truck more comfortable to drive by sealing the cab against drafts and water leakage.

Rubber Parts Repair

While specialty parts suppliers are doing an excellent job providing reproduction rubber parts for Chevrolet trucks, on early models especially, there may still be a few rubber items for which replacements are not available. The repair methods described here can be used when enough of the original rubber part is remains to serve as a basis for the repair, but the part is too badly deteriorated to use as is. This process does not apply to making new rubber parts.

If a cosmetic touch-up is all that's needed—to cover cracks or build up worn spots—the part can simply be dipped in Plastic Shield or a comparable product. Dipping rubber items to renew their finish only works when the original doesn't have large cracks or chips.

The procedure for repairing more badly damaged rubber starts with cleaning the part with a prep solution of the type used to clean metal in preparation for painting. This product is available at any auto parts store selling automotive refinishing products. When the prep solution has evaporated, a dam is built under the chipped or cracked areas using masking tape. If the rubber is torn, the sides of the tear should be pulled together for the repair. Sometimes the tear can be closed by clipping the edges together with a staple.

To fill the cracks and mend any tears, you'll use a two-part epoxy designed to repair chips in facia, fender flares, or other soft plastic or rubber parts on modern cars and trucks. Martin-Senour Flexible Bumper and Plastic Patch is formulated specially for this purpose. Other refinishing suppliers have similar products.

The filler is mixed with hardener in equal amounts just as you would with epoxy glue. After squeezing out two equal dabs of the filler and hardener onto a small square of cardboard, the two are mixed together. Now the filler can be spread over cracks or chips using a nail, toothpick or similar small applicator. The patch sets up quickly (about 15 minutes) and any excess can be sanded smooth with the surrounding surface. The patch product makes a permanent bond and has the pliability of fresh rubber. To give the entire rubber part a new look, and disguise the repair, use a semi-gloss paint designed for trim moldings on modern cars and trucks.

The procedures are a cosmetic repair and don't restore the softness and suppleness of new rubber. But where replacements are not available, these procedures make it possible to use an otherwise unusable part.

Window Glass Replacement

Breakage and cracks aren't the only reasons for replacing window glass in an older truck. Automotive safety glass turns cloudy along the edges with age and exposure to sunlight. In time, this cloudy band can extend several inches into the window, sometimes obscuring vision over nearly all the window area. If you've held off replacing cracked, cloudy, or even broken glass in your Chevrolet truck, thinking this was a job you'd have to take to a professional, there's no reason to live with the blemished glass any longer. Replacing side windows, including vent pane glass, calls only for basic mechanical skills and enough dexterity to avoid breaking the glass.

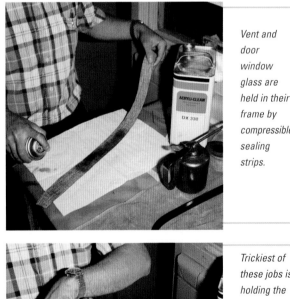

Vent and door window glass are held in their frame by compressible sealing strips.

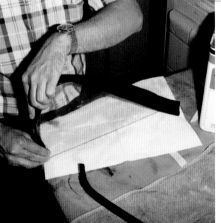

Trickiest of these jobs is holding the sealing strip in place around curved vent window glass from a 1952 or later Advance Design truck.

Compress the seal gently and carefully to avoid cracking the glass.

You will start by deciding which glass needs replacing. Let's understand that we're talking only about door window glass and vent panes in this chapter. Windshield and rear window glass, as well as rear corner windows on Advance Design five-window cabs, or on Suburbans, is held in place by rubber gaskets and requires a different technique than that presented here. Although it is possible for hobbyists to replace this gasket-retained glass, since windshields (particularly those that are one-piece or wrap around) are expensive, and in some

Because of the cost of new glass, windshield replacement (especially curved one-piece glass on newer trucks) is best left to professionals.

cases may be hard to find, so it's better to have these pieces installed by professionals.

The next step is removing the cracked, broken, or clouded glass. With door window glass, this requires removing the trim panels on the inside of the doors. These panels may be held in place by screws or clips. To remove the clips, you should use a tool designed for this purpose. These door panel clip removal tools are available from The Eastwood Co. and others. The inside door handle and window crank also need to be removed and these also are secured with clips or screws. To remove the clips, it is necessary to push in on the trim panel and slip the C-clips loose from the shank of the handle or window crank with a screwdriver or, preferably, the upholstery clip tool that has an insert on one end that fits the contour of the handle clips. When removing the last of the hardware, hold onto the trim panel so that it does not fall onto the ground.

When the door trim panels have been removed, you will be able to reach the window mechanism through the opening in the door. On trucks with vent panes, the vent pane frame needs to be removed in order to allow the door window glass to slide out of its channel at the rear of the vent pane assembly. The vent pane assembly is removed by loosening the screws that attach the vent pane channel to the inner door panel. With these screws removed, the vent pane assembly should pull up and out of the door.

Before attempting to remove the door glass, you will need to detach the weather seal that lines the lower edge of the window opening. This strip (which has a "whisker" appearance on older trucks and is made of rubber on more recent models) is typically held in place with clips and can be carefully pried loose.

Glass Removal

Now you can begin the process of removing the door glass itself. To do this, fit the window crank back on its lever and roll the window up or down until you see the screws that attach the window frame to the arm that raises or lowers the window. Exploded diagrams in parts catalogs or Assembly Manuals are helpful in seeing how these parts attach. Now position the window so that you can reach these screws with a wrench. Remove these screws, being careful not to drop them down in the bottom of the door. If this happens you may need a magnetic rod to fish" them out. Be sure to hold onto the window glass to keep it from falling down in the door. Once the window frame has been unbolted from the window regulator (the scissors-like mechanism that raises and lowers the glass), the glass and frame can be pulled up through the window slot in the door.

If the door glass is enclosed in a frame, as is the case with early Advanced Design and Task Force models, you will need to work the frame loose from the glass. The easiest way to do this is by squirting a few drops of gasoline along the edge of the window frame on both sides. Placing a small quantity of gasoline in an oil can will allow you to squirt the drops so that they penetrate the seal inside the window frame. The gasoline will soften the seal that holds the glass into the frame. Now you can remove the bolts that hold the upper frame channel to the lower channel and pull these two pieces apart. As the gasoline softens the channel seal you will be able to work the glass out of the upper channel. In some cases, this seal will have dried enough for the glass to pull out easily. In other cases, the seal may have hardened and you will have to pry out the glass. You can do this by gently tapping on the frame. Be very careful not to bend or break the channel. It will be used with the new glass

With the glass out of the frame, you will need to clean the channel. On early Advance Design trucks, the frame is painted whereas on Task Force series the door glass frame is bright metal. If the painted frame has surface rust, you will want to clean and refinish it. If the frame has more severe rust damage, it should be repaired or replaced. To give a bright metal frame a new look, the metal can be buffed following the instructions in the plating and buffing chapter.

Although replacement glass can be purchased at a shop that supplies and cuts automotive glass, the new windows will lack the factory markings. These markings, which include the manufacturer's name and sometimes the production date, are etched into factory glass and vehicles entering rigorous AACA or other national competition can lose points if fitted with glass that lacks these factory markings. Replacement glass with these markings is available from parts suppliers for your vintage Chevrolet truck and vintage auto glass suppliers. On years where tinted glass was offered, you may this glass available from your vintage Chevrolet parts supplier and decide to upgrade your truck with this glare resistant glass. Sometimes new-old-stock (NOS) glass can be found at swap meets or on eBay. If you buy glass from these sources, be sure to check the stock number (taken either from the original glass or a parts book) of the replacement glass and carefully inspect or inquire about the edge of the glass to make sure seal between the glass layers has not deteriorated and that the glass is free from clouding.

There is no "left" or "right" to side door glass. This means that the markings will be on the inside of the glass on one side and on the outside on the other. Small detail points like this are important in the rigorous upper levels of AACA competition.

Glass Fitting

As you prepare to replace the glass, you will need to gather several items. These include channel liner (a thin rubbery strip available from most shops that do glass replacement), windshield sealer/glue and new window channel weather seal. To install the new door glass a strip of channel liner is cut slightly longer than the glass and placed over the section of glass that is being fit into the channel. For most years, this will be the bottom edge, though on some models Chevrolet also enclosed the upper glass outline in a metal channel. To be sure the glass

doesn't work loose from the channel at some point in the future, you should spread a bead of glass adhesive in the channel before fitting the glass. Some adhesive will be squeezed out of the channel when the glass is inserted, but can be scraped off with a putty knife and the glass washed with prep solvent, a product used to prepare the surface for painting.

Now the glass can be pressed into the channel. If the fit is tight, you may have to tap the channel onto the glass. If you do this, place a hardwood board on the channel and rest the glass on another board. Tap very gently only against the wood so as not to crack the glass. Fitting glass in a channel that only covers the bottom of the glass is usually not difficult. Fitting glass into a frame can be more difficult and you may want to have this done at a shop which installs automotive glass. There the glass will be fitted into the frame using a clamping device. When the glass is seated in the frame or channel, you can cut off the excess channel liner and clean up the glue.

Fitting replacement glass into the vent frames follows the same process. If the vent frame is out of the truck, it is possible to force the glass in place by resting the frame on a block of wood, placing another block of wood (a short length of 2x4 works well) against the glass and tapping the wood gently with a hammer. Remember that glass is delicate; forceful tapping can easily crack or break the glass.

If the window channel liner is worn and needs replacing, this should be done before fitting the glass back in the doors. The procedure for installing window channel begins by measuring the old channel and cutting the new strip to this length. Next you will bend the new channel to the approximate contour of the old. If the old channel has not been removed, it can be pried out of its frame at this time. In some cases, the

Sealing the Cowl Vent on Advance Design Pickups
by Ronald Olsen

When I bought my truck, the cowl vent was sealed closed with silicone seal. Last summer I wanted the vent to open so I freed it up and of course it leaked when I washed the truck or it rained (not unheard of here in Oregon). The solution was to apply a bead of silicone seal under the cowl, between the cowl and the "water track." Surprise! No more leak. My truck's radio and speaker were out when I applied the silicone and made a great window to the underside of the cowl. Without the radio, this area is easy to work in. I am not sure the reason for the leak, but I was delighted that the fix was so easy. The rubber or foam vent gasket is apparently a draft seal and not a water seal.

channel may be held in place by rivets. In others it is press fit. If rivets were used, the new channel can be secured with pop rivets. If the channel was press fit, you can provide a more permanent attachment by putting dabs of adhesive on the back of the channel before pressing it in place.

Fitting the glass back in the doors is basically a matter of reversing the procedure you used to remove it. First, you will slip the glass and frame down in the window slot in the door. Next you will bolt the frame to the window slide. What's important here is to align the frame so that the glass doesn't bind in the channel. Cranking the glass up and down will test the alignment. Be sure to oil all moving parts of the window mechanism while the door panel is off and the mechanism is accessible.

The vent pane frame also installs in reverse order of which it was removed. If the hinge rivet was cut to remove the vent frame, a new rivet will have to be installed. These are available from vintage Chevrolet parts suppliers. With both the vent pane and door glass in place, roll up the door glass and close the vent pane to make sure the glass is fitted properly. Now roll the door glass all the way down and replace the weather strip that seals the glass at the window opening. Chances are the tiny clips that hold this weather strip in place are still in their sockets on the door. When fitting the weather strip into the clips, be very careful not to pry against the door glass. Localized stress of this type can crack the glass.

With the weather strip in place, the door panels and handles are replaced and the job is finished. New glass gives any vehicle a fresher look and improves visibility as well.

Windshield Leaks

Most leakage occurs in the left and right lower corners. The problem can be due to a poorly prepared weatherstrip or a deteriorated one; however, new windshields with new rubber

moldings are also prone to leak because the new glass is thinner than the original and new weatherstip retains the same channel dimensions.

Often, the windshield has been replaced at least once over the last 30 to 35 years. Perhaps the first time it was replaced there was a small water leak. The normal fix would have been to apply a urethane sealer between the cab and weatherstripping. This sealer would flow into the problem area and seal the leak.

A common reason for water leakage after windshield replacement is that the glass installer fails to clear the rubber weatherseal of all old sealers. Over time, these sealers harden. When the old sealer are not removed completely from the sealing surface after the weatherstripping, they cause that area to set above the windshield opening causing a leak. If you are preparing the weatherstripping yourself for re-installing, clean the weatherseal completely of all the old sealer and foreign material. Only then can you be assured of a windshield free of leakage. A good soft windshield weatherstripping can be used many times if it is prepared properly and has not dried up causing it to crack. New weatherseal avoids the sealer build-up problem, but there is still the issue of the thinner class.

The leak problem can be compounded if the metal ridge around the windshield opening that holds the weatherseal and windshield in place has rusted (or is missing in spots) due to earlier leakage. If this metal lip is corroded, metal repair may need to be done to rebuild it. In extreme cases, the cab may need to be replaced.

Should you find that leakage occurs after the new windshield is installed, you will, of course, have to reapply a bead of sealer between the weatherstripping and windshield in the area of the leak.

As the rubber gasket dries out it leaks causing the window channel to rust. If the rust is superficial, it can be cleaned and repainted, but where part of the channel has been eaten away, the damage is more serious and the metal will have to be repaired. Serious damage in this channel may require finding a different cab.

Pickups are working vehicles and the cargo box is where the work occurs, so it's not unlikely that extensive repair or rebuilding will be needed, especially if the goal is to return the truck to like-new condition. Fortunately, the design and stampings, especially of the narrow Stepside boxes changed little over the years, so new, reproduction steel parts are available from a number of vendors for Chevrolet pickup boxes of most years. It is often cheaper to purchase replacements than to have body work done on the box panels. Tailgates, which usually take a beating or are sometimes missing, can also be purchased new. Good used tailgates can sometimes be purchased at swap meets, and may be available on scrap yard trucks depending on the rust problem in your area. A variety of plain and louvered tailgate covers offer a low cost way of simply hiding tailgate damage. The louvered covers also provide a custom appearance. A nice finishing touch for the tailgate is the application of adhesive letters. These "Chevrolet" lettering kits are available in chrome, black, or white letters through several vendors.

The appearance of the box and bed wood is generally a matter of personal concern. If you plan to use your truck for hauling, it doesn't make sense to put in replacement wood, unless the bed wood is rotted. Sanding, filling, staining, and applying polyurethane varnish or paint will generally rejuvenate the original wood into a respectable looking bed. But, if you are building a show truck, you'll want to install new wood in the bed. Vendors offer replacement bed wood in pine, oak,

hickory, cherry, or pecan. Polished or plain stainless steel or chromed bed angle irons and bed strips can also be purchased to complete the show look, though these are not desirable for authenticity and could lead to a loss of points in closely scrutinized Vintage Chevrolet Club of America (VCCA) or Antique Automobile Club of America (AACA) competition. For those desiring to restore their trucks to factory standards, the bed wood and metal strips were painted the same color as the truck body. Bed wood installed in the trucks was made of pine and was not available in stained or varnished finishes.

If the box sides are solid, they can be sandblasted, straightened and reused.

This is how the box often looks starting out, with cracked, deteriorated and missing pieces of wood.

Pickup Box Removal and Inspection

Work on the pickup box almost always begins by removing the box from the frame. The box comes off easily by removing or cutting a few bolts. Its condition can be inspected much easier and the box can be worked on more conveniently when separated from the rest of the truck. The condition of the bed wood should be apparent, but the metal may look more intact than it really is. A cutting torch can be used to remove the bolts under the floor or a truck bed, but care should be taken to avoid letting the flame hit the bed side sheet metal. These large, flat expanses of metal can warp very quickly and be very difficult to repair.

You can easily determine the presence and extent of rust by poking a thin bladed screwdriver or ice pick into suspected areas, typically where you already see small holes or paint blisters. The bottoms of stake supports are particularly susceptible areas for rust. If the box sides are sound and not badly dented, you may decide to replace only the stake supports. These can be removed by drilling out the spot welds, purchasing new stake supports from one of the vintage Chevrolet truck parts suppliers and welding the new supports onto the side panel.

If the damage is more extensive, you face the decision of what to replace and what to repair. If your truck has the narrow Stepside box, you can unbolt and replace whatever pieces are badly rusted or dented as the sides, cross sills, and even tailgates are available in remanufactured form. Since most of these replacement pieces are manufactured offshore and have been in transport halfway around the world, it's likely that even the new parts will have minor scratches or dents that will need to be repaired in the restoration process. Entire new boxes are also available in knocked down form and need to be bolted together before painting and mounting on your truck.

If you are restoring your truck for show competition, you'll probably face the temptation to fill sport welds and other imperfections in the metal, with the aim of giving the box a mirror-smooth finish. However, for VCCA and AACA competition that holds vehicles closely to original standards, it is important not to disturb the spot welds and other markings made by the manufacturing process, since this is how these boxes came from the factory. After all, there are certain things that make a truck a truck, and spot welds joining the stake pockets to the box sides are among them.

Wooden Bed Restoration
By Bruce Horkey

One job that is nearly always required in restoring an old truck is replacing the wooden flooring in the pickup box. The wood may still be intact, but scarred and scraped—a condition that gives a truck a well-worked look. Whether you are restoring or rebuilding, you'll want to renew your truck's wooden pickup box flooring. This is a job you can do yourself; all the parts and pieces you'll need are available from a number of suppliers. When you're done you'll not only have the pride of your accomplishment, but you'll realize that nothing sets a vintage truck off like new wood in the pickup box.

All the narrow Stepside and many of the wide Fleetside boxes have wooden floors. The Fleetside boxes often have metal floors that are subject to extensive dent and rust damage. Where replacement metal floor pieces are available, a Fleetside box can be repaired in this way. However, if new metal flooring is not available, or if you would rather have a wood floored box, wooden flooring was available from the factory on Fleetside boxes as an option. To convert a metal floored Fleetside box to a wood floor, you will need to replace the front panel and rear cross sill as well as the bed support cross sills. These parts are all available.

Restoration of wooden bed floors in trucks from the 1930s to 1960s can be accomplished in several ways, but when it comes to winning show trophies, care and professional quality are all-important. To that end,, pickup box restorer and

Start by setting up a level work surface. Bruce Horkey

manufacturer of box wood parts nearly all Chevrolet pickups, Bruce Horkey mdescribes the step-by-step procedure he uses to build show-winning wooden pickup beds..

Preparation

Clean up the box and floor. Take pictures of all the details and make notes for reference at assembly time. Make notes also on sequence and fit, list all fasteners (size, type, and location). Remove the fenders, lights, and wiring. Order new

C-clamp the box sides onto horses using the lower lip of the box side. Bruce Horkey

wood, skid strips, and angle braces. If the box sides, front, or tailgate are badly dented or rusted and need replacing, also order these parts.

Disassembly

To make room for working underneath, remove the pickup box from the frame and set it on sawhorses or stands. Remove the old bed wood, skid strips, bolts, and cross members.

Scribe a reference line above and below the angles on the box sides for replacement reference. Measure from the bottom of the box side to the underside on the angle. Write down this measurement. Make notes on hole locations and angle location on the box side.

Center punch the spot welds attaching the angle pieces at the outer edges of the floor to the box. These welds will be

drilled out with a spot weld cutter. Set the depth of the cutter to drill only through the angle. After drilling out the spot welds, remove the old angle.

Cleaning and Metal Repair

Strip/sandblast the box metal, do any needed dent and metal repair work, refinish the box sides, front, and tailgate.

Set the width of the box at the rear crossmember according to the width of the front panel. Make sure the bedsides are square with the rear crossmember.

Clean the angle pieces along the sides of the bed and area around them. These will be the first items replaced.

Square the Box

Measure the box diagonally from corner to corner (driver's front to passenger's rear, passenger's front to driver's rear) to

Measure and lay out the box width to determine the location of the other box side. Bruce Horkey

Detail view of rear main crossmember. The box-to-frame bracket varies from metal to wood and location depending on vintage. A 1934-36 Chevrolet bracket is shown. Bruce Horkey

The rear crossmember, a U-shaped channel at the rear of the bed, fits into and attaches to the stake pockets. Bruce Horkey

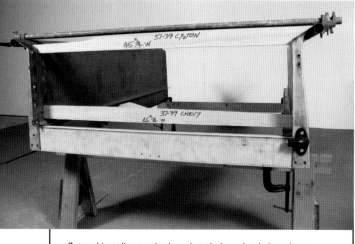

Cut and install spreader boards to help maintain box shape.
Bruce Horkey

Use carpenter's square to check squareness of the box.
Bruce Horkey

assure squareness. Push or pull the box sides to get them square. When the box is square, the measurements will be the same.

Replace Angle Braces

Set the cleaned or new angles in place, following notes made earlier, and mark hole locations to box side. (If you are working with angles that have no holes on the shorter side, note fender and stake pocket locations and decide where to drill holes to attach the angles to the box sides).

Drill holes in the box side and attach angles. (For originality, the angles should be spot welded in place instead of bolting).

Wood sits on the lip of the front bed panel and under the angle on the bedside Use a spacer to create clearance for the bed wood. This spacer board aligns the height of the rear cross member and front bed panel. Bruce Horkey

Use a carpenter's square to make sure sides are square to crossmember. Bruce Horkey

Fit New Bed Wood

Set edge boards in place and mark holes to attach angles to edge boards. Remove boards and drill holes with 3/8 diameter bit. Install edge boards and drop bolts through the angles. Loosely install the cross members.

Install one board and skid strip at a time. Install bolts, nuts, and washers loosely from the inside of the box by reaching over and under the boards. Install boards in an alternating pattern, first on one side of the box, then on the other.

188

Snug up bolts to maintain a square box. Bruce Horkey

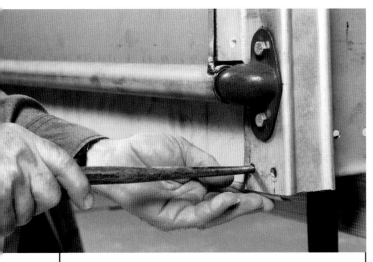

Insert a punch through holes to help maintain alignment.
Bruce Horkey

Slide tailgate onto hinge and install second hinge. Square up
tailgate to box sides. Bruce Horkey

Attach bracket for tailgate chains, if needed. Align with slot in
tailgate. Bruce Horkey

Install the center board and last two skid strips and bolts. Align the boards and adjust everything to fit.

Install Hardware

From the underside, loosely install the remaining nuts and washers loosely. Make one final check for alignment and squareness. Hand-tighten all nuts.

Replace Box on Frame

After you're satisfied with the fit, set the box on the truck frame. Note: Place a blanket over the front box panel to protect it and the cab from bumping together and scratching the finish.

Drop in the hold-down bolts and washers. Square the box on the frame and make alignment adjustments then bolt the box in place. Caution: don't over tighten the skid strip bolts. Now stand back and admire your work.

Install Fenders

Attach the front of the rear fender to the running board or stop. Adjust the rear of the fender and mark hole locations of you replaced the bedsides with parts lacking fender holes. Fenders were held on with 5/16 in. fasteners, so the holes need to be 11/32 in. On pre-1955 Chevy trucks there were usually one or two fender bolts that went through the center of

189

Set up tailgate to lie flush with box floor when open. Bruce Horkey

the bed to the box angle that is attached to the bed side. These could be used as reference holes for attaching the fenders.

Procedure for Varnishing Wooden Box Flooring
By Bruce Horkey

Although Chevy pickups didn't leave the factory with varnished flooring on the pickup box, most truck owners prefer a high-gloss finish on the pickup planking over the dull black or painted coatings that were applied to the wooden flooring as the box came down the assembly line. Actually, the varnish finish is important for more than just appearance. It also protects and in so doing extends the life of your truck's bed wood. Here are the steps to follow in applying a quality varnish finish.

To begin, you will need to gather the following tools and materials: file with safe edge (no teeth on one side), 120 grit or 280 grit sandpaper, tack cloth, Scotchbrite ultra fine pad, two varnish brushes, two 2 lb. coffee cans or similar containers, two qt. marine spar varnish, one qt. quality paint thinner, wipes, rubber gloves, a respirator, safety glasses, dust mask and saw horses. In order to minimize dust contamination in the wood finish, two work areas are needed: one to do the wood prep and finish sanding and another for a clean area to apply the finish.

The space you select to do the varnishing should have good ventilation (this is healthier for you and gives faster drying). Clean the area thoroughly. Sweep the floor well, then wet it down to settle the dust. Make sure your hands and contact surfaces arfe clean before handling the bed wood. Wearing rubber gloves minimizes contamination of both the wood and your hands.

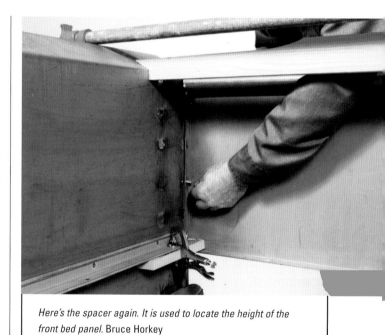

Here's the spacer again. It is used to locate the height of the front bed panel. Bruce Horkey

Parts Preparation

Pre-fit all wood before applying varnish, then with the file, stroke off the sharp edges of the boards. This will prevent the edges from snagging the brush and assure better adhesion for the varnish. When filing the edge of the groove, lay the file on the groove at a 45-degree angle and allow the safe edge (no teeth) to ride on the bottom of the groove. Now use the 120-grit sandpaper wrapped on a wood block to finish rounding all the edges. This will ease the edges and the finish will stay

Measure diagonally to maintain a square box. Bruce Horkey

on better. A sharp edge will be an area where the finish will be the weakest.

Sand the faces and edges in the direction of the grain with 12-grit sandpaper. After you are satisfied with the surface quality of the wood, vacuum off all surfaces. Then follow with a tack cloth, wiping the wood free of any dust or particles. Commercial tack cloths contain waxes to help pick up dust. Make certain to unfold and fluff up the tack cloth. Lightly wipe down each plank; you are only removing the dust so go easy on the cloth pressure. A light touch will help avoid transferring contaminants from the tack cloth to the piece. Now arrange the boards on saw horses, damp mop the floor to suppress dust, and get out the varnishing supplies.

Applying Varnish

Before applying the finish you must remove any oily film or residue to be certain of good adhesion. Use a quality, fast-drying solvent to remove any surface contamination. Allow the wood to dry completely before applying any finish. The solvent may raise the grain of the wood slightly. If so, take the 280-grit sandpaper and wisk off the raised wood fiber. Tack off

the boards again. After you are satisfied with the surface quality of the boards you can apply the finish.

Temperature and humidity affect all drying processes. The ideal temperature for varnishing is 68-72 degrees F. and the relative humidity should be around 35-40 percent. Avoid applying varnish in temperatures lower than 68 degrees F. Higher temperatures generally do not cause problems until they rise over 90 degrees F.

For the first varnish coat, pour 8 oz. of varnish into another container and gently mix in 2 oz. of thinner for a 75 percent/25 percent mix. A 2 lb. coffee can makes a good mixing container. *Do not shake or stir varnish vigorously.* Bubbles are another problem. They sometimes result from striking the brush off on the side of the can. Then the bubbly varnish drips back into the liquid surface. Bubbles can be avoided by striking the brush into an empty coffee can.

Apply the thinned varnish to the wood completely and evenly, coating all surfaces. After you've coated the complete board surface, lightly pull your brush the full length. This will even out a randomly applied finish. Spar Varnish is slow drying so it will self-level. Dry spots will be noticeable by their

191

Set edge boards in place, mark angle holes, remove and drill. Make sure all holes are the same distance from the box side. Bruce Horkey

After installing edge boards, loosely install the mid-crossmembers. Bruce Horkey

Working over and under the boards, loosely install the strips and boards. Bruce Horkey

dull, non-reflective appearance. Let this first coating dry overnight (eight to twelve hours). Drying time will depend on humidity, ventilation, and temperature. A low speed fan can be used to gently move air over the drying boards.

Cover and seal the unused varnish. Do not pour it back into the original unthinned product. Do not use any left-over varnish that has begun to gel.

When the first coat is dry, apply a second coat of 75 percent/25 percent thinned varnish. This will ensure proper varnish penetration and provide a more complete moisture barrier for the wood.

Once the second coat has been allowed to dry, remove the wood from the varnishing area and lightly sand in the direction of the grain with 280-grit sandpaper. Avoid cutting through the finish on the edges. Do not sand round edges. Go lightly on sanding pressure. The sanding is intended to level out any dust and imperfections on the surface. While sanding,

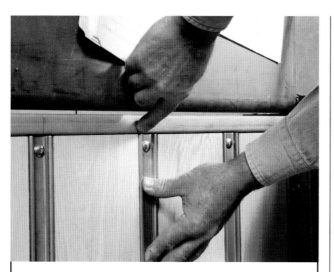

Once all boards are installed, equally space all pieces at the tailgate end. Then snug up the end row of bolts to hold all pieces in alignment. Move to the front and snug up this end row of bolts. Shift the mid-crossmembers to space these properly and snug up these bolts. Attach the remaining bolts using fender washers to span the gap between boards. Bruce Horkey

clean the sandpaper and board surface often to avoid loading the sandpaper. Replace the sandpaper as it loads up. Use only the Scotch Brite pad on rounded edges. Wipe off dust with a tack cloth. Bring the wood back to the varnishing area

For the third coat of varnish, you want to gently dilute and mix the solution to 90 percent varnish and 10 percent thinner ratio. You may want to coat only the backside, ends and edges and allow this coating to dry before applying the third coat to the face side. When the third varnish coating has dried thoroughly, move the wood away from the varnishing area and lightly sand with 280 grit sandpaper. Wipe the boards with a tack cloth to remove all dust. Then go over the wood again using a Scotch Brite pad to remove any remaining gloss from the last coat. Wipe down again with the tack cloth.

On the fourth coat, use a fresh can of varnish and a fresh, clean brush. Apply the varnish full strength first to the backside, edges, and ends—and allow the boards to dry. Then apply the varnish full strength to the face side. When the boards have dried, remove the wood from the refinishing area and again lightly sand following the grain with 280-grit sandpaper. Avoid cutting through the finish, especially along the edges and ends. Use the Scotch Brite pad to remove all remaining gloss.

The bed is now assembled and ready to fit onto the pickup frame. When you're satisfied with the fit, remove and disassemble to prep and finish all parts. Bruce Horkey

This rusted stake pocket will have to be replaced.

Now the stake pockets can be rewelded to a cleaned or new box side piece.

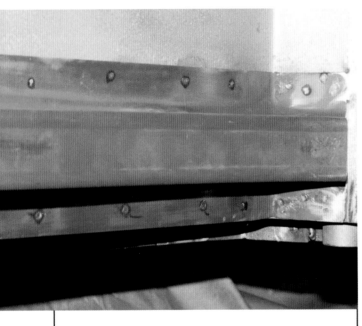

Stake pockets can be removed by grinding and drilling the welds.

Repeat this process for the fifth coat, except for sanding and buffing. Spar Varnish can be reapplied over a sound, old finish by cleaning and sanding to remove imperfections, contamination and gloss. Apply full strength, as in the fifth coat.

Put a Gloss on the Finish

When you are happy with the last coat and have given it at least 72 hours to dry (a week or more drying time is better), it's

Removing Angle Strips
by Mark Sharp

On Stepside boxes from 1973 and up, the angle strip bolts that go through the wood are apparently welded to the angle strip. If the bolts are being replaced when installing new bed wood they must be drilled out. I recommend that you use care when removing the nuts so that these bolts can be reused. The old wood must be destroyed to get it out from under the angle strips and the holes on the new outer boards will have to be slotted to the edge in order to be inserted under the angle strip. If the bolts are to be drilled out and replaced, I recommend using "ribbed neck" carriage bolts which can be pressed into the old bolt hole.

time to rub out the finish. For a satin finish, sand with the grain with 600-grit sandpaper and polish with an ultra-fine Scotch Brite pad. Rub down the surface with a clean cloth and you are through. A coating of paste wax will seal and preserve your efforts. The wax can be buffed to the desired sheen.

New, reproduction box sides are available with the stake pockets already in place.

Box sides and rear cross member set up for reassembly. Bruce Horkey's procedure of placing the box on horses makes the assembly process easier.

For a high-gloss finish, sand with 600-grit sandpaper followed by 1200-grit, always with the grain. Wrap the sandpaper around a wood block and use a few drops of liquid dish soap in water as a wetting agent. A rubber squeegee and towel help clear away the slurry. After sanding out all the nubs, swap the wood block for a cork block and give another even sanding, trying to get the surface as flat as possible. Pay special attention to the edges where the varnish can build up a little ridge. You can judge the flatness of the surface by looking at the reflection of a light on the board surface. If it looks as though the light is reflecting off the surface of a wind-swept pond, you have more sanding to do.

To complete the gloss finish, apply Meguiar's Mirror Glaze #1 (an automotive rubbing compound). Buff it out

Suburbans also have wooden floors that are replaced in essentially the same manner as pickups.

Notice that the inside box surfaces on Cameos are not painted body color.

using a low speed air or electric buffer with a waffle surface type foam pad. Wipe off all residue from the #1 compound, then buff again with #3 glaze and a fresh pad to bring the surface to a mirror finish. After the finish has cured for about 30 days you can apply a a coat of Carnuba paste floor wax to seal and preserve your efforts.

Ultra-violet light from the sun, ozone, detergent and air pollution all try to destroy the finish. Treat this wood like fine furniture. Remove dust with a soft cloth.

Painted Box Wood

The box flooring on Chevrolet trucks from 1947 to mid 1955 came from the factory with a dull black coating of a somewhat thin consistency. This means that if you are restoring your truck for VCCA or AACA competition, you will need to avoid the more finished looking varnished or painted planking. Mike Cavey, who has restored an AACA national prize winning truck of this vintage, says that he finds a mixture of linseed oil and lamp black creates the correct finish for the bed wood. The correct wood for the bed is yellow pine.

Later trucks had painted box wood. To achieve a quality-looking, durable painted finish on the box flooring, first prime the boards then apply a semi-gloss alkyd (oil) base enamel paint. The prime coating should be thinned slightly with mineral spirits and worked into all surfaces of the boards. When this coating has dried, the boards should be sanded lightly on the face with 280 grit sandpaper and wiped with tack cloth to remove all dust. Then a second prime coating should be applied, allowed to dry, and again slightly sanded. This is followed with the enamel paint, which is applied full strength to all surfaces of the boards.

Refinishing should be done after all machine work and hole drilling is completed. This will assure that all exposed surfaces are protected by the finish coating.

CHAPTER 18

PLATING TRIM

One advantage of restoring a truck, as opposed to a car, is that in most cases there's only a small amount of brightwork (chrome and stainless trim) to redo. Of course there are exceptions, most notably the later-Fifties deluxe cab models and the ultra-fancy Cameo with their chrome bumpers and grille and bright moldings around the windows. Cameo restorers also have to contend with plated diecast tail light housings, a chrome band at the front of the bed, and for 1957 and 1958, plated trim bands on the sides of the box. On most trucks, however, chrome trim is limited to the headlight rims, possibly the grille and front bumper, nameplates, door handles, and miscellaneous small knobs and control handles inside the cab.

In the 60s and 70s, stainless and aluminum replaced chrome on the grille, again simplifying this phase of the restoration process. Much of the brightwork on these later model trucks is available in reproduction form. With few exceptions, it is cheaper to buy new chrome parts than to have original pieces rechromed. Plating is an environmentally harsh process and a large portion of the cost you pay to have parts rechromed covers environmental expenses. Most reproduction chrome plated parts are manufactured in countries where environmental regulations are much laxer than is the case for the replating services.

Nothing brightens up a restored or upgraded truck like gleaming chrome and shining bright metal trim. Neglecting the brightwork will leave a truck looking shabby regardless of the quality of the painted finish. With a restoration, parts can be sent away for rechroming at any time. It is advisable to send parts out for rechroming well before final assembly is anticipated because two months or more can elapse between the time that you deliver or ship the parts to the plating shop and when they are ready to be picked up or arrive back at your door. When a truck is being made serviceable by rebuilding, sending parts out for rechroming is best done during refinishing.

Since having parts replated is expensive, you're going to want the best quality at an affordable price. You may have heard tales of woe from other restorers or have had unpleasant plating experiences or whose parts were lost or who claimed they received someone else's parts instead of their own. The section that follows should help you avoid these and other traps that can occur in the replating process.

Satisfactory Plating

It helps to think of the bright chrome on a plated part as being like a clear finish coating. The chrome plating doesn't cover surface imperfections. So pits or any damage on the surface of the plated part will be visible and in fact is enhanced by the bright metal coating. If you send parts for replating that are dented or pitted you're likely to receive brighter dented or pitted parts back. You contract with a plating service to restore your parts and then apply the bright chrome plating, but restorative plating is a time-consuming and expensive because it requires that the plating shop do all the work of straightening, buffing and filling pits in addition to doing the plating. The advice from plating services is to send them the best parts you can find. On this basis, they can deliver quality plating at an acceptable cost.

Straightening and locating missing trim parts is only the first step. To look like new, non-stainless trim has to be replated. John Hart

See the contrast in the replated grille. Yes, it's the same truck. John Hart

Bumpers also may need straightening and replating.
John Hart

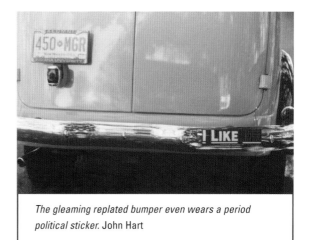

The gleaming replated bumper even wears a period political sticker. John Hart

Here's an example of someone finding better condition parts for plating. Let's say that you are restoring an Advance Design series truck like Mike Cavey's 1951 Chevrolet pickup featured throughout this book. The truck has a plated grille but the plating has lost its shine and the bars are rusted and pitted. Either the grille will have to be taken through an expensive restorative plating process or the plating service will simply remove the old plating and rust and apply the new bright coating over the pitted metal. You may not have specified that anything else be done, but you won't be satisfied with the results.

A better approach would be to locate a painted grille without rust (making sure the paint is original and not a new coating hiding metal work as well as pits) and have the paint stripped off and these uncoated bars plated. Of course, better parts are not always available. A plated grille was available as an option on standard trucks in the Advance Design series so there are plenty of unplated grilles to be found. Our example is only a partial solution, however, as straight, unpitted parts are not always available.

Types of Plating

Plating services are of two types: commercial services, which can be found through the Yellow Pages of larger city telephone books, and restoration plating shops which advertise in old car and truck hobby magazines. Commercial shops are usually less expensive, but they'll spent little if any time preparing the parts for plating, other than stripping off the old plating layers. They're usually not very interested in odd lots of parts and are rightfully reluctant to replate parts for vintage autos and trucks because they know from experience that restorers are likely to be dissatisfied with their service.

The first question a commercial plater will ask when you inquire about replating trim parts on your truck is whether or not any of these parts are diecast. Diecast is a man-made metal that melts at low temperatures and is therefore ideal for making molded trim parts. It was used for years to make tail light housings, trim plates, hood ornaments, control knobs, and other decorative items on cars and trucks. More recently manufacturers have replaced diecast with plastic. Most commercial platers will refuse to replate diecast, for good reason. The diecast metal is porous. This means that during the electrolysis process, where the old plating is stripped off and new copper, nickel, and chrome layers applied, chemicals from the electrolysis solution may seep into the diecast piece. As the chemicals leach out of the metal, they will be trapped by the plating layers. Unable to escape, the chemicals will bubble underneath the plating. Also, the gray, powdery pocks often seen in corroded diecast pieces cannot simply be ground or buffed smooth. Corrosion enters diecast like a cancer, eating deeply into the metal. To restore a corroded diecast part, the powdery pocks are often drilled out and replaced with brass or other non-corrosive metal. A commercial plater does not have the time or manpower to undertake a restoration process with diecast and knows that anything less will not result in customer satisfaction. So typically, the shop will simply say "No."

Commercial platering services can be an economical source for replating steel parts like bumpers and grille bars. For a truck that's not being restored to a show finish, a commercial plating will give acceptable quality—if you bring in good parts. The best parts for commercial plating are bumpers or other trim that was painted originally and is not dented or rusted. The plater will remove the paint and any surface rust in a chemical dip. Vintage trucks have an advantage over cars in that chrome bumpers and grilles were the exception on trucks in most years, so painted parts are relatively plentiful. As cautioned earlier, avoid buying parts for plating that have been repainted.

For replating die cast trim plates, hood ornaments, control knobs and other diecast parts, you'll need to contact a restoration plating service. Fortunately, there's not a great deal of diecast metal on a truck because replating these parts can be expensive. Unless you live near one of these services, you will probably make contact by phone or e-mail. Typically you will be asked to send the parts for an estimate, then wait several weeks (possibly two to four months) for the work to be completed. Often you will have a choice of quality with show chrome being the most expensive, but also giving the brightest shine and most perfect finish. As you think of quality, you should consider more than just the cost. The primary factor is your intended purpose for the truck. If your plans include entering the truck in show competition, quality is important at every step of the restoration process. If the truck will be driven and enjoyed, then show quality plating may not be desirable for two reasons. First, chances are you won't maintain the finish and chrome at its peak brilliance and so the show plating's glistening shine will soon be hidden under a coating of dust. Second, if you have other parts (the front bumper for example) redone by a commercial plating service, the difference in quality between show chrome on the trim and commercial plating on the bumper will be noticeable. It's better that all bright work be of a uniform grade.

The Plating Process

To understand the differences in plating quality, let's look at what happens when parts arrive at the plating shop. Typically, the parts are first dipped in a chemical bath to remove dirt, grease, paint, and other coatings. Next, they move through a series of baths where existing plating layers are stripped off by reverse electrolysis. Chrome plating is removed in one tank, nickel in another and so on until only bare metal remains. Now the parts go to a buffing room where the metal is ground down on a buffing wheel to smooth any pits or other surface imperfections. It's at this step that the quality of the parts becomes important. Buffing is a manual operation and is labor intensive. If parts need only minimal buffing to smooth the surface, the cost for this step will be low. Badly pitted parts will need extensive buffing which not only adds to the bill, but also can result in the shape of the parts being distorted as the buffer attempts to remove pits by cutting away the metal.

If the part being re-plated is an assembly, like a vent window lock with a spring, pin, and shaft in addition to the chrome plated handle the plater may not bother with disassembly. In this case, the chemical dipping and reverse electrolysis may remove the temper from the spring and parts of the assembly may interfere with proper buffing of the handle. It's important to disassemble items being replated as much as possible so as not to interfere with the replating process.

In restoration plating (which may be required if good quality parts are not available) rather than remove pits by buffing away the metal, a soft copper plating layer is applied, then the parts are buffed so that the copper coating becomes a filler thereby preserving the part's shape. Commercial platers do not perform the copper buildup step prior to buffing.

The bright metal looking instrument cluster on 1967-1972 Chevrolet trucks is actually plastic and the chrome plating is in reality a very thin layer of aluminum.

After buffing the parts go into the copper plating tank for the base copper layer. Depending on the desired quality, parts may stay in the copper plating tank anywhere from twenty minutes to four hours. The deep bluish luster that seems to gleam from far within top quality chrome plating results from a thick underlying layer of copper. With restorative plating, parts may be buffed again and sent through the copper plating step successive times. The copper plating and buffing process is kin to priming and sanding in preparing a show-quality finish.

After the copper layer, the parts receive a coating of nickel. The nickel plate assures a good bond with the chrome and helps gives the chrome its deep, rich brilliance. Parts will spend about twenty minutes in the nickel plating tanks. Between each plating step, the parts are rinsed thoroughly to keep chemicals in one tank from contaminating the next. Chrome plating is the final step and takes only a few minutes. When parts emerge from the chrome tank they are covered

This dented headlight rim purchased at the Hershey swap meet made an ideal test subject for restoring bright work.

Wooden dowels cut to the contour of the part work well to drive out dents. Work from the shallowest part of the dent to the deepest to avoid stretching the metal.

with a butter-colored film. The shiny chrome finish appears after the final rinse. Since the chrome plating is very thin and almost superficial, the secret to quality plating lies almost entirely with the thoroughness of the preparation and depth in the preceding copper and nickel layers.

To make your plating dollars stretch as far as possible, you should help the plater by sending the best quality parts and disassemble the parts fully. Commercial platers probably won't both with disassembly and restoration platers will charge for the time they spend on the disassembly process. An example of a small assembly that should be taken apart for plating would be the ventipane latch mentioned earlier. An example of a larger assembly would be a grille. Unless you want the plater to replate the grille intact (as could be the case with the grille of a mid-30s Chevy truck) you should remove the grille bars and send just the parts needing to be plated.

Replating Plastic Parts

On 1960s and later trucks, some of the interior trim (most notably the dash on 1966 and later trucks, as well as steering wheel hub, knobs, and air conditioning controls) have a chrome plated look, but the base material is plastic. In almost all cases, the bright finish on these parts will have dulled or disappeared and need to be replaced to return the truck's interior to its original appearance. The deterioration of the bright finish on these chrome plated plastic parts isn't caused by wear or corrosion, but results from the natural exposure to ultraviolet rays and atmospheric ozone. Although the bright appearance on these parts looks like chrome, they are not actually chrome plated (at least not in the restoration process). Rather, the a thin layer of vaporized aluminum is applied over the plastic in a process called vacuum metalizing. Several specialty companies offer this vacuum metalizing service for restoring chrome appearing plastic parts.

As in the actual chrome plating process, any surface imperfections will show up in the bright finish applied over plastic parts. For this reason, it is important to be alert to scratches, gouges, cracks, and breaks in the plastic. When scouting for parts without these defects on a parts truck or in a salvage yard, you need to be alert to the presence of a white, powdery substance that may have collected on the plastic where the finish has worn off. Areas where this white powder has collected are difficult to plate because the plastic had died, meaning the resins have evaporated. Plastic parts showing this white powdery residue should be avoided.

The guidelines for replating plastic parts (it's actually vacuum metalizing, not plating that we're talking about) are the same as for chrome plating. Send the best parts possible. Disassemble components (such as the dash) so that you send only the plastic unit. Ask the vacuum metalizer for a price estimate on the parts. With plastic plating you should also ask if the service applies a clear coat over the bright finish. The clear coat will protect the metalized finish from wearing off or disappearing over time due to sun exposure as occurred on the original part. Finally, be prepared to wait four to six weeks for the vacuum metalizing or plastic chrome plating service to return the parts.

Restoring Brightmetal

Most of the bright metal trim on Chevy trucks back to the 1940s is stainless steel or aluminum. This trim doesn't need to be replated, but it probably needs to be restored to its original luster and may need some straightening as well. While there are services that restore bright metal trim, you can do this work yourself at considerable savings. All you'll need is set of polishing and buffing wheels, an electric motor, and an array of polishing grits and buffing compounds. The expense to set

A few minutes of sharp pounding and the dent is beginning to disappear.

Smoothing out depressions he couldn't remove with the dowel, Jens worked the piece with a body hammer and dolly.

Another stubborn depression responded to a ball peen hammer.

up a buffing stand can be minimal if you have an extra electric motor on hand. If not, they're available at minimal cost at yard sales and auctions. Even if you buy a commercial buffing stand, you'll still be money ahead doing your own bright metal straightening and buffing. Polishing and buffing supplies are available from mail order restoration suppliers such as The Eastwood Company.

Before setting out to restore our truck's the bright metal, let's understand two key terms. In this setting *polishing* doesn't mean applying on the final sheen as it would if you were polishing the truck's finish. Instead, the polishing step is like sanding in that it removes the deeper scratches or repair marks. *Buffing* is the series of steps that produce the shiny luster that is our goal on these bright metal trim parts. Polishing can be done by hand using a series of progressively less coarse sandpapers. But hand polishing is slow and time consuming. A much faster method is to use an expander wheel (a flexible wheel that will conform to the contours of the part) mounted on an electric motor. Working a repaired area of a bright metal part with descending grit sandpaper belts fitted over the expander wheel will quickly smooth the surface to the stage where it can be brought back to a shiny finish. Buffing uses types of cloth wheels and mildly abrasive compound to remove small surface scratches and bring the surface to a high gloss.

This same polishing process can be used to prepare a chrome plated item for replating. However, the chrome finish is very hard and you'll make little progress attempting to remove it or repair underlying damage either by hand sanding or with an expander wheel. To polish chrome plated parts, you'll need to have the chrome plate stripped off first. Most commercial platers can do this. Just be sure to tag the parts for identification. When the parts come back with the plating removed, you can polish out the defects, saving some of the expense in the restoration plating process.

Polishing to Remove Surface Damage

The steps in restoring a damaged piece of bright metal trim, such as a dented aluminum grille surround on a 1969-1972 Chevy truck or the stainless steel window trim on a deluxe cab 1955-1957 pickup, begin by removing the trim piece. The next step is to straighten any kinks or dents. This is done using a drift, which can be an appropriate-sized flat-headed bolt, a hardwood dowel or small-headed hammer designed especially for this purpose and available from the source of the other polishing and buffing supplies) to flatten the dent.

A bolt head had the right contour for finish work.

You will work out the dent by tapping around the dented area in a spiral motion, starting at the outer edge of the dent and working in. When the surface feels and looks flat, it's time to polish the repair area with the expander wheel (or by hand with increasingly fine sandpaper) to smooth the marks made by the straightening process. The first polishing passes may reveal depressions and raised spots that need still need to be straightened.

For rough polishing, you would start with a 120 grit belt over the expander wheel, then use descending grits of 220, 320, 400 to smooth the repaired area to the point where it can be restored to a shiny finish by buffing. You'll have to determine the coarseness of the starting sandpaper. For less deep and severe scratches, gouges, or other surface imperfections,

The dent has nearly disappeared. After filing to remove high points from tool work, Jens smoothes the surface with 320 grit automotive sandpaper.

you would begin with a finer grit. Each time you change sanding belts you should work the part at a right angle to the previous passes. Remember to wear gloves to protect your hands from heat buildup on the parts and possible contact with the sanding wheel. Also wear a face shield to protect your eyes and face from flying debris.

The buffing process is used to remove the dull anodizing from aluminum as well as minor scratches on aluminum or stainless trim and restore the metal to its original brightness. Buffing is done with various grit compounds applied with cloth buffing wheels. Although the buffing wheels are made of cloth, they are available in varying coarseness. A combination of a rough cloth wheel and harsher grit provides more aggressive cutting for harder metals such as stainless steel. A smoother cloth and finer grit are used for finish buffing and for softer metals or plastic.

Buffing to Brighten the Trim

With hard metals like stainless, the buffing sequence begins by coating a sisal buffing wheel designed for fast, aggressive cutting with a coarse emery grit. Buffing is done in small sections until the whole part has been worked. At this stage it is important to watch out for rapid cutting that can cause localized heat build-up and distort the part's shape or burn holes in the metal. After coarse buffing, the part is worked again with a softer spiral wheel and milder grit. The typical buffing set up is a double arbor motor with a coarse wheel on one end of the shaft and a softer wheel on the other. With a dual arbor motor, it is not necessary to change wheels between every buffing step. The intermediate buff is followed by finish buffing using a soft loose section wheel and a coloring compound like white rouge to bring the metal to high luster.

He continues sanding with progressively milder paper.

Electro-plating on the StoveTop

I've been inside commercial plating shops and seen the elaborate equipment used to electro-plate metal parts. What a surprise, then, when I spotted an ad for a company selling do-it-yourself plating kits you could use at home on the stove top. Curiosity got the best of me and I decided I had to give the kit a try. A few days later the UPS man trotted up our front porch steps with a box about the size of a coffee carafe. The shipping label told me my Caswell electroplating kit had arrived.

For the trial run I'd cleaned up a pair of window pulls from our century-old Victorian house, a decorative eagle from my junk box, and a wrench from an old truck toolkit. In preparation for plating I wire brushed the window pulls to strip off several coatings of paint and pickled the wrench in Rusteco, a derusting chemical that's not only bio-degradable, but supposedly drinkable (I haven't done the latter test). The eagle went into the plating solution as is.

It took me a while to figure out the mixing proportions for the plating bath. The instructions called for 6% of one chemical and 20% of the other by volume. My non-mathematical mind kept trying to convert 6 and 20% measures into something simple like teaspoons and tablespoons. Finally, I reasoned that 6% of 100 % is just a tad over 1/20th, so that's how I mixed the solution, using my wife's quarter-cup measuring spoon. Adding slightly over half a quarter-cup of chemical A (6%), to 2 quarter-cups of chemical B (20%) and 7 1/2 quarter-cups of distilled water (74%). (To me this makes 100%.)

It worked.

The directions call for heating the mixture to 80 degrees F and maintaining that temperature for 5 to 15 minutes. I decided against using my wife's meat thermometer (reasoning I'd nickel plate the thermometer's metal probe) and couldn't find a glass thermometer— other than the oral and rectal units in our medicine cabinet), so I gauged the solution's temperature by placing the flat of my hand against the glass beaker holding the plating solution.

Fifteen minutes didn't produce much results, so I let the solution work (bubbles gurgling up from the metal) for about 45 minutes. If I approached the mouth of the plating beaker I could detect some odor, but the smell dissipated as I stepped away. Nor did my wife detect any offensive odor when she entered her kitchen, which is probably the most important test.

As the instructions advise, the plating finish matches the surface of the part before plating, dull on rough or brush finish parts, bright on polished parts. I consider the process a success. The window pulls have an attractive antique look and the wrench has a protective nickel coating on the section I plated. The kit appears ideal for a myriad of small items. Instructions say the solution can be reused—the possibly penalty being longer plating times. Ammonia neutralizes the solution so that it can be disposed of safely.

Besides the liter-sized nickel plating kit I tested, Caswell Plating supplies larger capacity kits with tank sizes up to 16 gallons and a range of plating solutions besides nickel, including copper, zinc, even gold. For information, contact Caswell Electroplating, 4336 Route 31, Palmyra, NY 14522, (313) 597-5140, or www@.caswellplating

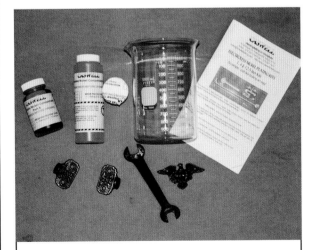

You won't restore you truck's grille this way, but it gave the wrench a nickeled look.

Caswell Plating offered a stovetop process, which I decided to try.

The surface is still rough, but the dent is gone.

Plastic parts can also be buffed to remove scratches and return to a factory-looking finish. Plastic tail light and parking light lenses are ideal candidates for the buffing process because if these are the original parts, they most likely are dull and scratched from dust and road debris. A soft wheel and special plastic buffing compound are used to avoid cutting into the plastic. When buffing plastic parts, it is important not to over-heat and melt the plastic. The Eastwood Company sells a tail light restoration kit that includes the correct compound and a string buff wheel that runs cool to damaging heat build up. Also when buffing plastic parts be careful not to remove part numbers or other detail features.

The typical errors made by first-time buffers are applying too much grit to the wheel and failing to clean the wheel before going to a milder grit. Putting too much compound on the wheel is not only wasteful, but clogs the wheel and prevents effective cutting. One sign of too much grit is black streaks on the work piece. These can be cleaned off with a soft cloth soaked in solvent. The easiest way to make sure that none of the harsher compound remains on the wheel as you move to a milder grit is to use a separate wheel for each buffing step. Lacking this, you can remove left over compound or extra build-up from the buffing wheel with a tool called a rake. Important: never take your eyes off the part while buffing.

Besides brightening and restoring trim and plastic items, polishing and buffing can also be used to produce a chrome-like finish on alternator housings, intake manifolds and any other aluminum parts. These components did not have a shiny finish from the factory, so polishing and buffing the castings to a high-gloss finish would not be done as part of restoration. However, giving engine components a shiny appearance appeals to many who aren't focused on restoration and want to display a shiny engine compartment at local shows. To give these cast aluminum parts a uniformly glossy finish, hand held

grinders can be used to polish small recesses that can't be reached by the expander wheel.

Although trucks don't use a lot of chrome and bright metal, upgrading the finish of these trim pieces will make an enormous difference in your truck's appearance. Indeed, you may find that if your truck is a standard model with mostly painted trim, you may want to add some of the bright work found on the deluxe models. In many cases this deluxe bright metal trim is available in reproduction form from vintage truck parts suppliers, but now that you know how to restore older, original trim, you might look for this deluxe model bright work at swap meets or salvage yards.

Note the use of a respirator, which should be worn in this process to prevent inhaling polishing grit.

Polishing has two main guidelines: keep the part moving and don't let it get caught by the wheel.

Collector trucks spend more time sitting than driving. Seeing a truck resting in storage may give us a good feeling, a sense that our truck is enjoying a well-earned retirement in which it will last forever. But in reality, storage can do more damage to a truck (or any collector vehicle) than regular driving. Deterioration resulting from storage can take many forms. The 1969 Chevy Longhorn pickup shown in numerous places in this book leaked automatic transmission fluid during the months it spent in the body shop. The cause—torque converters will drain during long periods of idleness. During winter storage, the air conditioning compressor seal has leaked Freon, something that would not happened if the seal had been lubricated from periodic use. Likewise with the water pump seal. A list of small maladies could be compiled that have resulted simply from storage. Then, too, storage brings the risk of the gasoline decomposing and a raft of troubles that can result.

Storage can be of two types, long term and short term. For many vintage trucks, long-term storage occurs during winter months (November through March or longer in some northern climates), but sometimes vehicles sit in prolonged storage lasting years. The longer the period of idleness, the greater the risk of dried out seals, electrical malfuction, gasoline spoilage and, depending on the storage conditions, mild to severe corrosion to body sheet metal and mildew of interior coverings. Many show trucks exist in a perennial state of long term storage with the truck only being started and driven out of its enclosed trailer onto the show area, then back into the trailer at the end of the show. Short-term storage is the time your truck spends sitting in the garage between occasions when you take it out on the road. For trucks that see frequent use, short-term storage may extend only a few days or a few weeks. Precautions for short-term storage are little more than keeping the truck out of the weather and performing routine maintenance. Preparations for long term storage are more involved to preserve the truck's mechanical condition and appearance.

Storage Settings

No vehicle should be stored outside for extended periods of time. Moisture from the ground will rot the truck from underneath while sunlight will fade the paint, dry out and crack vinyl interior coverings and deteriorate rubber on window and door weatherseal and the tires. Rain and dew will seep past the weather seal and welting as in the joints between the rear fenders and pickup box allowing rust to fester. Underneath the hood, condensation from temperature fluctuations will corrode wiring connections and enter the engine through the carburetor and intake valves as well as through the exhaust system. A truck that is stored outdoors can deteriorate

in a matter of months. The statement we often hear—it ran when I parked it, so it should run now—is false logic. Depending on the storage conditions, there's a greater likelihood that a vehicle, which has been sitting for some time, probably won't start or run, at least not run well.

Indoor storage isn't necessarily better. With a roof overhead but a dirt floor underneath, a truck may experience more moisture damage than if parked outside. This is particularly true of metal structures that can trap and hold condensation.

Optimal storage is warm, dry and dark with small temperature fluctuations year around. Unfortunately, not many of us have a storage facility that meets these conditions. But you don't need to bring your truck inside your house; there's a way to achieve all the conditions of optimal storage, even it the only storage you have for your truck is a tin-roofed, dirt floored shed.

Long-Term Storage

Your truck can rest in the dry, dark conditions of optimal storage is you seal it inside a CarJacket. These heavy (7.0 mil), non-breathable rip-stop polyethylene zippered bags hold light duty trucks as well as cars. The storage procedure is easy, just unzip to open the CarJacket and spread it out on spot where you want your truck to rest. You can use a CarJacket over an earthen floor if there are no sharp stones or other objects that might puncture the bag. In an earthen floor setting, it's better to lay down sheets of plywood or OSB and place the bag on top of that. Caution: the CarJacket is not meant for outside storage, only for storage within buildings. In outside storage, wind may whip the bag, damaging the vehicle's finish. Once the bag is spread out, the truck is driven into place and the

Before storage, top off the fuel tank to prevent condensation and add the proper amount to gasoline stabilizer.

You'll need to purchase a jacket big enough to enclose your truck. The Jacket package will include instructions, bags of desiccant to create a dry environment inside the jacket a protective cover for the antenna, and locks to keep unauthorized people from opening and looking inside the jacket.

truck in a CarJacket also deters theft by those who may not be curious about the lump inside the gray plastic bag.

To take the truck out of storage, simply unzip the CarJacket. This ultimate storage device is that easy to use. With care the same CarJacket can be reused year after year. The desiccant can be dried and reused by heating in a kitchen oven (open the cloth bag and spread out the desiccant pellets in a baking dish) for two hours at 425 degrees F. If a tear in the bag should occur, it can be mended with duct tape. CarJackets are available in a range of sizes from Pine Ridge Enterprises, 13165 Center Road, Bath, MI 48808 or by calling 800-5-CARBAG.

Preparation

Before placing your truck in a CarJacket or any long term storage setting, certain preparation steps need to be taken. The tires should be pumped to slightly over road pressure and the truck should be washed both underneath and on top and allowed to dry thoroughly. It's also a good idea to wax the finish; then when the truck comes out of storage it will be shiny and ready to go or show. Some collectors will apply wax to the chrome, but do not buff off the dried coating. The wax film will protect the chrome from oxidation (this step is not necessary if the truck is stored in a CarJacket). Along with the exterior, the interior should also be cleaned thoroughly.

Even if the oil in the engine looks fresh on the dipstick, before putting the truck in storage run the engine to operating temperature, drain the crankcase and refill with fresh oil. If the engine has an oil filter replace this also. A byproduct of combustion is acid that collects in the oil. Although the oil ceases to circulate through the engine during storage, vital parts such as bearings remained covered with a thin oil film. If the oil is contaminated with acid, this film also contains traces

sides of the bag pulled and zipped shut. Before sealing the bag closed, packets of desiccant (provided with the CarJacket) are placed inside with the vehicle. The desiccant will suck out the moisture and the truck will sit desert dry storage.

Unlike car covers, which are used to keep dust and dirt off the truck's finish, the CarJacket surrounds the vehicle, sealing out moisture and sunlight. For those who have experienced damage by rodents nesting in upholstery or engine exhaust or intake systems, the CarJacket ends that problem because rodents are not attracted to what they cannot smell and the bag emits only the aroma of fresh vinyl, which squirrels and mice apparently find unappetizing. Likewise, storing a vintage

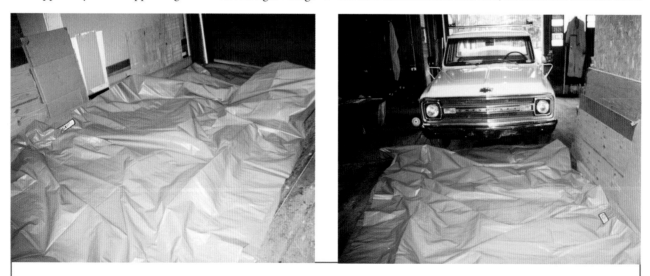

The first step is laying out the jacket in the location where the truck will be parked. The logo side of the jacket faces up.

of acid that can eat into bearing surfaces and other fine-tolerance parts. The way to prevent possible internal engine damage is simply to change the oil.

Likewise, anti-freeze also develops an acidic pH over time. The long-standing recommendation has been to flush the antifreeze and refill every three years, regardless of whether the truck is driven or in storage. There's also been a lively debate among collector truck and car owners over whether or not to drain the cooling system for storage. Advocates say a "dry" cooling system won't corrode. They're right if the truck is stored in a CarJacket. Otherwise condensation from ambient humidity will corrode engine water passages as much or more than slightly acidic anti-freeze.

If flushing and refilling the cooling system every three years is too much of a hassle, then the answer is Evans Coolant, a non-glycol based product that is *not* mixed with water. Besides solving the cooling system corrosion problem, Evans Coolant has a boiling point of 370 degrees—that's 110 degrees higher than modern pressurized cooling system with a 50/50 anti-freeze mixture! Here's a product with a dual advantage; no corrosion during storage and no overheating from boiling coolant, even under extreme temperatures.

There's a similar wet or dry debate over gasoline. Although modern gasoline breaks down much more rapidly than the more aromatic smelling stuff we used to burn, there has always been a problem with gasoline turning into a thick tarry goo in vehicles for left long periods without care. Drain the gasoline and you leave the fuel tank an empty canister and exposed to rusting from moisture condensation. Store the truck with the tank full and there'll be no condensation, but you'll risk of gooey gasoline and the enormous clean-up process that entails. Those advocating keeping the tank filled during storage, say

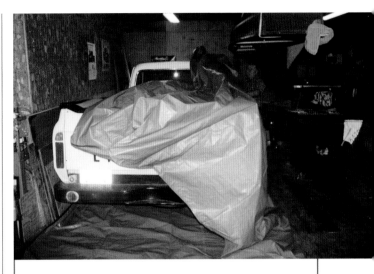
Now the jacket folds over the truck.

that the gasoline can be kept from breaking down by adding fuel preservative (available from auto supply stores and discount marts). The drain-the-fuel crowd isn't convinced. Fortunately, their problem—the risk of condensation in the fuel tank—has a simple solution already described: the CarJacket.

Not to be overlooked in any form of long-term storage, the battery should be disconnected and removed. Leaving the battery connected risks more than just a dead battery. A small discharge that might go unnoticed in normal operation can lead to a short that could cause a fire. Then there's the battery itself, which can better be preserved and maintained outside the truck. Steps to extending battery life are discussed later in this chapter.

With the truck inside the jacket, Jens can zip it shut.

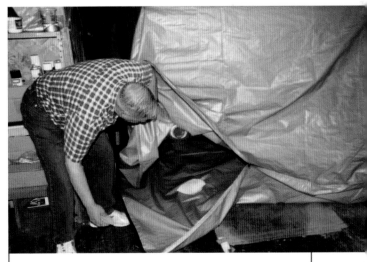
Before sealing the truck in its storage cocoon, Jens tosses in the desiccant.

Sealed in the CarJacket, the truck will sleep like an embalmed Egyptian mummy.

Other preparations include being sure the hand brake is *Off*. Parking a truck for an extended period with the hand brake set can cause the emergency brake shoes to seize to the drums or the cables—an awkward condition to have to repair before taking your truck out of storage. Although not required in the dry environment of a CarJacket, if your truck is going to sit for an extended period protected only by a cover, old blanket, or maybe just stashed in one corner of the garage, you'll do yourself a favor to spend a few minutes sealing the carburetor with a bread bag (or large food preservation bag) and the tail pipe with duct tape. Closing off the engine's entry and exit openings not only helps keep moisture from entering the engine, but also seals entry into the exhaust system for rodents. Mice have been known to nest not only in the muffler, but also in the engine itself.

Insurance

Not to be overlooked during long term storage is insurance coverage for the full amount of the truck's value. While highway coverage, liability and collision, are not necessary during storage, comprehensive coverage, with its protection against loss by fire and other risks, needs to be maintained. Equally important is making sure the insurance carrier not only has the truck listed for its true value, but that you have provided the insurer with a appraiser's statement of value. Asking your friend who's an old truck buff to write you a letter that lists a value figure won't do. You need to locate a certified collector vehicle appraiser (listed in hobby publications like *Hemmings*). The certified appraiser will inspect the truck with the thoroughness of a concours judge, checking the condition, authenticity, and other features of each of the truck's major areas (interior, trim, mechanical, body). From the checklist, the appraiser will compile a composite score on which the value can be based. The careful appraiser's close examination of each of the truck's features can prove extremely valuable, should damage occur to the car and the insurance company contest the car's insured value.

Short-Term Storage

The full regimen of preparations aren't needed for short term storage. However, a few preparation steps are advisable and cleaning should still be considered a must. The preparations consist of disconnecting the battery and covering the truck with soft fabric (optimally a professionally-made truck cover , but alternatively one or two full-size blankets) to protect the paint from airborne chemicals and the rubber, glass, and interior from sunlight. While the battery can be quite easily disconnected by removing the ground terminal, more convenient is to install a shut-off switch, either on the ground post of the battery or in the wiring harness. Disconnecting the battery prevents fire due to faulty wiring and it helps assure the car will start when you flip back the cover for a drive.

Assuming the car is only dusty it can be dry-cleaned by lightly wiping the finish with a mop-like product called a

When its time to remove the truck from the jacket, the enclosure can be folded and reused.

Realizing that the jacket is not going to fit back in its box, Jens uses the box to press out the trapped air.

California Car Duster, available from several suppliers. Usually it's not advisable to wipe anything across a dry, dusty finish because the dust particles, which are really tiny grains grit, will scratch the paint like sandpaper. The reason the California Car Duster can be used to clean a dry finish is that its 100 percent cotton mop strands are treated with a special paraffin wax that lifts the dust rather than brushing it off. The duster can be

used over and over by simply shaking the mop strands before and after use.

If the finish is really dirty, it should be washed. Dry washing is preferred because no water seeps into crevices and seams where it can cause rust. A product called Dri-Wash 'n Guard uses emulsifiers lift dirt and grime from the finish making it possible to wipe off the film without scratching the paint. This product is sold through independent distributors who are best contacted by calling the manufacturer, Enrivo-Tech International.

Extending battery life

Batteries in collector vehicles that are stored more than they are driven typically have very short lives. This isn't necessary. You'll get many years of life and service out of your truck's battery if you follow these three simple steps:

1) keep the case clean and dry
2) keep the electrolyte level above the plates
3) keep the battery fully charged.

Dirt and grease on the case create an electrical circuit that can cause the battery to discharge in a relatively short time. When you place your collector car in storage and remove the

A California Car Duster sweeps off dirt without scratching the finish. Oddly, the dirtier the duster gets, the better it works.

209

battery, wash the case with a cloth soaked in ammonia or a baking soda and water solution. When washing the case, be very careful that none of the solution gets into the cells as it will neutralize the electrolyte. Before storing the battery, be sure the case is wiped dry. Don't place the battery in a location (like a concrete floor) where it will pick up condensation.

Some electrolyte (the fluid in the cells) is lost each time the battery is charged. Make sure the electrolyte never falls below the top of the plates. If the plates are exposed to air, permanent damage to the battery will result. Distilled water should be used to fill the battery. On most batteries, the correct electrolyte level is indicated by a ring (1/4 to 1/2 inch above the plates) under the cell cap. Batteries discharge when they're not used, so they need to be charged on fairly frequent intervals. This is best done with a Battery Tender, a slow charger that monitors the battery's voltage and cuts out automatically when the battery reaches full charge. The advantage of the Battery Tender over a regular charger is that the Tender can be left hooked onto the battery and plugged into a an electrical outlet. It will begin charging automatically when the battery voltage drops to a certain level and shut off when the battery regains full charge. However, as mentioned earlier, the electrolyte level should be monitored periodically, even though the Battery Tender's slow charging rate minimizes electrolyte loss.

Batteries maintain their charge better in cool conditions than warm, so store the battery in as cool a location as possible. Never bring the battery inside a place it near the furnace. Assuming the battery is fully charged, it will survive sub-zero temperatures without freezing.

Before replacing the battery, wipe a light coating of grease (Vaseline is recommended) on the terminals. The grease won't disrupt the electrical contact and will prevent corrosion that does break the electrical flow.

Coming Out of Storage

Even though a CarJacket will deliver a truck from storage in virtually the same condition that it went in (the chrome will still be bright and shiny and there will be no trace of mildew or other humidity damage), there are still be items that need checking. Gaskets and seals can shrink during storage, especially in a low-humidity environment, so always check fluid levels (engine, transmission, brake reservoir, coolant) before operating the truck. You'll need to re-install the battery and you'll find that pouring a small amount of gasoline down the carburetor intake plus spraying a couple of shots of carburetor cleaner into the carburetor intake as the engine first cranks over will save grinding on the starter while the fuel pump replenishes the gasoline supply. Once the truck is running, let it idle for several minutes to reestablish good lubrication throughout the engine before applying power to move the truck from its resting spot. If you've stored the truck in a

CarJacket, you can fold up the bag, gather the desiccant and put these items away for the next storage season.

Trucks with bias-ply tires will ride a little bumpy for the first few miles after storage until the tires warm up and round themselves out again. Also after the first outing it's a good idea to check fluid levels and top up where necessary. If any leaks are detected they should be monitored to see if the gaskets seal as the truck is driven.

Periodic Care

In comparison with a daily driver that may roll up several thousand miles on the odometer in just a few months, a collector truck that is driven far fewer miles may seem to need infrequent maintenance. Actually, this is not the case. Caustic chemicals that collect in the crankcase as the engine oil breaks down are actually more damaging in a vehicle that is driven infrequently than in one which goes out on the road every day. As a result, you should change the oil and give the truck a complete lubrication at least once a year. The best time for this is right before putting the truck in storage. Trucks that see more than occasional use, should receive a complete lube and oil change every 2500 to 3000 miles.

If you use the owner's manual for your truck as a guide, you're likely to discover that your truck has several dozen grease fittings, which are located not just on the steering linkage and front suspension, but also on the spring shackles, universal joints, clutch and brake pedal shafts, and numerous other places. Take the time to service all these fittings; your truck will drive and ride smoother as a result. While servicing the engine and chassis in older trucks, remember to squirt a couple of drops of oil on the manifold heat valve and generator bushing cup and check the fluid levels in the steering box, transmission, rear end, and brake master cylinder.

On engines built prior to PCV systems, this annual maintenance check is also the time to wash the oil filler cap in solvent and a few drops of oil added to the wire mesh. The filler cap and screen ventilates the engine crankcase. The carburetor air cleaner (whether oil bath, wire mesh, or paper filter type) should also be serviced at this time. An oil bath filter is serviced by dumping out the old oil (pour the oil into a plastic milk jug or other suitable container and take it to a recycling center; don't pour the oil onto the ground) cleaning the oil reservoir and filter in solvent, then refilling the reservoir with fresh oil. A wire mesh cleaner is also washed with solvent and dried. A few drops of oil are squirted into the mesh before replacing this air cleaner on the carburetor. On engines using a paper filter air cleaner, the filter housing should be removed from the engine and washed in solvent. The filtering sponge at the PCV valve hose inlet should also be washed in solvent or replaced with a fresh filter. A new paper filter cartridge will be installed after the air cleaner housing is replaced on the carburetor.

On newer engines don't forget to check and change the PCV valve if the valve is clogged.

Like engine oil, antifreeze solutions contain additives that break down in time. This means that if the cooling system is not flushed periodically (annually is the recommended interval) and refilled with fresh antifreeze internal corrosion could result. Many collectors are also unaware that manufacturers recommend flushing and refilling the hydraulic brake system on an annual basis. The reason for this is that polyglycol brake fluid soaks up moisture like a sponge and you'll recall that the master cylinders on older trucks are vented (to prevent a vacuum from forming in the system) so moisture is easily absorbed into the brake fluid. One way to avoid this moisture problem—and to save the time flushing and refilling the brake fluid—is to use DOT 5 silicone fluid instead of the DOT 3 polyglycol product.

The annual truck care session concludes with putting a few drops of oil on the hood latch mechanism, hood hinges, rotary door latches, door hinges, seat track (on trucks with adjustable seats), and wiper linkage. The door latch striker should be lubricated with special stick wax.

Cleanup Tips

You may look at this heading and say "Hold it, I don't need to be told how to wash my truck." While that's probably true, you may discover a few techniques and "tricks" to caring for a collector vehicle that you haven't used in cleaning up that daily driver. The first is a warning that low-pressure water from the yard hose works is better for cleaning your truck than a high-pressure spray at the car wash which can force dirt and debris into seams and crevices. Better yet for cleaning the finish is the dry wash product, mentioned previously. Washing needs to be done underneath as well as on the visible surfaces. Glass Wax works better than commercial chrome cleaners for keeping chrome plating and bright work shiny. To make the windshield and cab windows sparkle, add a dash of kerosene to a bucket of clean water, wipe the mixture on the glass, and buff dry with a wad of newspaper. The combination of the kerosene film and newsprint will give the glass a mirror sheen. Rubber, including the tires, can be restored to a bright, black coloring with coating of ArmorAll, which also serves to protect the rubber against cracking.

On the inside of the cab, a damp cloth or sponge works well to clean vinyl seat coverings and to remove dust from door panels and the headliner. The rubber floor mat can be vacuumed, wiped down with a damp cloth, and renewed to its factory-freshness with ArmorAll. Other interior rubber (the gear shift boot on trucks with a floor shift), pedal pads and other items should also be given the rubber renewal treatment.

Under the hood, the engine compartment should be wiped down to clean off road dust and whatever oil film has developed. If the engine has gotten too grimy to be cleaned with a light wipe down, you can spray on a coating of Gunk, let the degreaser stand for ten to fifteen minutes, and wash off the grease film with the lawn hose. Be careful not to spray water on the distributor or other electrical parts. Used according to the directions on the can, Gunk will not harm paint.

Upkeep

It is wise to establish a cycle for checking wheel bearings, cleaning and gaping spark plugs, filing and resetting ignition points—routine maintenance of this sort. Be sure to do a maintenance run-through on these and other mechanical check points before a major trip if your truck is only driven occasionally. Remember, just because a truck spends much of its time not being driven doesn't mean that idleness assures that it stays in road-ready condition. Spending a few hours giving the truck a good check over before heading out of town is a better time investment than being stranded on the highway with fried ignition points or a dry wheel bearing.

Showing Your Truck

Special care is called for if you plan to enter your truck in show competition. Cleaning and waxing needs to be done with care and thoroughness that includes wiping wax residue out of cracks with a toothbrush and making sure that the chassis is as sanitary as the exterior. Beyond cleaning, show competition also requires close attention to the many small details that make your truck authentic for its period. These include such seemingly picayune items as the correct valve stem caps (plastic valve stem caps didn't appear until the early 1950s; trucks from

Many collectors make signs telling their trucks history to add to their display. The 1950 Chevrolet car/pickup seen here is a rare and unusual Australian Ute.

211

Some collectors add sideboards or door lettering indicating the truck's original occupation.

the 1940s should have metal caps) and spark plugs with plated bases on trucks from an era when the spark plug base was painted black.

In their enthusiasm for having an unusual show vehicle, some collectors dress their trucks out with accessories. While these add-ons can be great conversation pieces, they can also cost your truck points in show competition if the judges dispute their authenticity. In settings like this, the judge is supposed to ask the owner to produce documentation verifying that the accessory was a bone fide Chevrolet part, but if the judge thinks that add on is an after market item, you may not be given the chance to prove otherwise. One way to avoid this problem, and still display the accessory, is to make the documentation part of your display. This proof of authenticity can be accomplished by mounting pictures from dealer catalogs showing unusual accessory items in a display stand. The pictures will highlight the accessories for those viewing your truck while also alerting the judges to their authenticity.

A last tip for those entering prestigious AACA (Antique Automobile Club of America) competition. You are entitled to request a judges' evaluation after each competition round. You will not see the actual judging sheet, but you will be guided to those areas where the judges found fault. Correcting those oversights before the next competition will improve your chances for continued success.

Tool kits for Advanced Design Trucks

A 1948 model 3104 pickup would have these tools: a 2500 lb. capacity jack capable of a raised height of 15 1/8 in. and a lowered height of 6 1/2 in., a tire changing iron, lock for spare tire, wheel wrench, jack handle, plus the car tool kit which consisted of a canvas bag containing a spark plug wrench, 3 open-end wrenches, a 6 inch pliers, a 5 1/4 round shank screw driver, and a 10 oz. ball peen hammer.

Many states allow original tags to be used as historic license plates.

212

In 1990 when I was writing the first edition of this book, my uncle Mark asked for help selling a 1947 Chevrolet ton-and-a-half stake truck he still had on the farm. "There's surface rust, but no holes or rot. It runs and the mileage is around 40,000. Do you think I can get $450 for it?" Uncle Mark asked. I helped him place a couple of ads in publications of interest to old truck enthusiasts, but there were no takers. Today it would be a different story. Older heavier duty are now in demand, sought by restorers and in some cases by people who plan to fix them up and use them. By big iron I'm talking here about the medium duty class, trucks ranging from 1 ? to 2 tons, although some people also put one-ton trucks in this classification. The restoration of heavy-duty 3 ton and larger vehicles (semi tractors and the like) is an entirely different endeavor and, while certainly possible, likely to be beyond the grasp of most hobbyist restorers. One thing that separates light and medium duty trucks from the really big trucks is the requirement of a commercial drivers license. Trucks with a gross vehicle weight over 26,000 lbs. require a CDL. Why fix up a truck you can't drive?

The rise in popularity of the intermediate level trucks has come about, in part, because there's quite a lot in common between Chevrolet's medium duty models and their light duty brothers. For one, the cabs are the same, though the bigger trucks look different because of their larger, more massive grille, different fenders, larger wheels, and the fact that the cab perches higher in the air and requires steps to reach. The commonly shared cab means availability of all the repair panels, weather stripping and upholstery, even window glass. But there's where the commonality ends. For nearly everything else, you're looking at a distinct set of bigger truck parts, most of which are not going to be readily available in the catalogs of suppliers to light duty trucks.

Let's use as an example my son's 1968 C-50 dump truck shown on these pages. Notice that while the cab is the same as that from a 1967-1972 pickup the doors are different because they're arched at the lower front to clear the fender, which is two-piece, has a much larger wheel cutout and is unique to large trucks. If any of these parts need replacing, you'll be scouting for a parts truck or a vendor specializing in bigger trucks.

Light and Medium Duty Truck Differences

This may seem patently obvious, but ... bigger trucks are, um, *bigger*. They're taller, wider, longer, and heavier than the pickups. This makes them more of a challenge to store, park, transport and drive. Right off the bat, one should keep in mind that unlike a pickup, most medium duty trucks will not fit in the standard garage. They may not even fit the average driveway. These are important things to consider before bringing the oversize baby home!

See how stoutily a big truck chassis compares with a one-ton pickup of the same series.

You may need a rig like this to move the chassis. That's John Milliman on the John Deere.

Many of the bigger truck's components require special consideration as well. For example, the tires and rims generally weigh around 100 lb. each making them difficult, as well as dangerous, to deal with. And as long as we're talking about the tires and rims, the Budd wheels on the older trucks usually have two and three-piece rims. Some are even split rims. These older split style rims are dangerous, and even lethal for somebody who is not experienced and tries to take them apart in his garage. Split rims should be left to professionals.

Anyone contemplating restoring a bigger truck should be aware of the increased logistics involved, which can be quite different from those required by a light truck. Most hobbyist tools (floor jacks, jack stands, wrenches and the like) may not be capable of handling a heavy vehicle like a medium duty truck.. Before attempting a restoration, one is well advised to ensure the tools at hand can handle the job. You're going to need at least a ? in. drive socket set and may need 1 in. drive sockets for some applications. Likewise, other tools from crescent wrenches to screwdrivers will also need to be larger as well. Stroll into a service center for medium duty trucks and you will see the size of tools that you'll need.

Engines

Mechanically, you'll find a mixture of similarities and differences between light and medium duty models. Prior to World War II, all Chevrolet car and truck engines were essentially the same, but starting in 1941, a larger 235 ci. six became available to medium and heavy duty truck buyers. This engine is *not the same* as the later pressure-oiling "Blue Flame" 235 that Chevrolet installed in Corvettes and Powerglide-equipped

passenger cars in 1953 and was available across the line in 1954. This earlier truck 235 did not have the same overall length as the later car and truck 235, which may explain why the radiator shroud sheet metal has been cut on some trucks with a newer replacement engine, and it still has a partial splash oiling system and babbitt bearings. Once the insert bearing, pressure-oiling 235s came out, many bigger truck owners wisely replaced their babbitted 235s. For restorers wanting originality, it can be an obstacle to find one of those babbitted 235s, let alone locating someone to rebuild it. If strict originality is not important, a later 235 can be modified to look like the earlier one. Several parts vendors sell kits to make newer 235s look like the 216s that go into the light trucks, and that will do nicely for this application, too.

If it were just a matter of distinguishing between the 216 and two different 235s, our engine confusion might be minimal. But in 1950 when Chevrolet first introduced its Powerglide automatic transmission, it also brought out a "new" 235 for use with this transmission. This engine is also different from the earlier truck 235, though it still uses babbitt bearings, and was an option for truck buyers. Installed in trucks, this 235 had solid lifters. In cars with Powerglide, it had hydraulic lifters. This babbitt 235 physically resembles the later pressure-oiling Blue Flame engine. Here are the differences.

The newer style, pressure-oiling can be distinguished from 1941-1941 older-style 235s and 216s by the pushrod cover. On 216s and early 235s, the pushrod cover extends from the oil pan past the spark plug holes. This so-called tall pushrod cover surrounds the spark plug holes. Now here's the

Restoring big trucks is not for those with small garages.

confusion: both 1950 to 1953 babbitt bearing 235s and 1954 and later pressure-oiling 235s have a short pushrod cover that does not encircle the spark plugs. For a difference in detail, the 1941 to 1949 truck 235 looks identical to a 216 but has a threaded dipstick. Pressure-oiling 235s are best distinguished by the presence of a letter, either T or F, at the end of the engine serial number. T refers to the Tonawanda, New York, engine assembly plant and F to Flint, Michigan.

In 1954, Chevrolet also introduced a 261 ci. six for use in large and heavy duty trucks. The block for this engine is slightly taller than a 235, though both engines share the same crankshaft and have the same stroke (3 15/16 in.) The 261 has a larger 3 ? in. bore. This engine was called JobMaster and can best be recognized by a letter code at the end of the serial number, e.g. F 54 Q or T 54 Q for a Flint or Tonawanda 261 installed in a 1954 model year truck. These engines are, of course, pressure-oiling and have a rugged design, comparing favorably with larger GMC engines of the same period. Consequently, they are desirable for truck use and in hopped up form were even used as replacement engines in early six-cylinder Corvettes.

Beginning in 1955, both Chevrolet cars and trucks (both light and medium duty) could option the 265 V-8. As larger displacement variants of this small block V-8 engine became available, they were offered in both light and medium duty trucks. When the new generation six cylinder engine was introduced in 1963, the 230 ci. version was supplied standard in pickups and the 292 in larger trucks, though the 292 could be optioned in light duty models along with a cadre of V-8s.

Transmissions

Just about all the big trucks from 1947 to 1967 had the same 4-speed manual transmission—the venerable Muncie SM420. Because of its granny gear (for getting heavy loads moving) and rugged construction, it had a long production life and remains popular with off-road/4x4 enthusiasts. It's also popular with the pickup guys who are installing after-market rear-end upgrade kits that allow higher speeds. Although parts are starting to get hard to find, there are plenty of transmission specialists out there who are familiar with this transmission.

These trannies also have a plate on the side where a power take-off can be mounted. PTO's are used mainly to power hydraulic hoists (for dump trucks and grain trucks) or winches (tow trucks).

COE's have some unique shifter linkages, but usually, if the truck still has its tranny, it will still have all of this linkage, too.

The 5000 and 6000-series trucks also had the parking brake mounted on the back of the transmission. In this setup, the brake handle engaged a pad that acted upon a drum attached to the driveshaft right at the output from the transmission—a much more desirable set up than the lighter trucks (where the parking brake handle is attached to the rear brake shoes via cables). Larger trucks dispensed with parking brakes in the rear drums because often these trucks have long bodies. Running cables for parking brakes all the way to the rear axle would invite snagging, rust seizure and overall inefficiency. A lot of bigger truck restorers like to fit this arrangement into their 4000 series trucks as it eliminates the need for new parking brake cables, though a cable from the cab to the drive-shaft drum is still needed.

Rear Ends

To clear one something up that seems to be confusing for a lot of folks new to bigger trucks, a two-speed rear end will *not* give higher top speed. It produces a lower low-end ratio to make starting out under heavy loads. Medium-duty Advance Design trucks have a single-speed rear end ratio of 6:17. For comparison, the light truck rear axle ratio prior to 1960 was 4:11.

The Advance Design two-speed rear axle has an 8:10 low-range ratio and a 6:10 high-range. If you are not going to be hauling anything with your truck, you don't gain much by switching to a two-speed rear end. However, the dual-speed rear is very useful in working trucks.

If higher top speed is desired for cruising the Interstate (a medium duty truck is likely to have a comfortable cruising speed between 40 and 50 mph), merely switching to a lower ratio rear end out of a later model truck will hurt more than help. Remember that 235 up front. At best (when it was new) it was cranking out about 105 horsepower at 3,000 RPM. There's not a whole lot of grunt there to be pulling heavy loads or tall ratios. If more speed is desired, you're looking to install

an entire modern driveline, steering and brakes—not a project for the faint of heart.

Naturally, components like bearings, axles, differential gears and the like are going to be harder to find for these trucks than for their lighter-duty brothers. But they are available the patient searcher.

Brakes

Like everything else on these trucks, the brakes are going to be bigger to handle the heavier loads and increased braking power required. Brake shoes, wheel cylinders and all the other internal and external brake system parts are available from various parts sources—but be prepared for heftier price tags. On trucks with that nifty two-speed rear end, take a deep breath. It takes *four* wheel cylinders (two per side) at about $100 each. And no, they're not the same as the fronts.

In many cases, newer era medium duty trucks will have power brake boosters. Drum brakes with boosters have been used on medium and heavy-duty trucks up to modern times. A larger truck will have safe, sure stopping power with this drum brake booster setup. However, it will be necessary to inspect and replace brake lines, flex hoses, master and wheel cylinders as on a light-duty truck.

Front Ends

Larger trucks have used straight axle front ends for their ruggedness and simplicity. An exception occurred between 1960 and 1962, Chevrolet and GMC medium duty trucks used a beefed-up version of the torsion bar independent front suspension that is found under light duty trucks of those years.

Big trucks could also be equipped with the NAPCO front drive axle. The name, Big Brute, on this truck makes an apt description.

Big trucks often travel rough terrain under heavy loads, putting lots of stress on the suspension and when Chevrolet switched to a coil spring front IFS system, medium duty trucks reverted to beam axles. These straight axle front ends are the same design as on a small truck but the axle, springs, and all other parts are over-size and require a larger tool set.

Don't try this stunt with your rear drive truck.

metal has been reduced to junk and finding good, unaltered pieces can be a challenge. The difficulty of locating good, rust free replacement sheet metal pieces for the engine compartment also applies to forward sheet metal: front fenders, hood, and grille. Reproduction parts aren't available, so if the truck needs unrusted fenders or a straighter grille, you'll be exploring salvage yards, purchasing a parts truck, or finding someone with a stock of larger truck fenders and hoods.

Most sought-after among big truck collectors are the cab-over-engine models. The tall grille marks a 1939-1940 model.

NAPCO front drive axles were also available for medium duty trucks. Needless to say, any truck with drive axles front and rear was worked very hard and the likelihood of finding a medium duty truck with a NAPCO conversion providing traction at both axles is much slimmer than locating a NAPCO-equipped pickup, but big trucks with NAPCO front drive axles are out there. As with small trucks, a NAPCO front drive axle can be installed on an otherwise rear-wheel drive truck, but the front and rear axle ratios have to match. In many cases, NAPCO-equipped medium duty trucks have a history with the military. If they belonged to the Navy, they were probably used to offload LSTs, in which case running in and out of salt water and on sand beaches may have corroded and chewed up the axles gears and bearings. If you have the good fortune to stumble upon a NAPCO front-drive set up for a medium duty truck, or an intact truck so-equipped, inspect the front-drive unit carefully for severe use in the truck's history.

Sheet Metal

Not all larger trucks cabs interchange with pickups because wheel housings protrude into the floor on larger truck cabs. For this reason, doors may be different also. However the weather stripping, upholstery kits, glass and interior is the same. Sheet metal patch panels for repairing a pickup cab also work on larger trucks. Move forward of the firewall and the situation is different. Once you go bigger than a one-ton, the hoods, fenders, inner fenders, radiator shrouds are different (they're *bigger*!)—mainly to accommodate the larger tires and wheels found on the bigger trucks.

On a lot of 4000 and 6000-Advance Design series, the radiators have been moved forward to accommodate the longer engines when the engines were replaced. When this was done, generally, the radiator stands and shrouds were modified as needed and not with future restorers in mind! For a lot of these trucks, some of the interior engine compartment sheet

Bodies

Most of the medium duty trucks came out of the factory in the Cab and Chassis configuration. They had cabs (and everything in front), but they didn't have bodies (stake beds, bulk fuel tanks, van boxes, dumps, cranes, wrecker booms, and all the other work truck options) installed. It did not make sense to outfit trucks at the factory to meet every demand and fit every job. Industry practice was for dealers to order whatever specialty body the customer required from a variety of aftermarket suppliers and those dealerships selling medium and heavy duty trucks stocked aftermarket body supplier catalogs for this purpose. GM did offer a few standard bodies, the most popular being the platform/stake. These complete trucks were commonly purchased by farmers and freight hauling businesses, but even here a buyer might order a cab and chassis and install his old platform/stake body on the new truck when it arrived. Because of the usually hard use experienced by these trucks, original factory platform/stake bodies may need extensive reconstruction to replace bed wood, built new stake racks, and even to replace the wooden cross bracing. Often, only the

217

COE models in the Art Deco series use the same grille motif and headlights set in the fenders as the light duty models. Cabs on small and large trucks interchange.

metal hardware is re-usable, though it is helpful to have intact wood for patterns.

Some larger trucks, mainly in the 6000 series, were manufactured as Cowl and Chassis. Here the cab is missing and the truck only has its forward sheet metal (hood and front fenders, plus a cowl with instruments and steering shaft and wheel). Common uses of cowl and chassis configurations were for school busses, but milk trucks and moving vans are other examples.

Usually, older medium duty trucks sport a wide variety of professionally manufactured bodies as well as an amazing array of locally produced custom bodies. A lot of trucks even received hand-me-down bodies from older trucks whose mechanical components wore out before their bodies did.

The fact that bodies are not standardized on medium duty truck opens up a world of possibilities for the restorer who can, unlike his light duty truck restorer counterpart, mount just about anything that fits and have it be no less correct than any other truck in its class. If you find a special type of body you want to install on a medium duty truck, you do not have to be overly concerned about the length of the body in relationship to the length of the chassis of the truck. It was common to lengthen or shorten the chassis to fit the body. This is done by cutting the frame side rails and either splicing in an extra section or taking a length of frame out. The driveshaft would be lengthened or shortened accordingly. Shops modifying today's trucks for the same purpose would be able to do this work.

This COE is from the end of the Advance Design series. Note that while cabs interchange, the doors are different with a cutout in the lower section to clear the taller fenders.

Military Trucks

During World War II Chevrolet built a half-million military cars and trucks. The most widely produced and popular with collectors are the ton-and-a-half troop carrier and cargo trucks in 4x6 configuration. A number of these trucks ended up in construction settings and in service to highway departments, so they are not overwhelmingly difficult to find. While many had cabs like civilian trucks, some had military-style canvas tops. With military trucks, much of the sheet metal will be unique. A collector restoring one of these trucks should affiliate with other military vehicle collectors for parts sources, proper marking conventions and social gatherings, outings and events.

Chevrolet built large numbers of 2X4 military trucks during World War II some of which wound up with highway departments and construction companies after the war. As can be seen in these ads, (this page and next) Chevrolet built these trucks with both civilian and military cabs and front ends. Today, the military variety are sought after by collectors. Bob Christiansen

"WORK HORSE" of WORLD WAR II
And GMC Has Sent More Than 450,000 Into The Service

Acme News photo shows a convoy of GMC trucks carrying cargoes that carried the fight to Hitler

When a high-ranking Army Officer called the GMC 2½-ton "six-by-six" military truck the "Workhorse of the War," no name was ever more appropriately applied.

It works for the Artillery pulling guns and carrying ammunition. It helps the Engineers repair roads, bridges and damaged defenses. It works for the Signal Corps carrying poles and wire and radio equipment. It helps Ordnance repair tanks and trucks and arms of all types. It works for the Transportation and Quartermaster Corps transporting everything it takes to keep an Army on the offensive. It performs equally essential service for the Navy, the Marines, the Air Forces and the Coast Guard.

Is it any wonder, then, that our military forces have already requested and received more than 450,000 GMCs . . . that thousands more are going into Service each month!

★ ★ ★ ★ ★

In addition to being one of the largest producers of military vehicles, GMC is also building many commercial trucks for essential users. If you are eligible for a new truck, your GMC dealer will gladly help you fill out an application. Remember, too, that GMC is headquarters for the original Preventive Maintenance Service.

INVEST IN VICTORY . . . BUY MORE WAR BONDS

GMC TRUCK & COACH DIVISION
GENERAL MOTORS

Nice Ride: 1967 Chevrolet C-50 Dump Truck

Dump trucks have always seemed to me to be the most utilitarian of vehicles. When you want to unload, you pull a lever and off it goes. I was mesmerized by the dump action as a small child riding with my father in my uncle's dump truck. Impressions made early in life stick and I've been a dump truck admirer ever since.

When our son Anthony announced that he was on the hunt for an older dump truck to use with his home building business, he said, "I'm looking for a truck that's at least 30 years old because by then all the losers will have been sorted out." Usually the thinking goes the other way. People buy later model equipment believing that by doing so they'll escape the wear and mechanical failure of an older rig. Anthony usually takes a more practical outlook. Any old truck that's still running hasn't had all that tough a life, he maintained. Otherwise, it wouldn't be around. Besides, older stuff is easier to work on.

I got a chance to drive the "new" truck one day after work. Having owned a half-ton shortbox pickup and spent time behind the wheel of a slightly later 1969 ? ton Longhorn, I was familiar with the basic cab layout. But the Longhorn has power steering and an automatic transmission, so I had to get used to the dump truck's manual four-speed with its stump-puller 1st gear and the armstrong steering. I drove the dump truck around the neighborhood without a load, so I didn't get a chance to try to big truck moves like shifting the dual speed rear axle or pulling the dump lever to offload five yards of gravel. Still, the experience was fun and memorable. Back at the job site, Anthony demonstrated the dump action, which worked as well as the day the truck hauled its first load. Anthony was right. His nearly 40-plus-year-old truck must have lived a charmed life.

When our son, Anthony, decided he needed a dump truck for his home building business, he sought a truck at least 30 years old in the belief that all the weaklings had been sorted out. He settled on a mechanically fit 1968 Chevrolet C-50 that had miraculously escaped serious rust.

Although Anthony doesn't plan to restore his truck, which would defeat its purpose, he does plan cosmetic upgrades.

The chassis and dump mechanism are extremely rugged, another reason for selecting an older truck.

Whether big or small, trucks of this Chevy's vintage have exceptionally good styling. They're the first of Chevrolet's truly modern trucks. A feature of both the pickups and the heavier duty models in this vintage, GM put the gas tank inside the cab behind the seat. The curious thing about Anthony's truck is the seat height. For 6-plus footers like us, our heads almost touch the roof of the cab. Closer examination showed the reason. For more capacity, the big truck's gas tank bulges at the bottom. Not able to extend the cab, the engineers accommodated the bulge by raising the seat.

Now that there's a dump truck in the family it seems like every big job just got a little easier.

Final Thoughts

While the methods, skills and procedures used to restore a medium duty truck will differ very little from those of the light truck., locating replacement parts is going to be more difficult and informational resources nearly non-existent. The truck and its cadre of spare parts are going to require more room to store. Further, the parts are going to be heavier to move and harder to handle.

After the restoration is complete and the truck is ready to drive, registration and insurance will be required. Just about all of these bigger trucks were classified as commercial or farm vehicles. Although a lot of states authorize historic tags for antique commercial vehicles, it is still an issue to be researched by the individual restorer. The same goes for the drivers' licensing requirements. The cutoff for a Commercial Driver's License is 26,000 lbs. Medium duty trucks, generally, are below this limit, but unless you currently have or are prepared to qualify for a CDL, you'll want to research your truck's overall gross vehicle weight before putting a lot of time, money and effort into a truck you can't legally drive!

Big trucks may not be desirable as daily drivers, but the big truck restorer will derive as much satisfaction and enjoyment from his or her labors as redoing a light truck and will ultimately end up with a truck that's relatively speaking rarer and every bit as collectable.

Just remember: restoring a bigger truck is not for the faint of heart, weak of arm, or small of garage.

Advance Design Medium Duty Models Capture Collector Interest
By John Milliman, Stovebolt Page website (www.stovebolt.com)

A lot of pre-WWII medium duty trucks being worked on, but by far Advance Design models have captured the lion's share of collector interest in medium duty Chevrolet trucks, presumably because the supply of unrestored light Advance Designs is starting to dwindle. Of this group, the most popular (by a wide margin) seems to be the Advance Design COE. Collectors who find a short wheelbase Advance Design COE in good condition consider themselves blessed. Among the Advance Design series trucks, the nomenclature runs like this:

4000 Series (4400, 4401, 4500, etc.)—1 1/2-ton conventional trucks with flatbed and stake bodies. You'll find these on the farms, mostly. These are the most common of the medium duty trucks)

5000 Series—2-ton Cab Over Engine trucks. These COE models are rare and come in a plethora of wheelbases and bodies.

6000 Series—2-Ton conventional trucks. These are a little rarer than the 4000 series trucks and were built mostly as units for school buses and for heavier applications requiring longer wheelbases. The 6000 series are desired for their 2-speed rear axles and driveshaft-mounted parking brakes. Other than those parts, and the longer wheelbases, they can be hard to tell from the 4000 series.